AF668714

Principles and Theory of

GEOINFORMATICS

Principles and Theory of

GEOINFORMATICS

P. K. GARG

Professor

Civil Engineering Department

Indian Institute of Technology Roorkee

Roorkee–247667, (Uttarakhand), India

KHANNA BOOK PUBLISHING CO. (P) LTD.

Publisher of Engineering and Computer Books

4C/4344, Ansari Road, Darya Ganj, New Delhi-110002

Phone : 011-23244447-48 **Mobile:** +91-9910909320

E-mail : contact@khannabooks.com

Website : www.khannabooks.com

Price: ₹ 499.00

PRINCIPLES AND THEORY OF GEOINFORMATICS

P.K. Garg

Copyright © Khanna Book Publishing Co. (P) Ltd.

This book is sold subject to the condition that it shall not, by way of trade or otherwise, be lent, resold, hired out, or otherwise circulated without the publisher's prior consent in any form of binding or cover other than that in which it is published and without a similar condition including this condition being imposed on the subsequent purchaser and without limiting the rights under copyright reserved above, no part of this publication may be reproduced, stored in or introduced into retrieval system, or transmitted any form or by any means (electronic, mechanical, photocopying, recording or otherwise), without the prior written permission of both the copyright owner and the above mentioned publisher of this book.

ISBN: 978-93-86173-70-6

Edition: 2019

Published by:

Khanna Book Publishing Co. (P) Ltd.
4C/4344, Ansari Road, Darya Ganj, New Delhi-110 002
Phone: 011-23244447-48 **Mobile:** +91-9910909320
E-mail: contact@khannabooks.com

Printed in India by:
Vaibhav Products

PREFACE

Geoinformatics is a multidisciplinary subject which involves the use of cartography, geovisualization, GIS, remote sensing, photogrammetry, GPS, spatial statistics, geostatistics, multivariate statistics and other advanced tools and techniques. The emerging need of geospatial technology has created an unprecedented demand of trained manpower, world-wide, who can contribute to these areas.

My vast teaching and research experience at IIT Roorkee motivated me to write this book which concisely covers all the major topics of Geoinformatics; Photogrammetry, Remote Sensing, GPS and GIS, so that students understand the complete theory of land data collection & mapping, and subsequently the analysis from these maps. The book deals with the Earth surface data collection using various approaches from ground-based (GPS) to space-based (Remote Sensing). It also covers different technologies, approaches, processes, and methods related to data collection and analysis for various applications on the Earth surface. For each of the topics, the relevant theory & principles, and methods & analysis are presented in the book, in simple language with clear illustrations.

The book covers the course contents required mainly for UG (Civil Engg) and PG (Geoinformatics) as well as Computer Science, Information Technology, Geology, Geography, Environmental Science, Earth Science, students and research scholars. Today, geoinformatics has found applications in civil engg, natural resources management, disaster management, environment, geology, soil, forestry, agriculture, water management, urban, infrastructure development, 3D mapping, etc. The students will find the book useful as working principles and theory have been explained with simple mathematics.

I am thankful to the Khanna Publishing House, New Delhi for bringing out timely publication of the Book.

(Prof. P.K. GARG)

Professor, IIT Roorkee, Roorkee

and

Former Vice Chancellor,

Uttarakhand Technical University, Dehradun (UK)

CONTENTS

Contents **Page**

Preface *v*
List of Figures *xv*
List of Tables *xix*

CHAPTER 1: GEOINFORMATICS **1–13**

1.1 Introduction 1
1.2 Major Disciplines of Geoinformatics 3
1.2.1 Photogrammetry 4
1.2.2 Remote Sensing 4
1.2.3 Global Positioning System (GPS) 4
1.2.4 Geographic Information System (GIS) 5
1.3 Applications of Geoinformatics 5
1.4 Status of Geoinformatics in India 6
Review Questions 12
References 12

CHAPTER 2: PHOTOGRAMMETRY **14–61**

2.1 Introduction 14
2.2 Developments in Photogrammetry 15
2.2.1 Analog photogrammetry 16
2.2.2 Analytical photogrammetry 17
2.2.3 Digital photogrammetry 17
2.3 Types of Photographs 18
2.3.1 Aerial photographs 18
2.3.2 Terrestrial or Close-range photographs 20
2.4 Map Versus Aerial Photograph 20
2.5 Advantages and Disadvantages of Photogrammetry 22
2.5.1 Advantagees 22
2.5.2 Disadvantages 23

2.6 Acquisition of Aerial Photos 23

2.6.1 Aerial camera system 23

2.6.2 Flight planning 24

2.7 Geometric Properties of Aerial Photographs 27

2.8 Terms Associated with Vertical Aerial Photographs 28

2.9 Terms Associated with Tilted Aerial Photographs 29

2.10 Computation of Length of a Line 31

2.11 Determination of Scale of a Vertical Photograph 32

2.12 Types of Scale 34

2.12.1 Large scale photographs 34

2.12.2 Medium scale photographs 34

2.12.3 Small scale photographs 34

2.13 Relief Displacement of a Vertical Photograph 34

2.14 Stereoscopy 36

2.14.1 Vertical exaggeration 36

2.14.2 Stereoscopic model 37

2.14.3 Stereoscopes 38

2.14.4 Requirements of stereoscopic vision 39

2.15 Determination of Height from Vertical Aerial Photographs 40

2.15.1 Orienting a pair of photographs for stereo-viewing 40

2.15.2 Measurement of parallax by parallax bar 40

2.15.3 Derivation of relationship for height 42

2.16 The Scale of a Tilted Photograph 44

2.17 Ground Coordinates from a Tilted Photograph 45

2.18 Flying Height of a Tilted Photograph 46

2.19 Relief Displacement on a Tilted Photo 47

2.20 Tilt Displacement 48

2.21 Photogrammetric Systems 51

2.21.1 Data acquisition systems 51

2.21.2 Data reduction systems 52

2.21.3 Data presentation systems 54

2.22 Orthophotos 54

2.23 Applications of Photogrammetry 55

Review Questions 57

References 60

CHAPTER 3: REMOTE SENSING 62–177

3.1 Remote Sensing 62
3.2 Advantages and Disadvantages of Remote Sensing 63
3.2.1 Advantagees 63
3.2.2 Disadvantages 64
3.3 A Typical Remote Sensing System 64
3.4 Electro-magnetic Spectrum 66
3.5 Black Body Radiations 69
3.5.1 Planck's law 69
3.5.2 Wien's displacement law 70
3.5.3 Stefan-Boltzmann law 71
3.6 Interaction of EMR with Atmosphere 71
3.6.1 Reflection 72
3.6.2 Scattering 72
3.6.3 Absorption 75
3.6.4 Transmission 75
3.7 Atmospheric Windows 76
3.8 Spectral Signature 77
3.8.1 Water 78
3.8.2 Soils 78
3.8.3 Rocks 79
3.8.4 Vegetation 80
3.9 Using the Spectro-radiometer 80
3.10 Types of Orbits 82
3.10.1 Geo-synchronous orbits 83
3.10.2 Sun-synchronous orbits 83
3.11 Image Characteristics 84
3.11.1 Swath 84
3.11.2 Path-row number 85
3.11.3 Pixel 85
3.11.4 Digital number 85
3.11.5 Spectral band 86
3.11.6 Image histogram 86
3.12 Types of Resolutions 86
3.12.1 Spatial resolution 87
3.12.2 Spectral resolution 88
3.12.3 Radiometric resolution 89
3.12.4 Temporal resolution 91

3.13 Types of Remote Sensing images 91
3.13.1 Panchromatic images 92
3.13.2 Multi-spectral images 92
3.13.3 Hyper-spectral images 93
3.13.4 Colour composite images 94
3.14 Multi-concept in Remote Sensing 95
3.14.1 Multi-stage 95
3.14.2 Multi-resolution 96
3.14.3 Multi-spectral 96
3.14.4 Multi-detector 96
3.14.5 Multi-temporal 96
3.14.6 Multi-uses 96
3.15 Types of Sensors 96
3.15.1 Based on source of energy 97
3.15.2 Based on range of electro-magnetic spectrum 98
3.15.3 Based on imaging systems 105
3.16 Types of Remote Sensing Platforms 107
3.16.1 Based on height and area coverage 107
3.16.2 Based on spatial resolutions 108
3.17 Landsats 111
3.17.1 Return beam videcon camera 112
3.17.2 Multispectral scanner 112
3.17.3 Thematic mapper 113
3.17.4 Enhanced thematic mapper plus 114
3.18 SPOT 114
3.18.1 Along track multispectral scanner/Push broom scanner 117
3.18.2 Side viewing scanner 117
3.19 Indian Remote Sensing Satellites 117
3.19.1 Linear imaging self scanner 121
3.19.2 Wide field sensor/Advanced wide field sensor 122
3.20 IKONOS 123
3.21 QuickBird 123
3.22 OrbView 123
3.23 GeoEye
124
3.24 WorldView 124
3.25 Hyperspectral Imaging Systems 127
3.26 Interpretation of Remotely Sensed Data 128

3.27 Visual Interpretation of Remotely Sensed Data 129
3.27.1 Tone 131
3.27.2 Texture 132
3.27.3 Pattern 132
3.27.4 Shape 132
3.27.5 Size 132
3.27.6 Shadow 133
3.27.7 Site/Association 133
3.28 Digital Interpretation of Remotely Sensed Data 133
3.29 Image Pre-processing 134
3.29.1 Geometric correction 134
3.29.2 Radiometric correction 136
3.30 Image restoration 137
3.31 Image enhancement 138
3.31.1 Contrast enhancement 139
3.32 Image transformation 142
3.32.1 Image fusion 143
3.32.2 Vegetation indices 144
3.32.3 Tasseled cap transformation 145
3.32.4 Principal component analysis 147
3.33 Digital Interpretation of Remotely Sensed Data 149
3.33.1 Supervised classification 149
3.33.2 Unsupervised classification 153
3.33.3 Other classification techniques 155
3.34 Accuracy Assessment 160
3.35 Applications of Remotely Sensing 165
3.35.1 Geology 165
3.35.2 Hydrology and water resources 165
3.35.3 Land use and land cover 166
3.35.4 Natural hazards study 166
3.35.5 Site investigations and regional planning 167
3.35.6 Soil mapping 167
3.35.7 Transportation network mapping 167
3.35.8 Terrain mapping and analysis 168
3.35.9 Urban development 168
3.35.10 3-D city models 168
Review Questions 168
References 172

CHAPTER 4: GLOBAL POSITIONING SYSTEMS **178–215**

4.1 Introduction 178
4.2 History of GPS 178
4.3 Advantages and Disadvantages of GPS 180
4.3.1 Advantagees 181
4.3.2 Disadvantages 181
4.4 Coordinate Systems 181
4.5 Map Projection 183
4.5.1 Choosing a map projection 184
4.6 Datums 185
4.7 Various Segments of GPS 187
4.7.1 Space segment 188
4.7.2 Control segment 189
4.7.3 User segment 190
4.8 Working Principle of GPS 190
4.8.1 Trilateration 192
4.9 GPS Satellite Signals 193
4.9.1 Dilution of precision 194
4.9.2 Accuracy 195
4.9.3 Errors 196
4.10 Types of GPS Receivers 198
4.10.1 Code phase receivers 198
4.10.2 Carrier phase receivers 198
4.10.3 Geodetic receivers 199
4.10.4 Other classification of receivers 200
4.11 GPS Surveying Techniques 201
4.11.1 Static surveying 201
4.11.2 Rapid static surveying 203
4.11.3 Kinematic surveying 204
4.11.4 Stop and go kinematic surveying 204
4.11.5 Real time kinematic surveying 205
4.11.6 Differential GPS surveying 207
4.12 Applications of GPS 208
4.12.1 Civilian applications 209
4.12.2 Military applications 210
4.13 Future Uses of GPS Technology 210
Review Questions 212
References 213

CHAPTER 5: GEOGRAPHIC INFORMATION SYSTEMS 216–269

5.1 Introduction 216
5.2 Developments in GIS 217
5.3 Definitions of a GIS 221
5.4 Terminology Used in GIS 221
5.5 Advantages and Disadvantages of a GIS 223
5.5.1 Advantagees 223
5.5.2 Disadvantages 224
5.6 Components of a GIS 224
5.7 Basic Tasks of a GIS 226
5.8 Answers a GIS Can Do 228
5.9 Representation of Geographical Data 229
5.9.1 Points 229
5.9.2 Lines 229
5.9.3 Polygons 229
5.10 Converting the Geospatial Data 230
5.10.1 Scanning 230
5.10.2 Digitization 231
5.11 Data Models 233
5.11.1 Raster data 233
5.11.2 Vector data 234
5.11.3 Raster versus Vector 235
5.12 Topology and its Components 236
5.13 Geodatabase 239
5.13.1 Join 240
5.13.2 Relate 240
5.13.2 Relational database 240
5.14 Sources of GIS Data 241
5.14.1 Topographic maps 241
5.14.2 Thematic maps 243
5.14.3 Automated surveying 243
5.14.4 Photogrammetry 244
5.15.5 Remote sensing 245
5.14.6 Global positioning system 246
5.14.7 Light detection and ranging 247
5.14.8 Unmanned aerial vehicle/Drone 247

5.15 Interpolation of Data 249
5.15.1 Inverse distance weighted 249
5.15.2 Kriging 249
5.15.3 Natural neighbour 249
5.15.4 Spline 250
5.15.5 Trend 250
5.16 Various Operations in GIS 250
5.16.1 Measurement 251
5.16.2 Query 251
5.16.3 Raster operations in GIS 252
5.16.4 Vector operations in GIS 254
5.17 Free (Open) Source GIS Software 255
5.17.1 GIS data 255
5.17.2 Software 254
5.18 Applications of GIS 257
5.18.1 Civil engineering projects 258
5.18.2 Site selection 259
5.18.3 Urban planning 260
5.18.4 Terrain mapping and analysis 260
5.18.5 Water resources 260
5.18.6 Solid waste management 261
5.18.7 Natural resources management 261
5.18.8 Traffic and transportation engineering 261
5.18.9 Disaster management and mitigation 262
5.19 Future Uses of GIS Technology 262
Review Questions 263
References 265

List of Figures

Figures		Page
1.1	Concept of (a) Geoinformatics, and (b) Geomatics	3
1.2	Timeline of GIS, geomatics and geoinformatics	3
1.3	Geospatial technology contributing to major ongoing projects in India	7
1.4	Adoption of various geospatial technologies in different sectors in India	8
1.5	Geospatial service providers focussing on various sectors in India	8
1.6	The growth of India's geospatial market vis-a-vis rest of the world	9
2.1	Nadar's earliest surviving aerial image, taken above Paris in 1866 (left). Boston from a tethered balloon, 13th October, 1860, by James Wallace Black (right)	15
2.2	Major phases of development of photogrammetry	17
2.3	A typical vertical aerial photograph	19
2.4	Vertical, low oblique and high oblique photographs	19
2.5	Terrestrial or Close-range photogrammetry	20
2.6	Topographic map and aerial photograph	21
2.7	Route of flight lines	25
2.8	Photographs during a flight planning	26
2.9	(a) Geometry (b) Format of a vertical aerial photograph	27
2.10	(a) Representation of a titled photo (b) Parameters of a tilted photo	30
2.11	Length between two points from their coordinates	31
2.12	Scale of a vertical photograph in a flat terrain	32
2.13	Scale of a vertical photograph in undulating terrain	33
2.14	Relief displacement of a tower on a vertical photograph	35
2.15	Vertical exaggeration and stereovision	37
2.16	Recreation of 3D	37
2.17	(a) Lens stereoscope (b) Line diagram of lens stereoscope	39
2.18	(a) Mirror stereoscope; (b) Line diagram of mirror stereoscope.	39
2.19	(a) Base lining of a stereo-pair (b) Parallax bar measurements	41
2.20	Height determination from a stereo-pair using parallax bar reading	42
2.21	Geometry of a tilted photograph	44

2.22 Relief displacement on a tilted photo 47
2.23 Tilt displacement 49
2.24 (a) Analytical photogrammetric plotter, and (b) Digital photogrammetric workstation 52
2.25 Collinearity condition 53
2.26 (a) DEM and (b) Orthophoto 55
3.1 Stages of remote sensing 65
3.2 Propagation of electromagnetic waves 66
3.3 The electromagnetic spectrum 68
3.4 Power density of EMS at different temperatures and wavelengths 71
3.5 Four types of interactions: transmission, reflection, scattering and absorption 72
3.6 Various types of scattering with wavelength 74
3.7 Atmospheric transmission process 76
3.8 Atmospheric windows regions 77
3.9 Typical spectral signature curves 79
3.10 Spectral reflectance of various rocks 80
3.11 The spectro-radiometer 81
3.12 Sun-synchronous and geo-synchronous orbits 82
3.13 Swath width 85
3.14 Path-row of LANDSAT 85
3.15 Histogram of an image 86
3.16 Representation of an image 86
3.17 Spatial resolution of images 88
3.18 Optical ranges used by various images 92
3.19 SPOT panchromatic scene at a ground resolution of 10 m 93
3.20 Multispectral band images from SPOT satellites at a ground resolution of 20 m 93
3.21 Hyperspectral imaging with hundreds of narrow bands 93
3.22 False colour composite from multispectral SPOT images 95
3.23 True-colour composite of IKONOS image 95
3.24 Multi-stage remote sensing platforms 95
3.25 Classification of sensors 97
3.26 Passive and active remote sensing sensors 98
3.27 Sensor systems operating in the thermal IR region 99
3.28 Global sea surface temperature (SST) and sea ice cover of March derived from NOAA AVHRR thermal infrared satellite measurements in 2006-2008 102
3.29 Working of a SAR 103
3.30 Working of a LiDAR 104
3.31 Remote sensing sensors 107
3.32 Spatial resolutions and number of wavebands of various satellites 109
3.33 History of Landsats 111

3.34 Images of Landsat TM bands 114
3.35 Capturing the image using off-nadir capabilities of SPOT 115
3.36 Hyperion imaging spectrometer 127
3.37 Interpretation methods and analysis procedure 129
3.38 Image interpretation elements 131
3.39 Resampling methods 136
3.40 Histogram original (above) and after linear contrast enhancement (bottom) 139
3.41 Linear contrast enhancement on ETM+ images 140
3.42 Logarithmic contrast enhancement applied to a retinal fundus image 141
3.43 Original image (left), and after histogram equalisation (right) 142
3.44 Computation of NDVI values 144
3.45 The graph between red and infrared bands to depict tasselled cap transformation 145
3.46 Representation of Greenness, Brightness and Wetness components on three axes 146
3.47 PC1 and PC 2 components 148
3.48 Steps used in supervised (right) and unsupervised (left) classification techniques 150
3.49 Steps in supervised classification 151
3.50 Five important sampling techniques 160
3.51 Services of errors in remote sensing data 161
4.1 The history of satellite navigation 180
4.2 Coordinate system (a) rectangular, and (b) polar system 183
4.3 (a) Transferring Earth's three-dimensional curved surface to a two-dimensional flat surface 184
(b) Some project coordinate system onto a two-dimensional cartesian coordinate plane 184
4.4 The shape of the Earth and WGS 84 datum 186
4.5 Approximate layout of zones in Indian grid 186
4.6 Various segments of a GPS 187
4.7 Space segment 188
4.8 Control segment 189
4.9 User segment 191
4.10 Typical features on display of a GPS 191
4.11 Computation of distance 191
4.12 Determination of location from 1 satellite, 2 satellites, and 3 satellites using trilateration method 192
4.13 Carriers of GPS signals 193
4.14 Geometric dilution of precision 194
4.15 Position dilution of precision 195
4.16 Various accuracy levels 195
4.17 Various sources of errors in signals 197

4.18	(a) Navigational GPS receiver (b) Geodetic receiver	199
4.19	Static method	202
4.20	Real-time kinematic surveys	206
4.21	The DGPS survey	208
5.1	Dr. John Snow's cholera map of London's Soho-1954	218
5.2	Growth of GIS	220
5.3	Major components of a GIS	224
5.4	Abstracting real world into GIS layers	227
5.5	Sequence of operations in a GIS cycle	228
5.6	Point (trees), line (river), and polygon (water pond) features along with their coordinates	230
5.7	(a) Flat bed scanner, and (b) Wide-format, sheet-fed scanner	231
5.8	Heads up digitization process	232
5.9	Digitizing tablet	232
5.10	Raster and vector representation of features	233
5.11	Effect of grid cell size on shape of the feature	234
5.12	Topological spatial relationships	237
5.13	Topology of three basic types of features	238
5.14	Arc-node topology of polygon features	238
5.15	Topological relationships from three basic features	239
5.16	Joining two tables	240
5.17	Relating two tables	240
5.18	A relational database	241
5.19	A sample of topographic map at 1:50,000 scale	242
5.20	Latitude, longitude and contours values on a topographic map	243
5.21	Total station instrument	244
5.22	DEM of the area showing elevation values in feet	245
5.23	DEM created from stereo satellite images	246
5.24	The DEM of Mt St. Helen's by storing elevation values in a matrix of 30 meter grid cells of 466 rows by 327 columns (152, 382 values)	246
5.25	Data collection using Drone/UAV	249
5.26	Classification of spatial analysis functions	251
5.27	Local, focal, zonal and global operations in a GIS	253
5.28	Buffer zones around three types of features	254
5.29	Output from dissolve function	254
5.30	Various operations on vector layers	256
5.31	A glimpse of BHUVAN mainpage	257
5.32	Future directions and uses of GIS technology	263

List of Tables

Tables		Page
2.1	Difference between a map and an aerial photograph	21
2.2	Comparison between the analog, analytic and digital photogrammetric stereo-plotters	53
3.1	Principal divisions of electromagnetic spectrum	68
3.2	Primary regions of EMS along with their wavelength, frequency and energy	70
3.3	Details of atmospheric scattering processes	73
3.4	Major atmospheric windows used in remote sensing and their characteristics	77
3.5	Resolutions of some remote sensing sensors	89
3.6	Principal applications of Landsat TM bands	113
3.7	Principal applications of Landsat ETM+ bands	114
3.8	Characteristics of SPOT sensors	117
3.9	Some remote sensing satellites	119
3.10	Characteristics of high resolution satellites	125
3.11	Quantitative and qualitative details of image interpretation elements	131
3.12	Visual interpretation versus digital image analysis	134
3.13	Coefficients for tasseled cap transformation of Landsat MSS and TM data	147
3.14	Advantages and disadvantages of supervised and unsupervised classification techniques	154
3.15	Summary of some classifiers used for image classification	156
3.16	Advantages and disadvantages of different classifiers	159
3.17	A typical confusion matrix	163
4.1	GPS system with expected accuracy	196
4.2	A comparison of single and double frequency receivers	199
4.3	Guidelines for selecting the reference receiver and rover receiver during GPS survey	203
4.4	Summary of number of satellites, baseline lengths and observation times for static and rapid static methods	204
4.5	Advantages and disadvantages of various GPS survey methods	206
5.1	Advantages and disadvantages of vector and raster data models	236

ABBREVIATIONS

2D	Two Dimensional
3D	Three Dimensional
ACS	Atmospheric Correction Sensor
AFB	Air Force Base
ALISS	Advanced Linear Imaging Scanning Sensor
ANN	Artificial Neural Networks
AS	Anti-Spoofing mode
ASTER	Advanced Spaceborne Thermal Emission and Reflection Radiometer
AVHRR	Advanced Very High Resolution Radiometer
AVIRIS	Airborne Visible/infrared Imaging Spectrometer
AWiFS	Advanced Wide Field Sensor
B&W	Black and White
C/A code	Course/Acquisition-code
CAVIS	Clouds, Aerosols, Vapors, Ice, and Snow
CCD	Charge Coupled Device
DBMS	Database Management System
DEM	Digital Elevation Model
DGPS	Differential GPS
DN	Digital Number
DoD	Department of Defence
DOP	Dilution of Precision
DPW	Digital Photogrammetric Workstation
DSS	Decision Support Systems
ERTS	Earth Resources Technology Satellite
EDM	Electronic Distance Measurement
EMR	Electro-magnetic Radiations
EMS	Electro-magnetic Spectrum

EO	Earth Observations
ETM	Enhanced Thematic Mapper
ETM+	Enhanced Thematic Mapper Plus
FCC	False Colour Composite
FCM	Fuzzy c-means
FIR	Far Infrared
FOW	Field of View
GCP	Ground Control Points
GDOP	Geometric Dilution of Precision
GIS	Geographical Information System
GMS	Geostationary Meteorological Satellite
GOES	Geostationary Operational Environmental Satellite
GPS	Global Positioning System
HIS	Intensity, Hue (color), Saturation
HE	Histogram Equalization
HRG	High Resolution Geometrical
HRV	High Resolution Visible
HR-VIR	Visible & Infrared High-Resolution
ICT	Information and Communication Technology
IDW	Inverse Distance Weighted
IERS	International Earth Rotation Service
IFOV	Instantaneous Field of View
ILWIS	Integrated Land and Water Information Management
IoT	Internet of Things
IR	Infrared
IRNSS	Indian Regional Navigation Satellite System
IRS	Indian Remote Sensing Satellites
ISODATA	Iterative Self-Organizing Data Analysis Technique
IT	Information Technology
GLONASS	Global Navigation Satellite System
GNSS	Global Navigation Satellite System
GRASS	Geographic Resources Analysis Support System
LANDSAT	Land Satellites
LBS	Location-based Services
LiDAR	Light Detection and Ranging
LISS	Linear Imaging Self Scanning Sensor
MLE	Maximum Likelihood Estimates

MMU	Minimum Mapping Unit
NATMO	National Atlas Thematic Mapping Organisation
NavIC	Navigation with Indian Constellation
NAVSTAR	Navigation Satellite Timing and Ranging
NGIS	National GIS
NIR	Near Infrared
NOAA	National Oceanic and Atmospheric Administration
NRSC	National Remote Sensing Centre
OBSSR	On-Board Solid State Recorder
OCM	Ocean Colour Monitor
OLI	Operational Land Imager
PAN	Panchromatic
PCM	Possibilistic c-means
PP	Principal Point
QGIS	Quantum GIS
RADAR	RAdio Detection And Ranging
RBV	Return Beam Videcon
RDBMS	Relational Database Management System
RGB	Red, Green, Blue
rms	Root Mean Square
ROSA	Radio Occultation Sounder for Atmosphere
MIR	Middle Infrared
MODIS	Moderate Resolution Imaging Spectroradiometer
MSL	Mean Sea Level
MSS	Multispectral Scanner
NDVI	Normalised Difference Vegetation Index
OTF-AR	On-The-Fly–Ambiguity Resolution
PCA	Principal Component Analysis
P-Code	Precision-code
PPS	Precision Positioning Signals
PRN	Pseudorandom Noise
QZSS	Quasi-Zenith Satellite System
RFID	Radio frequency identification
RINEX	Receiver Independent Exchange Format
RTK	Real-Time Kinematic
SA	Selective Availability
SAGA	System for Automated Geo-scientific Analyse

SAR	Synthetic Aperture Radar
SCAT	Ku-band Pencil Beam Scatterometer
SOI	Survey of India
SPOT	Système Pour l'Observation de la Terre
SPS	Standard Positioning Signals
SRTM	Shuttle Radar Topography Mission
SST	Sea Surface Temperature
SVM	Support Vector Machine
SWIR	Short Wave Infrared
TCT	Tasselled Cap Transformations
TIN	Triangular Irregular Networks
TIR	Thermal Infrared
TM	Thematic Mapper
UAS	Unarmed Aerial Systems
UAV	Unmanned Aerial Vehicle
UTM	Universal Transverse Mercator
UV	Ultraviolet
VI	Vegetation Indices
WAAS	Wide Area Augmentation System
WGS-84	World Geodetic System-1984
WiFS	Wide Field Sensor

Chapter 1

GEOINFORMATICS

1.1 INTRODUCTION

In a rapidly changing world, **"Geoinformatics"** has a special significance, and is used for monitoring environment and human activities on the Earth's surface. Geoinformatics consists of two words; **"Geo"** which refers to **"Earth"** and **"Informatics"** which refers to **"Information Processing".** Hence, geoinformatics can be understood as the union of Earth sciences and Informatics (IGNOU, 2012). Wikipedia defines geoinformatics as "*...the science and the technology which develops and uses information science infrastructure to address the problems of geography, geosciences and related branches of engineering*". The art, science and technology dealing with the acquisition, storage, processing, production, presentation and dissemination of geoinformation is called geoinformatics (IGNOU, 2012). According to Burrough (1986) it is a powerful set of tools for collecting, storing, retrieving, transforming and displaying of spatial data from the real world.

Prakash (2006) defined geoinformatics as "the collection, integration, management, analysis, and presentation of geospatial data, models and knowledge that support disciplinary, multidisciplinary, interdisciplinary and transdisciplinary research and education". The four main tasks of geoinformatics are: (i) collection and processing of **geodata** (geodata is the contraction of geographic data), (ii) development and management of databases of geodata, (iii) analysis and modelling of geodata, and (iv) development and integration of logic and computer tools and software for the first three tasks. Geoinformatics may be defined in a relatively broad term as a number of different *technologies, approaches, processes, and methods* dealing with the issues mostly related to the Earth's surface for collaborative decision making (ESRI, 2014).

The term **'Geoinformatics'** is believed to have come in existence just few decades back as a result of the integration of four major disciplines; **Photogrammetry**, **Remote Sensing, Global Positioning System (GPS)** and **Geographical Information System (GIS) (Ehlers 2008).** Geoinformatics is a multidisciplinary science which can combine different types of dataset from various branches of *cartography, geodesy, photogrammetry, remote sensing, Laser, GPS, field, web-mapping, socio-economic, computer science, computer vision, mobile and* *game technology, intelligent system,* and *internet of things,* to generate results in the form of maps or reports which allow better *interpretation, management and decision making* about various human activities on Earth's surface (Oledzki, 2004).

For analyzing information related to Earth, geoinformatics combines geospatial analysis, geospatial models, geospatial databases, human-computer interaction, both wired and wireless networking technologies which are referenced to geographic location. It is the advancing science and technology, which can be used as a powerful tool for research and development to generate geocoded data and attribute database to help taking appropriate decision for planning (Oledzki, 2004). Geioinformatics research involves the use of modern information methods and technologies. Application programs, databases, the internet and software development constitute the foundation for the deployment of geoinformatics.

Geoinformatics is a valuable tool for planning and monitoring social, economic and technical processes. The dynamic progress of geoinformatics is strongly connected to the rapid development in information technology, especially software and computer graphics. The problem solving of geoinformatics is accomplished through GIS. The GIS is firstly introduced by Canadian researcher, Roger Tomlinson in 1968 (Marble and Peuquet, 1983). It is used to *visualize, query, analyze, and interpret geospatial data to understand the relationships, patterns, and trends, mostly* employed in the field of geography to explore and find the answers (ESRI, 2014). GIS being a powerful tool in spatial analysis; many disciplines have recently employed GIS to answer their research questions. Conceptualisation of geoinformatics is represented in Figure 1.1 (a).

There is another term i.e., '***Geomatics***', which was first used in Canada at Laval University in the early 1980s to describe the Geodesy, Engineering and Mathematics disciplines (IGNOU, 2012) realising the increasing potential of computing which was revolutionising surveys and representation sciences (Figure 1.1b). According to many sources, Geomatics is related to acquire and manage spatial data from the ***engineering point-of-view***. It consists of two words; **"Geo"** which refers to **"Earth"** and, **"Matics"** which refers to **"Mathematics"**. As per Wikipedia, *"Geomatics (or geomatics engineering), also known as surveying engineering (or geospatial science or geospatial engineering or geospatial technology), is the discipline of gathering, storing, processing, and delivering geographic information or spatially referenced information"*. In other words, it consists of products, services and tools involved in the collection, integration and management of geographic data. According to Konecny (2002) geomatics, composed of the disciplines of geopositioning, mapping and the management of spatially oriented data by means of computers, has recently evolved as a new discipline from the integration of surveys and mapping (geodetic engineering), merged with the remote sensing and GIS".

Michalak (2000) considers the term 'Geomatics' to be interchangeable with 'Geoinformatics'. However, some researchers are of the opinion that both Geomatics and Geoinformatics include geographical information and rely heavily upon the theory and practical implications of geodesy. The main focus of geomatics is on spatial information while the geoinformatics deals with the structure and nature of spatial information and also addresses the problems related to geography and geo-sciences. In time-line, GIS is the oldest one, followed by Geomatics, and the youngest is Geoinformatics, as shown in the Figure 1.2.

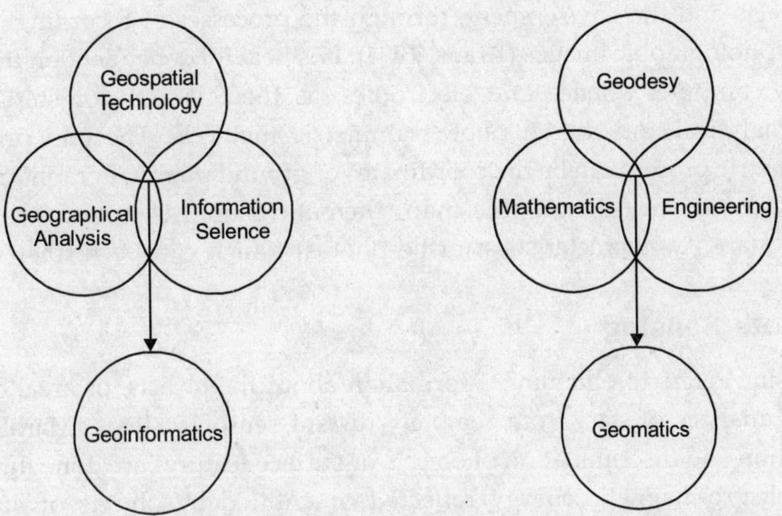

Figure 1.1: Concept of (a) Geoinformatics, and (b) Geomatics
(*Source: https://fatwaramdani.wordpress.com/2016/02/19/what-is-geoinformatics/*)

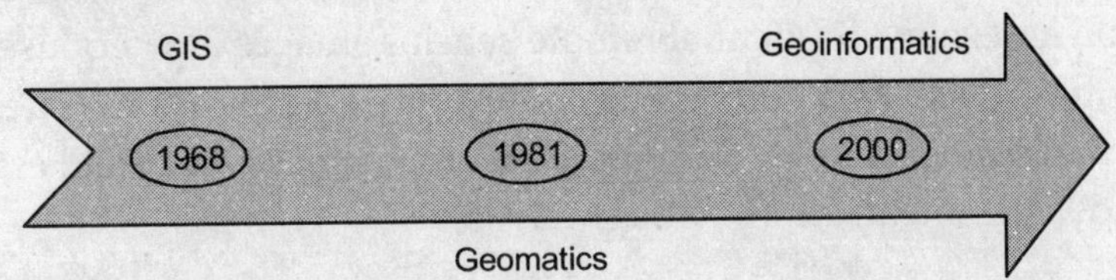

Figure 1.2: Timeline of GIS, geomatics and geoinformatics

Oledzki (2004) believes that the term geoinformatics is more easily understood, and is much better at conveying the essence of spatial research focusing on informatics. In about last four decades, geoinformatics has grown as a major tool for collecting information on almost every aspect on the Earth. In fact, with the availability of very high spatial resolution satellites in the recent years, applications of geoinformatics have increased manifold for a wide range of applications related to emergency services, public health, traffic and transportation, infrastructure, mineral and oil exploration, urban planning, land use, watershed management, environmental modelling, agriculture, meteorology, climate change, oceanography, atmospheric modelling, business, crime mapping, location based planning, telecommunications, navigation systems, military etc.

1.2 MAJOR DISCIPLINES OF GEOINFORMATICS

Geoinformatics consists of integration of four major disciplines (Ehlers, 2008); **Photogrammetry, Remote Sensing, Global Positioning System (GPS)** and **Geographical Information System (GIS),** as given below.

1.2.1 Photogrammetry

Photogrammetry is the art, science and technology of obtaining reliable information about physical objects and the environment, through the processes of recording, measuring, and interpreting photographic images (Kraus, 1994). It is heavily dependent on the developments in software, computer science and electronics, as there is a major shift observed from analog to analytical and digital photogrammetric methods. The end product from the photogrammetric process can be the coordinates of ground points, a graphical representation of the ground surface (topographic map, thematic map, 3D maps, etc.), or a rectified image with map-like characteristics (ortho-photos) which can be further used in GIS.

1.2.2 Remote Sensing

Remote sensing refers to obtaining information about the objects, or area, or phenomenon through the analysis of data from remotely distant sensor systems (Marble and Peuquet, 1983). Detection and discrimination of objects or surface features are done through recording of radiant electro-magnetic energy reflected or emitted by objects or surface material. Remote sensing systems provide an important source of spatio-temporal information on Earth surface at scales ranging from local to global, including land use, vegetation, surface temperatures, digital elevation models, soils, water, geology, roads, habitation, forestry, surface elevation and snow. Sequential remote sensing images are very useful in monitoring dynamic activities, such as flood, water pollution, deforestation, extent of forest fire, snow cover, urban sprawl studies, deforestation, crop acreage and yield estimation, drought monitoring and assessment etc (Burrough, 1986).

1.2.3 Global Positioning System (GPS)

The GPS provides three-dimensional position of objects on the Earth anytime, anywhere and in any weather condition, in addition to time data (El-Rabbany, 2006). Toady, it is considered as the most advanced and popular system of navigation. The technology has benefitted various applications like, highways, railroads, mining, geology, surveying and mapping, agricultural, environmental management, geodesy, power, telecommunications, health, law enforcement, emergency response, crustal movement, disaster response, weather, aviation, maritime, precise timing, automobile, navigation, tracking objects, sports, construction, recreation, etc. GPS are also used extensively by navy, airforce, army, coast guard, rescue and relief personals, civilian carriers, surveyors, commercial transport, hikers, and trekkers (Xu, 2010). World-wide, there are a large number users of GPS enabled gadgets, like mobile phones, wrist watches etc., for a variety of utility.

GPS has led to a new dynamism in the world of geographic information, and is able to monitor and analyze changes on the Earth surface. Citizens are now able to monitor the progress of a flight, or the arrival of a bus, using simple devices to access Web sites that broadcast such information in real-time (Ehlers, 2008).

1.2.4 Geographic Information System (GIS)

A GIS is an information system which is capable of integrating, storing, editing, interpreting, analysing, visualizing, querying, sharing and displaying spatially referenced data of the Earth to understand the relationships, patterns, and trends (Prakash, 2006). In a simple way, GIS consists of images that are geo-referenced to the Earth or have x, y coordinates and their attribute values that are stored in the database table. The spatial data generally is in the form of maps, such as topography, geology, soil types, forest and vegetation, land use, water, roads etc., stored as layers in a digital form. Integrating a database of multiple information layers using defined criteria can produce new thematic maps.

GIS capabilities have grown, while costs have decreased, because of the revolution toward personal computing and the development of crucial supporting software and digital base map resources. GIS application tools allow users to perform spatial query, statistical analysis, edit spatial data and create maps with the unique 3-D geovisualization capabilities (Doellner, 2005). It can be used for updating maps much easier than updating these maps manually. GIS has a great potential to be developed as an Expert System or Decision Support System (**DSS**) which helps decision makers and planners to provide best solution for solving complex problems (Eldrandaly, 2007).

1.3 APPLICATIONS OF GEOINFORMATICS

The geoinformatics technologies have witnessed significant developments over the last few decades, which have led to widespread use of the technologies in different fields and disciplines. Geoinformatics is central to all the disciplines which use spatial data recognised by their locations. It has now become an important tool for decision makers across a wide range of disciplines, researchers and academia, national survey and mapping organisations, industries, environmental agencies, and local and national governments (Ramprasad, 2013). Its applications are mainly oriented to real-world management problems pertaining to natural and man-made environments.

Geoinformatics is most useful for Government planning, like urban planning and land use management, agriculture etc. Other areas where the geoinformatics can bring revolutionary changes are climate change, oceanography, business location planning, archeological reconstruction, telecommunications, criminology, navigation etc. Geoinformatics today has become an important technology for industries and organisations as it enables them to acquire, process, analyse, visualise spatial information and produce outputs. For example, all major Telecom companies use geoinformatics technologies to lay their cables and locate mobile towers. Power sectors have identified geoinformatics technologies as the decision support tool for locating the electrical assets in towns to reduce the transmission loss and reduce electrical theft through consumer mapping.

According to Report on India's Geospatial Market and Prospects (2016) the applications of geospatial technology haves definitely found new avenues in recent times. Availability of real-time/updated information about assets and consumers is a key driver in usage of geospatial technologies. Satellite imagery and GIS are two of the most used technologies in the agriculture sector. Policy mandates drive usage of GPS, remote sensing and GIS in the areas of disaster management. Visualization and interpretation of disasters is the key to usage of digital maps. Majorly geospatial technologies are implemented for forest cover assessment and environmental modelling. GIS is widely used for asset management and network planning in electric utilities. Infrastructure development is aided by surveying and mapping related technologies, like total stations and GPS. Adoption of geospatial technologies in urban development is more towards data creation and monitoring. Usage of GIS and GPS is deriving help in project management and resource allocation in the water sector.

There are large number of benefits of using geospatial technologies, such as (i) better precision and accuracy, (ii) enhanced data safety, security and control, (iii) faster decision making, (iv) improved cost efficiency, (v) improved productivity, and (vi) increased transparency and planning (Report on India's Geospatial Market and Prospects, 2016).

1.4 STATUS OF GEOINFORMATICS IN INDIA

India has long been a leader in using modern spatial technologies and started its tryst with satellite images and GIS in the 1980s by having its own Indian Remote Sensing satellites and image-based mapping, and thus creating GIS databases for various applications. Geoinformatics is fast expanding its presence in India, and has become an important component of planning and decision making in various sectors, such as urban planning, natural resources, infrastructure, agriculture, forestry or location-based services. The emergence of Web 2.0 with the power of mapping and collaborative initiatives has helped change the way the geoinformatics tools and technologies can be used to generate maps, create interactive queries, analyse and visualise information for decision making purposes. There are many resource planning and business activities now which are unimaginable without input from geoinformatics (Ramprasad, 2013).

The *Digital India* project could help in connecting various projects, past and present, to bring India on a global platform. In various programs of the government, such as *Digital India, Smart Cities, Skill Development, Start-Up India, Make in India, National Mission for Clean Ganga, Interlinking of Rivers, Delhi Mumbai Industrial Corridor, Smart Power, and Agriculture*, geospatial technologies are poised to play a critical role (Vardhan, 2015, Datta, 2016). For instance, geospatial technology will act as the backbone for Smart City initiatives for Tier 1 cities and AMRUT for Tier 2 cities (Figure 1.3). Such projects of national significance would have major challenges related to project planning, conceptualization, design, implementation and monitoring. In all these phases of infrastructure and construction projects, geospatial technologies have a significant role to play.

India's ***'Vision 2020'*** envisages the nation evolving into an information society and knowledge economy built on the edifice of information and communication technology (ICT). ICT, including geospatial technologies is being integrated into planning and management to monitor, evaluate and apply spatial planning of natural resources, utilities, infrastructure and urban development and transport sectors, as well as developing decision support systems (DSS) in India (Sonnen, 2010).

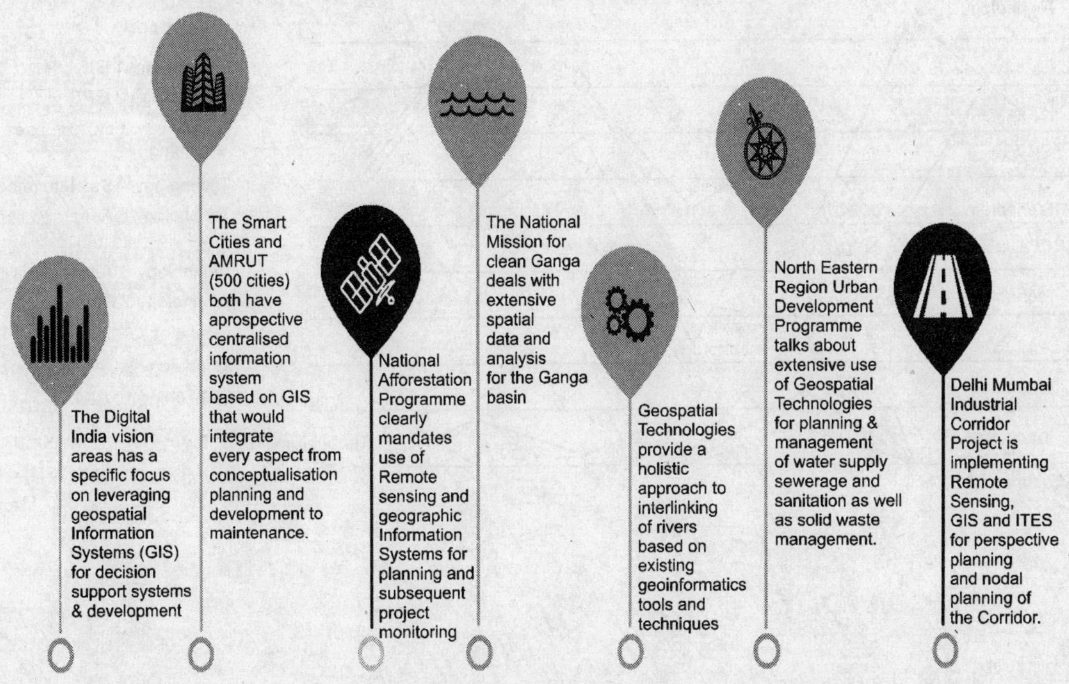

Figure 1.3: Geospatial technology contributing to major ongoing projects in India
(Source: Vardhan, 2015)

The Indian geospatial industry consists of two distinct but mutually supporting segments. The larger, international segment is geared to provide geospatial data and software development services for international organisations, primarily in North America and Western Europe. The other segment, i.e., the domestic segment which is largely funded, managed and controlled by national and state governments, caters to providing geospatial capabilities to the Indian data providers/users (Sonnen, 2010). The geospatial industry is presently witnessing tremendous opportunity within the country as the government has initiated several infrastructure projects and mandated the use of geospatial technologies. There are various other fields, such as, construction and maintenance of roads, railways and waterways, civil aviation, public utility services, education, health, command area development, flood control and management, urban renewal, urban water supply, rural water supply, etc., that essentially use geospatial tools and technologies for spatial planning, management and decision-making.

The adoption of various geospatial technologies in different sectors are presented in Figure 1.4, whereas Figure 1.5 shows the sectors where geospatial service providers are focussing currently as well as for future.

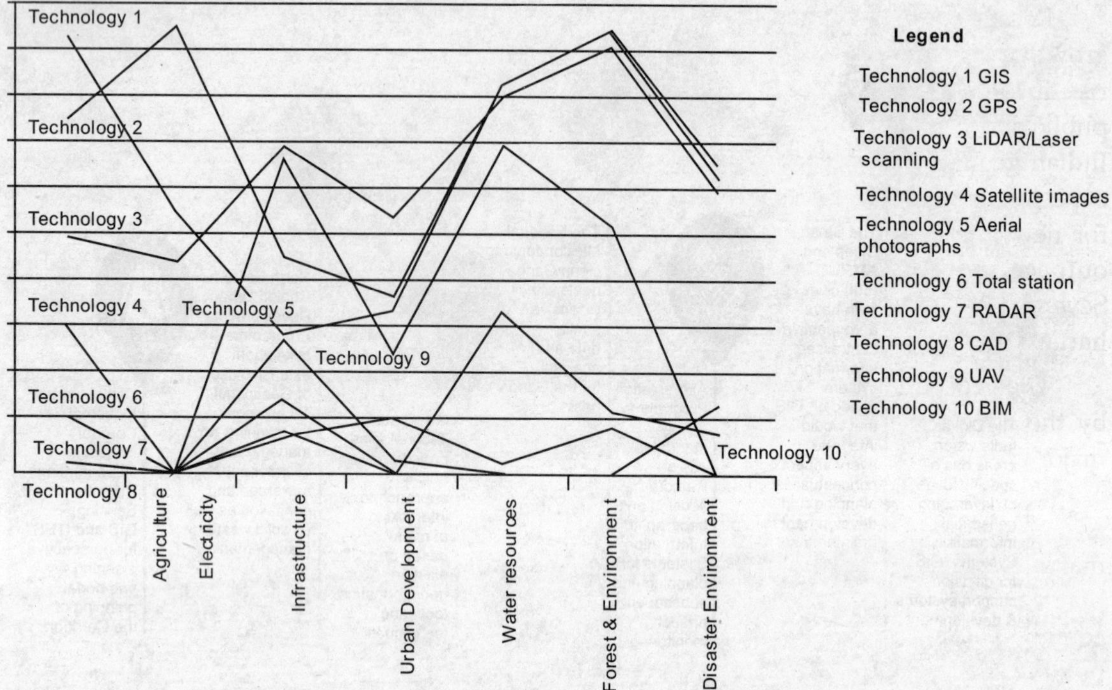

Figure 1.4: Adoption of various geospatial technologies in different sectors in India
(Source: Report on India's Geospatial Market and Prospects, 2016)

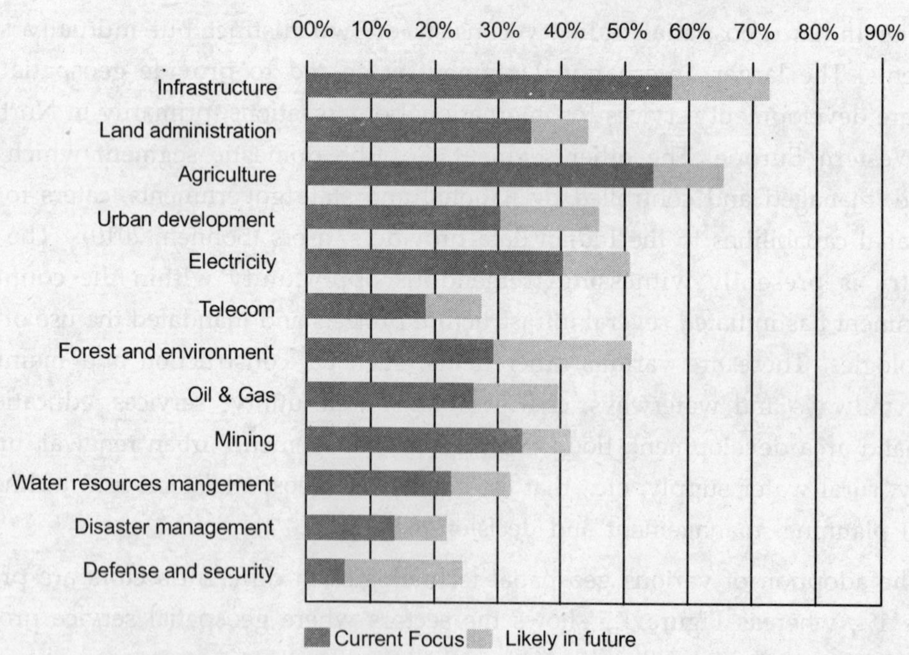

Figure 1.5: Geospatial service providers focussing on various sectors in India
(Source: Report on India's Geospatial Market and Prospects, 2016)

Recent surveys suggest that the Indian geoinformatics industry is witnessing higher growth rate than the average global growth rate than any other nation. The significant rise in demand for geospatial information is likely to give it more weightage in both public and private planning across sectors. Figure 1.6 shows the percentage growth for the Indian geoinformatics industry vis-a-vis worldwide growth. There is a significant increase expected in productive capacity after 2012 as India's geospatial industry builds out capacity for new international and internal markets. The growth of India's geospatial market will outpace growth rate for geospatial markets in the rest of the world (Sonnen, 2010). Several trans-national companies have outsourced their operations to India in order to harness the significant technical expertise in the geospatial sector (Ramprasad, 2013).

The geospatial data usage in India is supported to a large extent by initiatives set out by the government through its ministries and various departments. While defence is the major user of geospatial technologies, the initial lead for the usage of geospatial technologies in India was taken by the natural resources sector (Sonnen, 2010). Geographical information is a ubiquitous part of the governance. The primary role of Government is decision making in public interest which involves geographically related issues, therefore, GIS can play a critical role in all spheres of good governance. Several local governments have now come to depend on geospatial technologies to not only organise and manage spatial data, but also for dissemination of information and services to citizens (Ramprasad, 2013). Now, solutions such as decision support systems, asset management, enterprise wide risk assessment etc. have opened up avenues for this technology in almost every sector.

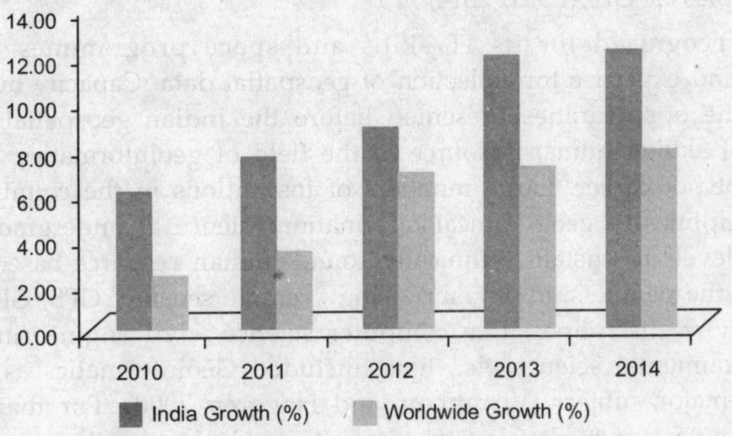

Figure 1.6: The growth of India's geospatial market vis-a-vis rest of the world

(Source: Sonnen, 2010)

Despite the acceptability that this technology has found amongst different stakeholders and end-users in India, the benefits of this technology are yet to go beyond specific projects to find applicability within the entire gamut of governance, decision-making and nation-building (Ramprasad, 2013). In relation to the development in the country, the actual demand for the application of geospatial technology domestically is far from adequate. Several potential sectors are yet to adopt the technology and make optimal use of its huge potential for better and cost-effective planning and management. It continues to be seen as a niche technology requiring huge investment and specific expertise leading to an aversion to adopt geospatial tools. The long terms benefits such as economy of time, effort, resources and cost for data collection and analysis are to be understood by the end-users.

The National GIS (NGIS) project was supported by Sam Pitroda, the then adviser to the Prime Minister on information technology, and the Planning Commission, and listed 1:10,000 mapping of the country as one of its primary focus areas (Datta, 2016). India visualizes starting of a National GIS as important step to map changes in natural resources, and to understand the complex interplay of social order and economic growth. GIS is technology-centric but needs to be decision-centric. This means that all types of decision makers, governments, enterprises, and citizens should have the ability to easily make use of readily available GIS data and applications that can help solve their problems (ESRI, 2014).

India has recognized that a strong organizational framework is essential for bringing focus and for institutionalizing National GIS and promoting geospatial technology use by government, enterprises, and citizens. The process of establishing and implementing the state and national vision will also provide considerable opportunities for the private sector to contribute to and be part of this national endeavor. The national and state GIS will also boost education and research in GIS with specific school, university, and research programs focused on training the leaders of tomorrow in spatial thinking concepts and the core principles of GIS (ESRI, 2014).

India is recognised for its IT skills and space programmes. It offers good infrastructure and expertise for collection of geospatial data. Capacity building is key to capitalise on the opportunities presented before the Indian geospatial industry. India has shortage of skilled human resource in the field of geoinformatics, so students can take this as hotspot career. Large numbers of institutions in the country offer courses in various disciplines of geographical information science at undergraduate as well as post-graduate levels to sustain technically sound human resource base. Geoinformatics is not only for the people studying surveying , remote sensing, GPS, GIS or geography, but recently more disciplines, like computer science, civil engineering, architecture, geology, environmental science etc., have included Geoinformatics as their minor or even as their major subject (Virrantaus and Haggrén 2000). For that reason, it has become more important to develop the contents of Geoinformatics curriculum towards more scientific and less related with traditional surveying and mapping. Ongoing advances in GIS functionality and the convergence of network computing and wireless communications with geospatial technologies are expected to further unleash the hitherto untapped potential for applications in development planning.

1.5 SUMMARY

We live in an era that is so dynamic and characterised by technological advancements that at times it goes beyond our imagination. In the rapidly changing world, geoinformatics has special applications. Knowledge in the form of spatial information or geoinformation pertaining to a region is of vital importance for decision-making at the economic, political and personal level. The value of geoinformation exhibits a high market potential and demonstrates economic benefits in many applications (Doellner, 2005). The significance of geoinformatics therefore can not be underestimated.

Geoinformatics is related to geocomputation and to the development and use of GIS or spatial decision support systems. It offers an integrated approach with information technology (**IT**) for acquisition, storage and retrieval, modelling, management and analysis, and presentation and visualisation of geo-processes (Ehlers 2008). Geospatial information is now recognised as an extremely important information layer at all decision levels. The scientific field of geoinformatics encompasses the acquisition and storing of geospatial data, the modelling and presentation of spatial information, geoscientific analyses and spatial planning, and the development of algorithms and geospatial database systems. Geoinformatics has gained significant importance to serve as basis for spatial decisions in many areas, such as navigation and positioning, telecommunication, real estate management, insurance business, and the planning and management of pipelines, residential and commercial districts as well as geomarketing strategies. It has now become an important tool for decision makers across a wide range of disciplines, researchers and academia, and also for national survey and mapping organisations, industries, environmental agencies, and local and national governments (Goodchild, 2009).

Significant progress has been made in recent years in automating the process of acquiring three-dimensional data. Laser-based equipment mounted in a vehicle, for example, can now be driven along busy city streets capturing not only images but also three-dimensional structures. Detailed digital models have been constructed for many of the world's large cities, and are available through sites, such as Microsoft Virtual Earth.

Geoinformatics is fast expanding its presence in India and elsewhere. Public perception towards geoinformatics industry is also changing. Today geospatial data and tools are familiar to virtually everyone on the well-endowed side of the digital divide. The general public has become quite familiar with the user interfaces of sites, such as Google Maps and MapQuest (Doellner, 2005). Services, such as Google Maps and Microsoft Virtual Earth have brought digital geographic information within reach of everyone, which for many years was viewed as the domain of highly trained experts (Goodchild, 2009).

In future, there will be many new sensors, systems and also new applications. Concentrated efforts in research and innovation become essential for the effective and economical use of geospatial data. Further research in geoinformatics is needed on the appropriate ways to represent three-dimensional structures – in effect, building ontology– in order to satisfy the various applications of three-dimensional representations. The integrated technologies, like Digital aerial photographs, LiDAR, Satellite images, GPS, RFID, Sensors, Internet, IT, IoT, UAV/Drone, GIS, etc, are expected to open new avenues and applications of geoinformatics to create interactive queries and analyse information with its different attributes for decision making purposes.

Review Questions

1. Explain the origin and meaning of "Geomatics' and "Geographic Information Science". How do they differ from Geographic Information Systems?
2. Discuss the major disciplines of Geoinformatics.
3. Write a short note on the status of Geoinformatics in India.
4. Describe the major application areas of Geoinformatics?

References

1. Burrough P A (1986), *Principles of Geographical Information Systems for Land Resources Assessment*, Clarendon Press, Oxford, 194 pp.
2. Datta, Anusuya (2016), Towards a National Geospatial Policy, Geospatial World, March 2016.
3. Doellner, J., (2005). Geo-visualization and real-time computer graphics. In J. Dykes, A.M. MacEachren and M. J. Kraak, eds. Exploring geovisualization. Amsterdam: Elsevier. Chapter 16, pp. 325_344.
4. Ehlers, M. (2008) Geoinformatics and digital earth initiatives: a German perspective, International Journal of Digital Earth, 1:1, 17-30, DOI: 10.1080/17538940701781975.
5. Eldrandaly, Khalid. (2007) *Expert Systems, GIS, and Spatial Decision Making: Current Practices and New Trends.* Chapter 8 in Expert Systems Research Trends, A. R. Tyler (Ed), Nova Science Publishers, Inc., USA.
6. El-Rabbany, Ahmed (2006) *Introduction to GPS: The Global Positioning System*, 2nd Edition, Artch House, Boston.
7. ESRI (2014), India's Vision for National GIS, ESRI, California, USA, Jan 2014
8. Goodchild, Michael F (2009) Geographic information systems and science: today and tomorrow, Annals of GIS, 15:1, 3-9, DOI: 10.1080/19475680903250715.
9. IGNOU (2012), MGY_001 Introduction to Geoinformatics IGNOU, School of Sciences, IGNOU, Delhi.
10. Konecny, G. (2002). Recent global changes in geomatics education. The International Archives of the Photogrammetry, Remote Sensing and Spatial Information Sciences, Vol. XXXIV, Part 6, pp. 9-14.
11. Kraus, K., (1994), *Photogrammetry*, Verd. DümmlerVerlag, Bonn.
12. Marble, D. F. and Peuquet, D. J. (1983), *Geographic Information Systems and Remote Sensing*, In R. N. Colwell (Ed.) Manual of Remote Sensing, Vol. 1, Falls Church, VA., ASPRS.
13. Oledzki, J.R. (2004) Geoinformatics: An Integrated Spatial Tool, Miscellanea Geographica Warszawa. Miscellanea Geographica—Regional Studies on Development, 11, 323-331.

14. Prakash, A. (2006). Introducing Geoinformatics for Earth System Science Education. Journal of Geoscience Education. Volume 54, 2006 - Issue 5.

15. Ramprasad (2013) Empowering India through Geospatial Technologies- select stories, (2013) FICCI, Editor-in-Chief and Publisher, Gateway Media Pvt. Ltd., Hyderabad 500004 (www.geospatialtoday.com)

16. Report on India's Geospatial Market and Prospects (2016), Published by Geospatial Media and Communications Ltd, Noida.

17. Sonnen, Dave (2010), India on a Roll, Geospatial World, Sept 2010.

18. Vardhan, Harsh (2015), How Geospatial Technologies are Contributing to Major Ongoing Projects in India?, Geospatial World, Oct. 2015.

19. Virrantaus, K. and Haggrén, H. (2000), Curriculum of Geoinformatics-Integration of Remote Sensing and Geographical Information Technology. International Archives of Photogrammetry and Remote Sensing, Vol. XXXIII, Part B6, pp. 288-294.

20. Xu, Guochang (2010) *GPS: Theory, Algorithms and Applications*, Springer Verlag.

Web Resources

Web Resources: http://www.wgsr.uw.edu.pl/pub/uploads/mcg04/35oledzki.pdf

Chapter 2

PHOTOGRAMMETRY

2.1 INTRODUCTION

Photogrammetry refers to the process of recording, interpreting and measuring from photographic images. The name "photogrammetry" is derived from the three Greek words **phot** which means light, **gramma** which means letter or something drawn, and **metrein**, the noun of measure.

The classical definition of photogrammetry is *it is the art, science and technology of obtaining reliable information about physical objects and the environment, through processes of recording, measuring, and interpreting photographic images and patterns of recorded electromagnetic energy and other phenomena.* It is a science and technology both as it takes information from an image and transforms this data into meaningful results.

Photogrammetry is an engineering discipline and is in a constant state of change, like other disciplines. As such, it is heavily dependent on developments in computer science and electronics. The ever increasing use of computers and software has had and will continue to have a great impact on photogrammetry. This becomes especially evident in the shift from analog to analytical and digital methods. Images used in photogrammetry can originate from a special (metric) camera, an ordinary camera or from digital sensors. These image can be recorded from a device mounted on an airplane (including helicopters), or on a tripod (terrestrial photogrammetry) which is set up on the ground. Photogrammetry is a skilled profession for the reason that it requires certain skills, techniques and judgments to be made for taking reliable measurements by the Photogrammetrists and experienced interpreters.

The photogrammetric process consists of project planning, image acquisition, image processing, and control data for image orientation, data compilation and derivation of results. The end product from the photogrammetric process can be the coordinate values of individual points, a graphical representation of the ground surface (topographic map, thematic map, etc.), or a rectified image with map-like characteristics (orthophotos). The most common use of photogrammetry is in the generation of base maps for various applications. Mapping using photogrammetry provides a cost-effective approach of establishing accurate base maps required for, such as urban planning, natural resources planning, terrain analysis, road alignment, forest management, etc. Aerial photographs have been successfully used to measure the 3-D location of points or features by creating three-dimensional model of the terrain/features. It is done by viewing the area from two different camera angles, thereby recreating the same conditions for 3D model, as it existed at the time of photography.

Modern photogrammetry includes airborne and terrestrial based light detection and ranging (LiDAR) data. Both these technologies are inherently being used to for various applications. With good contrast, good lighting and atmospheric conditions, photogrammetry is an excellent tool for mapping, but if vegetation or complex structures are present in the area, LiDAR may provide additional information for detailed and accurate interpretation. Photogrammetry has also been used along with images taken from a Drone (Unmanned Aerial Vehicle) for interpretation of large scale photographic images.

2.2 DEVELOPMENTS IN PHOTOGRAMMETRY

The conception of using photographs for purposes of measurement appears to have originated with the experiments of Aime Laussedat of the Corps of the French Army, who in 1851 produced the first measuring camera for its application to topography. The first known aerial photograph was taken in 1858 by a French photographer and balloonist, Gaspar Felix Tournachon, known as *Nadar*. In 1855, he patented the idea of using aerial photographs in map making and surveying, but it took him 3 years of experimenting before he could successfully produce first aerial photograph. It was a view of the French village of Petit-Becetre taken from a tethered hot-air balloon, 80 meters above the ground (Figure 2.1). In 1858, Laussedat, Meydenbauer in Germany carried out the first experiment in making critical measurements of architectural details on the basis of two photographs of the building.

Figure 2.1: Nadar's earliest surviving aerial image, taken above Paris in 1866 (left). Boston from a tethered balloon, 13th October, 1860, by James Wallace Black (right).

(Sources:http://profession alaerialphotographers.com/content.aspx?page_id=22&club_id= 808138 &module_ id=158950, History of Aerial Photography)

Besides hot air balloons, the improvement in technology made it possible to use kites, pigeons and rockets to carry cameras into the skies for air-photography. In 1882, the English meteorologist, E. D. Archibald was among the first to take successful photographs from kites. In 1889, Arthur Batut took aerial photographs from a kite, in Labruguiere, France. The first successful aerial photograph from a rocket mounted camera was taken by the Swedish inventor, Alfred Nobel in 1897. He is best known now-a-days for the Nobel prize. In 1903, Julius Neubranner designed a tiny breast-mounted camera for carrier pigeons.

The first aerial photography from an airplane piloted by Wilbur Wright was taken in 1909 by L. P. Bonvillain who took motion pictures of the military field at Centocelli, near Rome. During World War I (1914-1918), the battle maps used by both sides were created from aerial photographs, replacing the use of aerial photographs for sketching & drawing. After the end of war, aerial photographs were used for civilian purposes. Sherman Fairchild took a series of overlapping photographs and made an aerial map of Manhattan Island. This map was very popular and aerial photography became a successful commercial venture due to its civilian uses. Along with his successful development of aerial camera, Fairchild also designed and built airplanes with high-wings and stable platform to take aerial photographs. His innovation and strong commitment to the business of aerial photography brought more wide-spread use of aerial images. Before Fairchild died in 1971, he saw his cameras carried on Apollo 15, 16 and 17, and while astronauts explored the lunar surface, his cameras mapped the moon.

The development of the photogrammetry from year 1850 went through different cycles. Overall, there are four major phases of development in Photogrammetry (Figure 2.2. The first phase is related with the invention of photography which gave rise to new inventions and applications, followed by many experiments and investigations.

2.2.1 Analog Photogrammetry

The second phase of development was the era of analog photogrammetry form year 1900 to 1960, which led to the invention of analogue rectification and stereo-plotting instruments. During this era, airplanes and cameras were extensively used in the World War II (1939-1945), and established aerial survey techniques for military operations. World War II gave rise to new developments of aerial photography techniques, such as the application of radio control to photo flight navigation, and new wide-angle lenses & devices to achieve true vertical photographs. Photogrammetry thus became a popular surveying and mapping method. Optical or mechanical instruments were used to reconstruct the 3D geometry from stereo-images. The main product during this phase was topographic map. These methods use optical, mechanical and electronic components for modeling and processing. In this mode of processing, the data reduction is carried out using analog instruments (e.g., plotters such as Kelsh K-480 stereoplotter).

2.2.2 Analytical Photogrammetry

In 1950s, the third phase began with the use of computers; and thus analytical photogrammetry was developed for accurate photogrammetric measurements. Aerial triangulation was improved greatly, and the analytical plotters developed and made available in 1970s. Computer replaces the expensive optical or mechanical components. The resulting devices were digital/analog hybrids which use mathematical modeling assisted with digital processing. In this mode, the image coordinates are obtained using mono-comparators or stereo-comparators, and further processing is done through computer. Images used in both the above methods are in hard copy form (e.g., on film). The outputs were the topographic maps but in digital form.

2.2.3 Digital Photogrammetry

The fourth development phase is the transition from analog to digital photogrammetry. Digital Photogrammetry is also called softcopy photogrammetry, and is applied to digital images that are processed and stored in the computer. With the availability of good quality images with high resolution digital scanners and digital cameras, images in digital form are used in such systems. The modeling is based on same analytical principles except that they use digital images as input. Hence, digital methods use strengths of both analytical and image processing methods for analysis and stereo-plotting works (Grave, 1996). The entire process is carried out using digital photogrammetric software. The output of this is in the digital format: Digital Elevation Model (DEM), digital maps, digital othophotos stored in the computer. Digital photography is in wide-spread use for a diverse set of commercial, industrial, agricultural, governmental and private applications. The main advantage to extend from analog to analytical photogrammetry and then to digital environment is huge time and cost savings in deriving the useful results, and using the digital output as input into other analysis systems, such as GIS (Hassani and Carswell, 1992) .

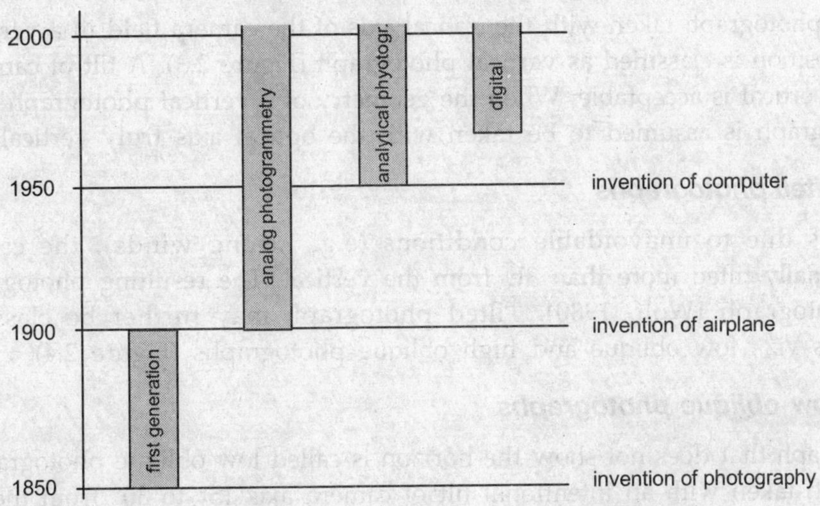

Figure 2.2: Major phases of development of photogrammetry

(*Source :Schenk, 2005*)

2.3 TYPES OF PHOTOGRAPHS

There are two main products in photogrammetry. Analog photogrammetric work requires **hard copy** photographic products. These products have a pre-defined scale and format. The format is generally square 23cm x 23cm. It generally involves the use of optical and mechanical systems to carry out analysis from hard copy products. Digital photogrammetric work requires **soft (digital) copy** of photographic products. Digital photographs are used in digital photogrammetry and all processing & analysis work is performed on computer using specialised software. These products don't have a defined scale and format, being digital in nature. Whether analog or digital, these photographs can be grouped into two categories, depending on the platform from air or ground used to capture them. These are aerial photogrammetry and terrestrial (close-range) photogrammetry (Robson et al 2014).

2.3.1 Aerial Photographs

Aerial photographs are taken with as **aerial** camera mounted in an aircraft and is usually pointed vertically towards the ground. Overlapping photographs of the ground are taken as the aircraft moves along a defined flight path. In digital photogrammetry, photographs or video are taken from a digital camera mounted in an airplane (Samson, 2003). Traditionally, these photos are processed in a stereo-plotter (hardcopy) or by automated desktop systems (digital), and used for topographic mapping and Digital Elevation Model (DEM) creation.

Aerial photographs which are normally used for mapping and photo-interpretation can be classified into two main categories viz., vertical and tilted photographs.

2.3.1.1 Vertical photographs

An aerial photograph taken with the optical axis of the camera held in a vertical or nearly vertical position is classified as vertical photograph (Figure 2.3). A tilt of camera axis upto ±3° from vertical is acceptable. When the geometry of a vertical photograph is considered, the photograph is assumed to be taken with the optical axis truly vertical (Figure 2.4).

2.3.1.2 Tilted photographs

Sometimes due to unavoidable conditions (e.g., strong winds), the camera axis is unintentionally tilted more than 3Ú from the vertical. The resulting photograph is called tilted photograph (Wolf, 1980). Tilted photograph may further be classified in two categorizes viz., low oblique and high oblique photographs (Figure 2.4).

2.3.1.3 Low oblique photographs

A photograph that does not show the horizon is called low oblique photograph. An aerial photograph taken with an intentional tilt of camera axis 15° to 30° from the vertical axis is referred to as low oblique photograph. This kind of photographs is often used in reconnaissance surveys.

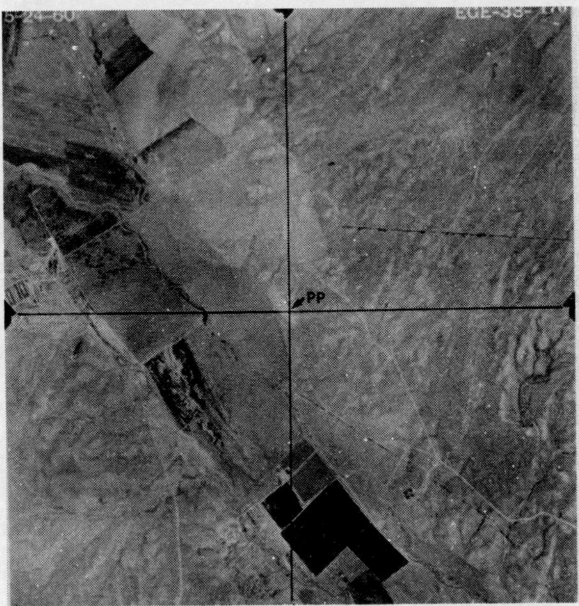

Figure 2.3: A typical vertical aerial photograph

2.3.1.4 High oblique photographs

A photograph in which the apparent horizon appears is termed as high oblique photograph. Apparent horizon is the line in which the Earth appears to meet the sky as visible from the exposure station. The high oblique photographs are obtained when the camera axis is intentionally inclined about 60° from the vertical axis. Such photographs are useful for mapping the international boundary and details of the territory on the other side as well as military applications.

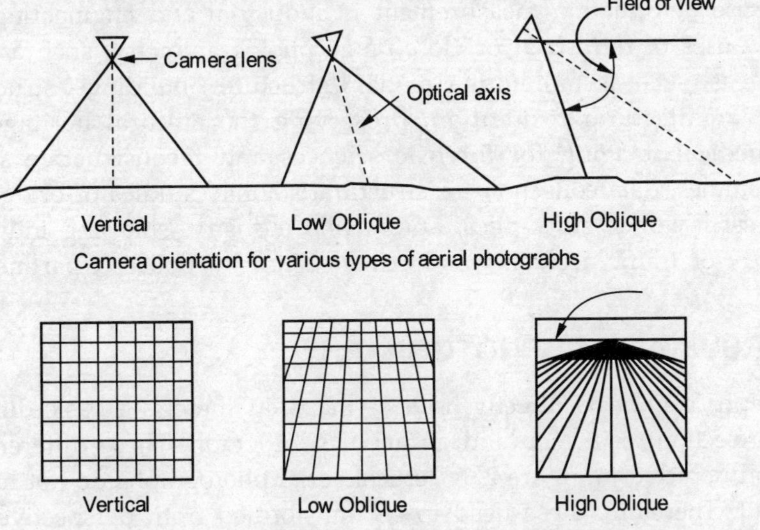

Figure 2.4: Vertical, low oblique and high oblique photographs (*Source: ASPRS, 1980*)

2.3.2 Terrestrial or Close-range Photographs

Terrestrial or close-range photographs are taken when the camera, either hand held or tripod mounted, is located on or near the ground,. The output may be photographs or non-topographic products, like 3D models, measurements, or point clouds. In computer vision science, this type of photogrammetry is sometimes called **Image-based modelling** (Robson et al 2014). Figure 2.5 shows the close range or terrestrial photographs of three points A, B and C, taken from three positions of cameras to determine the precise coordinates of three points.

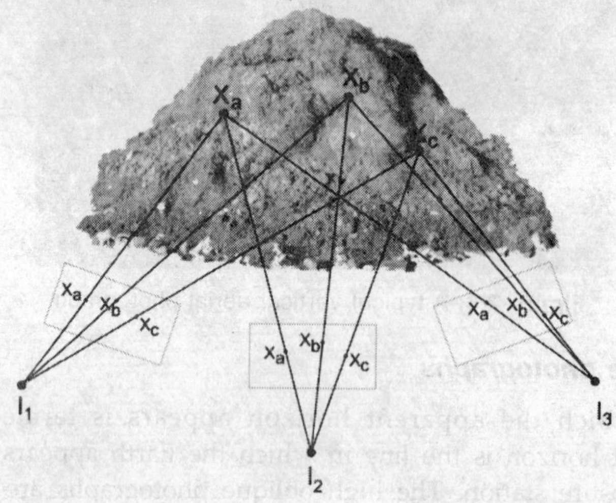

Figure 2.5 Terrestrial or Close-range photogrammetry (*Source: Wrozyhski, 2017*)

Close-range photogrammetry, employing wide range of cameras coupled with automated image measurement and mapping, has attracted wide usage over the past decade for precise deformation measurement in industrial and engineering applications. There are many uses of **terrestrial** or close-range photogrammetry, such as 3D modeling of objects or areas, such as monitoring of dam structures, buildings, structures, towers, or movie sets, architectural restoration, preserving the cultural heritage, location of monuments, medical imaging for forensic sciences and reconstructive surgery, facial reconstruction studies, data collection for structural stability studies of bridges and hydro-electric dams, earth-works, stock-piles, automobile industry, shipping industry, antenna calibration, study of traffic accidents and crime scenes by police departments, etc

2.4 MAP VERSUS AERIAL PHOTOGRAPH

Aerial photographs cannot be directly used as maps, as there is a basic difference in the plannimetry (projection) of a map and an aerial photograph. These differences are listed in Table 2.1, and depicted in Figure 2.6. Vertical aerial photographs do not have a uniform scale throughout. Therefore, these need to be transformed from perspective projection to the orthometric view before they can be used to prepare topographic maps. Such photographs are known as orthophotos (Moffit and Mikhail, 1980).

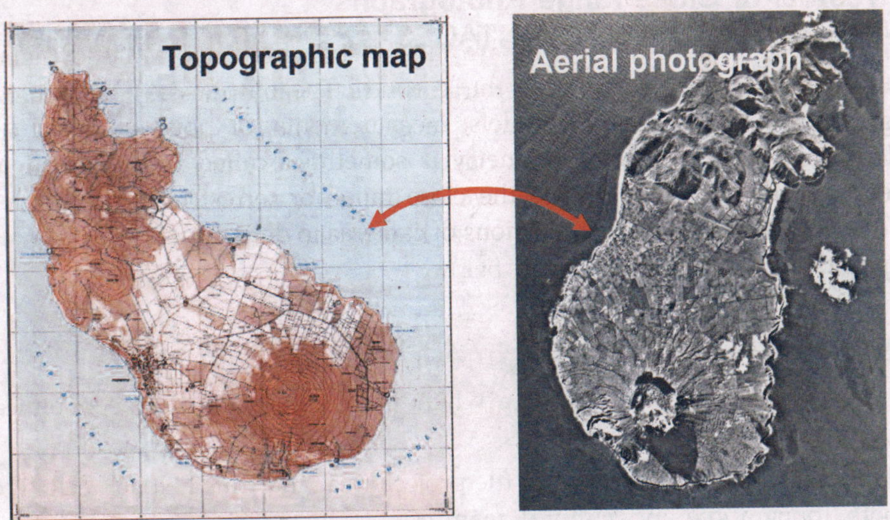

Figure 2.6 Topographic map and aerial photograph
(Source: https://www.scribd.com/document/277243918/Introduction-on-Photogrammetry-by-Koert-Sijmons)

Table 2.1: Difference between a map and an aerial photograph

S.No.	Aerial Photograph	Map
1	It is based on a Central projection.	It is based on an Orthogonal projection.
2	It is a real representation of the ground.	It is an abstract representation of the ground. Legend is needed to read it.
3	The scale of the photograph is not uniform.	The scale of the map is uniform throughout.
4	An aerial photograph has no geometric distortion at its centre but it increases towards the edges of the photograph.	A map is a geometrically correct representation of part of the Earth projected.
5	Relief displacement is present	Terrain relief is without distortion
6	Enlargement/reduction of the photographs can be carried out.	Enlargement/reduction of the map involves redrawing/remapping it a afresh.
7	It is comparatively difficult to read a photograph and identify the objects.	In a map, objects are shown with different symbols and colours, so easy to read and identify the objects with the help of Legend.
8	The objects and features are represented in their true shapes and sizes. sizes.	These are generall- epresented with different symbols and not with their actual
9	Aerial photography can be carried out for inaccessible and hazardous areas.	The mapping of inaccessible and hazardous areas is very difficult or impossible.
10	Information is explicit	Information is implicit

2.5 ADVANTAGES AND DISADVANTAGES OF PHOTOGRAMMETRY

The advantages of photogrammetry over traditional ground surveying are that it is the economical and efficient way of mapping a large area, no site access issues, provides a record of features at that instant of time; this is especially useful in rapidly changing sites such as mines, quarries and landfills. However, there are some disadvantages too (Wolf, 1980, Moffit and Mikhail, 1980, Kraus, 1994, Manugula et al 2018). A summary of the advantages and disadvantages is given below:

2.5.1 Advantages

1. It covers a relatively larger area which can be mapped more economically than the traditional survey methods.
2. It provides a bird's eye view of the project area, and thus helps in easy identifying both topographic and cultural features.
3. It provides a permanent pictorial record of the area that existed at the time aerial photographs were taken.
4. The sequential photographs of the same area may be used for monitoring the area.
5. The use of digital photographs ensures total flexibility of scale of mapping.
6. It is particularly suitable for areas that are unsafe, hazardous, forbidden properties (restricted arrears) and difficult access. Photogrammetry is an ideal surveying method for toxic areas where the safety of ground surveying staff is important.
7. It can effectively be used in the office for detail surveys of roads, including elevation data, as aerial surveys can be done without closing lanes, disturbing traffic or field staff.
8. The pictorial record minimizes the field work to acquire new information quickly. The measurements can be done in the office using these photographs.
9. Intervisibilty between control points and intervisibilty between the areas to be surveyed are not required, and thus minimising the cost of establishing the excessive control surveys.
10. The coordinates of every point in the mapped area can be determined with no extra cost.
11. Mosaic from aerial hotographs can be compiled in a short time to view and study the large area.
12. The photographs may be archived for future use. Same set of photographs can also be used for other studies, more efficiently and economically.
13. The technique is non-intrusive, and requires less manual effort for mapping the area.
14. It is cost-effective, providing high level of accuracy.
15. It provides speedy coverage of an area, and thus time-saving.

2.5.2 Disadvantages

1. Processing and analysis of aerial photographs require experienced photogrammetrists.
2. Photographic coverage requires advance flight planning as well as specialised equipment and aircraft.
3. Atmospheric conditions (winds, clouds, haze etc.) may affect the flight plan as well as quality of the photographs.
4. Seasonal conditions affect the aerial photographs, i.e., snow cover will obstruct the features.
5. The ground hidden by structures, such as buildings or by large tree canopies, and roads hidden by trees on both sides, cannot be mapped accurately.
6. Accuracy of contours and cross sections will depend on scale of photographs and accuracy & number of ground control points.
7. Aerial photography is expensive for developing countries, like India, particularly if repetitive coverage of an area is required for mapping and monitoring purposes.
8. For sensitive areas or restricted areas, aerial photography may not be allowed.

2.6 ACQUISITION OF AERIAL PHOTOS

It consists of system (hardware) such as camera system, and details of flight planning, as given below:

2.6.1 Aerial Camera System

The aerial camera is very important and sophisticated equipment used in the photographic acquisition process. **Analog camera is** a lightproof chamber or box in which the image of an exterior object is projected upon a sensitized plate or film through an opening usually equipped with a "lens," a "shutter" and a variable "aperture." The camera should be able to produce distortion free and high quality photos in a moving aircraft as the processing & analysis is done later on these photos. The images are recorded on stable film media (B&W or colour) in order to avoid shrinkage or expansion. The frame size in aerial film is usually 23cm x 23cm each, and the measurement errors on photographs/images will also depend on the sensitivity of the film to shrinkage or expansion. Hard copy photographs can be scanned through scanners, and converted into a digital format that can be imported into software for its processing. There are specialized scanners which preserve the radiometric and geometric characteristics of the scanned photographs.

Now-a-days, mostly digital cameras are used, therefore the data (photograph) is already in a digital format, and hence there is no need for the film and specialized scanner. Present day technology can provide digital cameras based on static field of CCD (Charge Coupled Device) sensors. The CCD can vary in storage capacity and resolution, which affects the clarity of the digital images. Two technologies are employed as the basis of airborne digital sensors – linear and area array CCDs. A high speed computer along with the specialised photogrammetric software is required for the analysis of digital aerial images.

2.6.2 Flight Planning

Successful execution of any photogrammetric project requires thorough planning prior to flying to take photographs of the project site. The first step in the design is to know the extent of the area, and decide on the scale of photographs and the required accuracy. The project area is marked on the topographic map to study the elevation range as well as the kind of features present in the area. It is required to know that focal length of the camera lens, photographic scale, size and shape of the area to be photographed, size of photograph, the amount of end lap and side lap, relief displacement, tilt of photographs, drift angle and ground speed of aircraft. Knowing the scale and focal length and average elevation (above *msl*) of the terrain, the flying height at which the aircraft would move can be computed. In fact, scale and flying height are inter-related to each other (Moffit and Mikhail, 1980). Higher the flying height, smaller the scale is and larger the area covered.

The number of flight lines, their locations, spacing between them (air-base), and their orientation are computed in advance which would depend on the characteristics of the area to be photographed and on the specifications of the flight mission. Other specifications to be known include end lap, side lap, area covered by one photograph, number of photographs covered in each flight line, total number of photographs, camera and film requirements (no need of film in case of digital camera system), speed of aircraft, tilt and crab tolerances, weather and meteorological conditions etc. Generally, wide lens cameras are preferred for the area that is smooth, and normal lens cameras are preferred for the area that is hilly or urban area (ASPRS, 1983)

The vertical photographs are usually taken by a series of parallel flight lines. The flight line is normally taken along the longer dimension of the area. After finishing recording of photographs along first flight line, the aircraft takes a semi-circular curve path (outside the project area) to enter into second flight line of project area and so on (Figure 2.7). Thus, it completes the photography of entire area in a zig-zag route. The flight line directions are generally planned in East-West or North-South direction. The land limitations, such as mountain range, lake, and sea-side may affect planning of the flight line directions. In these situations, flight lines are planed parallel to these details. All these processes are time-consuming and must be performed carefully. Any carelessness or mistakes might cause errors in the flight planning.

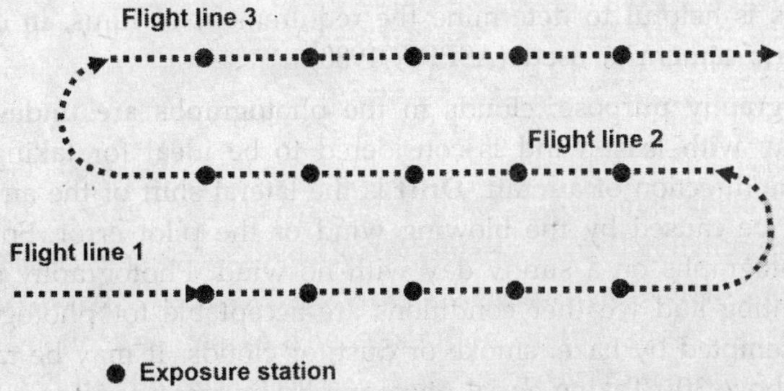

Figure 2.7: Route of flight lines

Controlling the aircraft speed is important for maintaining the necessary forward or end lap expected for the photographs. If the aircraft flies too fast, less forward lap than anticipated is obtained, while flying the aircraft too slow results in too much overlap between two successive photos. Little amount of overlap reduces the capability of using such photos for stereo-viewing and processing, while too much overlap results in too many unnecessary photos that may significantly enhance the project budget. Both situations are undesirable to the anticipated products and/or the project budget. Flying at a slower speed will allow for a better turning radius. Flying too slow becomes very inefficient with regards to fuel also. Best speed is one where lift and drag are equal, making it most efficient. The airbase or the distance between two successive photos along one flight line that satisfies the amount of end lap necessary for the project, is computed (Moffit and Mekhail, 1980). The distance between two successive exposure stations along a flight line is called the **air-base (Camera Base)**. Once the **airbase** is determined and the aircraft speed is decided upon, the time between two successive exposures is computed.

Photographs are normally exposed in such a way that the area covered by each successive photograph along a flight line overlaps a part of previous photograph. The positions of camera (Figure 2.8) at each exposure e.g., 1, 2, 3...are called the **exposure stations** and the altitude of camera at the instant of exposure is called **flying height**. Two successive photographs taken during a flight line is called a **stereo-pair**. This overlap between two successive photographs taken along a flight line is called **longitudinal overlap** or **forward overlap** or **endlap**. The amount of endlap is kept a minimum of 60%. This overlap is useful to generate 3D view of the common area between two successive photographs. The common overlap between three successive photographs is called **superlap** (Wolf, 1980).

Each flight line during photography of an area will cover some area on the ground in the form of a corridor, called a **flight strip**. The number of photographs covered during a flight strip is called **strip of photographs** which is uniquely numbered/coded. The overlap between two successive flight strips is called **lateral overlap** or **sidelap** which is kept between 20-40% (Figure 2.8). The photographs of two or more flight strips are called **block of photographs**. Knowing the total flight strips and the photographs covered by each strip, the total number of photographs required to cover the project area can be computed. This is helpful to determine the requirement of films, in case of conventional photogrammetric camera is used (ASPRS, 1980).

For photography purpose, clouds in the photographs are undesirable. Therefore, a clear sunny day with least wind is considered to be ideal for taking air-photos. Strong winds affect the direction of aircraft. **Drift** is the lateral shift of the aircraft from the flight lines that may be caused by the blowing wind or the pilot error. So, a good practice is to capture photographs on a sunny day with no wind. Photography shall be undertaken only when lighting and weather conditions are acceptable for photographs. Photography is not to be attempted by haze, smoke or dust, or clouds. It may be taken at any suitable solar altitude above 30_0. Taking aerial photography in urban territories is better at midday, when shadows are shortest. **Crab** is the angle formed between flight line and the edges of the photographs in the direction of flight. It occurs when the aircraft is not oriented with flight line. It reduces the effective width of photographic coverage (Kraus, 1994).

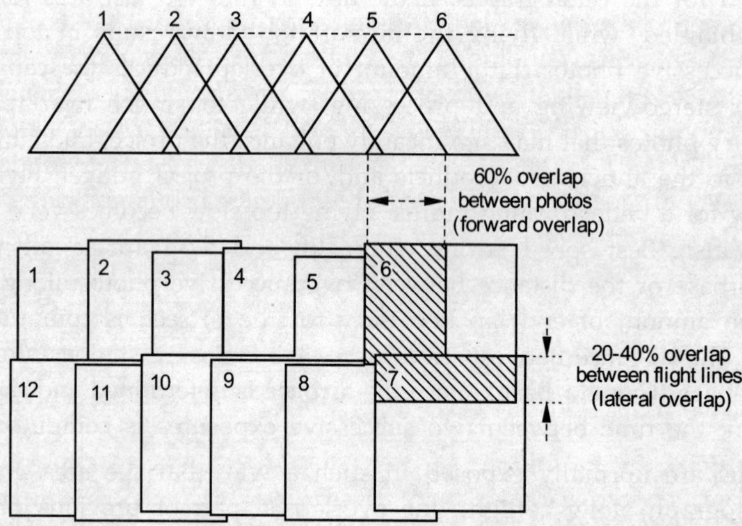

Figure 2.8: Photographs during a flight planning (*Source: ASPRS, 1980*)

In India, aerial photos are taken in the air by the authorised agency of Govt. of India, viz. **Survey of India (SOI),** Dehradun, and **National Remote Sensing Centre (NRSC)** Hyderabad. Users make a request to these agencies to obtain aerial photographs either from the archive or flying afresh through the area, subject to clearance from the Ministry.

The following processes are required in flight planning:

1. Developing the flight plan on a map, and computing the length and width of the area.
2. Planning the ground controls.
3. Compute the scale of the photograph using relationship:

$$S_{avg} = f / (H - h_{avg}). \quad ...(2.1)$$

4. Compute the coverage on the ground of one photo (*W*).

5. Compute the flight lines spacing as follows:
   Line spacing or distance between flight lines (SP):
   = Photo coverage (*W*) * (100 – amount of side lap)/100. ...(2.2)
6. Calculate the number of flight lines:
   $(N_1) = (WIDTH / SP) + 1.$ ...(2.3)
7. Always round up the number of flight lines, i.e. 6.4 becomes 7.
8. Start the first flight line at the North-South or East-West boundary of the project
9. Compute the distance between two consecutive photos (or airbase), as follow:
   Airbase (*B*) = Image coverage (*W*) * ((100 – amount of end lap)/100). ...(2.4)
10. When the camera exposes a photo, the aircraft has to move a distance equal to the airbase before it exposes the next photo. If the aircraft speed is (*v*), the time (*t*) between two consecutive photos is calculated as:
    Time (*t*) = Air-base (B)/Aircraft Speed (*v*). ...(2.5)
11. Compute number of images per flight line as:
    $(N_2) = (LENGTH / B) + 1.$ ...(2.6)
12. Always round up the number of photos, i.e. 20.3 becomes 21.
13. Add two images at the beginning of the flight line before entering the project area and two images upon exiting the project area in each flight line (to insure continuous stereo coverage), i.e. total of additional 4 images for each flight line.
    Number of images per flight line = $(LENGTH / B) + 1 + 4.$ ...(2.7)
14. Total number of images for the project = $N_1 \ x \ N_2$.
15. All the above data is essential in estimating the cost of the project.

2.7 GEOMETRIC PROPERTIES OF AERIAL PHOTOGRAPHS

Some important geometric properties of vertical aerial photographs are given below (Refer to Figure 2.9 a & b and Figure 2.12).

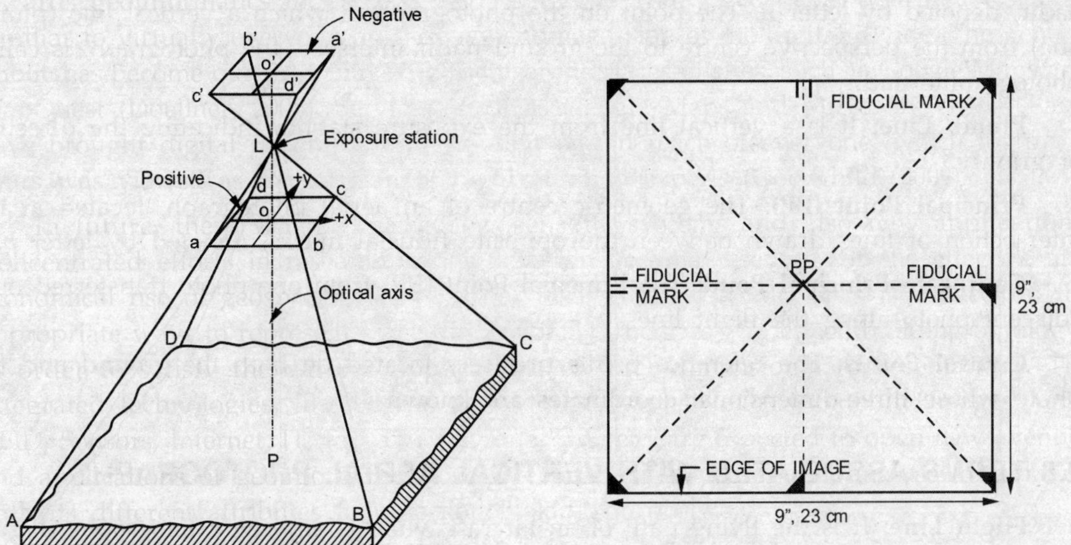

Figure 2.9: (a) Geometry (b) Format of a vertical aerial photograph (*Source: Wolf, 1980*)

Camera Axis: The camera axis represents the optical axis. It is a line passing through center of camera lens perpendicular both to camera plate (Negative) and photographic plane (Positive).

Exposure Station: Location of an aircraft in the air at the time of taking a photograph.

Fiducial Marks: Index marks, usually four, which are rigidly connected with the camera lens to form four sharp marks on the photographs.

Fiducial Axes: Straight line s joining opposite fiducial marks on a photograph. X axis is nearly in the direction of flight, and Y axis is perpendicular to the direction of flight.

Flying Height: The height at which the aircraft flies when photographs was taken. It has a direct relationship with the photographic scale, higher the flying height, smaller the scale. Flying height is always known prior to flying to the area.

Focal length: Distance from the optical centre of the lens to the focal plane, when the camera is focussed at infinity. Its value is known, as it is supplied by the manufacturer.

Ground Nadir: The point on the ground vertically beneath the perspective centres of the camera lens, denoted by letter N.

Perspective Centre: The point of origin or termination of bundles of perspective light rays.

Perspective (Central) Projection: All the projecting rays by a camera lens pass through a common point, called the perspective Centre. An aerial photograph is based on a perspective (central) projection. Due to relief variations of the ground objects, an aerial photograph differs geometrically from the map of the corresponding area.

Photograph Centre: The point on the photograph that is located at the intersection of the fiducial axes. In a perfectly adjusted camera, the photograph centre and the principal point are identical.

Photographic Nadir: The point on the photograph which corresponds to the ground nadir, denoted by letter *n*. The point on the photograph at which a vertical line (plumb line) from the perspective centre to the ground nadir intersects the photograph, is called photographic nadir.

Plumb Line: It is a vertical line from the exposure station, indicating the direction of gravity.

Principal Point (PP): The geometric centre of an aerial photograph, located at the intersection of lines drawn between the opposite fiducial marks, denoted by letter *p*.

Conjugate Principal Point: The Principal Point (PP) from one photo transferred onto adjacent photo along the flight line.

Control Points: The reference points precisely located on both the ground and the photo whose three-dimensional coordinates are known

2.8 TERMS ASSOCIATED WITH VERTICAL AERIAL PHOTOGRAPHS

Flight Line: It is the flying path of an aircraft while taking the photographs (Figure 2.7). It represents X axis for photographic measurements, while Y axis is perpendicular to it passing through the principal point of the photograph (Figure 2.8).

Floating Mark: A mark (dot or cross), associated with parallax bar or stereometers or stereoscopic plotting machines, seen as occupying a position in the three-dimensional space formed by the stereoscopic fusion of a stereo-pair and used as a reference mark in examining or measuring the stereo-model.

Orthogonal Projection: Maps are based on orthogonal (parallel) projections where the projecting rays are perpendicular to the line on the ground. The advantage of this projection is that the distances, angles or areas on the plane are independent of the elevation differences of the objects.

Orthophotos: An orthophoto is an aerial photograph that has been rectified by combining photogrammetric principles with Digital Elevation Model (DEM) data. An aerial photograph does not have a constant scale throughout the photograph, whereas the scale is uniform throughout in an orthophoto, and hence it can be used as an alternate to map.

Overlap: The common region (expressed as a percentage) by which one photograph covers the same area as covered by another. The overlap between aerial photographs in the same flight line is called "end lap," and the overlap between photographs in adjacent parallel flight lines is called "side lap (Figure 2.8).

Mean Sea Level (MSL): The average level of the sea surface, calculated as the arithmetical mean of hourly tide levels taken over an extended period and used as the standard for determining elevations.

Mosaic: The process of seamlessly joining several images together to form one large image, using a series of overlapping air photos. It is created to analyse the large area.

Parallax: The apparent displacement of the position of an object, with respect to a reference point, caused by a shift in the point of observation.

Photo Interpretation: An act of identifying the objects from images and judging their relative significance.

Scale: The ratio of a distance on a photograph or map to its corresponding distance on the ground. Scale may be expressed as a ratio (1:25,000), a fraction (1/25,000), or equivalence (1 cm = 250m).

Stereo-model: In two successive photographs, the overlapping part can be utilized for stereo measurements. The stereo-pair is used to create a stereo model that can be seen in 3D.

2.9 TERMS ASSOCIATED WITH TILTED AERIAL PHOTOGRAPHS

Azimuth: The horizontal angle measured clockwise about the ground nadir from a reference plane (usually the north meridian) to the principal plane. (The azimuth of a photograph is the ground-survey direction of tilt, while swing is the direction of tilt with respect to the photograph axes-

Isocentre: The point on the photograph where the bisector of the angle of tilt (t) strikes the photograph (located in the principal plane as well as on the principal line), denoted by letter *i* (Figure 2.10b). The isocenter is a unique point common to the plane of the tilted photograph, its principal plane, and the plane of the assumed truly vertical photograph taken from the same camera station and having an equal principal distance (i.e., the isocenter is located at the intersection of 3 planes).

Isometric Parallel: The photograph parallel that passes through the isocenter; also, the line of intersection between the plane of the photograph and a horizontal plane (or a truly vertical photograph) having an equal principal distance from the same perspective center (Figure 2.10a).

Principal Line: The line on the photograph which passes through the principal point and the nadir point (and the "isocentre") (Figure 2.10a).

Principal Plane: The vertical plane through the perspective centre containing the photograph perpendicular and the nadir point (and the "isocentre") (Figure 2.10a).

Swing: The angle about the principal point of a photograph, measured clockwise from the positive y-axis to the principal line at the nadir point, denoted by letter *s* (Figure 2.10a). Swing also refers to rotation of the photograph (or photo-coordinate system) around the photograph perpendicular (or photograph z-axis). In air navigation, swing represents aircraft rotation about the aircraft's vertical axis and is referred to as "yaw" or "crab."

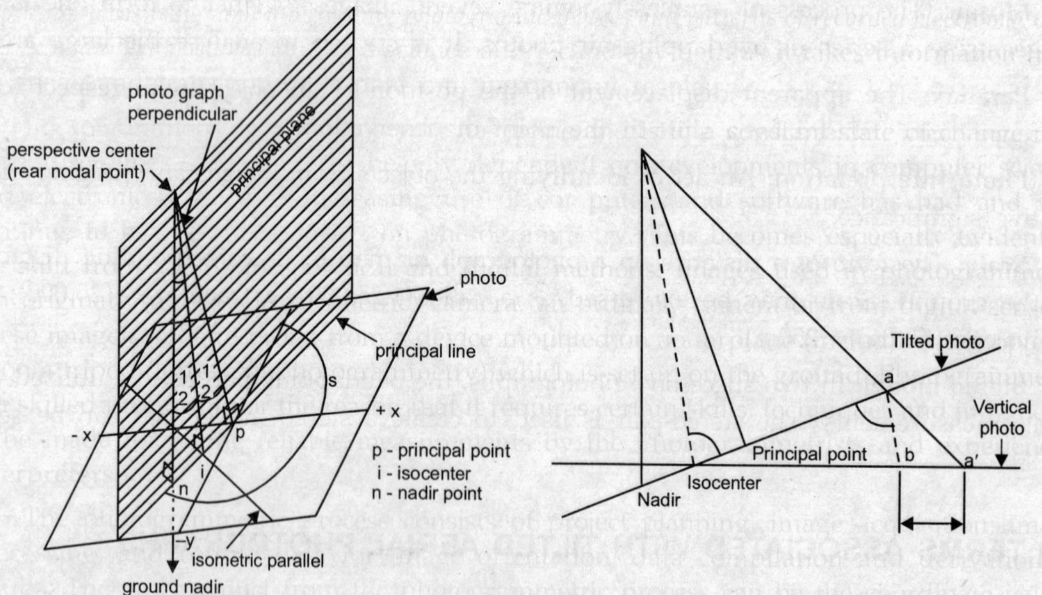

Figure 2.10: (a) Representation of a titled photo (b) Parameters of a tilted photo

(*Source: Moffit, and Mekhail, 1980*)

Tilt: The angle at the perspective center between the photograph perpendicular and the plumb line (Figure 2.10a).

Tilt Displacement: The displacement of images on a tilted photograph is radially outward (inward) with respect to the isocenter if the images are on the low (high) side of the isometric parallel. (The "low" side of a tilted photograph is the side closer to ground).

2.10 COMPUTATION OF LENGTH OF A LINE

Let the coordinates of two ground points *A* and *B* be (X_A, Y_A) and (X_B, Y_B) respectively. Their corresponding coordinates on the photograph for points *a* and *b* are (x_a, y_a) and (x_b, y_b), respectively (Figure 2.11). Here, *X* axis is along the direction of flight line and *Y* axis is perpendicular to flight line passing through the principal point of the photograph. *H* is the flying height of the aircraft, and h_A and h_B are the heights of *A* and *B* points with respect to *msl* (known from ground survey or contours on topographic map).

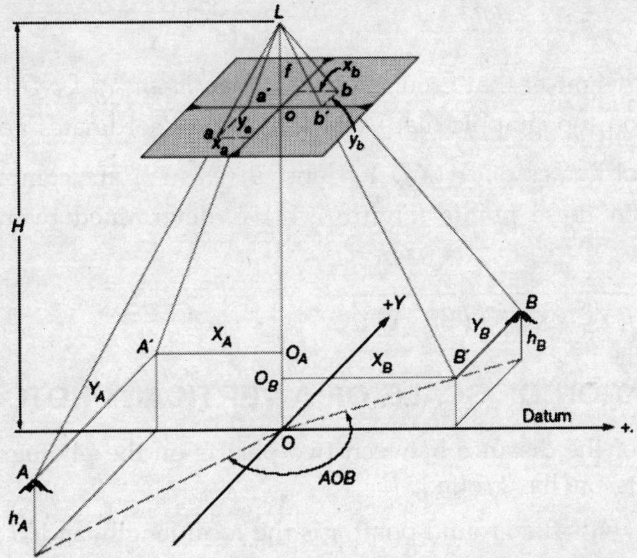

Figure 2.11: Length between two points from their coordinates *(Source: Schenk, 2005)*

For point (A) from similar triangles LA'O_A and La'o -

$$\frac{Lo}{LO_A} = \frac{x_a}{X_A} = \frac{y_a}{Y_A} = \frac{f}{H - h_A}$$

Similarly, for point (B) from similar triangles LB'O_B and Lb'o-

$$\frac{Lo}{LO_B} = \frac{x_b}{X_B} = \frac{y_b}{Y_B} = \frac{f}{H - h_B}$$

So

$$X_A = \frac{H - h_A}{f} . x_a \qquad ...(2.8)$$

$$Y_A = \frac{H - h_A}{f} . y_a \qquad ...(2.9)$$

$$X_B = \frac{H - h_B}{f} . x_b \quad \text{...(2.10)}$$

$$Y_B = \frac{H - h_B}{f} . y_b \quad \text{...(2.11)}$$

Since the flying height (H) of the aircraft and focal length (f) of the camera lens are already known, the ground coordinates of A (X_A, Y_A) and B (X_B, Y_B) can be computed using respective measured photographic coordinates (x_a, y_a) and (x_b, y_b). Their coordinates (x_a, y_a, x_b *and* y_b) should be used with caution in the relationship with proper algebraic sign depending on the quadrant these image points lie.

In general, the ground coordinates (X,Y) of any point can be related as:

$$X = \frac{H - h}{f} . x \quad \text{and} \quad Y = \frac{H - h}{f} . y$$

Where h is the height of that ground object above *mean sea level* (known from ground survey or contours on topographic map) whose ground coordinates are to be determined.

The ground coordinates of A (X_A, Y_A) and B (X_B, Y_B) are computed as above, and the distance between these points (Figure 2.11) is determined by using the following relationship:

$$L = \sqrt{(X_A - X_B)^2 + (Y_A - Y_B)^2} \quad \text{...(2.12)}$$

2.11 DETERMINATION OF SCALE OF A VERTICAL PHOTOGRAPH

The scale is a ratio of the distance between two objects on the photograph to the distance between same points on the ground.

In Figure 2.12, if A is the ground point, f is the focal length, and H is the flying height, scale S of the vertical photograph is computed as:

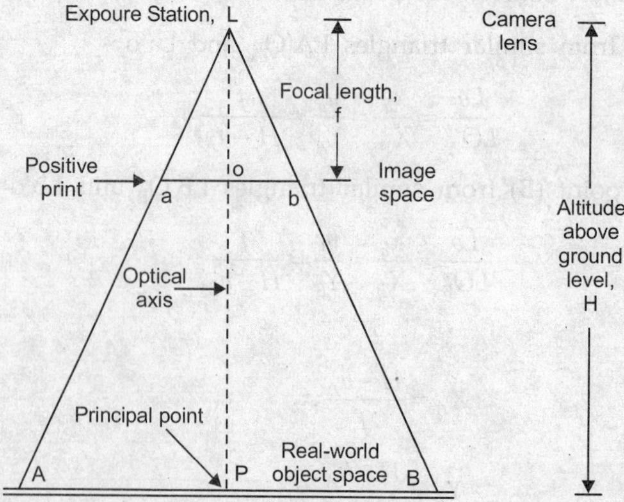

Figure 2.12. Scale of a vertical photograph in a flat terrain *(Source: Wolf, 1980)*

$$S = \frac{\text{Map distance}}{\text{Ground distance}} = \frac{oa}{PA}$$

Or $$S = \frac{oa}{PA} = \frac{f}{H} \qquad ...(2.13)$$

Let us consider two points A and B having elevation h_a and h_b, respectively above *mean sea level* (Figure 2.13). The scale of the photograph at point A may be written as:

$$\frac{ao}{AO_A} = \frac{Lo}{LO_A} = \frac{f}{H - h_A} \qquad ...(2.14)$$

Similarly, the scale of photograph at point B will be:

$$\frac{bo}{BO_B} = \frac{Lo}{LO_B} = \frac{f}{H - h_B} \qquad ...(2.15)$$

Scale at ground points C and D can be computed in a similar manner. It is concluded from above relationship that the scale of a photograph varies for points of different elevations, since f and H will be same for all the points in a given photograph. If all the points within a photograph are situated at the same elevation, scale will be constant and uniform throughout. But in general, there is height variation in the terrain. If the average elevation of the area is h_{av}, a more generalised relationship to compute the average scale S_{av} of photograph having points at different elevations may be written as:

$$S_{av} - \frac{f}{H - h_{av}} \qquad ...(2.16)$$

A more general expression for the scale may be written as -

$$S = \frac{f}{H - h}$$

Figure 2.13: Scale of a vertical photograph in undulating terrain *(Source: Schenk, 2005)*

So, photographic scale is directly proportional with the focal length of the camera lens. When a camera with larger focal length is used, a larger scale is obtained, and vice versa. It also varies inversely with the flying height. Scale decreases as the flying height increases and vice versa.

2.12 TYPES OF SCALE

Scale may be expressed as a ratio (1:25,000), or a fraction (1/25,000), or equivalence (1 cm = 250m). There are three broad categories of scale.

2.12.1 Large Scale Photographs

The aerial photographs with the scale 1:15,000 and larger are known as large-scale photographs. A large scale covers less area but shows more detail. Features on large scale photograph appear large. These photographs are used for regional planning such as new townships

2.12.2 Medium Scale Photographs

The aerial photographs with the scale ranging between 1:15,000 and 1:50,000 are usually considered as medium scale photographs. These photographs may be used for district level planning.

2.12.3 Small Scale Photographs

The photographs with the scale smaller than 1:50,000, are referred to as small scale photographs. A small scale shows the area in less detail but covers more area. Features on small scale photographs appear small. These photographs may be used for state level or national level planning.

2.13 RELIEF DISPLACEMENT OF A VERTICAL PHOTOGRAPH

It is the displacement of the objects on a vertical aerial photograph from their true horizontal positions. Aerial photograph is based on the central or perspective projection, and all objects on aerial photographs are displaced from their true positions, except the objects near the principal point where relief displacement is zero. Due to varying heights of different ground points, every point on the photograph is displaced from its original position. The higher objects, such as tall buildings, trees, towers, hills etc., are displaced away (outward) from the principal point, while the lower objects, such as valleys, depressions etc. are displaced (inward) towards the principal point. The direction of relief displacement is always radial from the principal point, and therefore it is also known as **radial displacement**.

In Figure 2.14, let AA_0 be a transmission tower with height h above ground. The a and a_0 respectively are the corresponding image points of tower on the photograph which has been taken from O. The aa_0 distance (d) on the photograph is called the relief displacement. The distance d can be computed as-

$$r = Ka$$

$$r_0 = Ka_0$$

$$R = K_0A_0$$

$$d = aa_0 = r - r_0$$

from similar triangles OKa_0 and OK_0A_0

$$\frac{r_0}{R} = \frac{f}{H}$$

$$r_0 = \frac{fR}{H} \qquad \text{...(2.17)}$$

from similar triangles OKa and $OK'0A$

$$\frac{r}{R} = \frac{f}{H-h}$$

$$r = \frac{fR}{H-h} \qquad \text{...(2.18)}$$

So relief displacement

$$d = r - r_0 = \frac{fR}{H-h} - \frac{fR}{H} \qquad \text{...(2.19)}$$

$$d = \frac{fR}{H(H-h)}(H - H + h) \qquad \text{...(2.20)}$$

$$d = \frac{f.R.h}{H.(H-h)}$$

But $\quad R = \left(\frac{H-h}{f}\right) r$

$$d = \frac{fh}{H(H-h)} \times \frac{(H-h)}{f}.r$$

So, $\quad d = \frac{rh}{H} \qquad \text{...(2.21)}$

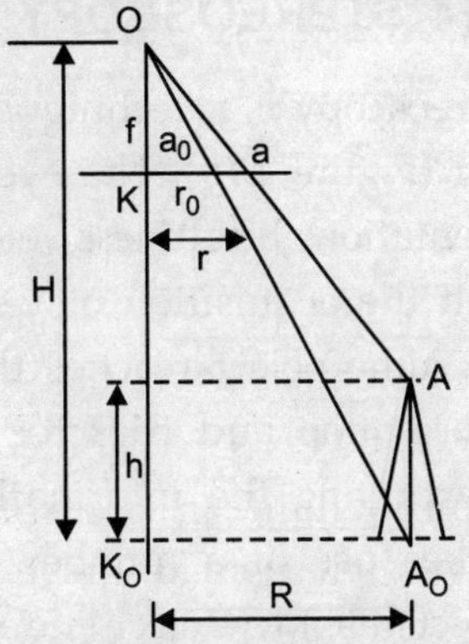

Figure 2.14: Relief displacement of a tower on a vertical photograph *(Source: ASPRS, 1980)*

It is seen that the relief displacement (d) is directly proportional to radial distance of displaced image point from principal point (r), as (r) increases (d) also increases. The relief displacement is maximum at the edges of photograph, and is zero at the principal point. It is therefore advisable that the objects situated at the edges of a photograph may not be selected for any measurement as it may have some error which is required to be eliminated before use. Relief displacement is directly proportional to the height of the object, as (h) increases (d) also increases. Whereas, (d) is inversely proportional to the flying height, as (H) increases (d) decreases. Relief displacement is also one of the main reasons; a photograph is not directly used as an accurate map.

From $$\frac{r}{r_0} = \frac{H}{H-h}$$

$$\frac{r}{H} = \frac{r_0}{H-h}$$

So relief displacement

$$d = \frac{rh}{H} = \frac{r_0}{H-h}h \quad ...(2.22)$$

If the relief displacement is known, the height of an object can be computed as:

$$h = \frac{dH}{R} \quad ...(2.23)$$

2.14 STEREOSCOPY

Stereoscopy is a technique for creating a model of depth perception by means of a stereo-pair (Figure 2.15). The eyes will see two images, which are only different in angle of view, orientation, brightness, etc. The perception of depth is a complex process which begins with the acquisition of visual information through the human eyes. When two images of the same object reaches the brain, it makes intelligent and meaningful output of the raw information and tries to fuse both the images into a single 3D image. The brain starts interpreting the information and also creates depth perception. For example, the brain makes use of a number of clues (e.g., colour, shape, size, pattern, texture, location of objects etc.) to determine relative distance and depth in perceived scenes, which are useful in interpretation.

2.14.1 Vertical Exaggeration

Vertical exaggeration simply means that vertical scale is larger than the horizontal scale. A final problem with three dimensional viewing of airphotos is vertical exaggeration. In stereoscopic viewing of a stereo-pair, the topographic features appear much taller than in reality and slope appears much steeper. It is the exaggeration of vertical heights with respect to the horizontal distances. The vertical exaggeration results due to wide spacing of camera position at the time of photography, as compared to the narrow spacing of the human eyes with respect to the normal viewing arrangement (Figure 2.16). The vertical exaggeration may be useful in photo-interpretation for identifying many features, such as slopes, low ridge and valley, topography, small depressions and elevations. It may be disadvantageous and somewhat disorienting to inexperienced viewers, particularly when quantitative estimation is to be done from the stereo-pair, such as slope estimation, heights of topographic features etc.

Vertical exaggeration occurs because of the difference in geometry when taking the airphotos and when viewing the airphotos. Factors affecting the vertical exaggeration are photographic and stereoscopic factors. The vertical exaggeration is fundamentally related to the ratio of air base with flying height (*B/H*).

It is directly proportional to air base (*B*), focal length (*f*), *h* is the distance from the eye at which the stereo model is perceived (approximately 45 cm). It is inversely proportional to flying height (*H*), and eye base (*b*) (approximately 6 cm). Vertical exaggeration ratio (*R*) is determined using the formula:

$$R = \frac{Bh}{bH} \quad \text{...(2.24)}$$

2.14.2 Stereoscopic Model

Two successive photographs which are taken from two different exposure stations, covering part of the common scene is called a **stereo-pair** or **stereoscopic images** or **stereogram**. Since the mental impression of three dimensions can only be obtained in the overlap portion of the photographs, the portion of scene in 3D which is common to both photographs is called **stereoscopic model** or **stereo-model**.

The term stereoscopic vision refers to the human ability to view 3D with both eyes using the basic principle that left eye will see left image and right eye will focus on the right image. It will allow interpreter to judge distance and depth in the overlap region. Human eyes, fixed on same object provide two points of observations which are required for parallax (Figure 2.16). Stereoscopic vision thus, is the observer's ability to resolve parallax differences between images of far and near objects.

In a similar way, 3D view can be created through stereoscopic process, using simple equipment, such as stereoscopes or sophisticated equipment, such as stereo-comparator, or digital photogrammetric system.

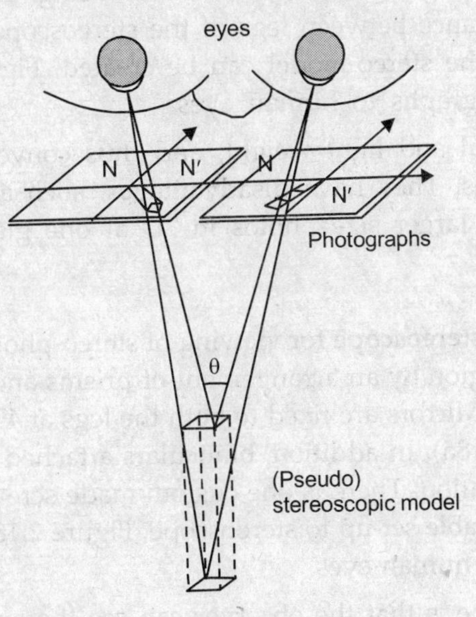

Figure 2.15: Vertical exaggeration and stereovision

Figure 2.16: Recreation of 3D photogrammetric system
(*Source: ASPRS, 1980*)

2.14.2 Stereoscopes

Stereoscopic vision is the basic pre-requisite for photogrammetry and photo-interpretation in 3D environment. Many applications need information extraction with stereo-images rather than mono-images. This requires two views of a single object from two slightly different positions. The photographs are taken from two different positions with overlap in order to reproduce the objects in a manner as they are individually seen by the eyes.

Stereoscope is an optical device for three-dimensional viewing of landscapes or individual objects. A stereoscope views a stereoscopic pair, depicting views of the left-eye and right-eye images of the same scene, to create a three-dimensional image. To do so, the photographs are to be properly oriented in the same manner as they were taken at the time of photography. Thereafter, each eye views the respective image, and these two images help creating a 3D view in overlap region. The fusion of these two images in the brain allows the judgement of depth or distance.

All stereoscopes deviate the rays from common points observed in the photographs. There are two simple instruments used for three dimensional studies of aerial photographs, i.e., **Lens stereoscopes** and **Reflecting** or **Mirror stereoscopes.**

2.14.3.1 Lens stereoscopes

Lens stereoscope is also called as **pocket stereoscope.** Because of its small size, it can be kept in the pocket, and is easy transportable in the field. Lens stereoscope consists of two plano-convex lenses with magnifying capability, mounted on a metallic frame (Figure 2.17a). The distance between two lenses is adjustable as per distance between users' eyes, and is approximately 65mm which is the average eye base of a human-being. The height of pocket stereoscope is normally 10cm. Distance between legs of the stereoscope and the focal length of lenses are so designed that the stereo-model can be created. Figure 2.17b shows the line diagram of rays from photographs to human eyes.

Lens stereoscopes are handy, economical and light weight, and thus convenient for the study of small format aerial photographs. They have disadvantages, such as limited magnification (2X–4X), and not viewing the larger size photos in 3D at one glance.

2.14.3.2 Mirror stereoscopes

Mirror Stereoscope is also called as **reflecting stereoscope** for viewing of stereo-photographs. It provides a view of almost entire overlap region by an arrangement of prisms and mirrors with increased distance to about 15 to 25cms. Mirrors are fixed to both the legs at 45Ú angle, alongwith two right angled prisms (Figure 2.18a). In addition, binoculars attached with the mirror stereoscope provide 3X to 8X magnification. There is one custom made screw on one foot which is adjustable in height to allow a stable set-up to stereoscope. Figure 2.18b shows the line diagram of rays from photographs to human eyes.

The main advantage of mirror stereoscope is that the observer can see the entire area from both the images, utilising the property of optics, even-though these photographs may not necessarily be located just below the lens. Mirror stereoscopes is however heavier to carry in the field. The mirror stereoscopes are most widely used in photo-interpretation and measurements, in combination with an instrument called, **parallax bar**. The measurements of points in the stereo-pair are done using parallax bar to determine the elevations of these points.

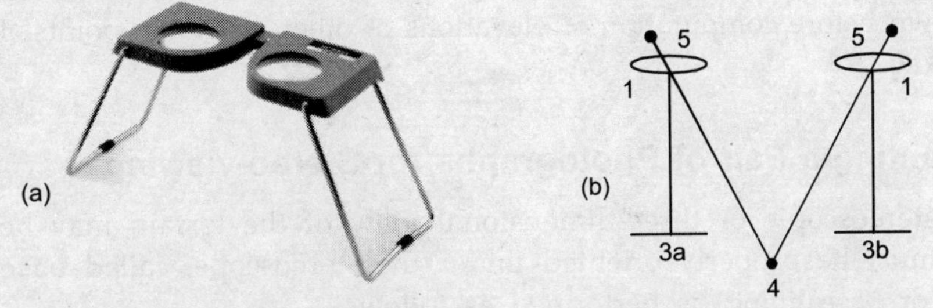

Figure 2.17: (a) Lens stereoscope (b) Line diagram of lens stereoscope

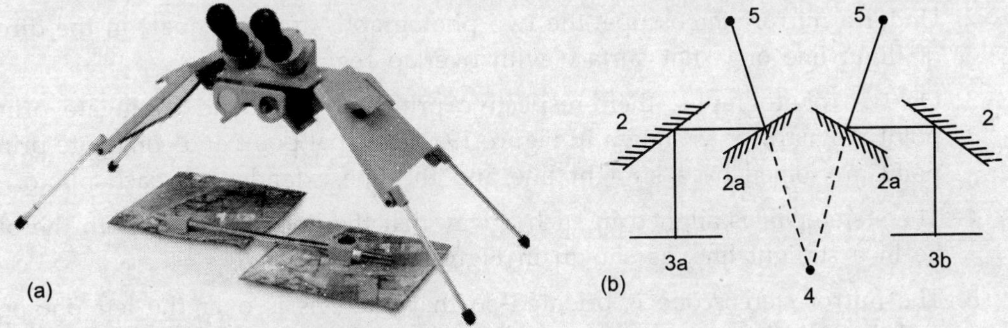

Figure 2.18: (a) Mirror stereoscope; (b) Line diagram of mirror stereoscope.

(1) lenses, (2) and (2a) mirrors, (3a) and (3b) identical points on the right and left photographs of a stereo-pair, (4) point at which the points 3a and 3b are seen stereoscopically, and (5) ocular axes of the observer.

2.14.4 Requirements of Stereoscopic Vision

To obtain a three dimensional model from the two dimensional photos, two photographs of an area must fulfill the following essential conditions:

1. Both the photographs must cover same common area, with minimum 60% overlap.
2. Time of exposure of both photographs must be nearly same.
3. Scale of two photographs should be the same.
4. The brightness of both the photographs should be similar.
5. Parallax must be present in the stereo-pair
6. Base to height ratio must have an appropriate value; the normal value is upto 2.0 but not less than 0.25. If this ratio is too small, say 0.02, the stereoscopic view will not provide a better depth impression. Base to height ratio increases when overlap decreases. Short focal length wide angle lens cameras give better base height ratio which is important in natural resource inventory and mapping.

2.15 DETERMINATION OF HEIGHT FROM VERTICAL AERIAL PHOTOGRAPHS

The elevation of various points in the overlap region of a stereo-pair may be determined with the help of parallax bar measurements. To do so the elevation of at least one control point is known before computation of elevations of other unknown points. The procedure is given below.

2.15.1 Orienting a Pair of Photographs for Stereo-viewing

Before the stereoscopic or three-dimensional view of the terrain may be created, the stereo-pair must be properly oriented under the stereoscope, called **base lining**. This orientation (or base lining) is performed as follows:

1. One photograph is kept over the other to visually assess the overlap region.
2. Under a mirror stereoscope, the two photographs are kept apart in the direction of flight line on a flat surface with overlap region inwards.
3. On two photographs, their respective principal point and conjugate principal point are marked, as shown in Figure 19a. Principal point and conjugate principal point are joined by a straight line and the line extended on each photo.
4. The stereo-pair is aligned in such a way that the line drawn on both the photos lie in a straight line, as shown in Figure 2.19a.
5. The mirror stereoscope is oriented so that left lens is over the left photograph and the right lens is over the right photograph. The line joining the centre of the lens should be almost matching with the direction of flight line.
6. Stereo-pair is seen through the stereoscope, and the distance between the photographs may be adjusted slightly till two images are fused in the brain and a 3D model of the overlap region is created.
7. At the first attempt, it might appear a bit difficult to see the stereo-vision. However with little more adjustments and practice, it will appear to be easy.
8. The two photographs are now properly oriented (this process is known as base lining).
9. The identification of features on photographs is much easier and more accurate with three-dimensional view. The visual interpretation elements (size, shape, shadow, tone, and surrounding objects) will still be applied to identify the objects; but now with the addition of relief, a more natural view is seen.
10. Points on left and right photos can be measured by parallax bar. The difference between two measured distances by parallax bar will provide parallax differences between two points.

2.15.2 Measurements by Parallax Bar

Stereometer or **Parallax bar** is used to measure the difference of parallax between any two points, more accurately and precisely. The change in position of an image from one photo to the next is caused by aircraft's motion, called **stereoscopic parallax, x-parallax**, or **simply parallax**. There are two important aspects of stereoscopic parallax; (i) parallax of any point is directly related to the elevation of the point, and (ii) parallax is greater for high points than for low points.

The parallax bar consists of a pair of glass graticules, one is attached on left side and another to a rigid bar. Each graticule has three small identical marks (cross, dot or circle) etched on the glass, called **floating marks**. The left hand graticule can be clamped at any required distance over a rigid bar so that overlap area is covered by the separation of two floating marks. The separation of two index marks (i.e., floating marks) can be changed by the rotation of micrometer screw to measure parallax difference on a stereo-pair of photographs (Figure 2.19b). The right hand graticule can be moved with the help of a micrometer screw having a least count as 0.01mm.

The points on stereo-pair are selected whose parallax bar readings are to be measured for the computation of heights of these points. The stereo-pair already oriented in the direction of base line is viewed in stereo and the floating marks of parallax bar are kept at a point (left mark on left image and right mark on right image) whose parallax bar measurements are to be taken. To create stereo-model of the point, the micrometer screw of the parallax bar is rotated. The floating marks on clear glass will move away or come closer. While further rotating micrometer screw, at a given instant, these marks start to fuse together into a single mark. If micrometer screw is rotated further, these marks move closer together and appear to rise. If the screw is rotated in opposite direction, these marks move apart and appear to fall. When the floating marks appear to be a single mark, resting exactly on terrain, main scale and micrometer screw readings are read and added together, called **parallax bar reading** at that point. Several parallax bar readings at that point are taken and average value used in the computation. Similarly, the parallax bar readings of other points are taken.

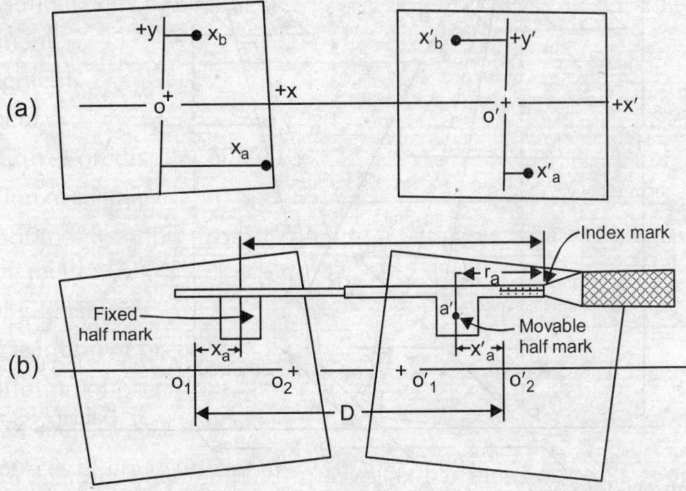

Figure 2.19: (a) Base lining of a stereo-pair (b) Parallax bar measurements (*Source: Kraus, 1994*)

2.15.3 Derivation of Relationship for Height

The **absolute parallax** of a point imaged on both photos of the pair is determined as the algebraic difference between two distances. These distances are measured from the corresponding principal point (or Y axis) of the two images (left photo, and right photo), parallel to the direction of flight (air base), called x-parallax. Figure 2.19a shows a stereo-pair where locations of two points a and b are marked with their X-coordinates. Let the distance on left photo be x_a and x_b and on right photo be x'_a and x'_b .

The **absolute parallax** of a point is determined as the algebraic difference between two distances of that point on the stereo-pair. The absolute parallax of ground points A and B are computed as given below. Let the average parallax bar readings at a and b points are P_A and P_B respectively, measured with parallax bar. The difference in absolute parallax of p_a and p_b can be related with the difference in parallax bar readings. It is to be noted that the value of parallax has been used with proper sign.

$$p_a = x_a - x'_a$$

$$p_b = x_b - (-x'_b) = x_b + x'_b \qquad ...(2.25)$$

$$\Delta p = p_b - p_a$$

$$\Delta p = (x_b + x'_b) - (x_a - x'_a) \qquad ...(2.26)$$

Δp = difference of parallax bar readings at a and b ($P_A \sim P_B$)

The absolute parallax of A (p_a) is determined using measurements of x-coordinates on stereo-pair. Since the elevation of a ground point A (h_a) is known from reference map or field observation, the elevation of unknown point (say B) is to be determined (say h_b) using parallax bar measurements. The images of A on the stereo-photograph are a and a' and that of B are b and b'.

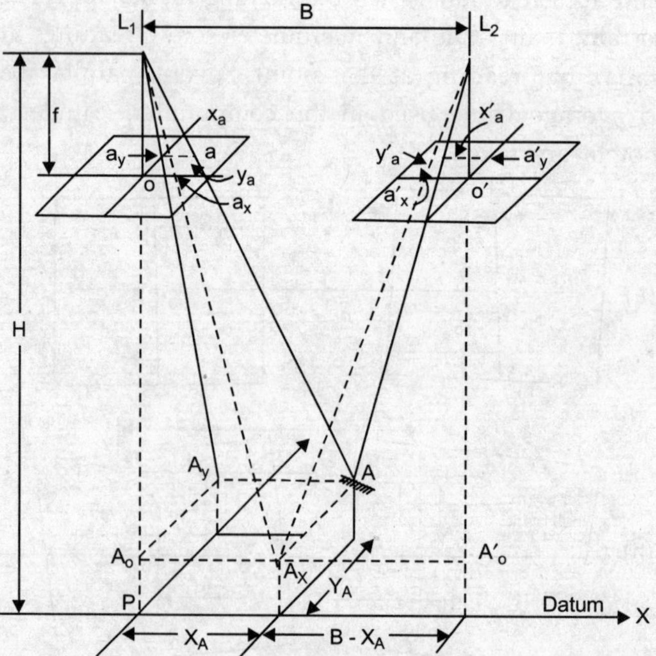

Figure 2.20: Height determination from a stereo-pair using parallax bar reading (*Source: Wolf and Dewitt, 2000*)

From Figure 2.20, the absolute parallax p_a at point A is related as follows where B is air base b is the eyebase, f is the focal length of camera lens, H is the flying height.

$$\frac{b}{B} = \frac{f}{H - h_c} \quad \text{...(2.27)}$$

Substitute in elevation differences formula and recognizing that $P_a = b$

$$p_a = \frac{fB}{H - ha} \quad \text{...(2.28)}$$

Similarly the absolute parallax p_b is computed as -

$$p_b = \frac{fB}{H - h_b} \quad \text{...(2.29)}$$

Parallax differences:

$$\Delta p = p_b - p_a$$

$$= \frac{fB}{H - h_b} - \frac{fB}{H - h_a} = \frac{fB(H - h_a) - fB(H - h_b)}{(H - h_a)(H - h_b)}$$

$$= \frac{fB(h_b - h_a)}{(H - ha)(H - h_b)} = \frac{p_b(h_b - h_a)}{H - h_a}$$

So $$h_b - h_a = \frac{\Delta p(H - h_a)}{p_b}$$

$$\Delta p = p_b - p_a$$

$$h_b = h_a + \frac{\Delta p(H - h_a)}{p_a + \Delta p} \quad \text{...(2.30)}$$

$p_a = (x_a - x_a') =$ Absolute Parallax of point A

$\Delta p =$ difference of parallax bar readings at a and b points (P_A~P_B)

Since, it is difficult to measure the coordinates of all the objects on the photos, so these coordinates can be replaced by the parallax bar readings (P_A and P_B) at points a and b.

Using the above relationship (Equation 2.30), elevation of point B (h_b) can be computed.

In a similar way, elevation of another unknown point C (h_c) can be computed using the relationship given below.

$$h_c = h_a + \frac{\Delta p(H - h_a)}{p_a + \Delta p} \quad \text{...(2.31)}$$

Where $\Delta p = P_A \sim P_C$

It is evident from above relationship that the elevations of various points can be computed by knowing the elevation of at least one ground point and using absolute parallax of that point as well as parallax bar readings. This method however determines the approximate height of the points. The errors in the determination of height may be due to several reasons –

1. Locating and marking the flight line on photos.
2. Orientation of stereo-pair for parallax measurement.
3. Parallax and photo co-ordinate measurements.
4. Shrinkage and expansion of photographs.
5. Difference in flying height of stereo photographs.
6. Tilt may be present on photos.
7. Error in the height of known ground control.

2.16 THE SCALE OF A TILTED PHOTOGRAPH

The scale of a tilted photograph changes throughout the photograph. Figure 2.21 shows the geometry of a tilted photograph. The scale is too small on the high side and too large on the low side. The scale also changes along the principal line (i.e., in the direction of tilt), but it does not change along any line perpendicular to the principal line. The points situated at different distances from the isometric parallel will have different scales, but points equidistant from and on the same side of the isometric parallel (i.e., points along any line which is parallel to the isometric parallel) will have the same scale.

In Figure 2.21, all the standard notations have been used to represent various points in a tilted photograph. The *o* is the principal point and *n* is the nadir point on the photo. Here, *y*-axis is rotated till the new *y* -axis or the *y* ′-axis coincides with the principal line having a positive direction *(no)*. Let this angle of rotation be è=180° - *s*, where *s*=swing angle

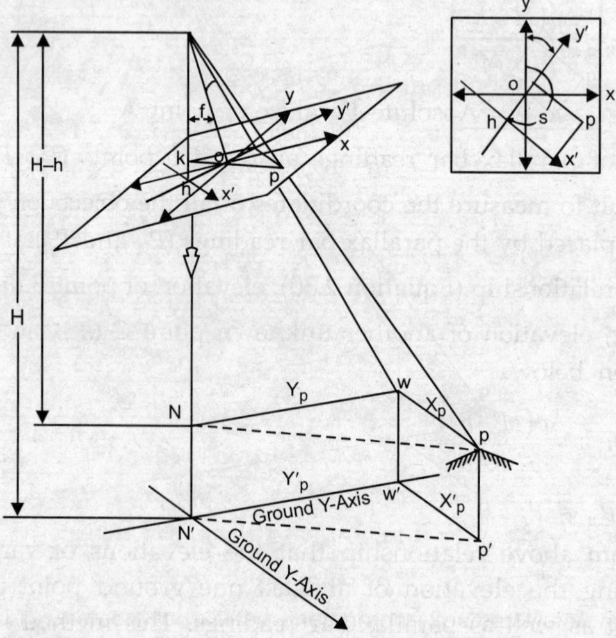

Figure 2.21: Geometry of a tilted photograph (*Source:Mikhail at al 2001*)

Let P be the point lying at an elevation h_p above the datum, p is its image on the tilted photo. Its photo-coordinates be (x, y) and measured coordinates with respect to axes defined are (x', y') by collimation marks. Since è *is* measured clockwise, it must be negative. From p point a perpendicular pw is dropped to the principal line. Co-ordinates in rotated system can now be derived. On translating x' axis from o to w, the co-ordinates of point p on tilted photo after translation are-

$$\left.\begin{aligned} x' &= x\cos\theta + y\sin\theta \\ y' &= -x\sin\theta + y\cos\theta + on \\ &= -x\sin\theta + y\cos\theta + f\tan t \end{aligned}\right\} \quad ...(2.32)$$

$$on = f\tan t \quad ...(2.33)$$

A perpendicular line is dropped from w as wk on Ln. In fact, this denotes a horizontal line, Ln being a vertical line). Since wp is perpendicular to the principal line, it is also a horizontal line. Therefore, the plane made by kwp points is a horizontal plane. Also, $PP' = WW' = NN' = h_p$ (from construction on the ground), and therefore, plane formed by NWP points is also horizontal.

In similar triangles Lkp and LNP, we can write

$$\frac{kp}{Np} = \frac{Lk}{LN} = \frac{Lk}{H-h}$$

But $Lk = Ln - kn = f\sec t - y'\sin t$.

Therefore,

$$\frac{kp}{NP} = \frac{f\sec t - y'\sin t}{H-h}$$

But kp/NP = scale for a point lying in a plane kwp. Since p lies on this plane, so scale of tilted photo (S_t) at p is-

$$S_t = \frac{f\sec t - y'\sin t}{H-h} \quad ...(2.34)$$

Where S_t is the scale of a tilted photograph at a point whose elevation is h, f is focal length, t is the tilt angle, H is the flying height above datum, and y' is the y- co-ordinate of the point with respect to a set of axes whose origin is at the nadir point and whose y' axis coincides with the principal line.

The above equation does show that scale is a function of tilt only, and scale variation occurs on a tilted photo even over flat terrain.

2.17 GROUND COORDINATES FROM A TILTED PHOTOGRAPH

The coordinates of a ground point P (X, Y) can be derived by assuming that (Figure 2.21) (i) Y-coordinate axis lies in the principal plane, and (ii) X-coordinate axis passes through ground nadir point (N'). Therefore, ground nadir point is the origin of coordinates. Let us assume -

$wp = x'$, and $WP = X$

$nw = y'$, and $NW = Y$

The relationship of scale using the property of triangles *kwp* and *NWP* is given as-

$$kp/NP = wp/WP = \text{scale}$$

But $$\frac{wp}{WP} = \frac{x'}{X} = \frac{f\sec t - y'\sin t}{H-h} \quad \text{...(2.35)}$$

$$\frac{kw}{NW} = \frac{kw}{Y} = \frac{nw\cos t}{Y}$$

$$\frac{nw\cos t}{Y} = \frac{y'\cos t}{Y}$$

$$\frac{y'\cos t}{Y} = \frac{f\sec t - y'\sin t}{H-h} \quad \text{...(2.36)}$$

From Equation 2.35 $$X = \frac{H-h}{f\sec t - y'\sin t}.x' \quad \text{...(2.37)}$$

From Equation 2.36 $$Y = \frac{H-h}{f\sec t - y'\sin t}.y'\cos t \quad \text{...(2.38)}$$

Where X, Y are ground co-ordinates of a point. x', y' are co-ordinates of the same point on tilted photo with respect to axes whose origin is at the nadir point and whose y' axis coincides with the principal line, and t is the angle of tilt.

2.18 FLYING HEIGHT OF A TILTED PHOTOGRAPH

The flying height of a tilted photograph can be derived in a similar way as that for a vertical photograph. The photo-coordinates of the end points (say A and B) of a control line on the ground with respect to defined axes are taken and ground length AB computed. Here A and B are like ground control points (GCPs) lying in the area whose coordinates are known. Photographic length of line ab is measured directly on photo. Ratio formula of photographic length to known ground length is used to get the first approximation of flying height as-

$$\frac{f}{H_{app} - h_{AB}} = \frac{ab}{AB} \quad \text{...(2.39)}$$

where, f is the focal length, h_{AB} is the avg. elevation of A and B.

By using H_{app}, together with other data, one can solve the following equations-

$$\theta = 180^o - s$$

$$x' = x\cos\theta + y\sin\theta \quad \text{...(2.40)}$$

$$y' = -x\sin\theta + y\cos\theta + f\tan t \quad \text{...(2.41)}$$

From Equation 2.37 $$X = \frac{H-h}{f\sec t - y'\sin t}.x'$$

From Equation 2.38 $$Y = \frac{H-h}{f\sec t - y'\sin t}y'\cos t$$

Using above equations, first set of ground co-ordinates are determined and the distance between AB computed. This computed distance is used for better approximation of flying height H, and a new value of H is determined using the following relationship.

The procedure is iterative and repeated till computed value of length agrees with the known ground length within the desired precision.

$$\frac{H - h_{AB}}{H_{app} - h_{AB}} = \frac{corrected\ AB}{computed\ AB} \quad ...(2.42)$$

2.19 RELIEF DISPLACEMENT ON A TILTED PHOTOGRAPH

Figure 2.22 shows the relief displacement on a tilted photograph. On a tilted photo, relief displacement is radial from the nadir point (*n*). The amount of relief displacement depends upon: (i) flying height, (ii) distance from nadir point to image, (iii) elevation of ground point, and (iv) position of point with respect to principal line and to the axis of the tilt. Compared to an equivalent relief displacement on vertical photo, the relied displacement on a tilted photo will be (i) less on the half of the photograph upward from the axis of the tilt, (ii) greater on downward half of the photo, and (iii) identical for points lying on the axis of the tilt.

Image displacement due to the tilt tends to compensate relief displacement on the upward half and will be added to relied displacement on the downward half. The value of relief displacement is computed with sufficient accuracy, as tilt in near-vertical photos rarely exceeds 3°. In case of tilted photos, the radial distance should be measured from the nadir point and not from the principal point.

$$d = \frac{rh}{H} = \frac{rh}{H - h} \quad ...(2.43)$$

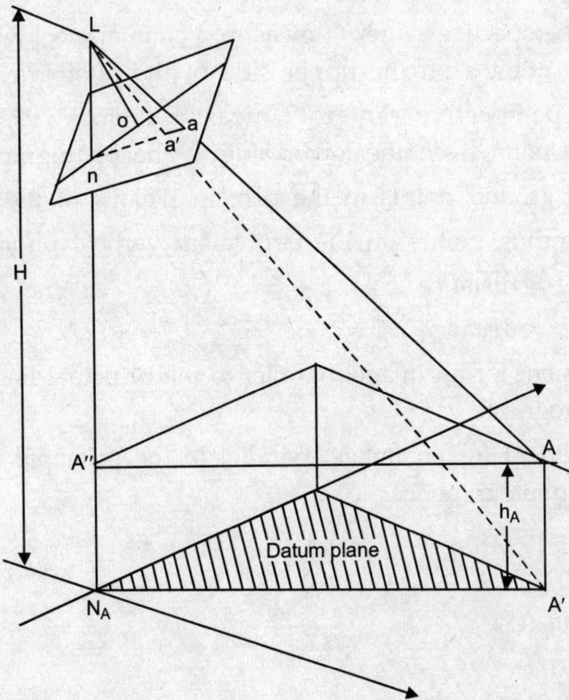

Figure 2.22: Relief displacement on a tilted photograph *(Source: ASPRS, 1980)*

2.20 TILT DISPLACEMENT

The tilted photo and its equivalent vertical photo are identical along the isometric parallel, where they intersect. At any other position on the tilted photo, the image of a point will be displaced either outward or inward with respect to its equivalent position on the vertical photo. The characteristics of a tilted photograph are-

1. Displacement due to Tilt is radial from Isocenter
2. Displacement due to tilt is zero on a truly vertical photos, but increases proportionally as tilt angle increases.
3. Tilt displacement on slightly tilted photos is usually less in magnitude than displacement from elevation differences, but tilt is much more difficult to detect, calculate, and correct.
4. Images on "up side" of a tilted photo are displaced toward photo center
5. Images on "down side" of titled photo displace away from photo center

From Figure 2.23

t = angle of tilt

p = principal point

i = isocenter

n = nadir point

o = perspective center (lens)

j = focal length of photograph

a = angle at the perspective center O measured counter-clockwise from the photograph perpendicular to any point a on the upper side of the photograph

= angle at the perspective center O measured clockwise from the photograph perpendicular to any point b on the lower side of the photograph

a,b = images of ground points in the principal plane of the photograph

a', b' = corresponding points on the equivalent vertical photograph

$+r$ = distance ia = distance ic

$-r$ = distance ib = distance ie

d = the displacement for an image, parallel to the principal line and due to tilt, on the upper side of a photograph

d' = the displacement for an image, parallel to the principal line and due to tilt, on the lower side of a photograph

So

$$\tan (t/2) = (pi)/f \quad ...(2.44)$$

$$(pi) = f \tan (t/2)$$

$$\tan (t) = (pn)/f \quad ...(2.45)$$

$$(pn) = f \tan (t)$$

The displacement has been computed as:

$$d = ia' - ic$$

$$d = ia' - (ia) = ia' - (ip + pa) \quad ...(2.46)$$

$$d' = ie - ib'$$

$$d = ib - ib' = (pb\text{-}pi)\text{-}ib' \quad ...(2.47)$$

$$d = f\left[\tan(\alpha + t) - \tan\alpha - 2\tan\frac{t}{2}\right] \quad ...(2.48)$$

$$d' = f\left[\tan\beta - \tan(\beta - t) - 2\tan\frac{t}{2}\right] \quad ...(2.49)$$

In somewhat simpler equations, the image displacement has also been computed as:

$$d = \frac{(ia)^2}{\frac{f}{\sin t} - ia} \quad ...(2.50)$$

$$d' = \frac{(ib)^2}{\frac{f}{\sin t} - ib} \quad ...(2.51)$$

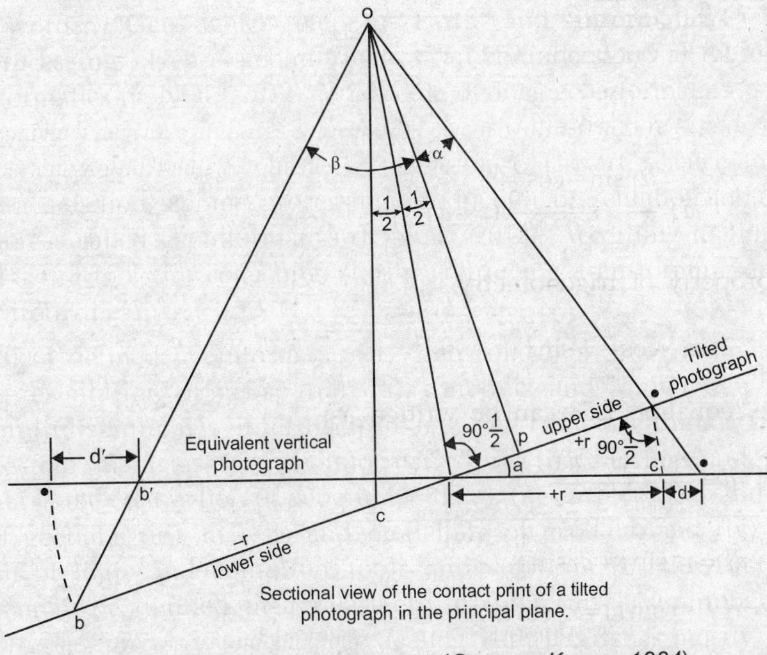

Figure 2.23: Tilt displacement (*Source: Kraus, 1884*)

Considering the isocenter, *i*, as the center of rotation, an arc is drawn from point *a* on the tilted photograph so as to intersect the equivalent vertical photograph at a point *c*. The distances *ia* and *ic* are therefore equal and the isosceles triangle *iac* is thereby formed having two sides equal to *+r*.

$$\angle\ Oip = 90^o - \frac{t}{2}$$

In the isosceles triangle *iac*,

$$\angle\ iac = 90^o - \frac{t}{2}$$

Therefore lines *Oi* and *ac* are parallel (corresponding opposite interior angles) and, triangle *Oia'* is therefore similar to triangle *aca'* Therefore

$$\frac{d}{r+d} = \frac{ac}{Oi} \qquad \text{...(2.52)}$$

Since $ac = 2r\sin\frac{t}{2}$ and

$$Oi = \frac{f}{\cos\frac{t}{2}}$$

Substituting, in equation 2.52, we get

$$\frac{d}{r+d} = \frac{2r\sin\frac{t}{2}}{\frac{f}{\cos\frac{t}{2}}}$$

$$d = \frac{2r\sin\frac{t}{2}\cos\frac{t}{2}}{f}(r+d) \qquad \text{...(2.53)}$$

By the property of trigonometry,

$$2\sin\frac{t}{2}\cos\frac{t}{2} = \sin t$$

Therefore, equation 2.53 can be written as:

$$d = \frac{r\sin t(r+d)}{f}$$

$$df = r^2\sin t + dr\sin t$$

$$d(f - r\sin t) = r^2\sin t$$

so

$$d = \frac{r^2\sin t}{f - r\sin t} \qquad \text{...(2.54)}$$

Dividing the numerator and the denominator of equation 2.54 by sin t, we get-

$$d = \frac{r^2}{\frac{f}{\sin t} - r} \qquad \text{...(2.55)}$$

This form of the equation applies to both sides of the photograph when the algebraic sign of r is observed. The equation is usually expressed in an approximate form when computing the value of d for either 2.55 side of a single lens photograph having a tilt angle of less than 3°.

$$d = \frac{r^2 \sin t}{f} \qquad ...(2.56)$$

This equation is logical due to the fact that the subtractive value of r in the denominator of previous equation has only a small effect on the value of d because of the much larger values of r^2 and $\sin t/f$.

2.21 PHOTOGRAMMETRIC SYSTEMS

In general, a photogrammetric system is defined by its three components; Data acquisition, Data reduction, and Data presentation.

2.21.1 Data acquisition Systems

These are employed to procure the data or information. The data can be acquired in terms of images or films into two categories: **Conventional imagery** and **Non-conventional imagery**.

In conventional data acquisition system, the system has a lens and an image plane, such as frame photographs, which is based on the central projection of the object onto an image plane. A non-metric camera is often used for conventional photography. These cameras are not especially made for the photogrammetric purposes. In these types of cameras, the elements of interior orientation are not known or partially available (Wolf and Dewitt, 2000).

In non-conventional data acquisition system, the system uses Holograms, X-rays, TV systems etc. In these cameras, the elements of interior orientation: the focal length and location of the centre of the photograph are known. The metric cameras are specially designed for photogrammetric applications, which are further classified as single and stereometric cameras. A single metric camera is mounted on a tripod, whereas a stereometric camera consists of two identical metric cameras mounted rigidly at the ends of a fixed base for photographic work (Egles and Kesser, 2001).

Digital close range photogrammetry is the latest development in photogrammetry, which is especially used to obtain 3D spatial information about objects placed near the camera. The introduction of digital cameras into close range photogrammetry has given rise to on-line systems, which facilitate both real time and near-real time 3D coordinate measurement. With the availability of wide range of digital cameras, including camcorders and video cameras, these cameras are utilised considerably as data acquisition systems in close range photogrammetry (Samson, 2003).

2.21.2 Data reduction systems

Data processing systems are used for data reduction from geometric information (e.g., image coordinates) on the image to object space information. The data reduction deals with the process of extracting desired information from photographs. Depending on the type of input used and the desired output, there are three alternatives for data reduction: **analog, analytical** and **digital** (Hassani and James, 1992). In the earlier stages, analogue approach was used in which the imaging geometry was reconstructed by orienting two images in such a way that a 3D model of the object is formed through optical or mechanical devices. A flow diagram of the processes involved is given in Figure 2.24a. The analog method employs complex instruments, which physically model the geometric relationship that existed between the image and the object at the time of data acquisition.

Photogrammetric operations can also be performed by mathematical modelling. This method is called analytical, numerical or computational photogrammetry. With development in optics and mechanics, the analog photogrammetric instruments have improved to attain high accuracy. With the evolution of computers, analogue instruments have been replaced by analytical plotters, where single or a pair of photographs is placed which digitally records image coordinates (using mono or stereo-comparators) (Grave, 1996).

In digital or soft copy photogrammetry, digital images are used with wide range of data processing operations in Digital Photogrammetric Workstation (DPW) not available with hard copy images. The developments in digital photogrammetry have resulted in digital photogrammetric workstations and specialised software. Some of the well known digital photogrammetric systems are LH Systems, Z/I Imaging, and ERDAS. DPWs are more user friendly than the analytical plotters. DPWs have image processing capabilities, such as enlargements, reductions, contrast enhancements, etc. DPW is more reliable and potentially more accurate since no calibration procedures are necessary (Manugula et al 2018). Flow diagram of the processes involved is shown in Figure 2.24b. DPWs have the potential to automate photogrammetric applications, such as aerial triangulation, DEM generation, and orthophoto production. As more photogrammetric procedures will be automated, the operation of a DPW requires less specialized operators (Egles and Kasser, 2001).

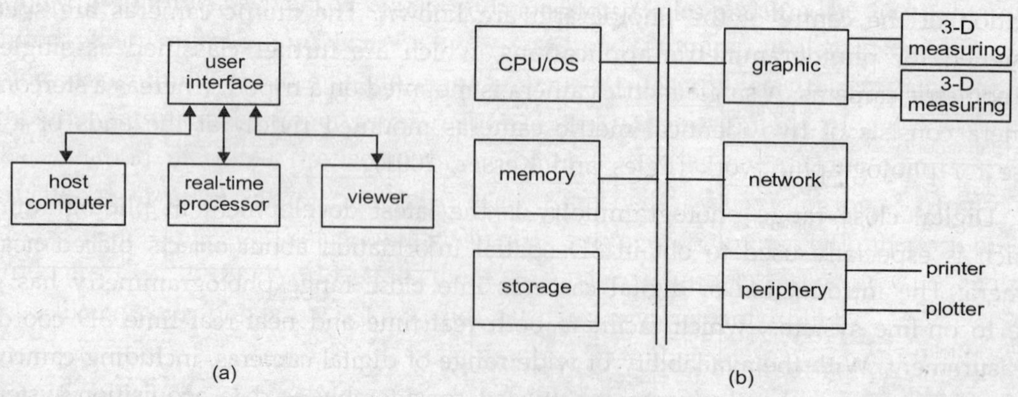

Figure 2.24: (a) Analytical photogrammetric plotter, and (b) Digital photogrammetric workstations (*Source: Schenk, 2005*)

Table 2.2 shows the differences between the various types of photogrammetric stereo-plotters.

Table 2.2: Comparision between the analog, analytic and digital photogrammetric stereoplotters

Characteristics	Analog	Analytic	Digital
Image	Film	Film	Pixels
Plotter	Analog	Analytical	Computer
Model Construction.	Mechanical	Mechanical/Computer	Computer
Stereo Viewing	Optical	Optical	Varies
Output	Mech/CAD	Mech/CAD	CAD
Aerotriangulation	Very limited	On/off line	Semi-automatic
Orthophoto	Very limited	Unavailable	Automatic
Limitations	Focal length Film format	Film format	None
Accuracy	Average up to ±15µm	Very high up to ±3µm	Same as scanning accuracy
Cost	Very high	Very high	Reasonable to high

The relations between image points and object points are described through numerical calculations based on the **collinearity equations**. The collinearity conditions specify that the exposure station, ground point and its corresponding image points, all must lie along a straight line. In Figure 2.25, let *L* be the exposure, *P* be the location of a point in object space whose corresponding point in image plane is *p*. Therefore, *L p P* represents the collinearity condition. The basic transformation equation describing the relationship between two mutually associated 3D coordinate systems is given by (Wolf and Dewitt, 2000).

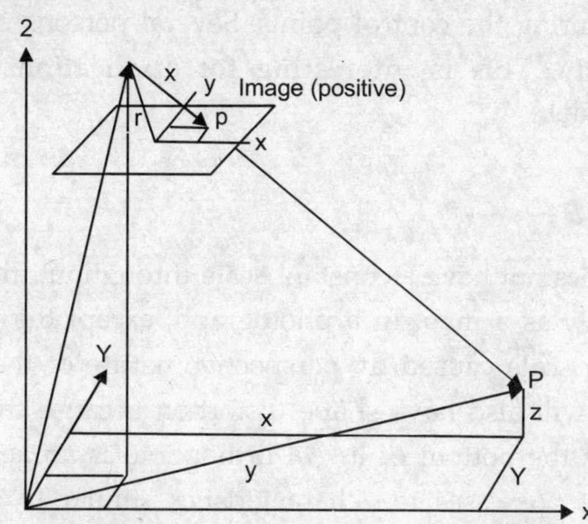

Figure 2.25: Collinearity condition (*Source: ASPRS, 1980*)

$$X = -f\frac{m_{11}(X - X_L) + m_{12}(Y - Y_L) + m_{13}(Z - Z_L)}{m_{31}(X - X_L) + m_{32}(Y - Y_L) + m_{33}(Z - Z_L)} \quad ...(2.57)$$

$$Y = -f\frac{m_{21}(X - X_L) + m_{22}(Y - Y_L) + m_{23}(Z - Z_L)}{m_{31}(X - X_L) + m_{32}(Y - Y_L) + m_{33}(Z - Z_L)} \quad ...(2.58)$$

Where x, y, z are the coordinates of image point, X, Y & Z *are the* coordinates of object point, and X_L, Y_L and Z_L are the coordinates of exposure station L in XYZ coordinate system. f is the focal length of the camera, m_{11},.. m_{33} are the elements of rotation matrix.

2.21.3 Data Presentation Systems

The introduction of digital photogrammetry has changed the world of photogrammetry completely. The advances in electronics and computer science have permitted new approaches to obtain photogrammetric solutions more effectively, while the basic mathematics, optical theory and many of the basic practices remain the same.

Data presentation consists of preparing and presenting the results in the form of contour maps, pictorial representation of objects, digital model, three-dimensional (3D) spatial coordinates etc. A typical digital photogrammetric system comprises of standard hardware components, such as stereo-viewing devices and a 3D mouse with a core of specialized photogrammetric software. Such systems carry various operations, such as vector, raster and attribute data storage and processing, image handling, compression, processing and display, including several photogrammetric applications, such as image orientation, generation of digital elevation models (DEM) (Ebner et al, 2003).

Digital Photogrammetric Workstations (DPWs) offer more flexibility in viewing and measuring several images simultaneously. It is possible to increase the roaming capabilities of DPWs beyond the stereo-model, such as DEMs, databases, and design data. It would further enhance the efficiency and user friendliness of DPWs. This is a great advantage in identifying and measuring the control points. Several persons can stereoscopically view a model simultaneously. This is interesting for applications where design data is superimposed on a model.

2.22 ORTHOPHOTOS

An aerial photograph does not have a constant scale throughout the entire image; therefore, it cannot be used directly as a map. In a photograph, except the principal point, all other points have variation in scale caused by perspective nature of the photograph. A feature, such as a tall building, will also have shape distortion because the top of the feature will have a larger scale than the bottom of it. An orthophoto is an aerial photograph that has been rectified so that it possesses the characteristics similar to a map. The rectification process is performed by combining photogrammetric principles with DEM data (Wolf and Dewitt, 2000).

An orthophoto is an image of the terrain created in such a manner that the scale is uniform and shapes of the objects are not distorted throughout, while preserving the characteristics of image. Map revision or map updation becomes easy using orthophotos. Production of DEM is faster and less expensive. Orthophotos have been used for many years for a diverse range of applications, including GIS. Cartographic overlay in a GIS can be added to enhance the interpretability. The disadvantage of orthophoto is that the elevations of surface (topography) and also the height of every feature (buildings, trees etc.) above that surface should be known to create an accurate DEM, otherwise there may be some error. Figure 2.26 shows the DEM generated (left) from an orthophoto (right).

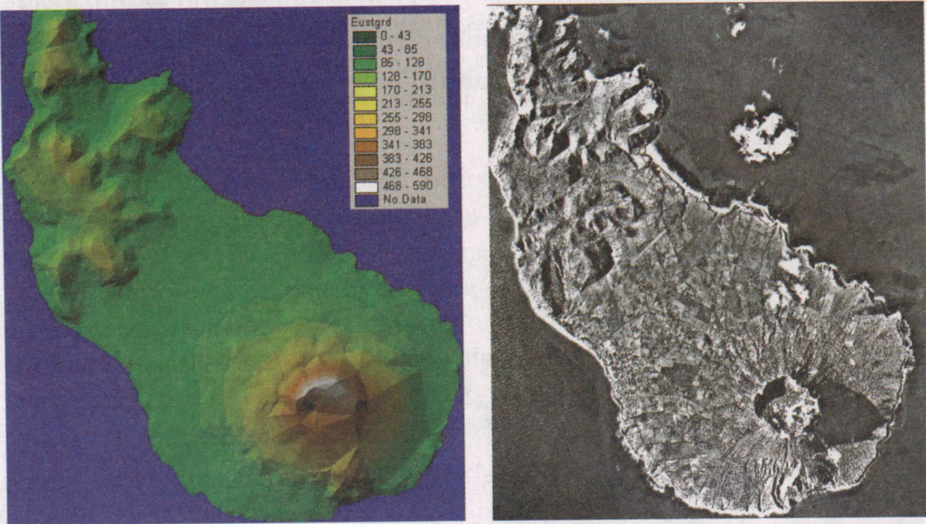

Figure 2.26: (a) DEM and (b) Orthophoto

(Source: https://www.scribd.com/document/277243918/ Introduction-on-Photogrammetry-by-Koert-Sijmons)

In past, orthophotos were produced with a photogrammetric stereo-plotter, but today with the advent of digital photogrammetric methods, orthophotos can now be produced on a desktop PC using the appropriate photogrammetric software. An orthophoto is produced by computing the scale and position distortions of each pixel of aerial photograph, re-scaling and re-positioning the pixels in a new computer generated image. This process is called **differential rectification**. Photo-mosaics are best known, but composites with orthophotos, called orthophoto maps are also used, especially now with the possibility to generate them with methods of digital photogrammetry (Hassani and Carswell, 1992).

2.23 APPLICATIONS OF PHOTOGRAMMETRY

Photogrammetry is widely accepted as one of the best methods to acquire Earth surface data, but its high operational costs limit its application in surveying and mapping, particularly when the area is to be monitored at regular interval. However, with the development of digital photogrammetry in the 1990's, as well as the lower cost of computer hardware and digital cameras, the operational and processing costs came down, making photogrammetry more accessible to several engineering fields.

Aerial photography is an important source of information for landscape studies. There are numerous potential applications of air-photos. Mapping from aerial photographs is invaluable for military intelligence, preparation of topographic maps, classification of soils, interpretation of geology and preparation of composite pictures (mosaic) of the ground (ASPRS, 1980, Koh and Grahm, 2002, Samson, 2003). Photogrammetry can be used for large number of applications, including landfill or gravel pit monitoring, determining the location of ore bodies or determining proposed locations for utilities. It is applied to civil engineering in topographic mapping, road alignment, canal alignment, deformation measurements, experimental measurements and inventorying. Aerial photographs have been used in transportation studies, such as identify vehicle types, estimate traffic flows, identify parking areas on city streets, etc.

Aerial photographs have been widely used for land use mapping and monitoring changes in land use over time. These photos as visual aid can support local administration and decision makers to check construction or deforestation activities. Aerial photos can support the management of land use on the slopes and hills to take preventive measures from landslides and earthquakes. These photographs are frequently used in managing natural disasters, such as earthquakes, volcanic eruptions or floods to take relief measures. Insurance companies also make use of aerial photographs to assess the damage and verify the insurance claims.

Urban development and the landscape studies can be aided with aerial photographs. Large scale aerial photos have gained popularity among planners, developers and engineers for most urban and land development applications. Information from aerial photos is used for analysis, strategic planning and evaluation in urban planning and engineering. Town developers need to study the impact of expansion and development of urban centres on the landscape and the impact on the environment by analysing photographs of different years. Such photographs are vital to plan new facilities (for example an airport) and associated support infrastructure i.e. more houses, upgrade of roads, etc. By specifying a set of criteria that represents desirable locations for the business or public facility, aerial photographs can be used to identify sites that satisfy the project requirements. Aerial photographs have often been used to locate businesses or public facilities, such as schools, banks, bus stations, fire stations etc.

Aerial photographs are used to estimate the housing density. This approach can be extended to produce estimates of population density, if information is available on average household size. Municipalities use large scale air-photos (1:5000) to identify unauthorised buildings/constructions as well as encroachment of land.

In archaeology, aerial photography is found ideal for locating the lost monuments and tracking features, especially those that are not visible at ground level, and those that can only be seen under certain conditions. They are usually discovered through (a) Crop marks and Parch marks, and/or (b) Soil mark. Crop marks are signs of a sub-terrain feature that show up as irregularities in the crop pattern, and are best studied in summer. Parch marks occur in dry summer, and usually the crop may simply show up a different colour. Soil marks are best studied in winter when no crops are growing or grasses have largely died-off; both rainy and dry conditions are conducive to picking out buried features. Soil marks typically show up as darker areas, and may indicate underlying stonework, the outline of prehistoric features, such as barrows, monuments, and ditches.

One of the greatest benefits of aerial photography concerning the environment is the assessment of its change over time. Aerial photographs provide vital records of changes over seasons and years to study local effects of climate change and risks to local ecosystems. Aerial photographs can highlight the impact of changes in their environment, such as die-off of certain vegetation, drying of rivers, or the increase of invasive species.

Some of the other uses are given below (Shenk, 2005):

1. Land surveying for site development and planning
2. Hydrographic surveying to map shore lines
3. Create topographic maps, including base maps for GIS work
4. Route (road or railways) survey and selection
5. Flood control and dam site selection
6. Canal, pipeline and transmission line surveying
7. Vegetation, water and environmental management
8. Creating orthophotos
9. Creation of Digital Elevation Models (DEMs)
10. Computation of coordinates
11. Earthwork volume estimation
12. Used in many other fields e.g., archaeology, forestry, agriculture, geology, military intelligence, traffic management, accident investigation, etc.
13. Manufacturing industries
14. Police investigation
15. Plastic surgery and medical sciences

Review Questions

1. What is meant by photogrammetry? Why photogrammetry is important in mapping the resources?
2. Discuss the historical developments in Photogrammetry.
3. Explain different classifications of photogrammetry.
4. Discuss the types of aerial photographs alongwith their uses. What are low oblique and high oblique photographs? What are the basic advantages of using vertical air photos?
5. Explain the advantages and disadvantages of aerial photographs.
6. Discuss the basic differences between an aerial photographs and a map.
7. What is flight planning? Why is it necessary? What are the factors that affect the flight planning?
8. How do you plan and compute various parameters of flight planning, discuss?
9. An aerial camera makes an exposure at a shutter speed of 1/500 sec. If the aircraft speed is 480 km/hr. How far will the aircraft travel during the exposure?

10. A project area is 20 km long in the east-west direction and 15 km wide in the north-south direction. It is to be covered with vertical aerial photographs having a scale of 1:12000. End lap and side lap are to be 60% and 30%, respectively. A camera of 152.4mm focal length with a 23 cm square format was to be used. Compute the number of photographs necessary for the project.
11. A project area of size 10 km by 6.5 km in east-west and north-south direction respectively is to be covered with 1: 8,000 scale in photograph with side lap of 30% and end lap of 60%. A camera with 152.4 mm focal length camera is to be used. Compute the total number of photographs.
12. A rectangular area 14.5km in north-south direction by 9.5km in the east-west direction is to be covered with aerial photography having a scale of 1:6000. End lap and side lap are to be 60% and 25%, respectively. A camera having a 230mm square format is to be used. Compute the total number of photograph in the project, assuming that the flight strips are parallel with the east and west project boundaries and that the coverage of the first and flight lines is 75% within the project boundary. Also add two photos at the ends of each strip to ensure complete coverage.
13. Define crab. How does crab differ from the drift?
14. Define the following terms with the help of neat sketch.

    (i) Exposure station, (ii) Air base, (iii) Camera axis, (iv) Focal length of camera lens, (v) Principal point, (vi) Fiducial marks, (vii) Flying height, (viii) Nadir point (viii) Conjugate principal point, (ix) Mean sea level, (x) Flight line, (xi) Floating marks (xii) Mosaic.
15. Derive a relationship to determine the horizontal ground distance between two known points using aerial photographs.
16. Define scale of a photograph. What are major categories of scales? Derive an expression to compute the scale of a photograph in a flat terrain.
17. Draw a neat sketch, and establish a relationship to compute the scale of a photograph in an undulating terrain. List the parameters on which scale of a photograph is dependent. Explain why the scale of a vertical photograph is not uniform.
18. Evaluate if the distance of a line on the photographic known as 1 cm, what is its equivalent distance on the ground if the photographic scale is 1: 10,000.
19. What is the area covered by an aerial photograph taken at a height of 12,000m above the average ground with a camera having a focal length of 152mm and a 23cm square format?
20. What is meant by relief displacement? How do you use the formula of relief displacement to determine the height of objects?
21. Derive a relationship to compute the relief displacement in vertical aerial photograph. Why is this displacement radial from principal point?

22. At the bottom of a valley, the scale of a vertical photograph is 1:8000. The focal length of the lens used to capture the photograph is 152mm. A road intersection on the same photograph is 4950m above the valley floor and 10cm away from the principal point. What is the relief displacement of the road intersection with respect to the bottom of the valley?
23. Define the following terms with the help of diagram.
    (i) Longitudinal overlap, (ii) Side lap, (iii) Superlap, (iv) Stereo-pair, and (v) Stereo-vision
24. The air base of a stereo pair of vertical photos is 1400m and flying height above average ground is 2440m. The camera has a focal length of 152.4 mm and a 23 cm format of photographs. Compute the percentage end lap?
25. What is stereoscopy? Explain the concept of vertical exaggeration in stereo-pair. Describe how you visualise 3D from a stereo-pair.
26. Discuss the construction and uses of pocket stereoscopes and mirror stereoscopes.
27. With the help of neat sketch, explain the process of base lining of a stereo-pair. Why is it necessary?
28. Discuss how the height of an object above ground can be determined using stereo parallax measurements.
29. What is parallax in stereo-photographs? State how this is created to view the stereo-vision.
30. Explain the working principle of a parallax bar with the help of a neat sketch.
31. Define absolute parallax. Describe the procedure to compute the absolute parallax from stereo-photographs.
32. Calculate the stereoscopic parallaxes of points A through D, given the following measured coordinates.

Points	Coordinates (mm)	
	x (left photo)	x'(right photo)
A	59.94	–27.18
B	68.05	–21.61
C	99.57	9.91
D	100.37	8.52

33. Which point is the highest in elevation?
34. Establish a relationship to compute the height of an object using single aerial photographs.
35. In a tilted photograph, define the following terms with the help of sketch.
    (i) Azimuth, (ii) Angle of tilt, (iii) Isocentre, (iv) Isometric parallel, and (v) Swing

36. Derive an expression to compute the scale of a tilted photograph.
37. Establish a relationship to compute the ground coordinates from a tilted photograph.
38. How do you compute the flying height of a tilted photograph? Derive the expression.
39. What is tilt displacement? Derive a relationship to compute the tilt displacement.
40. Discuss various Photogrammetric systems along with their advantages and disadvantages.
41. Write a short note on
    (i) Collinearity equations
    (ii) Orthophotos
    (iii) Applications of photogrammetry

References

1. ASPRS, (1980), *Manual of Photogrammetry*, ASPRS publication, 4th Ed., p. 1056.
2. ASPRS, (1983), *Multilingual Dictionary of Remote Sensing and Photogrammetry*, ASPRS publication, p. 343.
3. Ebner H, Heipke C, Mayer H, and Pakzad, K., (2003) *Photogrammetric Image Analysis*, ISPRS Conference on "Photogrammetric Image Analysis" (PIA '03), Munich, Sept. 17-19, 2003.
4. Egels, Yves and Kasser, Michel, (2001), *Digital Photogrammetry*, CRS Press.
5. Grave, Cliff, (1996), *Digital Photogrammetry: An Addendum to Manual of Photogrammetry*, ASPRS Publication.
6. Hassani, Mahmoud and Carswell, James, (1992), *Transition from Analogue to Digital Photogrammetry*, Journal of Advances in Remote Sensing, Vol I. No. 3 –VII.
7. Koh, Alexander and Graham, Ronald (2002), *Digital Aerial Survey: Theory and Practice*, CRC Press.
8. Kraus, K., (1994), *Photogrammetry, Verd. Dümmler Verlag*, Bonn.
9. Manugula, S S and Bommakanti, Veeranna Bommakanti (2018), *Photogrammetry, GIS & Remote Sensing*, Ebooks2go Inc.
10. Mikhail, Edward M, Bethel, James S and McGlone, J Chris (2001), *Introduction to Modern Photogrammetry*, John Wiley & Sons.
11. Moffit, F.H. and Mikhail, E., (1980), *Photogrammetry*, 3rd Ed., Harper & Row Publishers, New York.
12. Phillipson, Warren R. (1996), *Manual of Photographic Interpretation*, ASPRS Publication.

13. Samson, A. A., (2003), M. Tech. Thesis, Dept. of Civil Engineering, IIT Kanpur, India.

14. Schenk, T. (2005), *Introduction to Photogrammetry*, Department of Civil and Environmental Engineering and Geodetic Science, The Ohio State University 2070 Neil Ave., Columbus, OH 43210.

15. Sijmons, Koert, Introduction on Photogrammetry, ITC, Netherland. https://www.scribd.com/ document/277243918/Introduction-on-Photogrammetry-by-Koert-Sijmons

16. Thomas, Robson, S.O., Kyle, Stephen and Boehm, Jan, (2014) Close Range Photogrammetry and 3D Imaging, Walter de Gruyter, GmbH, Berlin.

17. Wilkinson, Benjamin E., DeWitt, Bon A. and Wolf, Paul R.(2014), 4th Ed, Elements of Photogrammetry with Application in GIS, McGraw-Hill Education India Pvt.Ltd - New Delhi

18. Wolf, P., 1980, *Elements of Photogrammetry*, McGraw Hill Book Co, NY.

19. Wolf, P.R. and Dewitt, B.A. (2000), *Elements of Photogrammetry with Applications in GIS*. 3rd Ed., McGraw-Hill Education, New York.

20. Wrozynski, R., Pyszny, K., Sojka, M., Przybyla, C. and Murat-Blazejewska, S. (2017), Ground Volume Assessment using 'Structure from Motion' Photogrammetry with a Smartphone and a Compact Camera, Open Geosciences formerly Central European Journal of Geosciences, Vol 9, Issue1.

Web Resources

http://www.durban.gov.za/City_Services/engineering%20unit/Surveying_ Land_Information/Documents/AerialPhotogrammetry.pdf

http://www.state.nj.us/transportation/eng/documents/survey/Chapter7.shtm#7.3 Introduction to Photogrammetry by T. Schenk, Autumn Quarter 2005

http://professionalaerialphotographers.com/content.aspx?page_id=22& club_id=808138& module_id=158950, History of Aerial Photography.

Chapter 3

Remote Sensing

3.1 INTRODUCTION

Any living organism whose sense organs are well developed can interact with its environment better. Human-beings have five well developed sense organs (natural sensors): eye, ear, nose, skin and tongue along with highly developed sensing systems – the brain and the nervous system, and these are called as natural remote sensing. The word "**remote**" means "**from a distance**." "**Sensing**", in this case, means "**to record**." So a basic definition of remote sensing is to record from a distance. For example, with eyes it is possible to gather information about the surroundings from a distance. Human beings can see only through the visible light which forms only a very narrow band of the electro-magnetic spectrum. It is because human eyes are not sensitive to the wavelengths below the violet and above the red region of the electromagnetic spectrum (Gibson, 2000).

Remote sensing refers to obtaining information about an object, area, or phenomenon through the analysis of data acquired by a device that is not in contact with the object, area, or phenomenon under investigation (Lillesand and Kiefer, 1994). Remote sensing can be defined as the *"art of science & technology of obtaining reliable information about the physical objects and environment through the process of recording, measuring & interpreting images/data obtained from remotely distant sensor systems"*.

In remote sensing interactions between the Earth surface and the electromagnetic energy take place. Detection and discrimination of objects or surface features are done through recording of radiant energy reflected or emitted by objects or surface material. All features on the Earth's surface reflect and absorb the Sun's radiant energy. They also emit and reflect back parts of that energy. The amount and type of radiation that is emitted and reflected from the Earth's features depends on the properties of those objects or material. Various objects emit and reflect different amount of energy in different parts of electromagnetic spectrum, depending on the property of the material (structural, chemical, physical), surface roughness, angle of incidence, intensity and wavelength of radiant energy (Gibson, 2000). Various sensors gather the data and efficiently absorb the reflected energy of the Earth surface. These sensors onboard remote sensing satellites play an important role in data capture and dissemination.

Remote sensing is a branch of physics, namely reflectance spectroscopy which has now found extensive applications in almost every field of human activity. It is basically a multi-disciplinary science which includes combinations of sensor/satellite launch, photography, spectroscopy, electrical, electronics & telecommunications and computer. All these technological aspects combined together act as one fully integrated system in itself, known as **Remote Sensing System**. All these parts are equally important for successful operation of the system (Colwell, 1983).

Remote sensing systems provide a very important source of spatio-temporal information on Earth surface processes at scales ranging from regional to global. A wide range of parameters can be measured from remote sensing images, including land use, vegetation types, surface temperatures, soils, water, geology, forestry, surface elevation and snow. Sequential remote sensing images are useful in monitoring flood, water pollution, deforestation, extent of forest fire, snow cover, urban sprawl studies, crop acreage and yield estimation, drought monitoring and assessment, wasteland mapping, mineral prospects, forest resource survey etc. Today, remote sensing image have become an integral part of the resources management system. The remote sensing applications are growing very rapidly with the availability of high-resolution and very high resolution data from the state of the art satellites, like Landsat, IRS-1C/1D/P4, IKONOS, WorldView, QuickBird, GeoEye etc. The advancement in computer hardware and software in the area of remote sensing also enhances various applications. Integration of remote sensing data with other thematic layers generated from various sources is an added advantage for complex modelling and applications in **Geographic Information System (GIS)** (Eastman, 1999, Lillesand et al, 2004).

3.2 ADVANTAGES AND DISADVANTAGES OF REMOTE SENSING

Remote sensing images are available at different resolutions, providing global, national, regional and local level information at specified interval of time. There are large number of benefits derived from these data, depending on the objective and application of the study, as well as time, funds and expertise available. Remote sensing images provide latest information of the area and saves time. Some of the advantages and disadvantages are given below.

3.2.1 Advantages

1. Provides data of large areas
2. Provides data of very remote and inaccessible regions

3. Easy and rapid collection of data
4. 3D of the terrain can be produced.
5. Terrain visualisation can be done in the laboratory.
6. Images of any area are obtained repetitively over a period of time so that natural changes in the landscape can be monitored and analyzed.
7. Area can be seen in colour with the help of multi-spectral images.
8. Images of poor contrast may be digitally enhanced.
9. Images can be quickly analysed with the help of software.
10. Relatively economical production of thematic maps from satellite images.
11. Results are in raster format which can be directly used in GIS alongwith other data.

3.2.2 Disadvantages

1. The interpretation of imagery requires skill.
2. Needs field verification of analysis with the ground data
3. Data from multiple sources at different resolutions may create confusion
4. Objects can be misclassified if sufficient ground truth data are not available.
5. High resolution images are expensive, if multiple scenes are required for study.

3.3 A TYPICAL REMOTE SENSING SYSTEM

A remote sensing system has various components (Figure 3.1), as given below:

(a) The source of illumination (the Sun).
(b) The atmosphere through which signals travel.
(c) The emitted or reflected signals (from an object or phenomenon)
(d) The atmosphere
(e) The sensor (from a satellite platform), and
(f) The ground receiving station
(g) The archival section
(h) The data products
(i) The data interpretation and analysis
(j) Applications

Electromagnetic radiation from the sun (A) interacts with the atmospheric constituents and gets absorbed, scattered or transmitted. Interaction of radiation (signal) with the ground object by which information is obtained and the transmission channel which reduces the signal strength, are given due considerations in remote sensing. The reflected energy again interacts with the atmosphere to finally reach the sensor system (Jenson, 1986). The analog signals are converted into digital signals, and transmitted back to ground receiving station. From ground receiving station, signals are pre-processed and sent to data archive centre where these are stored and given to users on demand. The users then carry out the interpretation and analysis of images, and apply the results to the application in hand.

Most of the remote sensing system for natural resources applications takes day light images. It means, the Sun is the source of illumination of ground objects. Remote sensing images can be taken either in passive or active mode. The **passive systems** depend upon external source of illumination (such as Sun), while the **active systems** have carry their own source of energy (such as **RADAR** or a camera with a flash gun). Passive systems take images during daylight only, while the active systems are ready to take images, anytime, anywhere (Colwell, 1983).

Next important component is atmosphere (B) as the electromagnetic radiation travels a long distance from the Sun to the object on Earth (C), and then back from object to sensor, following the Snell's Law. During both the travels, scattering, absorption and transmission processes take place, affecting the quality of electromagnetic radiation.

The most important component of a remote sensing system is the sensor/detector on board satellite (D) which records the variation of radiant energy reflected or emitted by objects on Earth surface. Different types of sensors are available, which are sensitive to different parts of the electromagnetic spectrum. The data or image is formed of the object in accordance to the response of detector to the incident energy. The function of a sensor is to covert analog signals into digital signals so that these are machine readable. These sensors fall in two broad categories-image forming and non-image forming type of sensors.

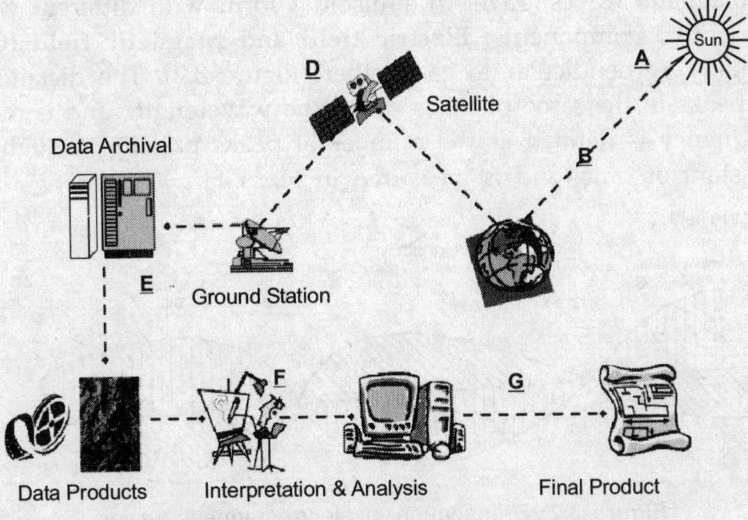

Figure 3.1: Stages of remote sensing

(Source: http://www.nrcan.gc.ca/node/9295)

Through telemetry, satellites transmit the reflected and emitted electromagnetic energy from the Earth's features to the ground stations (E). The images are raw and unprocessed, and they need to be digitally enhanced and combined to highlight particular Earth feature (Jain, 1989). Ground communication stations are the radio telemetry links between satellites and the Earth, and fall into two general categories; (i) those having the sole function of receiving the sensor and attitude data from the satellites and (ii) those which, in addition to receiving the sensor and attitude data, can receive satellite house-keeping data, and transmit commands. The function of recording system (E) is to convert the energy detected by sensor into a form which can be perceived. This is done by dividing the incoming energy by filters into different wavelength bands, and then converting energy in each wavelength band into electrical signal (E). The electrical signal is processed to give radiometric data for each band, which is then recorded on digital tapes. These data are again pre-processed and supplied to the users on their request (E).

Various remote sensing software are available to process and analyse these data (F) and covert them into useful thematic maps for various applications. The data are converted into various thematic maps as per need of the application (G).

3.4 ELECTROMAGNETIC SPECTRUM

The Electromagnetic Spectrum (EMS) forms a very broad spectrum varying from very low frequency to very high frequency or from very long wavelength to very short wavelength. It does not require a material medium to propagate. In empty space, it travels with the velocity of light, which is the highest signal velocity that can be attained. This signal velocity of electromagnetic radiation (EMR) coupled with its low atmospheric attenuation provides a unique advantage to the electromagnetic waves to be used as signals in satellite remote sensing.

All electromagnetic waves travel in sinusoidal form with different wavelength and frequency. It has two components; **Electric field** and **Magnetic field** (Colwell, 1983), which are mutually perpendicular to each other (Figure 3.2). The distance between the two successive peaks in the same phase is called the **wavelength**, and is measured in cm, mm or ìm. **Frequency** is defined as the number of peaks passing through a given point at any given instant of time, and is measured in Hz, GHz.

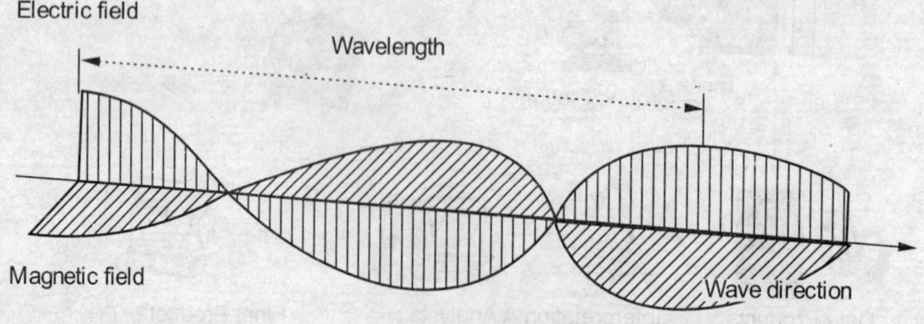

Figure 3.2: Propagation of electromagnetic waves

The frequency (*í*) and wavelength (λ) and velocity (c=2.9979x 10^8 m/s) of the electromagnetic radiation can be related as-

$$\lambda = c/f \qquad ...(3.1)$$

The wavelength of the emitted radiation is inversely proportional to its frequency. Lower is the wavelength, higher the frequency.

All electromagnetic waves travel with a wide range of frequencies, wavelengths, and photon energies. These radiations bear different names, based on differences in their behaviour in the emission, transmission, and absorption and also based on their different practical applications. There is no precise boundary between any of these contiguous portions, so the ranges have some overlap. Electromagnetic radiation reveals its presence when it interacts with the objects (Castleman, 1996).

The EMS ranges from the shorter wavelengths to the longer wavelengths (Figure 3.3). It consists of γ-ray and X-ray regions and part of the Ultraviolet region, visible region, Infrared region, radiowaves and microwaves. Table 3.1 presents the broad part of electromagnetic spectrum of various wavelength regions and their applications. It is to be noted here that the spectrum is much beyond these parts which are shown in Figure 3.3 and Table 3.1.

Ultraviolet (UV) radiation (0.3 to 0.4 μm) is absorbed by Ozone at an altitude of between 20 and 40 km. Some Earth surface materials fluoresce or emit visible light when illuminated by longer wavelength of UV radiation.

Part of the electromagnetic spectrum that human eyes can detect is the **visible spectrum**. The visible region (0.4 to 0.7μm wavelengths) occupies only a very small portion of the spectrum; the longest is red and the shortest is violet. There is a lot of radiation around us which cannot be detected by human eyes, but these can be measured by sensors. This is the only portion of the spectrum that can be associated with the concept of **colours**. **Blue**, **green**, and **red** are the **primary colours** or wavelengths of the visible spectrum. All other colours can be formed by combining blue, green, and red in various proportions. Energy reflected from the Earth during daytime is recorded as a function of wavelength, being maximum energy reflected at 0.5μm wavelength. It corresponds to the green band of the visible region, and is called the **reflected energy peak.**

In the next portion, the **infrared (IR)** region encompasses the wavelength range from approximately 0.7μm to 100μm; more than 100 times as wide as the visible portion. The infrared region can be divided into two categories based on their radiation properties. The NIR and SWIR are also known as the **Reflected IR**, referring to the main infrared component of the solar radiation reflected from the Earth's surface. The MWIR and LWIR are known as the **Thermal Infrared**. Reflected IR region (0.7μm to 3.0μm) is used for remote sensing purposes in similar ways as the visible region. The region from 0.7 to 0.9μm is detectable with film, and is called the **photographic IR band**. The thermal IR region (3.0 μm to 100μm) is quite different than the visible and reflected IR portions, as this energy is emitted from the Earth's surface in the form of heat. Principal **atmospheric windows** occur in the thermal region.

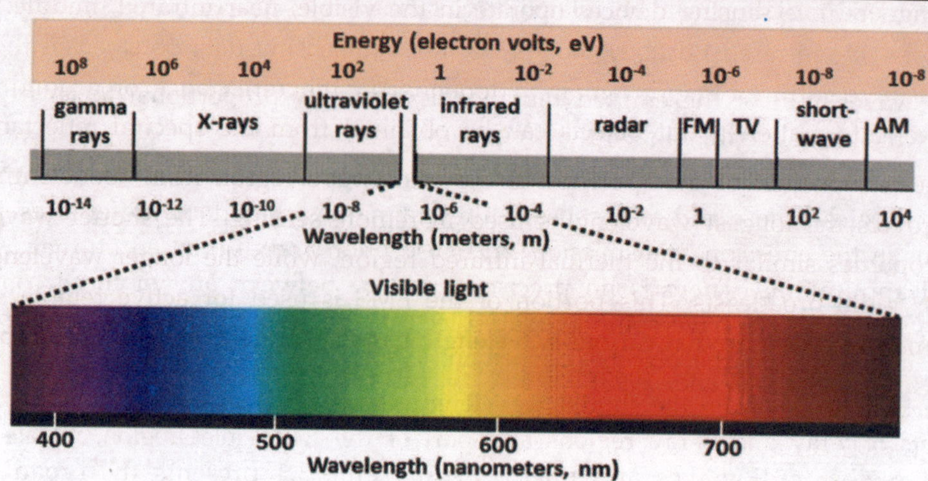

Figure 3.3: The electromagnetic spectrum (Source: Castleman, 1996)

Table 3.1: Principal divisions of electromagnetic spectrum

Wavelength	Description
Gamma (γ) rays	Gamma rays used in medical sciences.
X-rays	X-rays used in medical sciences.
Ultraviolet region (0.3- 0.4μm)	This region is beyond the violet portion of the visible wavelength. UV radiation is largely scattered by earth's atmosphere, and hence not used in field of remote sensing.
Visible region (0.4-0.7μm) **Violet** (0.4-0.446μm) **Blue** (0.446-0.50μm) **Green** (0.50-0.578μm) **Yellow** (0.578-0.592μm) **Orange** (0.592-0.620μm) **Red** (0.620-0.7μm)	The light which our eyes can detect. This is the only portion of the spectrum that can be associated with the concept of colour. Most important portion of spectrum used in optical remote sensing.
Infrared region **NIR** (0.75-1.4μm) **SWIR** (1.4-3μm) **MIR** (3-8μm) **LWIR** (8-15μm) **FIR** (15-100μm)	Infrared region is longer than the red portion of the visible spectrum. Reflected IR (0.7μm-3.0μm) is used for remote sensing. Thermal IR (3μm-14μm) is the radiation emitted from Earth's surface in the form of heat.
Microwave region (1mm30cm) **L band** (15cm-30cm) **S band** (7.5cm-15cm) **C band** (3.75cm-7.5cm) **X band** (2.5cm-3.75cm) **Ku band** (1.7cm-2.5cm) **K band** (1.13cm-1.7cm) **Ka band** (0.75cm-1.13cm)	This is the longest wavelength used in remote sensing. The shortest wavelengths in this range have properties similar to thermal infrared region. The main advantage of this spectrum is its ability to penetrate through fog and clouds.
Radio waves >30cm	This is the longest portion of the spectrum, mostly used for commercial broadcast and meteorology.

Optical remote sensing devices operate in the visible, near infrared, middle infrared and short-wave infrared portion of the EMS. Remote sensing data obtained in the visible and reflective infrared regions mainly depends on the reflectance of ground objects. Therefore, information about objects can be obtained from the spectral reflectances.

The next portion of the spectrum is the **microwave region** from about 1mm to 1m which covers the longest wavelengths used in remote sensing. The shorter wavelengths have properties similar to the thermal infrared region, while the longer wavelengths are used for radio broadcasts. This portion of the EMS is used for active remote sensing. Radar images are acquired at various wavelength bands. Longer wavelengths can penetrate clouds, fog and rain (Vane, 1993).

3.5 BLACK BODY RADIATIONS

All objects with a temperature above absolute zero (^{0}K, or -273.15ºC) emit energy in the form of electromagnetic radiation. A blackbody is a theoretical or model body which absorbs all radiation falling on it, reflecting or transmitting none. Characteristically the black body is a perfect absorber of electromagnetic radiation and also a perfect emitter over all wavelengths. On the contrary, a white body is a non-absorber and non-emitter, it is a perfect reflector (Colwell, 1983). As a matter of fact, in the natural world we do not come across a perfect black body or a white body. Natural bodies show behaviour intermediate between a perfect black body and a perfect white body; the grey body. Emissivity is defined as the ratio of absorbed radiation energy to total incoming radiation energy as compared to a theoretical black body (which absorbs everything), and thus is a measure of absorptivity. The emissivity of a perfect black body is 1, while the emissivity of a perfect white body is zero.

The characteristics of blackbody radiation can be described in terms of several laws (Jenson, 1986):

3.5.1 Planck's Law

According to quantum physics, the energy of an electromagnetic wave is quantized, i.e., it can only exist in discrete amount. The basic unit of energy for an electromagnetic wave is called a **photon**. The energy E of a photon is proportional to the wave frequency f –

$$E = h f \quad ...(3.2)$$

Where h is the Planck's constant = $6.62606957 \times 10^{-34}$ joule second.

Planck's radiation law can also be written in terms of wavelength as-

$$\mathrm{E} = h\ (\mathrm{c}/\lambda) \quad ...(3.3)$$

The energy E radiated is inversely proportional to the wavelength of EMS, as product (h*c) is a constant quantity. Lower the frequency, higher will be the energy carried by the photons and electrons. Since, X rays, γ rays etc., have higher frequency due to their lower wavelength, that's why they are able to penetrate through skeleton/human body, and useful in medical sciences. Table 3.2 gives the details of primary regions of electromagnetic spectrum along with their wavelength, frequency and energy levels.

Planck's law determines the spectral energy density of the emission at each wavelength ($E_{\ddot{e}}$) at a particular absolute temperature (T). The spectral radiance can also be measured per unit wavelength (λ) instead of per unit frequency. In this case, spectral energy is given by:

$$E_{\lambda} = \frac{8\pi hc}{\lambda^5 \left(e^{(hc/\lambda kT)} - 1\right)} \quad \text{...(3.4)}$$

where h = Planck's constant = 6.26 X 10^{-34} Js(joule-second)

c = velocity of light = 2.9979 X 108 m/s = 2.9979 X 10^{14}m/s

λ = wavelength of radiation

k = Boltzmann's constant = 1.38 X 10^{-23} J /K

T = Absolute temperature of the radiating body in degree Kelvin (K)

Table 3.2: Primary regions of EMS along with their wavelength, frequency and energy

S.No.	Region	Wavelength (Cm)	Frequency (Hz)	Energy (eV)
1	Radio	> 10	< 3 x 10^9	< 10^{-5}
2	Microwave	10 - 0.01	3 x 10^9 - 3 x 10^{12}	10^{-5} - 0.01
3	Infrared	0.01 - 7 x 10^{-5}	3 x 10^{12} - 4.3 x 10^{14}	0.01 - 2
4	Visible	7 x 10^{-5} - 4 x 10^{-5}	4.3 x 10^{14} - 7.5 x 10^{14}	2 - 3
5	Ultraviolet	4 x 10^{-5} - 10^{-7}	7.5 x 10^{14} - 3 x 10^{17}	3 - 10^3
6	X-Rays	10^{-7} - 10^{-9}	3 x 10^{17} - 3 x 10^{19}	10^3 - 10^5
7	Gamma Rays	< 10^{-9}	> 3 x 10^{19}	> 10^5

3.5.2 Wien's Displacement Law

It states that the frequency of the peak of the emission increases linearly with absolute temperature (T). Conversely, as the temperature of the body *increases*, the wavelength at the emission peak *decreases*. When the temperature of a blackbody increases, the overall radiated energy increases and the peak of the radiation curve moves to shorter wavelengths (Figure 3.4). The maximum radiation is evaluated from the Planck's formula, the product of the peak wavelength and the temperature is found to be a constant.

$$\lambda_{max} = \frac{b}{T} \quad \text{...(3.5)}$$

Where, T is the temperature and b is a constant of proportionality, known as Wien's displacement constant = $2.898{\times}10^{-3}$mK.

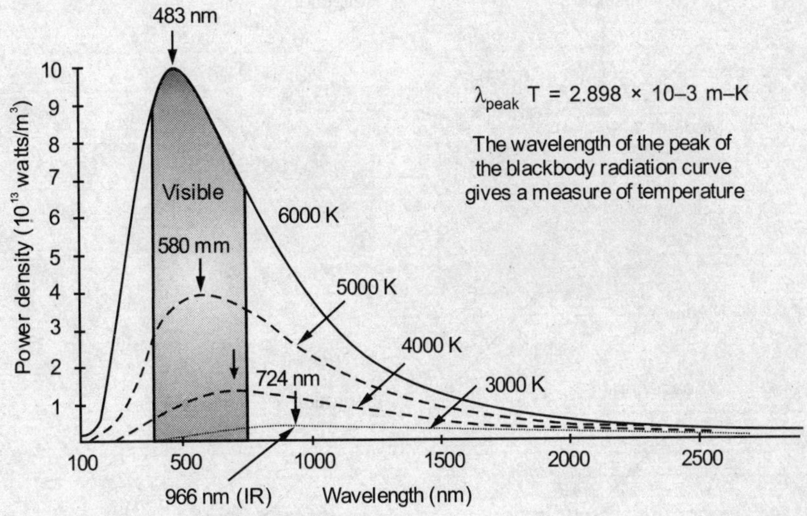

Figure 3.4: Power density of EMS at different temperatures and wavelengths
(*Source: http://hyperphysics.phy-astr.gsu.edu/hbasees/quantum/radfrac.html*)

3.5.3 Stefan–Boltzmann Law

It relates to the total energy emitted *(E)* to the absolute temperature (*T*), as the wavelength of the peak of the blackbody radiation curve decreases in a linear fashion as the temperature is increased (Figure 3.4). The Stefan-Boltzmann law states that the total amount of energy per unit area emitted by an object is proportional to the fourth power of the temperature.

$$E = \sigma T^4 \qquad ...(3.6)$$

where σ is Stefan–Boltzmann constant = 5.67×10^{-8} W / (m^2 K^4)

The Sun produces more spectral energy at 6,000 ^{0}K than the Earth at 300 ^{0}K. As the temperature increases, the total amount of radiant energy measured increases and the radiant energy peak shifts to shorter wavelengths.

3.6 INTERACTION OF EMR WITH ATMOSPHERE

When electromagnetic radiation strikes a material/object, it is called incident radiation. For Earth, the strongest source of incident radiation is the sun. The full moon is the next strongest source, but its radiant energy is only about a millionth that of the sun. Four types of interaction take place: reflection, scattering and absorption and transmission (Figure 3.5) when EMR strikes the matter/objects. These interactions depend upon the compositional and physical properties of the medium, the wavelength or frequency of the incident radiation, and the angle at which the incident radiation strikes a surface (Castleman, 1996).

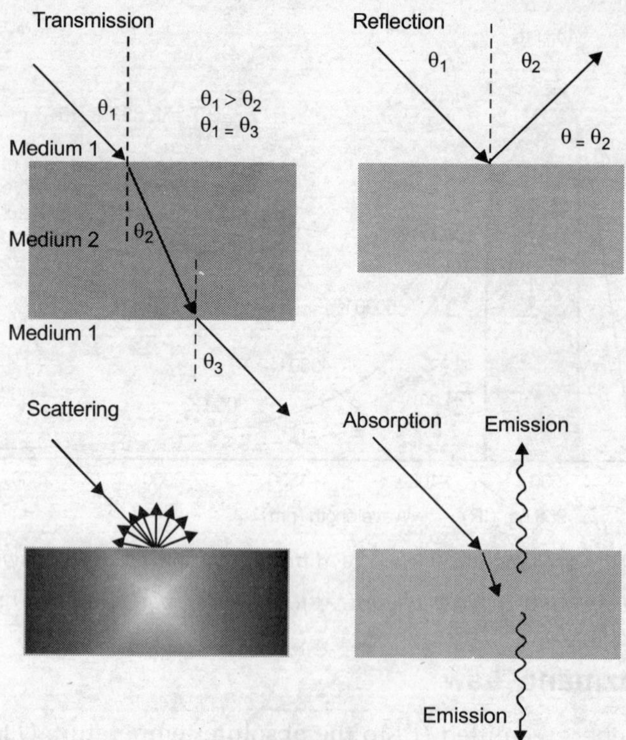

Figure 3.5: Four types of interactions: transmission, reflection, scattering and absorption (*Source: Colwell, 1983*)

3.6.1 Reflection

Reflection also called **specular reflection** is the process whereby incident radiation bounces off the surface of a substance in a single, predictable direction. The angle of reflection is always equal and opposite to the angle of incidence. Reflection is caused by surfaces that are smooth relative to the wavelengths of incident radiation. These smooth, mirror-like surfaces are called specular reflectors. Specular reflection causes no change to either EMR velocity or wavelength. It is the reflected portion of radiation which is recorded by the sensor system. The amount of reflected energy will depend upon the nature of the material of the object, wavelength region, and the atmospheric condition.

3.6.2 Scattering

Scattering is the process by which small particles suspended in a medium of a different index of refraction diffuse a portion of the incident radiation in all directions. With scattering, there is no energy transformation, but a change in the spatial distribution of the energy. Scattering also called **diffuse reflection** occurs when incident radiation is dispersed or spread out unpredictably in many directions, including the direction from which it originated. In the real world, scattering is much more common than the reflection. It is important only in the visible and near infrared regions.

Scattering occurs with surfaces that are rough relative to the wavelengths of incident radiation. Such surfaces are called diffuse reflectors. The velocity and wavelength of electromagnetic waves are not affected by scattering. Scattering produces **blurring** of the targets in remotely sensed images due to spreading of the reflected radiation by scattering, resulting in a reduced resolution image. Scattering of radiation by the constituent gases and aerosols in the atmosphere causes degradation of remotely sensed images. Most noticeably, the solar radiation scattered by the atmosphere towards the sensor without first reaching the ground produces a **hazy appearance** of the image.

Essentially three types of scattering takes place in the atmosphere: Rayleigh scattering, Mie scattering and non-selective scattering (Gibson, 2000). It will depend on the wavelength of the incident radiant energy, and the size of the gas molecule, dust particle, and/or water vapor droplet encountered. The atmospheric scattering processes are summarized in Table 3.3.

Table 3.3: Details of atmospheric scattering processes

Scattering Process	Wavelength dependence	Approximate particle size (μm)	Kind of particles
Rayleigh	λ^{-4}	< 0.1	Air molecules
Mie	λ^0 to λ^{-4}	0.1 to 10	Smoke, fumes, haze
Non-selective	λ^0	> 10	Dust, fog, cloud

3.6.2.1 Rayleigh scattering

Rayleigh scattering mainly consists of scattering from atmospheric gases. It is primarily caused by air particles i.e., O_2 and N_2 molecules. Rayleigh scattering takes place when the dimension of the particles is much smaller than the size of wavelength λ.

$$\text{Scattering} \propto 1/\lambda^4 \qquad \text{...(3.7)}$$

Since, scattering is inversely proportional to the fourth power of the wavelength, radiation in the shorter blue wavelengths is scattered much more strongly than radiation in the red wavelengths (Figure 3.6). It is due to this reason that Rayleigh scattering causes the sky to appear blue. The red colour of the sky during the sunset is also caused by Rayleigh scattering. As the sun approaches the horizon and its rays follow a longer path through the denser atmosphere, the shorter wavelength radiation is comparatively strongly scattered out of the line of sight, leaving only the radiation in longer wavelengths, red and orange, to reach our eyes. This is because blue light is scattered around four times as much as red light, and UV light is scattered about 16 times as much as red light (Jenson, 1986).

Because of Rayleigh scattering, multispectral remote sensing data taken in the blue portion of spectrum is of relatively limited use. In case of aerial photography, special filters are used to cut out the scattered blue radiation due to haze present in the atmosphere.

3.6.2.2 Mie scattering

Mie scattering (Figure 3.6) occurs when diameter of the particle is roughly equal to the size of wavelength (λ). Mie scattering is caused by pollen, dust, smoke, water droplets, and other particles in the lower portion of the atmosphere. It is also called **large particle scattering**. Mie scattering may or may not be strongly wavelength dependent, depending upon the wavelength characteristics of the scattering cross sections. In remote sensing, Mie scattering usually manifests itself as a general deterioration of multispectral images across the optical spectrum under conditions of heavy atmospheric haze. The greater the amount of smoke and dust particles in the atmospheric column, the more violet and blue light will be scattered away and only the longer orange and red wavelength light will reach our eyes. The influence of the Mie scattering is most affected in the lower 4.5 km of the atmosphere (Lillesand et al 2004).

3.6.2.3 Non-selective scattering

Non-selective scattering is produced when the particles in the lower atmosphere are several times bigger than the diameter of the radiation being transmitted. This type of scattering is non-selective, i.e., all wavelengths of light are scattered, not just blue, green, or red (Figure 3.6). Thus, large particles of smoke, water vapor, water droplets, ice crystals, which make up clouds and fog banks, scatter all wavelengths of visible light equally well, causing the cloud to appear white. It also takes places when the lower atmosphere contains suspended aerosols of diameter at least 10 times larger than the wavelengths under consideration (Colwell, 1983). Scattering can severely reduce the information content of remotely sensed data to the point that the imagery looses contrast, and at times it becomes difficult to differentiate one object from another.

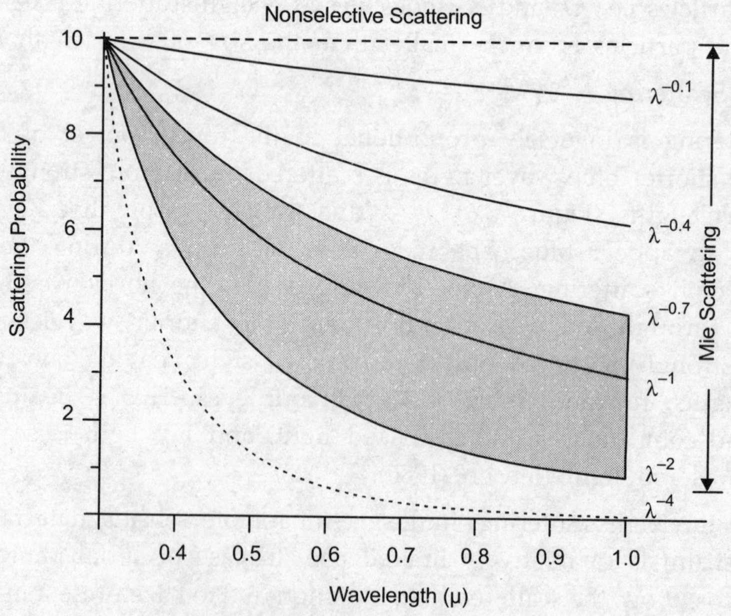

Figure 3.6: Various types of scattering with wavelength

(Source: http://what-when-how.com/remote-sensing-from-air-and-space/atmospheric-absorption-scattering-and-turbulence-visible-imagery-remote-sensing/)

3.6.3 Absorption

It is the process by which incident radiation is taken in by a medium. For this to occur, the substance must be opaque to the incident radiation. A portion of the absorbed radiation is converted into internal heat energy, which may be subsequently emitted at longer thermal infrared wavelengths.

A photon of electromagnetic radiation can be absorbed by a molecule when its frequency matches with one of the available transitional energies. Absorption of ultraviolet (UV) in the atmosphere is mainly due to electronic transitions of the atomic and molecular oxygen and nitrogen. These atoms play an important role in the absorption of solar ultraviolet radiation in the thermosphere. The primary gases that are responsible the atmospheric absorption of energy are ozone, water vapour and carbon dioxide (Gibson, 2000). The photochemical dissociation of oxygen is also responsible for the formation of the ozone layer in the stratosphere. Ozone in the stratosphere absorbs about 99% of the harmful solar UV radiation shorter than 0.32 µm, and is responsible for protecting us from damaging radiation that causes skin cancer.

There is very little absorption of the electromagnetic radiation in the visible part of the spectrum. The absorption in the infrared (IR) region is mainly due to rotational and vibrational transitions of the molecules. The main atmospheric constituents responsible for infrared absorption are water vapour (H_2O) and carbon dioxide (CO_2) molecules. The water and carbon dioxide molecules have absorption bands centred at the wavelengths from near to far infrared (0.7 to 15 µm). In the far infrared region, most of the radiations are absorbed by the atmosphere. The atmosphere is practically transparent to the microwave radiation. Atmospheric absorption affects mainly the visible and infrared bands. Absorption reduces the solar radiance within the absorption bands of the atmospheric gases. Hence, atmospheric absorption may alter the apparent spectral signature of the target being observed.

3.6.4 Transmission

In contrast to the absorption, transmission is the process by which incident radiation passes through the atmosphere and reach the surface; the substance is thus transparent to the radiation (Jenson, 1986). Refraction or deflection from a straight-line path with change in its velocity and wavelength (frequency always remains constant) may take place during transmission of EMR passing through material media of different densities (e.g., air to water). Visible wavelengths are able to penetrate to the Earth's surface with little atmospheric interaction (Figure 3.7). Radio wavelengths have little interaction with the atmosphere and easily penetrate to the surface.

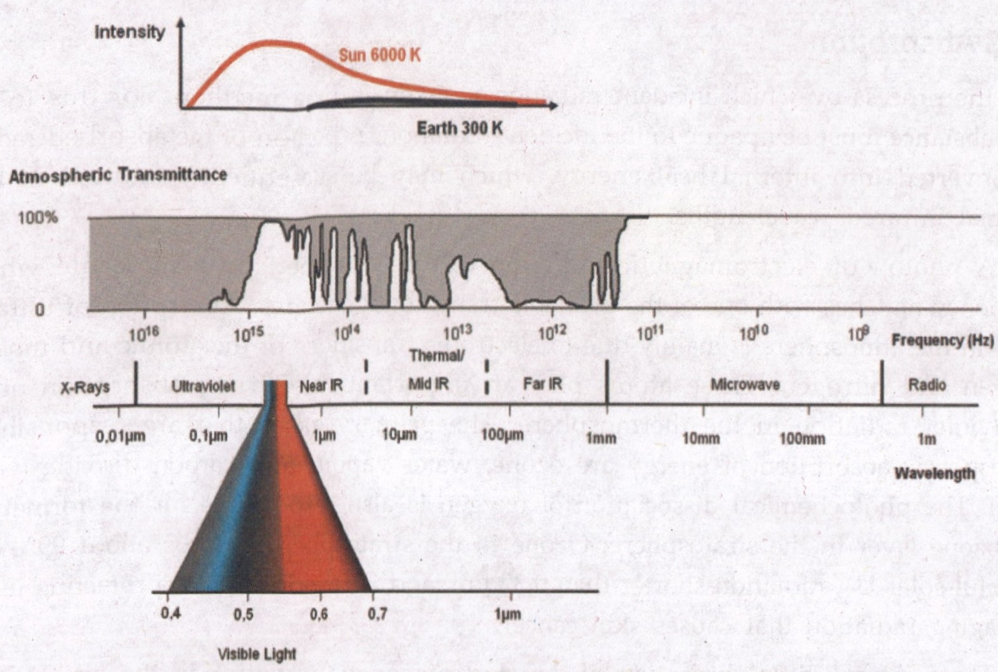

Figure 3.7: Atmospheric transmission process *(Source, Albertz, 2007)*

3.7 ATMOSPHERIC WINDOWS

In optical remote sensing, many wavelengths within the visible and infrared portions of the electromagnetic spectrum (400-2500 nm) penetrate the Earth's atmosphere where they can interact with the Earth's surface and reflect light back to the sensor. Those regions in the atmosphere where transmission of EMR from source to object and back to the sensor is maximum, and absorption & scattering processes are minimum, are called **atmospheric windows** (Colwell, 1983). Each type of molecule has its own set of absorption bands in various parts of the electromagnetic spectrum. As a result, only the wavelength regions outside the main absorption bands of the atmospheric gases can be used for remote sensing. Such regions are found to be very suitable in remote sensing (Figure 3.8), as sensors are designed to capture the reflected radiation in these wavelength regions. Within these ideal ranges, certain wavelengths of light are absorbed by atmospheric gases and water to create wavelength ranges where little incoming radiation makes it to the surface. It is therefore important to design a sensor that will detect reflected light in the specific regions where atmospheric windows occur (Liilesand et al 2004).

The wavelength bands used in remote sensing systems are usually designed to fall within these windows to minimize the atmospheric absorption effects. These windows are found in the visible, near-infrared, certain bands in thermal infrared and the microwave regions (Table 3.4).

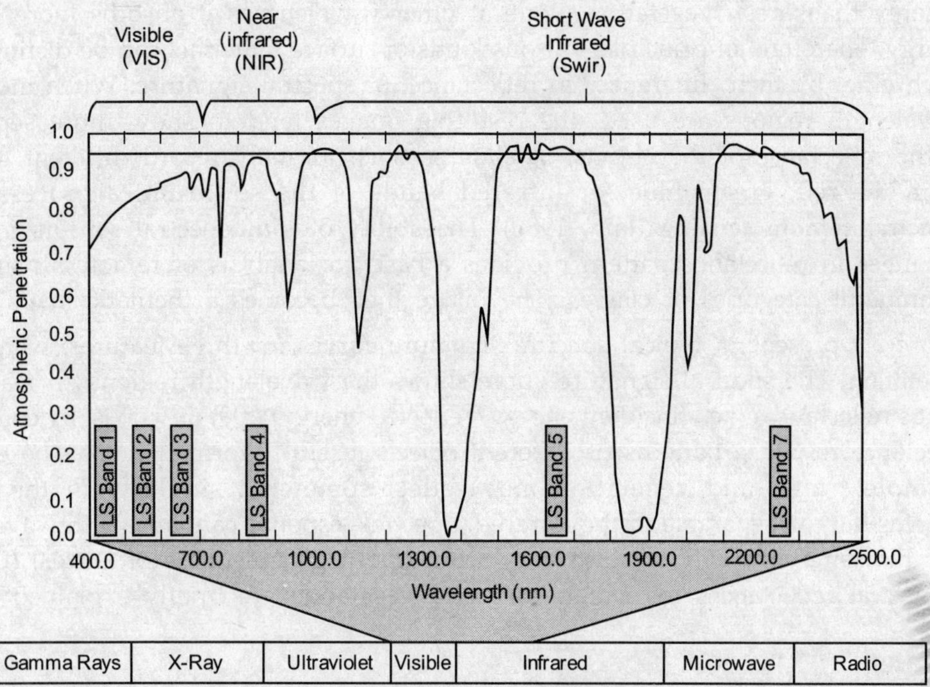

Figure 3.8 Atmospheric windows regions

(*Source: http://www.harrisgeospatial.com/Support/SelfHelpTools/HelpArticles/HelpArticles-Detail/TabId/2718/ArtMID/10220/ArticleID/17333/Atmospheric-Windows-and-Optical-Sensors.aspx*)

Table 3.4: Major atmospheric windows used in remote sensing and their characteristics

Atmospheric window	Wavelength (μm)	Characteristics
Upper ultraviolet, Visible and photographic	IR 0.3-1.0 approx.	95% transmission
Reflected infrared	1.3, 1.6 and 2.2	Three narrow bands
Thermal infrared	3.0-5.0 and 8.0-14.0	Two broad bands
Microwave	>5000	Atmosphere is mostly transparent

3.8 SPECTRAL SIGNATURE

Spectral signature is the variation of reflectance or emittance of a material with respect to wavelengths (i.e., reflectance/emittance as a function of wavelength). For any given material, the amount of solar radiation that is reflected will vary with wavelength. Every object reflects and emits EMR over a range of wavelengths due to its own chemical composition and physical properties (Lillesand and Kiefer, 1994). This EMR from objects over different wavelengths help in separating distinctly various objects on the Earth based on their reflected response for a given wavelength, called spectral signature (Figure 3.9).

Two objects may exhibit different reflectance in a certain wavelength region, and due to this difference, these two objects create different tone (colour) and texture, and thus are easily identifiable from an image. For example, at certain wavelengths, sand reflects more energy than green vegetation while at other wavelengths it absorbs more (reflects less) energy. Therefore, in principle, various kinds of surface materials can be distinguished from each other by their differences in reflectance, or spectral signature. When more than two wavelength regions are used, the resulting images tend to show more separation among the reflectance of the objects. Satellite sensors normally record different reflected energy in the red, green, blue, or infrared bands of the spectrum, a process called **multispectral remote sensing** (Jain, 1986). The ability of multispectral sensors to detect small changes in reflectance pattern provides a basis for analysis of remote sensing data into meaningful categories or classes. The image then becomes a thematic map.

Figure 3.9 presents a typical spectral signature curves for three features; water, soils and vegetation. The spectral signature curve shows the wavelength regions on x-axis and percentage reflectances (i.e., (incident energy/reflected energy)*100) on y-axis. By comparing the reflectance response patterns of different objects, useful information may be derived. For example, water and vegetation may reflect somewhat similarly in the visible wavelengths but are separable in the infrared. Spectral response can vary with wavelength, even for the same object. It can also vary with time (e.g., greenness of leaves) (Colwell, 1983). Spectral reflectances for water, soils and vegetation are briefly explained below.

3.8.1 Water

In longer wavelength, visible and near infrared radiation is absorbed more by water than shorter visible wavelengths. Thus, water typically looks blue or blue-green due to stronger reflectance at these shorter wavelengths, and darker at red or near infrared wavelengths. If there is suspended sediment present in the upper layers of the water body, then this will allow better reflectivity and a brighter appearance of the water. The apparent colour of the water will show a slight shift to longer wavelengths. The reflectance of suspended sediment can easily confuse with shallow (but clear) water, since these two phenomena appear very similar. Chlorophyll in algae absorbs more of the blue wavelengths and reflects the green, making water appear greener in colour when algae are present (Gibson, 2000). The topography of the water surface (rough, smooth, floating materials, etc.) can also lead to complications for water-related interpretation due to potential problems of specular reflection and other influences on colour and brightness.

3.8.2 Soils

Soils tend to have reflection properties that increase approximately with the wavelength. They normally have high reflectance in all the bands. This of course is dependent on factors, such as the colour, constituents and especially the moisture content. As water is a relatively strong absorber of all wavelengths, particularly those longer than the red part of visible spectrum. Therefore, as soil moisture content increases, the overall reflectance of that soil tends to decrease (Lillesand et al 2004). Soils rich in iron oxide reflect proportionally more of the red than other visible wavelengths, and therefore appear red (rust colour) to the human eye. A sandy soil, on the other hand, tends to appear bright white in the image because visible wavelengths are more or less equally reflected; when slightly less blue wavelengths are reflected this results in a yellow colour.

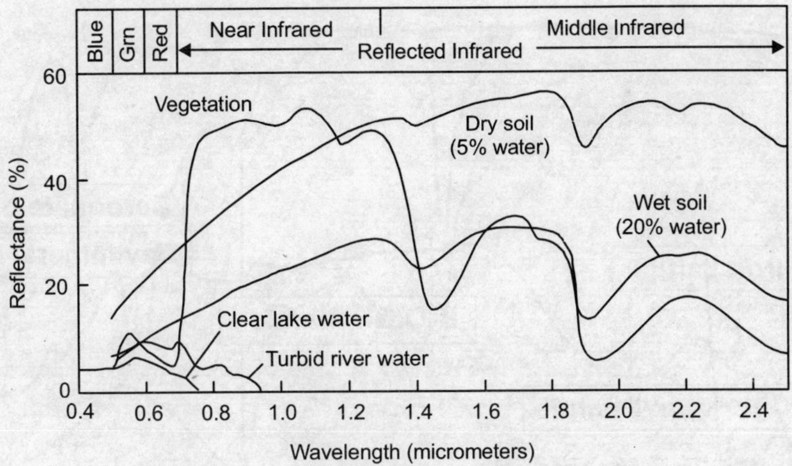

Figure 3.9: Typical spectral signature curves
(*Source: http://web.sonoma.edu/users/f/freidel/techniques/exer/rem_sens/remsen_e.html*)

3.8.3 Rocks

Analysis of spectral reflectance provides information on the distribution of key minerals, while spectral emittance analysis displays silicate compositional variations among the main lithologies (Rowan et al., 2005). The spectral reflectance features of rocks and minerals over the wavelength range of 0.40-2.5 μm are determined by important factors, such as chemical composition, grain size and color (Figure 3.10). The middle infrared region of the spectrum (1.1 and 2.5 μm) can provide more information about the mineralogical composition. Opaque minerals have very distinct effect on the spectra of rocks, because they have low reflectance from rocks. Basic, mafic and intermediate igneous rocks show low reflectance as compared to acidic igneous rocks (Gupta, 1991).

The sedimentary rocks generally have water absorption bands at 1.4 μm and 1.9 μm, clay-shale have additional absorption features from 1.2-2.3 μm region, carbonaceous shale and pure siliceous sand do not show any spectral features. Sandstone containing iron oxide exhibits absorption feature at 0.87 μm region which is related to Fe3+. Limestone and calcareous rocks exhibit absorption range at 1.9 μm and 2.35 μm, respectively (Rajesh, 2004). In most of the metamorphic rocks, such as marbles and quartzites, spectral reflectance curves exhibit absorption features at 1.4 μm and 1.9 μm, respectively. Spectral reflectance curves of all metamorphic rocks reflect feature of water or hydroxyl-like that of igneous rocks. Schistose rocks exhibit feature of ferric and ferrous (Sabins, 1996). Spectral ranges of 1.55-1.75 μm and 2.08-2.35 μm are very helpful for distinguishing vegetation from hydroxyl and iron oxides.

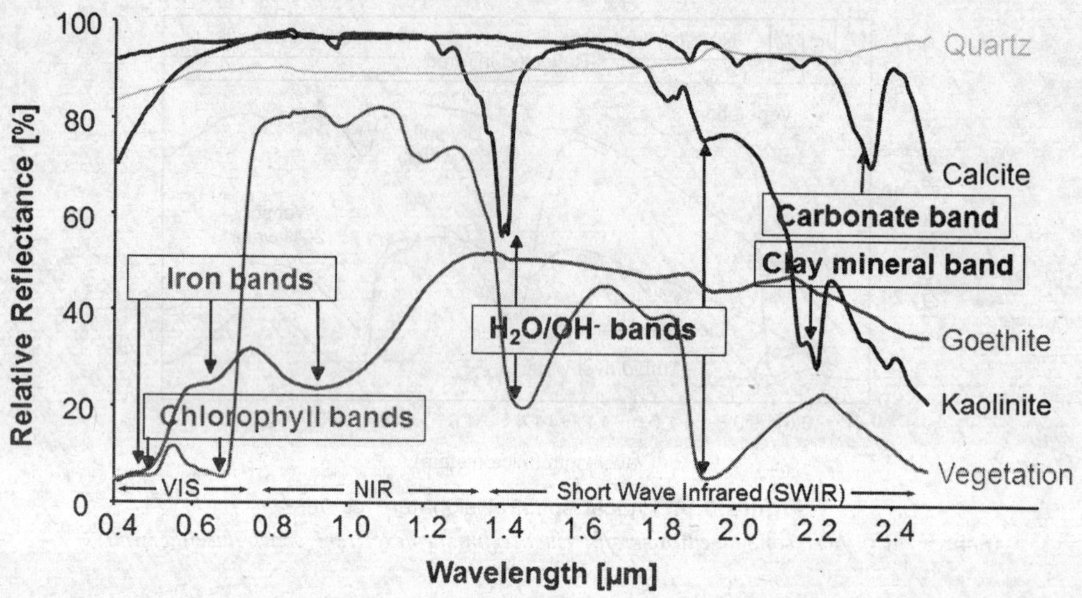

Figure 3.10: Spectral reflectance of various rocks
(*Source: http://instruct.uwo.ca/earth-sci/300b-001/remote.htm*)

3.8.4 Vegetation

A chemical compound in leaves, called chlorophyll, will strongly absorb radiations in the red and blue wavelengths but reflects in green wavelengths. Leaves appear "greenest" when chlorophyll content is at its maximum. In autumn, there is less chlorophyll in the leaves, so absorption is less and proportionately more reflection of red wavelengths, making leaves appear red or yellow. The internal structure of healthy leaves act as excellent diffuse reflectors of near-infrared wavelengths. In fact, the health of leaves can effectively be measured and monitored in near-IR reflectance.

3.9 USING THE SPECTRO-RADIOMETER

Ground truth data collection for various remote sensing applications requires proper field-based instrumentation. It is necessary that such instruments meet the requirements of radiometric performance, such as spectral and spatial parameters, sampling/averaging rate, signal-to-noise ratio, dynamic range, linearity, etc. **Spectro-radiometer** (or **Radiometer** or **Ground Truth Radiometer**) is a field-based instrument that measures the intensity of radiation in several wavelengths of electromagnetic spectrum, such as infrared or microwave (Figure 3.11). It also helps in measuring the differences in the reflectance pattern of various objects (or **spectral signatures**) as a function of wavelength. The reflected radiation of various objects is measured in the field through spectro-radiometer in different wavelength regions, and these values are plotted on a graph, representing spectral signature of features.

The Space Application Centre (Indian Space Research Organisation, Bangalore) has also designed, developed and commercialized Ground Truth Radiometers (Manjul, 2002, Manjul and Kulkarni, 2004) for spectral signature studies. These instruments operate in 400-3000 nm and are being extensively used for field and laboratory applications. Measurement of irradiance can be made using a coated plate with Barium Sulphate in each of the bands, and this value is the reference value for the computation of percentage reflectance. These readings of Barium Sulphate plate are considered as 100% reflected radiation at that moment of time. The Barium Sulphate plate being a Lambertian Surface reflects radiations in all directions evenly. The reflected radiance can be measured by holding the radiometer vertically over the object at around 1.5m from the ground. Radiometer is portable, easy-to-operate, and low cost, environmental friendly, and produces consistent and reliable data sets, after the calibration.

Figure 3.11: The Spectro-radiometer
(Source: https://www.spectravista.com/ger1500/)

The readings are normally taken between 8 am to 10.30 am and 3 pm and 5 pm, such that neither the sun elevation is too low nor too high. This is to avoid the extreme values as a result of high intensity due to high sun elevation, and low intensity due to low sun elevation. The presence of cloud also makes a significant difference in the reflectance values. Thus cloudy days and cloudy period in a day are avoided. The spectral response of the target also depends on orientation of the Sun (solar azimuth), the height of the Sun in the sky (solar elevation angle), look angle of the spectro-radiometer, and the distance between the instrument and the target.

The radiometer is placed approximately 1.5 meter above the sample terrain and the reflectance for each band is collected. This process is repeated for all the sample sites to take several readings at each sample location, and average value is finally taken. The percentage reflectance for each sample in a wavelength band is calculated with respect to the reflectance values obtained from the Barium Sulphate plate. This process is also repeated for several locations of the same sample for better accuracy.

The measurements of reflectance in narrow spectral bands under *insitu* conditions have many applications in remote sensing. The measurement of spectral reflectance also provides useful inputs to the design and calibration of remote sensing sensors. The databases created in the field would be helpful to possibly decide the sensor parameters, such as optimal number of spectral bands, optimal ground resolution, and actual required dynamic range of input flux reflected from terrain surface, etc. Such instruments can also provide data for radiometric and atmospheric corrections of satellite images, which requires field reflectance measurements of the targets with illumination and viewing geometry equivalent to that of the imaging sensor of interest. Other possible applications are:

- Inputs into models for plant growth, estimating crop biomass & crop yield, estimating leaf area index and crop loss due to disease, insect infestation, etc.
- Effects of drought on plant growth and yield.
- Soil moisture and fertility studies.
- Irrigation scheduling studies.
- Water pollution and contaminants
- Land surface reclamation studies.
- Mineral mapping
- Ground truth for remote sensing image analysis.

3.10 TYPES OF ORBITS

From the point of view of periodicity of satellite movement, orbits can be classified as **geo-synchronous (geo-stationary) and sun-synchronous (polar)**, as shown in Figure 3.12 (Lillesand, 2004). Remote sensing applications generally use near polar, sun-synchronous satellites. The near polar satellites provide global coverage, whereas the geo-synchronous satellites are useful in communication and weather-related studies. Images from sun-synchronous satellites have good spatial resolution required for resource surveys and thematic mapping, while larger area is covered by images from geo-synchronous satellites with poor spatial resolution.

A space-borne remote sensing platform is placed in an orbit in which it moves continuously. From geometrical characteristics point of view, orbits of the space-borne platform can be circular, elliptic, parabolic or hyperbolic. In practice, it is difficult to establish and maintain an exactly circular orbit, therefore, the so-called nominally circular orbits are slightly elliptical. Parabolic and hyperbolic orbits are not used for terrestrial remote sensing.

3.10.1 Geo-synchronous Orbits

Geo-stationary or geo-synchronous orbit is the one in which the satellite covers one revolution in the same time as that for the Earth to rotate once about its polar axis. The satellites revolve in the same direction as that of the Earth (West to East) at an angular velocity equal to the Earth's rotation rate. In order to achieve this orbital period, geo-synchronous orbits are generally at high altitude of 36,000 km above equator (Figure 3.12). These make an inclination of 0° from equatorial plane. The satellites moving in these orbits are called **geostationary satellites** (Gibson, 2000). Thus from any point on the equator, the satellite moving in such orbit appears to be stationary. INSAT series of satellites launched by Indian Space Research Organization, Department of Space, Government of India is an example of these satellites.

Geo-stationary or geo-synchronous satellites, like INSAT, Meteosat, GOES, GMS etc., are used for communication and meteorological purposes. Satellites in the geo-synchronous orbit are located at any particular longitude to get a constant view of that particular region, thus providing frequent images in a day. For example, the GOES East and GOES West satellites are placed in orbits over North America (normally at 75° W and 135° W, respectively), INSAT 3-A is located at 93.5° E longitude over India, the Japanese Geostationary Meteorological Satellite (GMS) is located over New Guinea, and Meteosat over Europe. These images are very useful in weather forecasting and meteorological studies. The signals from these satellites are used for communication and television broadcast spurposes. Because of the very high altitude, they can cover 45-50% of the area of globe.

3.10.2 Sun-synchronous Orbits

Sun-synchronous or **Polar orbits** are usually low orbits (approximately 700-900km from equator) as compared to the geo-synchronous orbits. Sun synchronous orbits maintain a constant angle between the aspect of incident sun and viewing by the satellite, so that the sun-lit portion of the Earth is always below the satellite. These orbits maintain nearly 87° inclination from the equatorial plane. The satellites in such orbit are called **sun-synchronous** or **polar satellites** as their orbital plane is passing close to poles (Figure 3.12) (Colwell, 1983). Consequently the orbital period is less, which typically varies from 90-103 minutes, covering several orbits per day (Table 3.5). Therefore satellites in the polar orbits make more than one revolution around the Earth in a single day. The National Oceanic and Atmospheric Administration (NOAA) series of satellites, like NOAA 17, NOAA 18, IRS, Landsat, SPOT are all examples of polar orbiting satellites.

The satellite retraces its path when an orbital cycle is completed by a satellite, and is known as **repeat cycle** of the satellite. Due to the rotation of the Earth on its own axis, each time in a new orbit the satellite observes a new area. The satellite's orbit period and the rotation of the Earth together will allow to complete coverage of the Earth's surface, after a few days, known as the **revisit period**. Revisit period (refer to Table 3.5) is the time elapsed between two successive views of the same area by the same satellite. In polar orbit, the satellite travels from North to South poles, and the Earth turns below it about its axis, so entire Earth is covered.

Now-a-days using the steerable sensors, a satellite-borne instrument can view off-nadir areas before and after the orbit passes over a ground. In view of this, off-nadir viewing capability of the satellites, revisit time can be reduced considerably than the orbital cycle. The revisit time is important especially when frequent images of an area are required to be analysed, such as floods, earthquake etc. In near- polar orbits, areas at high latitudes will be imaged more frequently than the equatorial zone due to the increasing overlap in adjacent swaths as the orbit paths come closer together near the poles.

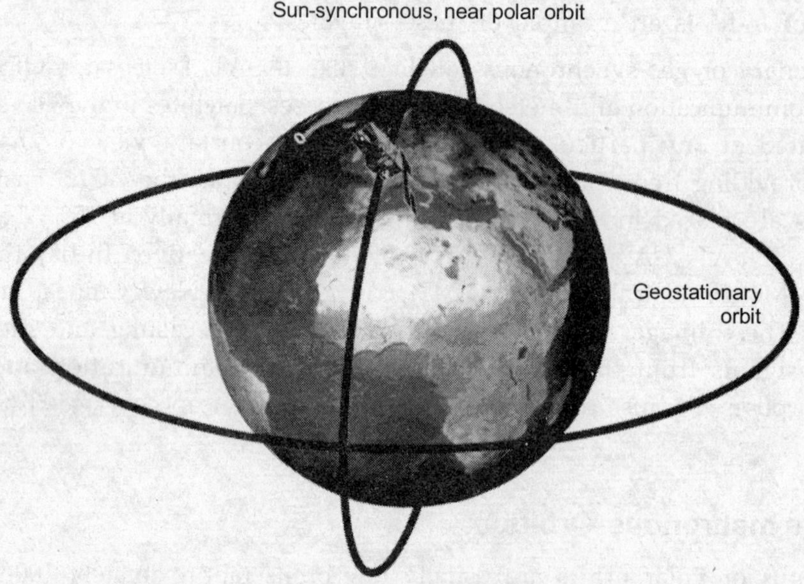

Figure 3.12: Sun-synchronous and geo-synchronous orbits

3.11 IMAGE CHARACTERISTICS

3.11.1 Swath

The satellite moves north to east in the orbit and collects EMR of the ground objects. The width of the area covered on the ground when satellite sensor scans the Earth surface while moving in a orbit is called a swath (Figure 3.13). Imaging swaths for space-borne sensors generally vary between tens and hundreds of kilometres wide, for example, it is 185 km wide by earlier Landsats. As the satellite orbits the Earth from pole to pole, due to rotation of the Earth (from west to east) the satellite appears shifting westward. This apparent movement allows the satellite swath to cover a new area with each consecutive pass. The sensor of the satellite will collect the reflected signals across (West to East) the motion of the satellite in the orbit, called **scan line**.

3.11.2 Path-row Number

Since the reflected radiations from the ground are continuously recorded by the sensor, each orbit is given a unique number for identification of the ground scene/area, called **Path number**. These signals are sent to ground receiving station where these contiguous signals are truncated as per scenes and recorded on magnetic media; each scene having roughly a square shape (it is not perfectly square) with same length as swath (e.g. one Landsat MSS scene covered 185 km x 185 km on the ground). The length of the scene defines the **Row number**. Thus, each scene can be located with its unique Path-Row number (Figure 3.14).

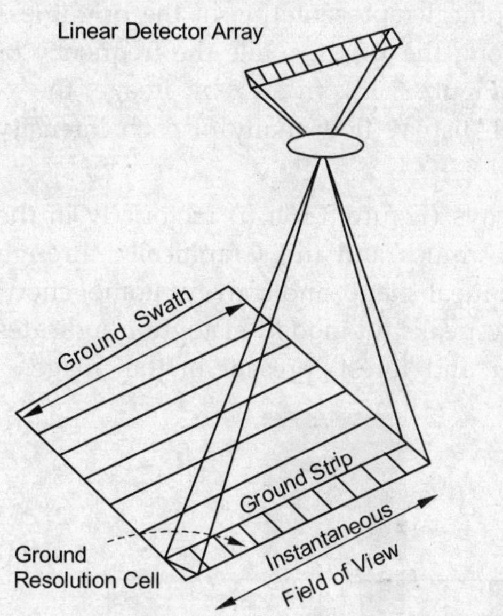

Figure 3.13: Swath width

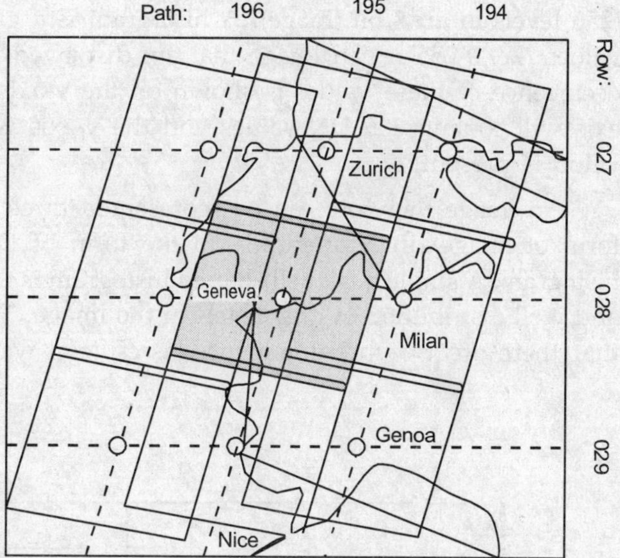

Figure 3.14: Path-row of LANDSAT

3.11.3 Pixel

The word pixel is made from "picture element". It is smallest element in an image (Figure 3.13). As the image is composed of row and columns, one small grid is called a pixel. The number of pixels in an image may be computed by multiplying rows and columns present in the image.

3.11.4 Digital Number

Digital Number **(DN)** in remote sensing systems, is a variable assigned to a pixel, usually in the form of a binary integer in the range of 0–255 (i.e. a byte) in an 8 bit image. The range of energy examined in a remote sensing system is broken into 256 grey levels in an 8 bit image (2^8). DN value is very important as digital analysis of remote sensing images is based on these values.

3.11.5 Spectral Band

The sensors are designed to operate in narrow wavelength ranges to gather the information. These wavelength range from a referred to as a **channel** or a **band**. The number of bands imaged by the sensor may be grouped as panchromatic (single band), multispectral (more than one band), or hyperspectral (usually over 100 bands).

3.11.6 Image Histogram

Image histogram is a powerful tool to portray information of an image. In raw imagery, the useful data often occupies only a small portion of the available range of digital values (256 levels in an 8 bit image). A histogram is a graphical representation of the brightness values (i.e. 0-255) in an image that are displayed along the x-axis, while the frequency of occurrence of these values is shown on the y-axis (Figure 3.15). In an 8-bit image, the x-axis will contain 256 DN values and the y-axis will display how many of each intensity value is present.

An image therefore can be represented three ways (Figure 3.16): (i) Pictorially in the form of image (ii) Numerically in the form of DN values and (iii) Graphically through histogram. A single peak bell shaped histogram is the ideal shape, and conveys homogenous and well distribution of grey levels in the image. Two peaks (bi-model) histogram indicates that there are two pre-dominant classes (e.g. water and forest) present in the image.

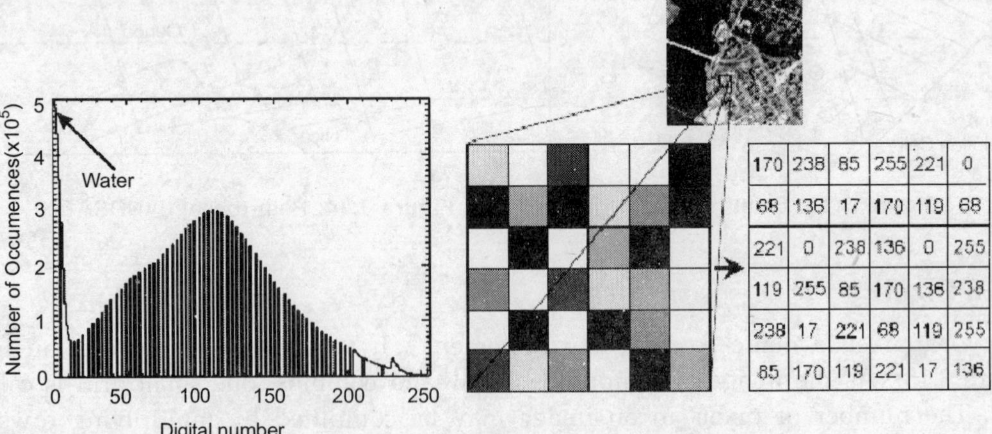

Figure 3.15: Histogram of an image.

Figure 3.16: Representation of an image

3.12 TYPES OF RESOLUTIONS

An image can be described better in terms of its resolution. In general, the resolution is the minimum distance between two objects that can be distinguished in the image. Objects closer than the resolution appear as a single object in the image. In remote sensing, the term resolution is used as the capability to identify the presence of two objects. In qualitative terms, resolution is the amount of details that can be observed in an image. An image showing finer details is said to have finer resolution as compared to the image that shows coarser details. In remote sensing, three different types of information are needed, such as spatial information, spectral information and radiometric (intensity) information. This information from an object is gathered by using the multispectral sensors/ scanners.

Four types of resolutions are therefore considered important in remote sensing work. They are: Spatial resolution, spectral resolution, radiometric resolution and temporal resolution (Gibson, 2000, Lillesand et al 2004). The different resolutions of some popular satellite systems are presented in Table 3.5.

3.12.1 Spatial Resolution

A digital image consists of an array of pixels, and each pixel contains information about a small area on the land surface. Spatial resolution is a measure of the area or size of the smallest dimension on the Earth's surface over which an independent measurement can be made by the sensor (Table 3.5).

It is the minimum separation between the two objects that a sensor can record distinctly. The geometric properties of the imaging system are usually described by the instantaneous field of view **(IFOV)**. The instantaneous view of the ground seen from the detector of a sensor is also called a pixel (Figures 3.13 and 3.16). The IFOV is dependent on the altitude of the satellite; higher the altitude, larger is the IFOV. The spatial resolution specifies the pixel size of satellite images covering the Earth surface (Figure 3.17). High spatial resolution images are < 4 m, while low spatial resolution images are >30 m pixel size. An IFOV value however is not in all cases a true indication of the size of the smallest object that can be detected. An object of sufficient contrast with respect to its background can change the overall appearance of a given pixel so that the object becomes detectable. Due to this reason, the features smaller than spatial resolution, such as roads, canals, railway lines and drainages are detectable on images.

Based on the spatial resolution, satellite systems can be classified as.(i) Low resolution systems, (ii) Medium resolution systems, and High/very high resolution systems. Remote sensing systems with spatial resolution more than 1km are generally considered as low resolution systems, e.g., Moderate Resolution Imaging Spectroradiometer (MODIS) and Advantage Very High Resolution Radiometer (AVHRR) sensors. The moderate resolution systems have the spatial resolution between 100m –1km, for example, IRS WiFS (188m), band 6 i.e., thermal infrared band, of the Landsat TM (120m), and bands 1-7 of MODIS having resolution 250-500m. High resolution systems have spatial resolution approximately 5-100m, such as Landsat ETM+ (30m), IRS LISS-III (23m MSS and 6m Panchromatic) and AWiFS (56-70m), SPOT 5 (2.5-5m Panchromatic) are some of the high resolution sensors. Very high resolution systems are those which provide less than 5m spatial resolution. GeoEye (0.45m for Panchromatic and 1.65m for MSS), IKONOS (0.8-1m Panchromatic), and QuickBird (2.4-2.8 m) are examples of very high resolution systems.

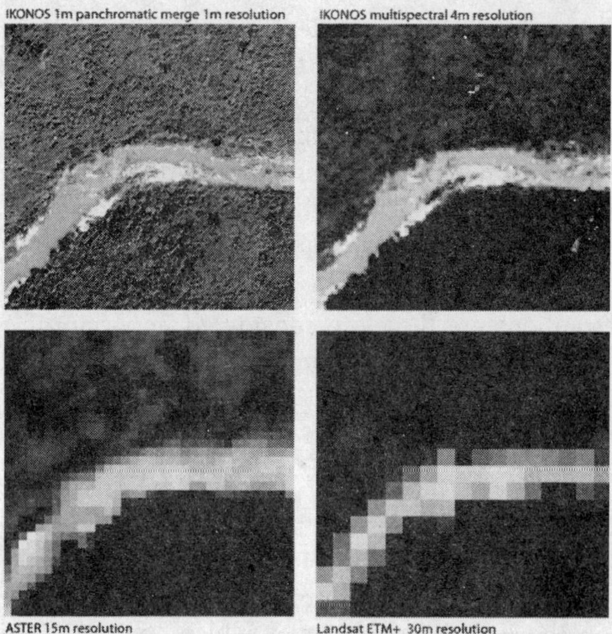

Figure 3.17: Spatial resolution of images

3.12.2 Spectral Resolution

While the human eye only recognizes the visible spectrum of light, a satellite can, depending on the type, depict radiations differently in many spectral regions. The spectral resolution is the ability of a sensor to define fine wavelength intervals or the ability of a sensor to resolve the energy received in a spectral bandwidth to characterize different constituents of earth surface. The finer the spectral resolution, the narrower the wavelength ranges for a particular channel or band. Many remote sensing systems are multi-spectral that record energy over several wavelength ranges at various spectral resolutions. These satellites have between three and eight bands and are therefore called multispectral, for example Landsat, SPOT and IRS.

In remote sensing, spectral resolution is determined by the bandwidth of the channels used. High spectral resolution is achieved by narrow bandwidths which are collectively likely to provide more accurate spectral signature for discrete objects than the broad bandwidths. The number of bands and position of bands, both are important aspect in defining the spectral resolution. Generally surface features can be better distinguished from multiple narrow bands, than from a single wide band. Broad classes, such as water and vegetation, can be easily separated using broad wavelength ranges like visible and near-infrared. However, for more specific class viz., vegetation type, rock classification etc, much finer wavelength ranges, and hence finer spectral resolution are required.

In remote sensing analysis, images are available with high spectral resolution- 220 bands, medium spectral resolution 3 - 15 bands, and low spectral resolution-3 bands. For example, IRS LISS-III uses 4 bands, and Hyperspectral sensors detect more than hundreds of very narrow spectral bands. The higher the spectral resolution, the narrower is the wavelength range for a specific band, and therefore, the more bands there are. With a higher spectral resolution single objects can be perceived better and spectrally distinguished.

3.12.3 Radiometric Resolution

Radiometric resolution is determined by the number of discrete levels into which signal strength may be divided (quantization). With a given spectral resolution, increasing the number of quantizing levels (Table 3.5) or improving the radiometric resolution will improve the discrimination between the objects.

If the radiometric resolution is finer or higher, the small differences in reflected or emitted radiation can be measured accurately, but the volume of data will be larger. Radiometric resolution depends on the wavelengths and the type of the sensor/ spectrometer. For example, the Landsat-MSS (from Landsat 1-3 has 6 bits (64 grey values), IRS-LISS I-III: 7 bits (128 grey values), Landsat-TM (from Landsat 4-5) and SPOT-HRV: 8 bits (256 grey values), Landsat-ETM & ETM+ (from Landsat 6-7): 9 bits (only 8 bits are transmitted), IRS-LISS IV: 10 bits (only 7 bits are transmitted), and IKONOS and QuickBird: 11 bits data.

3.12.4 Temporal Resolution

Temporal resolution is related to the time interval between two successive visits of a particular scene by remote sensing satellite (Table 3.5). Smaller the revisit time the better is the temporal resolution of the sensor system. High temporal resolution may be < 24 hours - 3 days, medium temporal resolution between 4-16 days, and low temporal resolution > 16 days. For example, the temporal resolution of IKONOS is 14 days, Landsat 7: 16 days, and SPOT: 26 days, while Meteorological satellites, such as METEOSAT 7 every half an hour and METEOSAT 8 with 15 min have extremely shorter repetition rates.

Multi-temporal image from satellites are more suitable for monitoring dynamic surface features or processes like the seasonal changes of vegetation, growth and development of agricultural crops, floods, the expansion of cities over decades, deforestation, and so on (Colwell, 1983, Gupta, 1991). To monitor changes with time, temporal resolution is also an important consideration when determining the resolution characteristics of a sensor system. For agricultural applications, the use of time as a discriminant parameter may allow crops over large areas to be identified with sensors possessing spatial and spectral resolutions that are too coarse to identify them on the basis of the spectral and morphological characteristics alone. Many times, images may have cloud cover present on it on the day of pass. In such cases, next clear image of the area/activity would be available when there is no cloud cover. In order to reduce the temporal resolution to monitor the area/activity, images of that can be taken for analysis from various satellites.

3.13 TYPES OF REMOTE SENSING IMAGES

Remote sensing images can be divided into two broad types, depending on the media: hard copy or photographic products (B&W, colour) and soft copy (Digital product). The digital image is the original product from the sensor. Depending upon the range of wavelength used for capturing them, the images are classified into three main types (Figure 3.18).

Table 3.5: Resolutions of some remote sensing sensors

Satellite	Sensors	Resolution		
		Spectral Bands (µm)	Spatial (m)	Temporal (days)
LANDSAT-1, 2 and 3*	RBV	Blue-green (0.475-0.575) Orange-red (0.580-0.68) Red to Near-Infrared (0.69-83)	80 40*	18
	MSS	Green (0.5 to 0.6) Red (0.6 to 0.7) NIR (0.7 to 0.8) NIR (0.8 to 1.1) TIR (10.4 to 12.6)*	80	
LANDSAT-4, and 5	MSS	Same as LANDSAT -1 and 2	80	16
	TM	Blue (0.45-0.52) Green (0.52-0.60) Red (0.63-0.69) NIR (0.76-0.90) NIR (1.55-1.75) Thermal (10.40-12.50) Mid-IR (2.08-2.35)	30 120	
LANDSAT 7	ETM+	Blue (0.45-0.52) Green (0.52-0.60) Red (0.63-0.69) NIR (0.77-0.90) NIR (1.55 - 1.75) Thermal (10.40-12.50) Mid-IR (2.08-2.35) PAN (0.52-0.90)	30 60 15	16
LANDSAT 8	Operational Land Imager (OLI)	(0.43 - 0.45) Blue (0.450 - 0.51) Green (0.53 - 0.59) Red (0.64 - 0.67) NIR (0.85 - 0.88) SWIR 1(1.57 - 1.65) SWIR 2 (2.11 - 2.29) PAN (0.50 - 0.68) Cirrus (1.36 - 1.38)	30 15	16
	Thermal Infrared Sensor (TIRS)	TIRS 1 (10.6 - 11.19) TIRS 2 (11.5 - 12.51)	100 100	
SPOT-1, 2 and 3	HRV	Green (0.50 – 0.59) Red (0.61 – 0.68) NIR (0.78 – 0.89)	20	26 4-5 days by using steering capabilities
	PAN	(0.50 – 0.73)	10	
SPOT-4	HR-VIR	In addition to HRV and PAN MIR (1.58-1.75)	20	26 4-5 days by using steering capabilities

SPOT-5	2 HRG sensors	Green (0.50 – 0.59) Red (0.61 – 0.68) NIR (0.78 – 0.89) SWIR (1.58 – 1.75) Pan (0.51 – 0.73)	10 10 10 10 5	26 4-5 days by using steering capabilities
SPOT-6 and 7		Pan (0.45–0.75) Blue (0.45–0.53) Green (0.53–0.59) Red (0.62–0.69) NIR (0.76–0.89)	1.5 8.0	26 4-5 days by using steering capabilities
IRS-1A	LISS-I, and LISS-II A/B (3 sensors)	Blue (0.45-0.52) Green (0.52-0.59) Red (0.62-0.68) NIR (0.77-0.86)	72.5 m LISS-I 36 m LISS-II	22
IRS-1B	LISS-I and LISS-II	same as for IRS-1A		22
IRS-1C & 1D	LISS-III	Green (0.52-0.59) Red (0.62-0.68) NIR (0.77-0.86) NIR (1.55-1.70)	23.5 23.5 23.5 70	24
	PAN	(0.50-0.75)	5.8	24 (5)
	WiFS	Red (0.62-0.68) NIR (0.77-0.86)	188	5
IRS-P3	WiFS	Red (0.62-0.68) NIR (0.77-0.86) NIR (1.55-1.70)	188	5
	MOS-A MOS-B MOS-C	(0.75-0.77) (0.41-1.01) (1.595-1.605)	1500 520 550	Ocean surface
IRS-P4 (Oceansat-1)	OCM MSMR	(0.40-0.90) 6.6, 10.65, 18, 21 GHz (frequencies)	360x236 105x68, 66x43, 40x26,34x22(km for frequency sequence)	2 2
IRS-P6 Resourcesat-1	LISS-IV	Green (0.52-0.59 Red (0.62-0.68 NIR (0.77-0.86	5.8 5.8 5.8	24 (5)
	LISS-III	Green (0.52-0.59) Red (0.62-0.68) NIR (0.77-0.86) NIR (1.55-1.70)	23.5 23.5 23.5 23.5	24
	AWiFS	Red (0.62-0.68) NIR (0.77-0.86) NIR (1.55-1.70)	70 70 70	5
IRS-P5 Cartosat-1	PAN-F PAN-A	(0.50-0.75) (0.50-0.75)	2.5 2.5	2-line stereo camera
Cartosat-2	PAN camera	(0.50-0.85)	< 1	
Oceansat-2	OCM SCAT ROSA	(0.40-0.90) 8 bands 13.515 GHz GPS occultation	360 x 236 25 km x 25 km	2

**Landsat 3 MSS has 5 bands data and RBV data has 40 m spatial resolution*

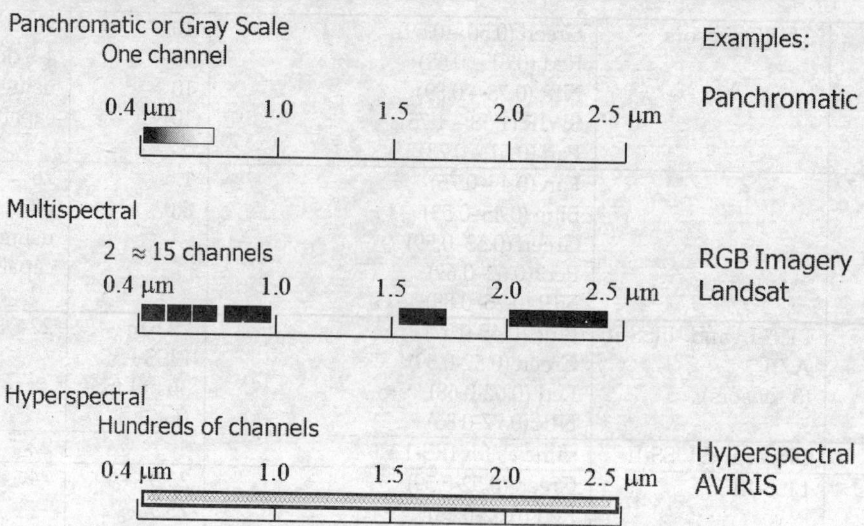

Figure 3.18: Optical ranges used by various images

3.13.1 Panchromatic Images

These images are usually displayed as a grey scale image (such as SPOT, QuickBird), consists of one band with a slightly larger range in visible part of the electromagnetic spectrum. A panchromatic image may be interpreted similar to a black-and-white aerial photograph. The radiometric characteristics are utilized in its interpretation, as the main parameter. Figure 3.19 shows the B&W panchromatic image from SPOT satellite. In this Figure, the urban area at the bottom left and a clearing near the top of the image have high reflected intensity, while the vegetated areas on the right part of the image are generally dark. Roads and blocks of buildings in the urban area are visible. A river flowing through the vegetated area, cutting across the top right corner of the image can be seen. The river appears bright due to sediments while the sea at the bottom edge of the image appears dark.

3.13.2 Multi-spectral Images

These images consist of several bands of data (3-10 bands), such as from Landsats. For visual colour display, each band of the image which is a grey scale image is displayed and three bands are combined at a time to generate a **colour composite image**. Interpretation of a colour composite image will require the knowledge of the spectral signature of the objects in the scene. The multi-spectral images in three individual bands are shown in Figure 3.20. The area covered is the same as that shown in the panchromatic image (Figure 3.19). Both the band 1 (green) and band 2 (red) bands look almost identical to the panchromatic image. In contrast, the vegetated areas appear brighter in the band 3 (near infrared) band due to high reflectance of leaves in the near infrared wavelength region. Several shades of grey can be identified corresponding to different types of vegetation. Water features (both the river and the sea) appear dark in the band 3 (near IR) band.

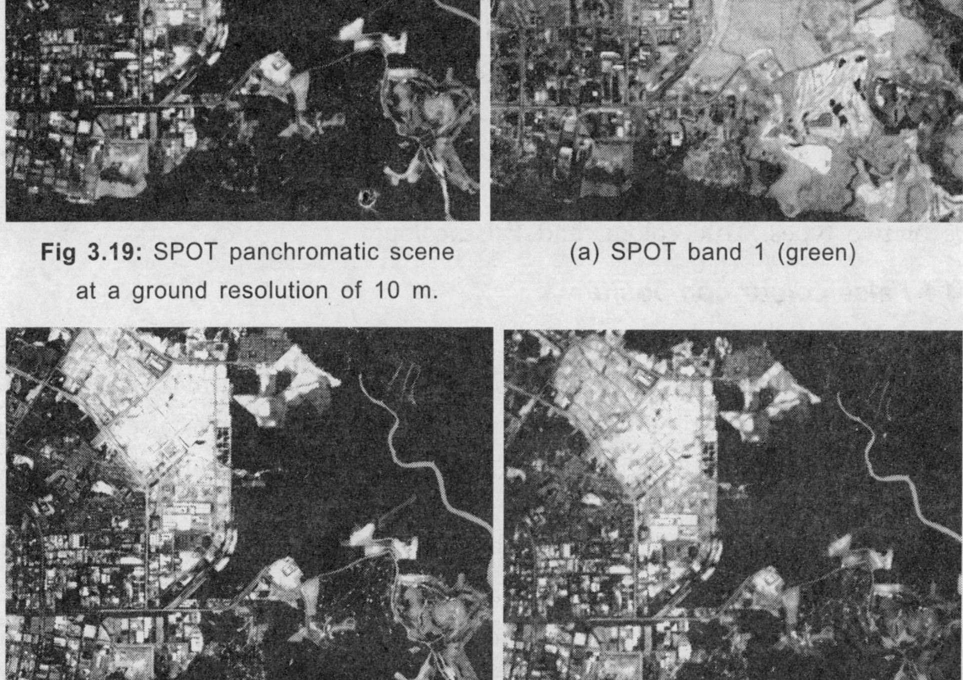

Fig 3.19: SPOT panchromatic scene at a ground resolution of 10 m.

(a) SPOT band 1 (green)

(b) SPOT band 2 (red)

(c) SPOT band 3 (Near IR)

Figure 3.20: Multispectral band images (a), (b) and (c) from SPOT satellites at a ground resolution of 20 m.

(Source: Figures 3.19, 3.20 & 3.22, https://crisp.nus.edu.sg/~research/tutorial/opt_int.htm)

3.13.3 Hyperspectral Images

Multispectral imagery generally refers to images in 3 to 10 bands, where each band is obtained using a scanner/sensor/radiometer. The hyperspectral imagery consists of much narrower bands (10-20 nm) to record the images in hundreds or thousands of bands (Figure 3.21). These images are recorded by an imaging spectrometer, such as Airborne Visible Infrared Imaging Spectrometer (AVIRIS).

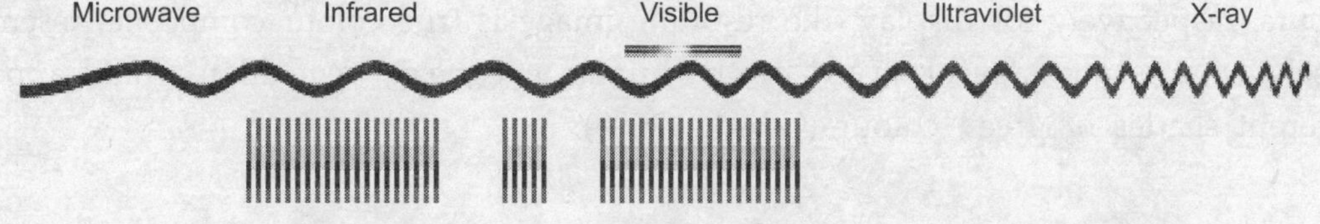

Figure 3.21. Hyperspectral imaging with hundreds of narrow bands

3.13.4 Colour Composite Images

Human visual system can differentiate thousands of colours but only few grey levels. Colour composite images are generated with minimum 3 bands data. However, a pseudo colour image can be generated with a single band B &W image, where the range of DN values are segmented into homogenous classes and each class is assigned a different colour. In displaying a colour composite image, three primary colours (red, green and blue) are used. If three primary colours are superimposed in different proportions, then number of colors is produced. If three primary colours are superimposed in equal amount, then grey colours ranging from black to white are produced. Each spectral band is associated with a separate primary colour which results in a colour composite image. Colour composites can be of two types; True colour, and False colour.

3.13.4.1 False colour composite

The colour assignment for any band of a multispectral image can be done in an entirely arbitrary manner. When the colour of an object in the displayed image does not have any resemblance to its actual colour, the resulting image is known as a false colour composite **(FCC)** (Lillesand and Keifer, 1994). There are many possible combinations of producing false colour composite images, however, a common false colour composite scheme for displaying a SPOT multispectral image is band 3 (NIR) in red, band 2 (red) in green, and band 1 (green) in blue colour.

Figure 3.22 shows a FCC image from SPOT multispectral bands already shown in Figure 3.20. In Figure 3.22, vegetation appears in different shades of red colour, depending on the types and conditions of the vegetation. It allows vegetation to be detected readily from FCC image, as it has a high reflectance in the NIR band as compared to Red band. Clear water will appear as dark-bluish (higher green band reflectance), while turbid water will appear as cyan (higher red reflectance due to sediments), as compared to clear water. Bare soils, roads and buildings may appear in various shades of blue, yellow or grey, depending on their composition.

3.13.4.2 True colour composite

In a multispectral image, the three primary colour bands (red, green, blue) may be combined to produce a "**true colour**" or "**natural colour**" image. For example, if bands 3 (red band) in red, 2 (green band) in red and 1 (blue band) in blue colours are assigned of a Landsat TM image or an IKONOS multispectral image (Figure 3.23) are assigned R, G, and B colours, respectively for display, the resulting image is true colour composite, resembling closely what is normally observed by the human eyes, e.g., vegetation would appear in different shades of green colour (Gibson, 2000).

Figure 3.22: FCC from SPOT images

Figure 3.23: True colour composite of IKONOS image

(*Source: Figure 23, http://gisknowledge.net/topic/remote_sensing_and_dia/tutorial_true_ colour_ composite.htmMulti-concept in Remote Sensing_*)

3.14 MULTI-CONCEPT IN REMOTE SENSING

The **multi-concept** is an important approach and one of the key concepts in remote sensing (Colwell, 1983), as applied to data acquisition and analysis. It includes multi-stage (height), multi-resolution (pixel size), multi-spectral (bands), multi-detector (sensors), and multi-temporal (date), and multi-uses (applications).

3.14.1 Multi-stage

It includes satellite data, high altitude data, low altitude data, drone data, balloon data, and ground observations. Each of the platforms will provide data/images at different scales as well as different ground coverage (Figure 3.24). Lower platform covers small

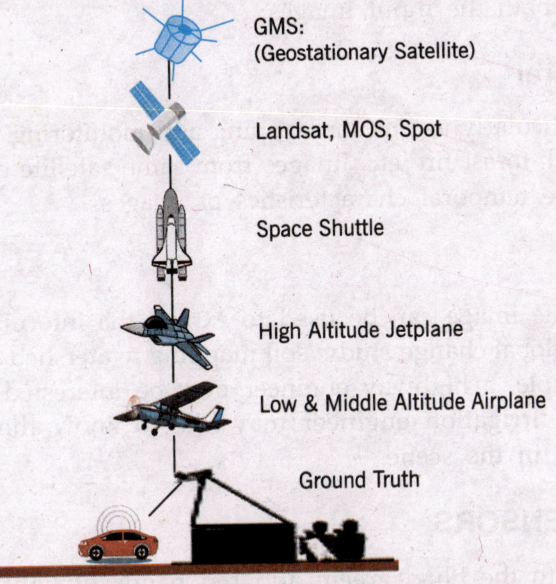

Figure 3.24: Multi-stage remote sensing platforms

area with greater details, as compared to higher platform. The selection of data/image will depend on how much details are required to be mapped. Many times, a combination of data would help in more reliable and accurate classification, particularly where ground verification is essentially required.

3.14.2 Multi-resolution

It means images collected at different spatial resolution which defines the pixel size. Higher the resolution, more detailed is the information about the ground features but lesser is the area covered, and vice versa. Higher cost of the images is also associated with the higher resolution, and therefore the selection of such image for the study may be done in an economical manner. For example, if the urban region is to be demarcated, medium resolution image would be sufficient, but if individual house is to be mapped then very high resolution image would be required.

3.14.3 Multi-spectral

Such images are needed to correctly identify various objects on the ground as they look differently in each wavelength region, depending on the reflected and emitted energy in that wavelength region. Moreover, minimum three bands data are required to generate colour composite, as human eye is more sensitive to colours for identification of features as compared to individual B&W band data.

3.14.4 Multi-detector

These images taken from various sensors are helpful in accurate mapping of features. These sensors provide data at different resolutions and different wavelength region of the same area thus enable to recognise the objects. Moreover, data fusion techniques are very popular to merge data from two sensors and get the resultant image which has the best information out both the input images.

3.14.5 Multi-temporal

These images are particularly useful for mapping and monitoring the dynamic events and features, such as flood, forest fire etc. Images from same satellite or different satellites can be used to reduce the temporal characteristics of images.

3.14.6 Multi-uses

It means that the same image can be used to extract the information related to various applications, such as global change study, soil mapping, watershed analysis, and vegetation monitoring. For example, a highway engineer may be interested in mapping only road network, whereas an irrigation engineer may like to know the rivers, canals, ponds, reservoir etc., present in the scene.

3.15 TYPES OF SENSORS

Our eye is sensitive to the blue, green, and red bands of light, known as the visible spectrum, but other wavelengths are present that our eyes cannot sense. Satellites, however, have sensors that record the reflected radiation not only the visible spectrum, but also infrared, near infrared, and thermal infrared bands, microwave bands. The reflected radiations from the objects are captured by the device onboard satellite, called **sensor**. There is normally more than one sensor in a satellite. The function of these sensors is to convert analog signals into digital signals. Figure 3.25 summarizes the types of sensors being used in remote sensing (Colwell, 1983, Gibson, 2000, Lillesand et al 2004). There are two broad categories of sensors which are further sub-classified.

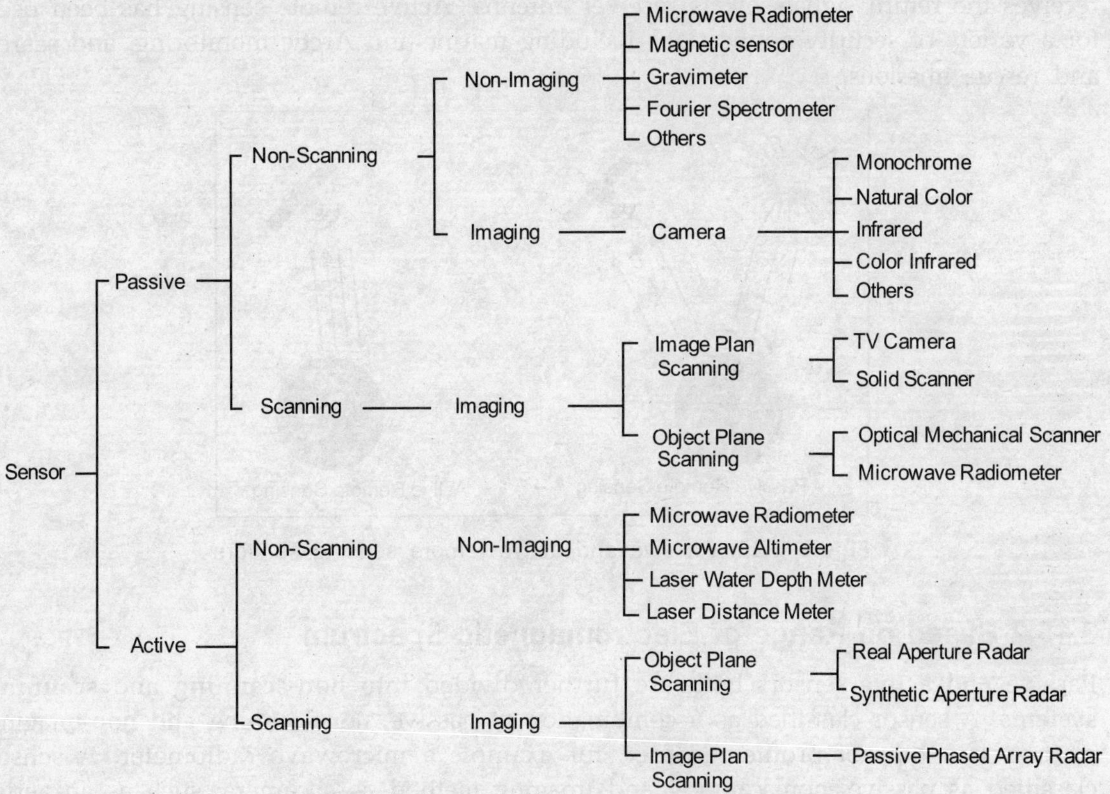

Figure 3.25: Classification of sensors

3.15.1 Based on Source of Energy

There are two types of sensors based on the source of energy; passive sensors and active sensors.

3.15.1.1 Passive sensors

The Sun, a natural source, provides a useful and important source of energy for remote sensing. The Sun's energy is either reflected, as it is for visible wavelength or absorbed and then re-emitted (for thermal infrared wavelength). A sensor that depends on an external (natural) source to illuminate the target to be sensed is called a **passive sensor**. In visible light, the sun illuminates the target and the reflected light from the target is detected by the sensor (Figure 3.26). Most sun-synchronous satellites employ passive sensors. Landsat MSS is an example of passive sensor.

3.15.1.2 Active sensors

An **active sensor** consists of both the sensor and the source to illuminate the target (Figure 3.26). These sensors have the advantage of obtaining data any time of day or season. The majority of active sensors operate in the microwave portion of the electromagnetic spectrum, which makes them able to penetrate the atmosphere under any conditions. The Synthetic Aperture Radar (SAR) is an example of active sensor which transmits microwave pulses from its transmitter antenna to illuminate the target and receives the return signals by its receiver antenna. Active remote sensing has been used for a variety of security applications including marine and Arctic monitoring, and search and rescue missions.

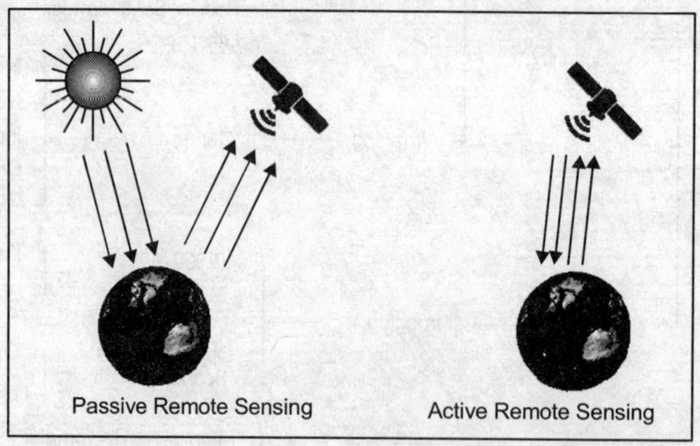

Figure 3.26: Passive and active remote sensing sensors

3.15.2 Based on Range of Electromagnetic Spectrum

Passive and active sensors both are further divided into **non-scanning** and **scanning systems**. A sensor classified as a combination of passive, non-scanning and non-imaging method is a type of profile recorder, for example a microwave radiometer. A sensor classified as passive, non-scanning and imaging method, is a camera, such as an aerial survey camera or a space camera. Sensors classified as a combination of passive, scanning and imaging are classified further into **image plane scanning sensors**, such as TV cameras and solid state scanners, and **object plane scanning sensors**, such as multispectral scanners (optical-mechanical scanner) and scanning microwave radiometers.

3.15.2.1 Optical sensors

The optical remote sensing devices operate in the visible, near infrared, middle infrared and short wave infrared portions of the EMS within a range 300 nm to 3000 nm, e.g., bands of Landsat MSS, IRS P6 LISS IV, SPOT sensors work in optical range of EMS. It will be discussed in more details later, including the applications.

3.15.2.2 Thermal sensors

Thermal infrared energy is emitted from all objects that have a temperature greater than absolute zero. All objects, both natural and manmade, emit infrared energy as heat. Even in complete darkness and challenging weather conditions, thermal imaging gives users the ability to detect very subtle temperature differences. Water, rocks, soil, vegetation, and the atmosphere all have the ability to conduct heat directly through them (thermal conductivity) onto another surface and to store heat (thermal capacity). Some materials respond to changes in temperature more rapidly or slowly than others (thermal inertia).

Human eyes cannot detect differences in thermal infrared energy because they are not sensitive to this region to the infrared (0.7-3.0μm) or thermal infrared energy (3.0-14μm). The main difference between infrared and thermal infrared is that the infrared is reflected energy, whereas the thermal infrared is emitted energy. Absorption by water and other gases in the atmosphere restricts the sensors to record thermal images in two wavelength windows; 3 to 5 μm and 8 to 14 μm, and that's why the interpretation and processing of thermal IR imagery is difficult.

Thermal sensors record the energy emitted from the Earth features in thermal range of EMS (3μm to 5μm and 8μm to 14μm). The 3μm to 5μm range is related to high temperature phenomenon, like forest fire, while 8μm to 14μm range is related with the general Earth features having lower temperatures. Thermal remote sensing is very useful to measure the surface temperature and thermal properties of targets, for fire detection and thermal pollution studies, e.g., the last five bands of Advanced Spaceborne Thermal Emission and Reflection Radiometer **(ASTER)** and band 6 of Landsat ETM+ are thermal. The ASTER launched in 1999 onboard **TERRA** satellite provides high-resolution images of the Earth in 14 different bands of EMS, with the resolution ranging between 15 and 90 meters. ASTER data are used to create detailed maps of surface temperature of land, emissivity, reflectance, geology and elevation. Useful reviews on thermal remote sensing are given by Gupta (1991) and Sabins (1996). The details of various thermal sensors are given in Figure 3.27.

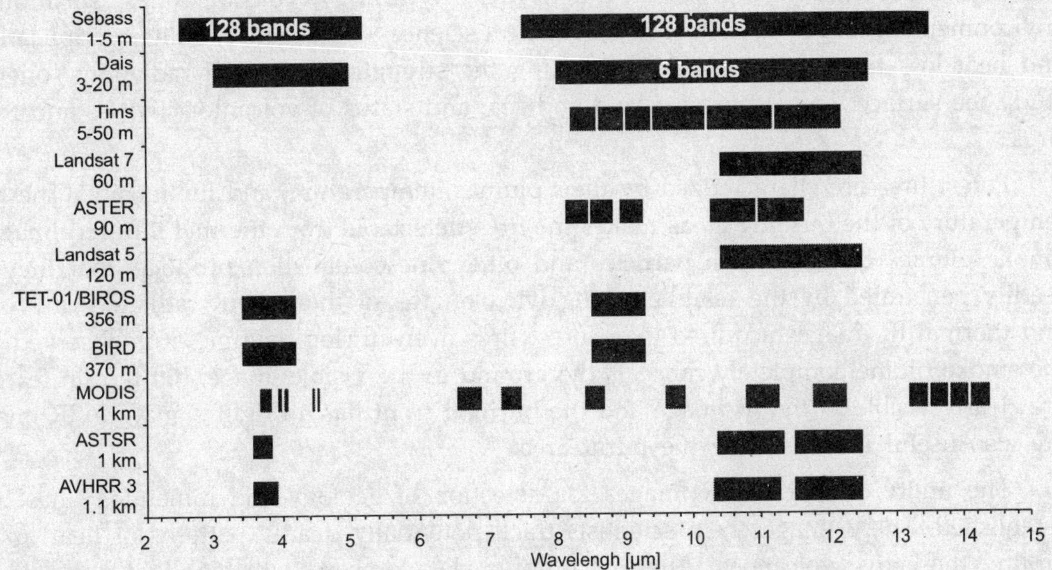

Figure 3.27: Sensor systems operating in the thermal IR region *(Source: Morisette et al 2002)*

Landsat Thematic Mapper 4 and 5 sensors were launched on July 16, 1982 and March 1, 1984, respectively, and collected 120 x 120 m thermal infrared data (10.4 - 12.5 µm) along with two bands of middle infrared data. The (National Oceanic and Atmospheric Administration) **(NOAA)** Geostationary Operational Environmental Satellite (**GOES**) collected thermal infrared data at a spatial resolution of 8km x 8 km for weather prediction. Entire earth is imaged every 30 minutes both day and night by the thermal infrared sensor. The NOAA Advanced Very High Resolution Radiometer (**AVHRR**) collected thermal infrared local area coverage data at 1.1 x 1.1 km and global area coverage at 4 x 4 km. Sensors such as the NOAA-AVHRR, ERS-ATSR and **TERRA-MODIS** are equipped at 3.8 µm wavelength that can be used for the detection of fire and hot spots.

Applications of thermal images

Thermal property of a material is representative of upper several centimetres of the surface. In thermal remote sensing, the measured emitted radiations would help to identify surface materials and features such as rock types, soil moisture, geothermal anomalies etc. The ability to record variations in infrared radiation has advantage in understanding phenomena where minor temperature variations may be significant in environment. Thermal data can be acquired during the day and during the night. For some applications it is useful to have data from both the times. However, for many applications night-time or more specifically pre-dawn images are preferred as during this time the effect of differential solar heating is the minimal (Gupta, 1991).

Thermal images were first developed for military uses, and later these images have been adopted by law enforcement, fire and rescue teams, security professionals, maintenance operations, coal fire team, etc. Besides the measurement of regular surface temperature, infrared sensors have been used for detection of forest fires or other warm/hot objects, or monitoring volcanic activities, hydrology, coastal zones, seismology, environmental modelling, meteorology, medical sciences, intelligence/military applications, and heat loss from buildings. By examining the strength of thermal radiations, one can study the surface temperatures of land and sea, and status of volcanic activities and forest fires.

Forest fires are characterized by their plumes, temperature, and luminosity. The high temperature of the burning areas makes the fires detectable from thermal infrared imaging. Smoke plumes consist of ash particles and other fine combustion products that they are readily penetrated by the relatively long wavelengths of thermal IR radiation. In visible and thermal IR images acquired over forest fires even during daytime, it is observed that the smoke plume completely conceals the ground in the visible image, but terrain features are clearly visible in the IR image and the burning front has a bright signature. IR images are also useful in estimating the burnt area.

The utility of thermal IR images for detection of geology and mineralogy has been established. These images help scientists track potentially deadly patterns of heat in and around the active volcanoes. Thermal infrared data processed to highlight hotspots can alert administrators and planners about the forecast of volcanic activity before it becomes hazardous. In high resolution thermal IR images, active volcanoes stand out as bright spots, and these become further brighter in a time series images as they ramp up for an eruption. The speed with which the volcanoes cool down can give a clue to the scientists about their geological composition. Through thermal infrared images, it is possible to monitor and map eruption clouds, tropospheric plumes, hot spots and active lava flows. Post-eruptive studies may also be undertaken effectively using thermal infrared images.

In practice, thermal data prove to be complementary to other remote sensing data. Thus, though still not fully explored, thermal remote sensing has potential for a variety of applications. Some other applications are-

Agriculture - Thermal imaging, due to its higher temporal and spatial resolution, play an important role in various fields of agriculture, such as monitoring irrigation scheduling, soil salinity stress detection, plants disease detection etc. Detection of water stress in crops and evapo-transpiration are significant inputs in the management of agricultural practices. However, the use of thermal images has some drawbacks viz., it is more expensive and thermal measurements depend on environmental and weather conditions.

Forestry - Thermal infrared imaging is used in forestry to map and monitor forest cover in terms of vegetation stress and evapotranspiration which is important in environmental management, making vegetation a simple and effective way to reduce urban heat islands. Quantitative information about forest canopy structure, biomass, age, and physiological condition can be extracted from thermal infrared data. Change in surface temperature can be measured by an airborne thermal infrared sensor by repeatedly flying over the same area a few times.

Sea surface temperature (SST) - Ocean surface water temperature has increased due to climate change, runoff from impervious surfaces and thermal effluents from industrial processes. The temperature of the sea surface is an important parameter in the upper ocean that governs biological activity, the exchange of gas, heat, and momentum with the atmosphere, ecological and biogeochemical processes; it controls water metabolism and specifies the habitat area for aquatic life. Information about SST is required by scientific, commercial, and social interest activities, such as weather forecasting, air–sea interaction modeling, climate change studies, fisheries, and coastal zone management. Sea surface temperature is a key climate and weather measurement obtained by satellite microwave radiometers and IR radiometers.

An algorithm for estimating land surface temperature and emissivity spectra using multi-spectral thermal infrared images from the Advanced Spaceborne Thermal Emission and Reflection Radiometer (ASTER) has been developed (Gallespie et al 1998 and Schmugge et al 1998). SST was derived from infrared (IR) observations collected by the AVHRR sensors (Figure 3.28). If the water neighboring to a current has different temperature, the flow patterns in the sea are easily observed with AVHRR data. Sea surface temperature measurement is being used in many ways; such as determining where to release stranded sea turtles, at appropriate temperature, or identifying commercial fishing locations in the sea.

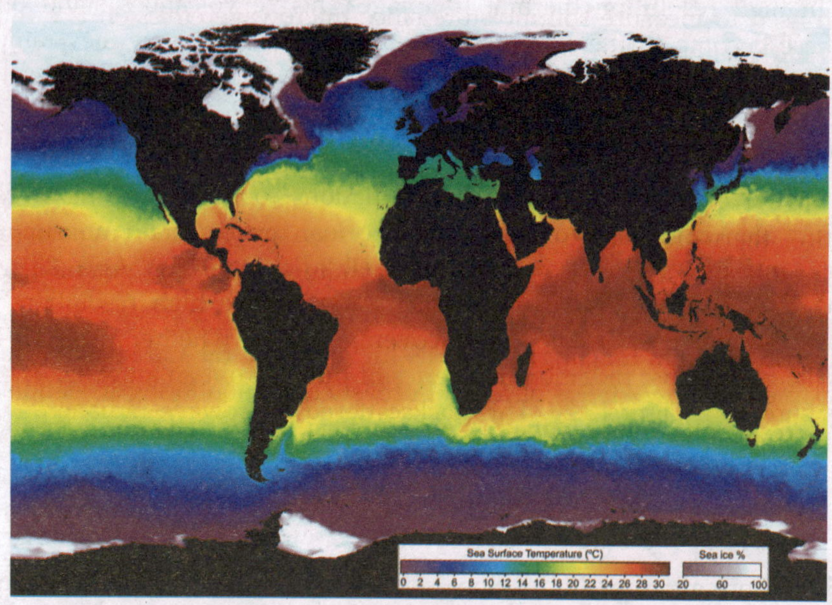

Figure 3.28: Global sea surface temperature (SST) and sea ice cover of March derived from NOAA AVHRR thermal infrared satellite measurements in 2006-2008. (*Source: http://www.euroargo-edu.org/argoeu_4.php.*)

3.15.2.3 Microwave sensors

The microwave region falls between the IR and radio wavelengths, and has a range extending from approximately 0.1 cm to 1 meter. The microwave sensors, having their own sources of energy, record the backscattered microwaves and operate independent of weather and solar radiations e.g., RADARSAT (Sabins, 1996, Calla, 2010). Microwaves have special properties that are important for remote sensing because of their long wavelengths, as compared to the visible and infrared. Microwave radiations can pass through clouds, tree canopies, haze, dust, and the rainfall as these are not susceptible to atmospheric scattering which affects the shorter optical wavelengths. These sensors therefore have the capability to collect imagery day and night, under almost all weather and environmental conditions. The microwave sensors could be passive or active, as described below:

(a) Passive microwave sensors

These detect the naturally emitted microwave energy within its field of view. This emitted energy is related to the temperature and moisture properties of the emitting object or surface. Passive microwave sensors are typically radiometers or scanners, and they operate in the same manner as other radiometers/scanners, except that an antenna is used to detect and record the microwave energy. Because the wavelengths are so long, the energy available is quite small as compared to optical wavelengths. Thus, the field of view is large to detect enough energy to record a signal. Therefore, most passive microwave sensors have low spatial resolution. The passive microwave sensors can be used to measure atmospheric profiles and to determine water and ozone contents in the atmosphere. These sensors are also used to measure soil moisture since microwave emission is influenced by moisture content. Oceanographic applications of such sensors include mapping sea ice, currents, and surface winds as well as detection of pollutants, such as oil slicks.

(b) Active microwave sensors

They provide their own source of microwave radiations to illuminate the target/object. These sensors are generally of two distinct categories: **imaging and non-imaging**. An active, scanning and imaging sensor is RADAR (**RA**dio **D**etection **A**nd **R**anging), for example Synthetic Aperture Radar (**SAR**), which can produce high resolution, imagery, day or night, independent upon the cloud coverage. SAR, whether used air-borne or space-borne, emits microwave radiation in a series of pulses from an antenna. The working of a RADAR is shown in Figure 3.29. This backscattered microwave radiation is detected, and the time required for the energy to travel to the target and return back to the sensor determines the distançe or range to the target. By recording the range and magnitude of the energy reflected from all targets, a two-dimensional image of the surface can be produced. The intensity in a SAR image depends on the amount of microwave backscattered by the target and received by the SAR antenna (Castleman, 1996).

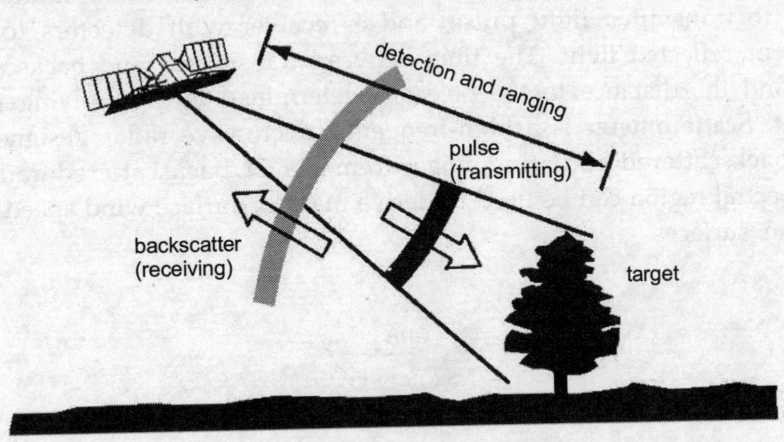

Figure 3.29: Working of a SAR

(*Source: http://labs.cas.usf.edu/geodesy/sar.html*)

Since the physical mechanisms responsible for this backscatter is different for microwave, the interpretation of SAR images requires the knowledge of how microwaves interact with the targets. Because of the speckle and quite different imaging conditions, the SAR images cannot be compared directly with optical images having the same spatial resolution. The spatial resolution of 10m and larger is not sufficient for topographic mapping, as the information contents of SAR images is below the information contents of optical images with the same resolution. Due to these differences, radar and optical data can be complementary to one another as they offer different perspectives of the Earth's surface providing different information content.

Other examples of active sensors include **ERS-1** launched in 1991, **J-ERS** satellite launched in 1992, **ERS-2** in 1995, and Canada's advanced satellite **Radarsat-1** launched in

1995 and **Radarsat-2** launched in 2007, IRS-P4 (**Oceansat-1**), **Oceansat-2, RISAT-1, RISAT-2, TerraSAR-X** Radar Satellite launched in 2007. SAR images have been used frequently for the generation of maps of tropical forests. But interferometric SAR (InSAR) images can be used for the generation of height models. So images from ERS-1 and ERS-2 have been used for DEM generation. The Shuttle Radar Topography Mission (**SRTM**) launched in 2000 uses InSAR which measures Earth's elevation with two antennas to create digital elevation models of Earth. The SRTM also provides a homogenous DEM covering the Earth from 56° southern up to 60.25° northern latitude.

Non-imaging microwave sensors include **altimeters, LiDAR** and **scatterometers**. In most cases, these are profiling devices which take measurements in one linear dimension, as opposed to the two-dimensional representation of imaging sensors. Radar altimeters transmit short microwave pulses and measure the round trip time delay to targets to determine their distance (range) from the sensor. Radar altimetry is used on aircraft for altitude determination and on aircraft & satellites for topographic mapping and sea surface height estimation. Light Detection and Ranging (LiDAR) is an active microwave sensor that measures ground height (Figure 3.30). In addition, it can provide coordinates of the points. It consists of a sensor that uses a laser (light amplification by stimulated emission of radiation) to transmit a light pulse, and a receiver with detectors to measure the backscattered or reflected light. The time between transmitted and backscattered pulses is recorded, and the distance to the object is determined by multiplying time with the speed of light. **Scatterometer** is a high-frequency microwave radar designed specifically to measure backscattered radiation, measurements of backscattered radiation in the microwave spectral region can be used to derive maps of surface wind speed and direction over the ocean surfaces.

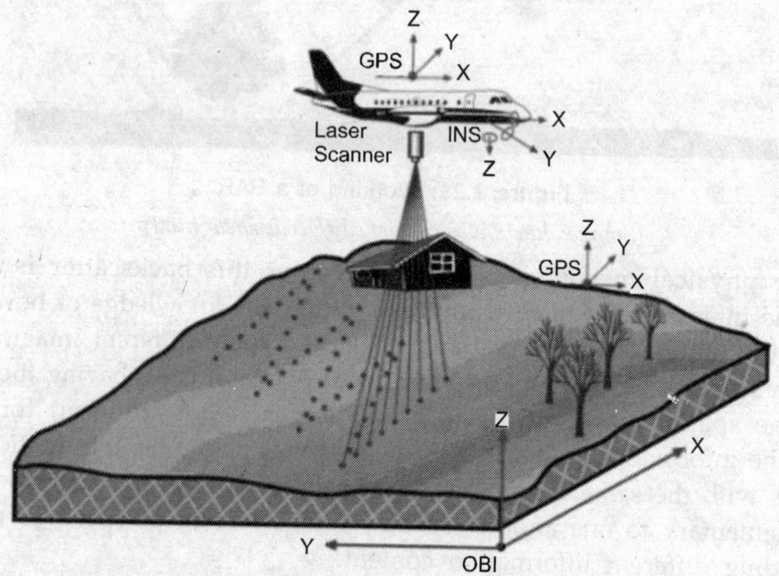

Figure 3.30: Working of a LiDAR

(*Source: http://forsys.sefs.uw.edu/fusion.html*)

Applications of microwave images

Microwave sensors can be used for study of crops, agriculture, urban land use and land cover, geology and hydrology, forest cover, snow and ice, soil moisture and soil types, Snow studies, hydrocarbons, etc., (Calla, 2010). Its potential has been scientifically established in various sectors, like discrimination of crop types, crop condition monitoring, soil moisture retrieval, delineation of forest openings, fire scar mapping, monitoring wetlands and snow cover, coastal wind field measurement, wave slope measurement, ship detection, substrate mapping, and slick detection (Kasischke et al., 1997). Many studies have demonstrated the use of Synthetic Aperture Radar (SAR) remote sensing to retrieve biophysical characteristics from forest targets (Richards, 1990), and established useful relationships between backscattering coefficients and the above-ground biomass (Imhoff, 1995). These relationships may provide a method of monitoring forest ecosystems which play such a vital role in carbon storage.

For ocean applications, active as well as passive sensor both can be used for determination of salinity sea surface temperature, suspended sediment concentration, shoreline detection, sea ice identification, ocean colour and bathymetry studies, wave heights, and the detection of Tsunami. For atmospheric applications, the microwave remote sensing can be used for profiling the moisture and temperature in the atmosphere which is essential for delineating meso-scale climatic systems. The application for studying the minor constituents in the atmosphere is considered important for stratospheric research. These applications have a potential for using microwave data for Indian monsoon studies, and monsoon temperature profile. Microwave sensors are being used for planetary exploration, the planets like Mars and Venus, and satellites like Moon have been explored to detect presence of frozen water on Moon (e.g., very successful **Chandrayan Mission of India**) and presence of buried channels under sand dunes on Mars (Calla, 2010).

Microwaves are sensitive to the moisture content, as they are capable of penetrating into the ground itself. The depth of penetration is function of moisture content in the soil. The microwaves are sensitive to the presence of moisture in the soil as well as in vegetation or any material which absorbs moisture. This is due to the variability of dielectric constant of the dry material and that of water. The dielectric constant of dry soil varies between 2-3 depending upon the texture whereas the dielectric constant of pure water is around 80 at room temperature and at around 1 GHz. Thus the dielectric constant will vary between dielectric constants of dry soil and of the saturated soil which is around 30. The moisture content in soil can be assessed by measuring the dielectric constant of the soil.

3.15.3 Based on Imaging Systems

There are two classes; imaging sensor systems and non-imaging sensor systems (Richards and Jia, 2013), as explained below.

3.15.3.1 Imaging sensor systems

These are of two types: framing systems and scanning systems. In framing systems, images of the targets are taken frame by frame. These include imagers, like photographic film cameras and return beam videcon. The scanning systems include across track scanners and along track (push broom) scanners. Imagers and scanning altimeters/sounders are used for three dimensional topographic mapping. Multispectral scanners/thematic mappers are used for limited spectral resolution with high spatial resolution mapping. Imaging spectrometers are meant for high spectral and spatial resolutions. Imaging radiometers and imaging scatterometers (microwave) are used for high accuracy intensity measurement with moderate imaging resolution and wide coverage (Jenson, 1986).

In the framing type, entire frame of image is acquired instantaneously in the basic image unit e.g., in a frame camera used in photography. In scanning type, the information is acquired sequentially from the surface in bits of picture elements or pixels, point by point and line by line, which may be arranged after acquisition into a frame format.

3.15.3 2 Non-imaging sensor systems

These include (i) sounders and altimeters for the measurement of locations and topographic profiles with high accuracy, (ii) spectrometer and spectro-radiometer for the measurement of high spectral resolution along track lines or swath, and (iii) radiometers, scatterometers and polarimeters for high accuracy intensity measurements and polarization changes measurements along track lines or wide swath (Richards and Jia, 2013).

Non-imaging types of sensors are used to record a spectral quantity or a parameter as a function of time or distance (such as Gamma radiation, magnetic field, temperature measurement etc.) They are mostly used for ground observation and in study of atmosphere and meteorology. These sensors do not form image and as such, are not used in operational remote sensing but give detailed information on spectral characteristics of the target.

The most popular sensors used in remote sensing are the camera, solid state scanner, such as the CCD (charge coupled device) images, the multi-spectral scanner and in the future the passive synthetic aperture radar. Laser sensors have recently begun to be used more frequently for monitoring air pollution by laser spectrometers and for measurement of distance by laser altimeters.

The internal geometry of design of a space-borne multispectral sensor is quite different from an aerial camera. Figure 3.31 shows six types of remote sensing systems; digital frame area array, scanning mirrors, linear pushbroom arrays, linear whiskbroom areas, and frame area arrays. A linear array, or pushbroom scanner is used in many space-borne platforms, such as SPOT, IRS, QuickBird, OrbView, and IKONOS. The geometric distortions in the images, such as skew caused by the rotation of the Earth, are required to be corrected before analysis of the imagery. Several air-borne systems also employ pushbroom technology where each line of imagery is captured at a time, corresponding to an instantaneous position and attitude of the aircraft.

The internal geometry of images captured by space-borne scanning systems is much more complex. Across-track scanning and whiskbroom systems are more similar to a LiDAR scanner than to a digital array sensor. Each pixel is captured at a unique time, and there is a stack of recording pixels, one for each spectral band, which are required to be precisely co-registered pixel-by-pixel to create an accurate multispectral image.

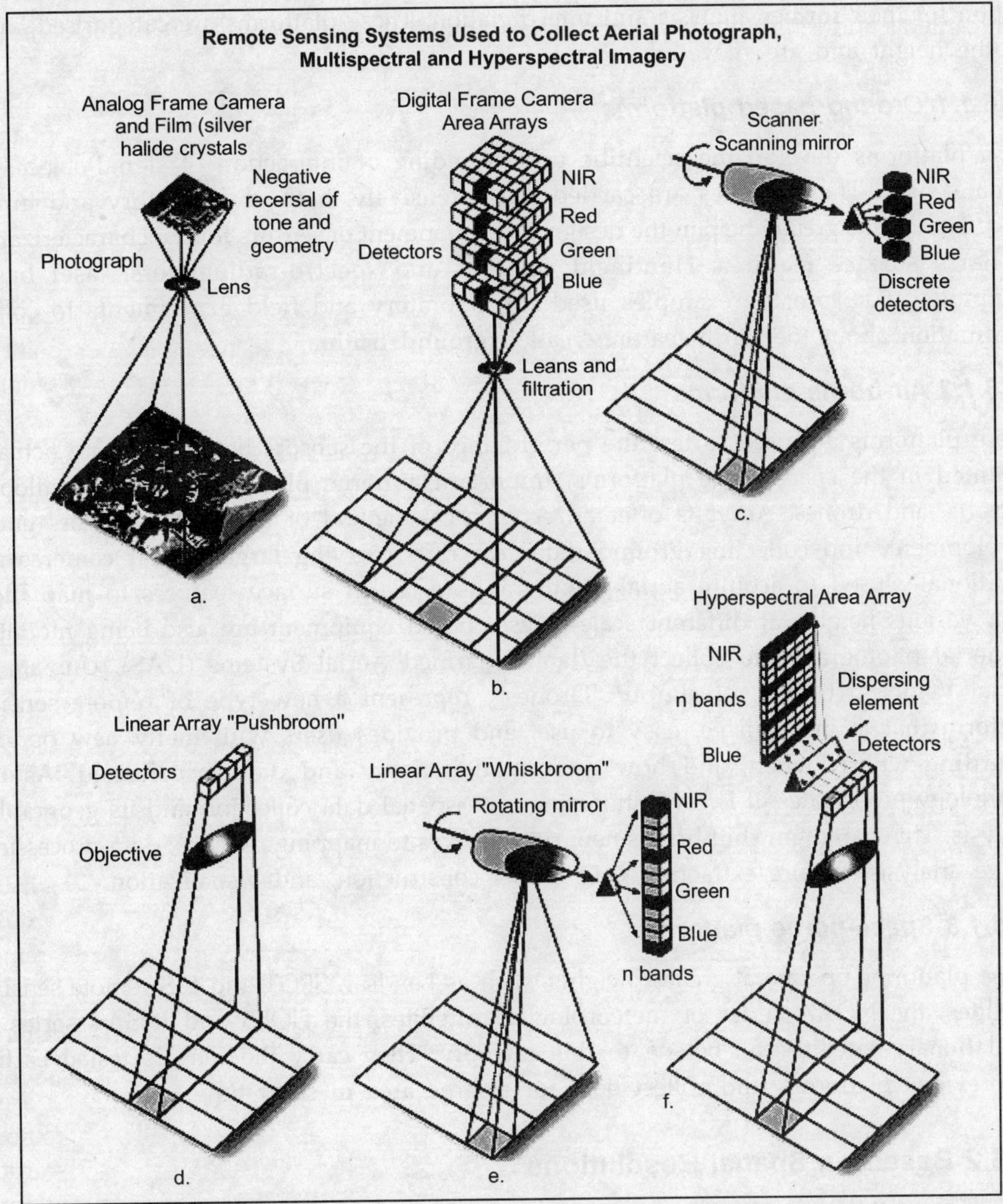

Figure 3.31: Remote sensing sensors *(Source: Jensen, 2007)*

3.16 TYPES OF REMOTE SENSING PLATFORMS

3.16.1 Based on Height and Area Coverage

Essentially three different types of platforms are used to mount the sensors to collect information on Earth's surface features, and transmit the same to an earth receiving station for their further analysis and interpretation. These platforms are categorised based on the height and area covered:

3.16.1.1 Ground based platforms

Such platforms develop the scientific understanding of interaction of signal-object and signal-sensor. These studies are carried out extensively, both at laboratory and in the field. The results greatly help in the design & development of sensors for the characterization of Earth surface features. Handheld cameras and spectro-radiometers, laser based equipment, GPS are the examples used for laboratory and field experiments to collect information about the Earth features, called **ground truth**.

3.16.1.2 Air-borne platforms

These platforms are used to test the performance of the sensors before they are actually mounted in the space-borne platforms. Important airborne platforms include– balloons, aircrafts, and drones. Aircrafts offer an economical method of testing the sensors under development, and collecting ground data. Aircrafts carrying large format cameras are traditionally used to acquire aerial photographs of Earth surface features to map them from various heights at different scales. Laser based equipment are also being mounted on aerial photographs to collect the data. Unarmed Aerial Systems (UAS), Unmanned Aerial Vehicles (UAVs), or simply "Drones", represent a new type of remote sensing platform that is inexpensive, easy to use, and provides users with many new options regarding where, when, and how geospatial imagery and data is collected. As the technology proliferates, it is revolutionizing both spatial data collection and its geographic analysis. This paradigm shift brings new perspectives to mapping practice, data processing, image analysis, feature extraction, 3-D model construction, and visualization.

3.16.1.3 Space-borne platforms

These platforms operate at greater heights, such as Landsat, SPOT and IRS remote sensing satellites, the NOAA series of meteorological satellites, the GOES and INSAT series of geostationary satellites; all belong to this category. They carry the sensors tested earlier on previous platforms, and collect data for a large area in short time.

3.16.2 Based on Spatial Resolutions

Different satellites are designed and launched based on their intended use and orbit. Satellite imagery employed in various research works ranges from 1000 m to <1 m in resolution (Figure 3.32). The resolutions of today's satellite systems vary, and are classified as:

- Low resolution: larger than 100 m spatial resolution
- Medium resolution: 5 - 100 m spatial resolution
- High/very high resolution: under less than 5 m spatial resolution

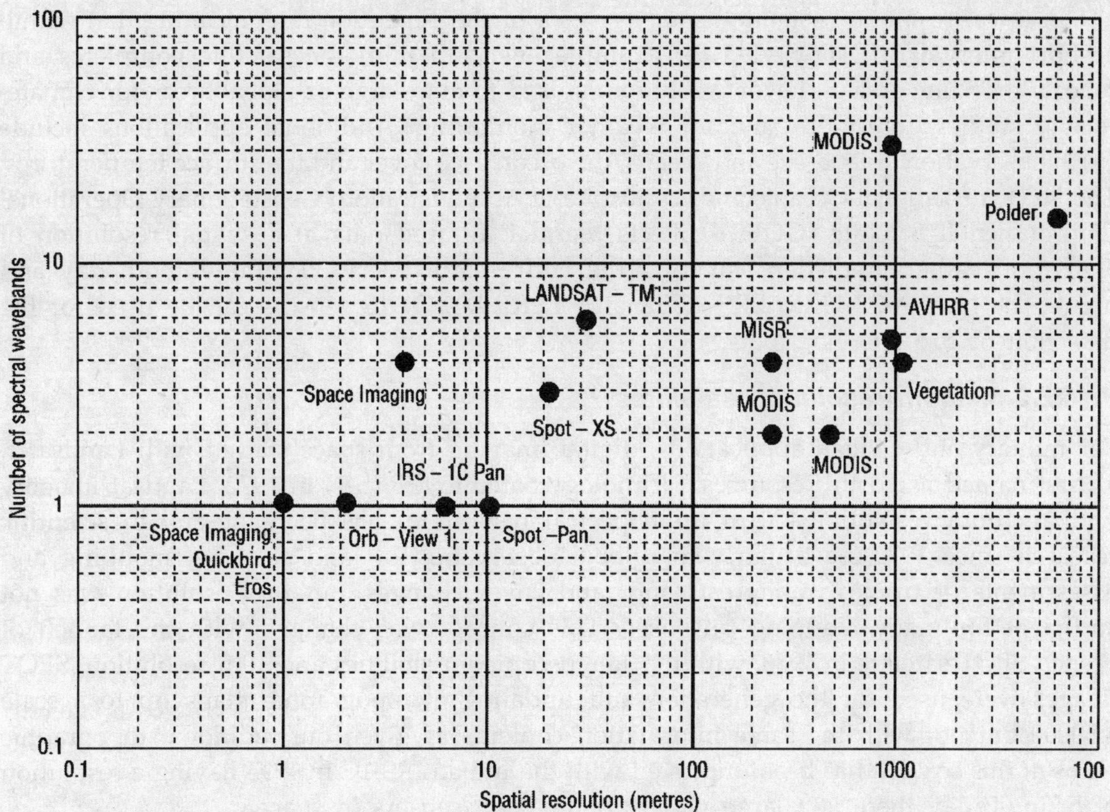

Figure 3.32: Spatial resolutions and number of wavebands of various satellites

Although free data sets and free satellite imagery are available online, many of these resources are at lower resolutions (e.g. MODIS, Landsat), limited by the available dates. High to medium resolution imagery provided via Google Earth or Indian site BHUVAN that is increasingly being used in scientific research greatly help in the selection of field sampling locations for classification. Image analysis based on Google Earth images, however, has limitation, as multi-spectral bands are not available for digital analysis. The very high resolution images from IKONOS, QuickBird, OrbView and EROS A1 are operated by private companies (e.g. GeoEye, DigitalGlobe) that have provided much-needed access to satellite imagery for many research areas. As an example, Figure 3.32 presents the spatial resolutions and wavebands of all the three types of satellites.

3.16.2.1 Low resolution satellites

ERS-1 and ERS-2, launched in 1994 and 1995, respectively provided 1km spatial resolution images from ATSR-1 and ATSR-2 sensors in 4 and 6 bands. VEGETATION sensor of SPOT-4, launched in 1998, provided 1.15km spatial resolution images in 4 bands. MODIS (Moderate Resolution Imaging Spectrometer) in EOS-1 satellite, launched in 1999, provided data in 30 spectral bands at 250m, 500m and 1km spatial resolutions. The NOAA Advanced Very High Resolution Radiometer (**AVHRR**) collects thermal infrared local area coverage data at 1.1 km and global area coverage at 4 km spatial resolutions.

A lower resolution satellite usually gives a higher repetition rate, meaning that within a short interval (METEOSAT-8 for example every 15 min) the satellite completes and repeats the same area. A lower resolution is used to map large or global areas for climate-related studies, forest fire, and for weather monitoring. Additional applications include Earth observation of land use and oceans, the ocean's ice cover and the surface temperatures. The **NOAA** (National Oceanic and Atmospheric Administration) Geostationary Operational Environmental Satellite (**GOES**) collects thermal infrared data at a spatial resolution of 8km for weather prediction, covering the entire earth every 30 minutes both day and night. The NOAA-AVHRR, ERS-ATSR and **TERRA-MODIS** sensors can be used for the detection of fire and hot spots.

3.16.2.2 Medium resolution satellites

For military and civilian applications, digital imaging from space started with Landsat-1, at first named as Earth Resources Technology Satellite (ERTS-1) in 1972. Landsat imagery with medium resolution (30 m multispectral resolution) has been integral in scientific research since 1972, particularly for global observation of land surfaces. mapping and assessments of tropical rainforests and land cover changes, but the resolution was not sufficient for many mapping purposes. This concept was changed with the launch of French SPOT satellite in 1986, with the stereoscopic possibilities and 10m resolution. SPOT images were used for the generation and updating of topographic maps up to a scale 1:50000 but not with the same information contents as given on traditional topographic maps at this scale. It has been improved with the Indian IRS-1C in 1995 having a resolution of 5.7m. Today there is a large variety of imaging sensors in space.

3.16.2.3 High/Very high resolution satellites

High resolution data is mainly used for mapping smaller areas of the Earth's surface. The next major change came with the launch of very high resolution IKONOS in 1999. Such data has become available commercially and privately satellites, such as IKONOS or QuickBird at ≤ 5 m resolution for topographic and thematic mapping. High-resolution imagery is typically used to map regional-to-local areas, but often such imagery is expensive and cost-prohibitive. High-resolution imagery, as well as long-term, time-series data are essential for conservation, economic, and social research and applications (Richards and Jia, 2013, Shang and Gruen, 2006, Poon and Fraser, 2006, *https://www.satimagingcorp.com/services/resources/*).

DigitalGlobe was founded 1993 under the name World View Imaging Corporation, becoming Earth Watch Incorporated in 1995, and lastly DigitalGlobe in 2002. In October 2001, the DigitalGlobe successfully launched the world's highest-resolution commercial satellite, QuickBird, (Refer to Table 3.10), and further built an extensive business serving both governmental and commercial markets. Its agreement was to provide high-resolution imagery to the Keyhole Corporation, acquired by Google in 2004, a vital component in the creation and commercial success of Google Earth and beginning the proliferation of online mapping portals.

DigitalGlobe announced to build next generations, high-resolution imagery satellites, WorldView-1 and WorldView-2 (Refer to Table 3.10). In January 2007, DigitalGlobe acquired Globe Xplorer, a leading online imagery provider. By early 2009, DigitalGlobe announced several other strategic agreements expanding availability of high-resolution imagery to online portal, navigation, and applications. It has extended its service agreement with Google continuing Google and DigitalGlobe's relationship to pioneer wider global imagery accessibility. A new partnership with Microsoft provides high resolution satellite and aerial imagery for its Virtual Earth Platform.

3.17 LANDSATS

Landsat is the longest running satellite program for acquisition of earth observation imagery. The Earth Resources Technology Satellite (ERTS) launched by US in July 1972 was renamed Landsat in 1975. Since then, the Landsats have provided the vast amount of medium resolution multispectral images to study and analyse the land use/landcover, vegetation and agricultural crops, water, soils, geology and other Earth resources. Landsat has been one of the most important and demanding sources of medium resolution multispectral images globally (*https://landsat.usgs.gov/*). The date-wise history of Landsats is given in Figure 3.33. For other details refer to Table 3.5 and Table 3.9.

The launches of Landsat 2 and Landsat 3 followed in 1975, and 1978, respectively. The first three satellites were identical and their payloads consisted of a multispectral Scanner (MSS) and two video cameras called Return Beam Videcons or (RBVs). One scene covered an area of 170 km x 185 km, as the satellites operated at an altitude between 907-915 km in sun-synchronous polar orbit with 103 minutes of orbital period and revisit time of 18 days.

Landsat 4 was launched in 1982. Landsat 5 was launched in 1984, and it continued to deliver high quality global data of Earth's surfaces (Wulder et al, 2008). LANDSATs 4 and 5 were equipped with two multispectral sensors, i.e., a multispectral scanner (MSS) and a Thematic Mapper (TM). The altitude of the orbit was 705 km with 99 minutes orbital period, and revisit time of 16 days. Other parameters were same as earlier satellites.

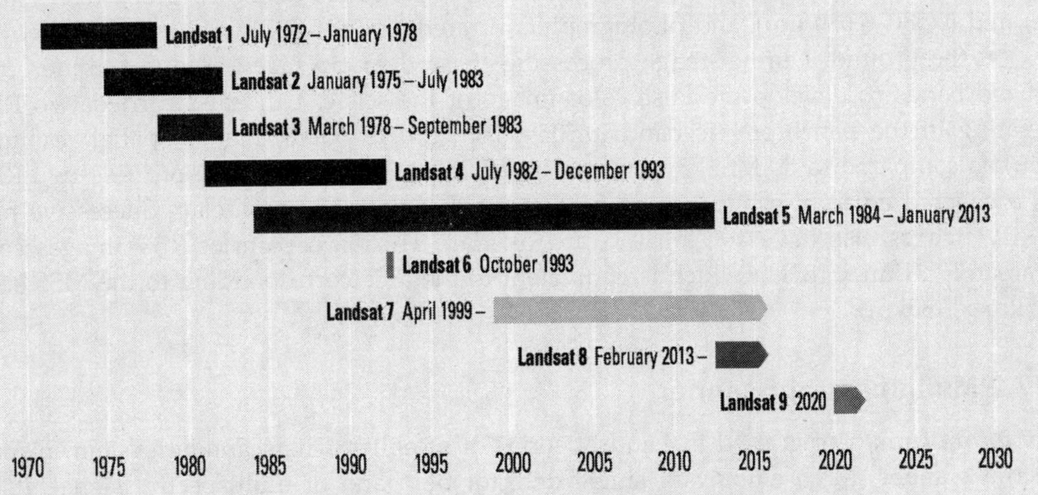

Figure 3.33: History of Landsats (*Source: https://landsat.usgs.gov/landsat-missions-timeline*)

Landsat 6 was launched October 5, 1993, but was lost during launch. Landsat 7 was successfully launched in April 1999 which has 8 separate spectral bands with spatial resolutions ranging from 15-60 m, and a temporal resolution of 16 days. It was equipped with a multispectral sensor known as the Enhanced Thematic Mapper Plus (ETM+). ETM+ provides data in one panchromatic band. Other parameters were same as Landsat-4 and -5 satellites.

Landsat 8 was launched in 2013, which continue to provide daily global data. It was launched in sun-synchronous orbit at an altitude of 705 km, circling the orbit every 98.9 minutes, covering the entire globe every 16 days. It has two sensors. The Operational Land Imager (OLI) operates in nine spectral bands, including a pan band with resolution of 30 m in multispectral and 15m in pan, while Thermal Infrared sensor **(TIR)** operates in two spectral bands: (10.6 - 11.19 μm) and (11.5 - 12.51 μm) with 100 m resolution.

Landsat 9 is planned to launch in late 2020.

Some important sensors/scanners onboard Landsats are explained below (*https://landsat.usgs.gov/)*.

3.17.1 Return Beam Videcon Camera

The payloads of the first two satellites included a series of three return beam videcon (RBV) cameras that took pictures in the visible and infrared bands. The resolution of the image was 80m covering 185 x 185km area. The resolution of the images acquired by Landsat 3 was raised to 40m, but the cameras took images in a single panchromatic spectral band (0.5-0.75μm) only. Return beam videcon was an electron imager, and works like a television camera. When the shutter is opened and closed, its optical system frames an image on a photo conducting plate just like a photographic camera frames the image on a photochemical film. A fine electron beam from the electron gun scans the pixels line by line. Being a framing device, the return beam videcon collects a full frame data practically instantaneously.

Landsat-1 and -2 carried three RBVs with spectral filters to record green (0.475–0.575 μm), red (0.580–0.680 μm), and photographic infrared (0.698–0.830 μm) images of the same area on the ground. During image processing these data are taken as due to blue, green and red bands to develop the false color image of the scene. Landsat-3 carried two RBVs operating in the panchromatic band (0.505–0.750 μm) to obtain higher spatial resolution (40m) as compared to its MSS ground resolution (80m). Moreover, each of these two RBVs has a covered adjacent ground area of 99km x 99km with 15Km sidelap. Successive pairs of RBV images also have a 17km forward overlap. Thus two pairs of RBV images cover an area of 181km x 183km which is equivalent to the area corresponding to the MSS scene (185km x 185km).

3.17.2 Multispectral Scanner

This form of imaging is used in Landsat series of satellites. The scanning system in muti-spectral scanner (MSS) employs a single detector per band of multispectral signal. It has a scanning mirror fixed at 45° to the axis of its rotation with 2-3^0 steering capability. Since the rotating mirror scans the swath line by line perpendicular to the track (flight direction), the scanner is called **across-track scanner**. The field of view (FOV) is restricted by an aperture so that the mirror will receive signals in almost nadir view from 2000 ground resolution cells that makes one scan line. The signal received by the rotating scanning mirror from a ground resolution cell contains spectral information in different bands. The detectors with their designed apertures are so placed that they now receive the spectral information from the ground resolution cells in the specified bandwidths of various color components of the white signal. The signals are transmitted to the ground receiving stations or stored in magnetic tapes till a ground receiving station is within its range for transmission / reception.

These mechanical sensors collected information in four spectral bands and over a 185 x 185km area. Since this instrument was developed after the three RBV cameras, these bands were numbered from 4 to 7. MSS of Landsat 3 included an additional spectral band in the thermal infrared band.

3.17.3 Thematic Mapper

The Landsat Thematic Mapper (TM) sensor provides multispectral imagery in seven spectral bands at 30m resolution, covering 185km x 185km area. Figure 3.34 illustrates the images taken in various spectral bands of Landsat TM system. It is observed that the greatest amount of information about the natural environment can be seen in near-infrared and red wavelength bands. Water is strongly absorbed by infrared wavelengths, and is thus highly distinctive in that region. In addition, plant species typically show their greatest differentiation here. In the red band, chlorophyll absorbs energy for photosynthesis. Thus in this band, vegetated and non-vegetated surfaces can be readily distinguished. A traditional false color composite (**FCC**) can be derived from the green, red, and infrared bands of TM (as opposed to the blue, green, and red bands of natural color images). This combination works well in the interpretation of the cultural landscape as well as natural and vegetated surfaces. However, it is increasingly common to include other bands that are more specifically targeted to the differentiation of surface materials. For example, Landsat TM band 5 is very useful in determining soil and leaf moisture differences, while TM band 7 targets the detection of hydrothermal alteration zones in bare rock surfaces. Landsat TM band 6 has a spatial resolution of 120m, while the remaining bands have a spatial resolution of 30m. Their principal applications are given in Table 3.6.

Table 3.6: Principal applications of Landsat TM bands

Band	Spectral band	Applications
1	0.45 – 0.52 µm	Ground/plants differentiation, coastal zones
2	0.52 – 0.60 µm	Vegetation
3	0.63 – 0.69 µm	Plant species differentiation
4	0.76 – 0.90 µm	Biomass
5	1.55 – 1.75 µm	Snow/cloud differentiation
6	10.41 – 12.5 µm	Thermal
7	2.08 – 2.35 µm	Lithology

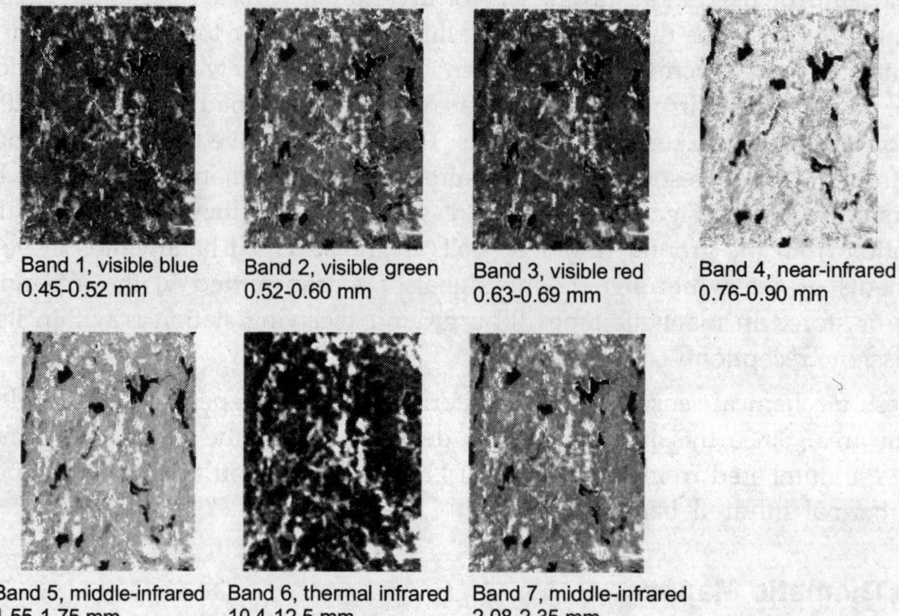

Figure 3.34: Images of Landsat TM bands

3.17.4 Enhanced Thematic Mapper Plus

The enhanced thematic mapper plus (ETM+) scanner is an enhanced version of the TM. It has a high-resolution panchromatic band with 15 m resolution. It also provides images in 7 multispectral bands with 30 m resolution in other band and 60m in thermal band. The principal applications are given in Table 3.7.

Table 3.7: Principal applications of Landsat ETM+ bands

Band	Spectral band	Resolution	Applications
1	0.441 – 0.514 µm (Blue)	30 m	Ground/plant differentiation, coastal zones
2	0.519 – 0.601 µm (Green)	30 m	Vegetation
3	0.631 – 0.692 µm (Red)	30 m	Differentiate plant species
4	0.772 – 0.898 µm (NIR)	30 m	Biomass
5	1.547 – 1.749 µm (SWIR-1)	30 m	Snow/cloud differentiation
6	10.31 – 12.36 µm (TIR)	60 m	Thermal
7	2.064 – 2.345 µm (SWIR-2)	30 m	Lithology
PAN	0.515 – 0.896 µm	15 m	

3.18 SPOT

SPOT (*Système Pour l'Observation de la Terre*) (System for Earth Observation) a high-resolution optical imaging Earth observation satellite system was initiated by the **CNES** (*Centre National d'études Spatiales* - the French Space Agency) in the 1970s. The SPOT was launched in sun-synchronous orbit with an inclination of 98.7° from equator and an altitude of 832 km. The inclination of the orbital plane combined with the Earth's rotation around the polar axis allows a satellite to cover entire Earth every 26 days. It provides data in panchromatic band image at 10 m spatial resolution as well as multi-spectral three band images at 20 m spatial resolution (Holand et al 2003). Refer to Table 3.5 and Table 3.9 for additional details. The SPOT was designed to explore the Earth's resources, detecting and forecasting phenomena, such as climatology and oceanography, and monitoring human activities and natural phenomena *(https://www.satimagingcorp.com/services/resources/ and www.eoedu.belspo.be/en/ satellites/spot.htm).*

The SPOT satellites have been another important source of medium-resolution multispectral images with improved resolution over Landsat images. SPOT also had the capabilities to collect stereo- images for 3D study of Earth. Images of the pair are captured on successive days by the same satellite viewing off-nadir. Off-nadir viewing capability is shown in Figure 3.35 where from 4 different times, the satellite captures the same area. These images are very useful for creating 3D model of the area. The disadvantage is that those days the satellite will miss the images of areas down below it. The availability of stereo imagery is limited, as their collection requires special control on the satellite. Traditional photogrammetric techniques can be used to successfully create topographic 3D data of inaccessible areas of the world.

SPOT 1 was launched by Ariane 2 on 21 February 1986. Two days later, SPOT 1 transmitted its first image with a resolution of 10-20m. SPOT 2 was launched in 22 January 1990. SPOT 3 was launched on 25 September 1993 which has ceased operations, due to problems with stabilization.

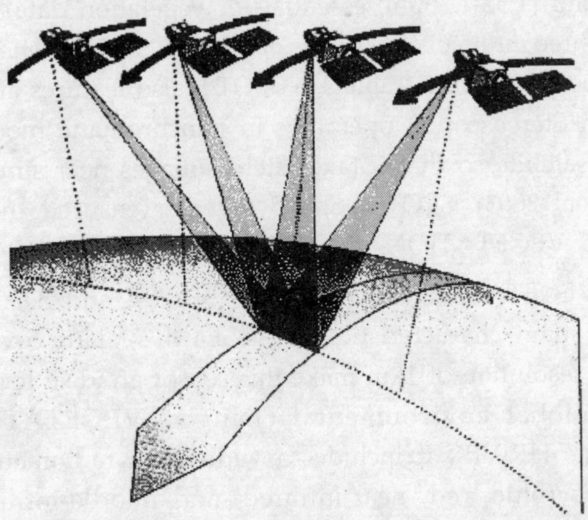

Figure 3.35: Capturing the image using off-nadir capabilities of SPOT

(Source: https://crisp.nus.edu.sg/~research/tutorial/spot.htm)

Sensors in all these satellites were identical, including two identical optical imaging instruments High Resolution Visible (HRV) which operated in two modes (panchromatic and multispectral), either simultaneously or individually. The characteristics of HRV are given in Table 3.8. The panchromatic band has a resolution of 10 m, and the multispectral 3 bands operating in Green, Red and NIR wavelengths, have a resolution of 20 m with a scene covering an area of 3600 km^2. Panchromatic sensor covers the visible and NIR part of the electromagnetic spectrum. The orientation of each instrument's strip-selection mirror can be remotely steered by the ground stations, offering an oblique viewing capability up to angles of $\pm 27^0$ from the satellite's vertical axis (Holland et al 2003). In this way, the temporal resolution is shortened from 26 to 4-5 days for the temperate zones.

In March 1998, the SPOT 4 satellite with same geometric imaging characteristics (a swath of 60 km with oblique viewing capability of 27° on either side of the vertical) as the earlier SPOT satellites was launched. It operated at an altitude of 822km in sun-synchronous polar orbit with period of revolution of 101 minutes and a repeat cycle of 26 days. The performance of SPOT 4 has been increased by adding a new SWIR band. SPOT 4 carried two identical optical instruments Visible & Infrared High-Resolution **(HR-VIR)** sensors. The characteristics of HR-VIR are given in Table 3.8. This sensor had all bands of HRV sensor plus one additional band in MIR region (1.58-1.75μm) with 20m ground resolution. SPOT 4 had also onboard the first VEGETATION instrument, developed for observations of vegetation at global level.

SPOT 5, launched in May 2002, provided further improved quality of images. SPOT 5 has 2 High Resolution Geometrical **(HRG)** instruments offering a higher resolution of 2.5-5m in panchromatic mode and 10m in multispectral mode. It was designed to have shortwave infrared band (1.58-1.75μm, essential for vegetation data) at a resolution of 20 m, in addition to first three multispectral bands of SPOT 4 HR-VIR sensor. The characteristics of VEGETATION sensor is given in Table 3.8. SPOT 5 also features an imaging instrument HRS (High-Resolution Stereoscopic) operating in panchromatic mode, pointing forward and backward of the satellite so that it takes stereo-images near simultaneously to create 3D relief (Holland et al 2003). SPOT 4 and 5 together ensured the provision of high-resolution images and VEGETATION global images.

The aim of the VEGETATION instrument in SPOT-4 and 5 is to provide accurate measurements of the main characteristics of the Earth's plant cover. Practically, daily global coverage and a resolution of 1km make this sensor an ideal tool for observing long-term regional and global environmental changes. VEGETATION sensor works independently from the HR-VIR. It includes a wide-angle radiometric camera operating in four spectral bands (blue, red, near-infrared, and middle-infrared). With its wide 2,250km swath, this instrument is thus capable to cover almost all of the Earth's dry land in just one day.

Table 3.8: Characteristics of SPOT sensors

High Resolution Visible (HRV) Sensor			
Mode	**Band**	**Spectral band**	**Resolution**
Multispectral	B1	0.50 – 0.59 µm (green)	20m
	B2	0.61 – 0.68 µm (red)	20m
	B3	0.78 – 0.89 µm (near IR)	20m
Panchromatic	PAN	0.50 – 0.73 µm	10m
Visible and Infrared High Resolution (HR-VIR) Sensor			
Mode	**Band**	**Spectral band**	**Resolution**
Multispectral	B1	0.50 – 0.59 µm	10m
	B2	0.61 – 0.68 µm	10m
	B3	0.78 – 0.89 µm	10m
	SWIR	1.58 – 1.75 µm	20m
Monospectral	PAN	0.51 – 0.73 µm	5m (or 2.5m in supermode)
VEGETATION Sensor			
Mode	**Band**	**Spectral band**	**Resolution/Applications**
Multispectral	B0	0.43 – 0.47µm (blue)	1165m Oceanographic applications/
	B2	0.61 – 0.68 µm (red)	1165m Atmospheric corrections
	B3	0.79 – 0.89 µm (near IR)	1165m Vegetation photosynthesis activity
	MIR	1.58 – 1.75 µm (middle IR)	1165m Ground and vegetation humidity

SPOT 6 and SPOT 7 were launched on 08 September 2012 and 30 June 2014, respectively to provide continuity of high-resolution images. The Indian Space Research Organization (ISRO) launched SPOT-6 on a Polar Satellite Launch Vehicle. The satellite provided Panchromatic (0.45–0.75) µm at 1.5m resolution, and multispectral in Blue (0.45–0.53), Green (0.53–0.59), Red (0.62–0.69), NIR (0.76–0.89) µm at 8m resolution, covering an area 60km x 60km, as well as color merged products at 1.5m, resolution. SPOT-6 and SPOT-7 have identical sensors and operating characteristics. They can provide a daily revisit everywhere on Earth with a 60 km × 60 km swath.

Two types of scanners onboard SPOT have been briefly explained below.

3.18.1 Along Track Multispectral Scanner/Push Broom Scanner

These scanners are employed by the SPOT system. In this type of scanner, the scan direction is along the track (direction of flight), and hence called along track scanner. Development of charge-coupled device (CCD) has contributed to the successful design of such scanners. It is also called **push broom scanner** because the detectors are analogous to the bristles of a push broom sweeping a path on the floor. SPOT series of satellites extensively use this type of payloads for scanning the Earth surface. For multispectral scanning, the along track scanner accommodates one line of detector array for each spectral band.

The sensor elements consist of an array of as many silicon photodiodes arranged in a line, as there are ground resolution cells (corresponding to IFOV). Each silicon photodiode, in turn, is coupled to a tiny charge storage cell forming a CCD. When light from a ground cell strikes a photodiode in the array, it generates a small current proportional to the intensity of light falling on it and the current charges the storage cell placed behind the diode. The output signals are correlated with the shift pulses, and digitized to reconstitute the image.

3.18.2 Side Viewing Scanner

The across track and along track scanners are used in passive remote sensing in visible, and infrared regions of the electromagnetic spectrum. These scanners always receive signals in the nadir view. However, if the user demands to observe a dynamic scene frequently, then there is a provision in SPOT satellites to steer the cameras to look off-nadir at the required scene, some days before to some days after the normal nadir viewing date.

3.19 INDIAN REMOTE SENSING SATELLITES

The launch of the India's first civilian remote sensing satellite **(IRS)-1A** in March 1988 marked the beginning of a successful journey in the course of the Indian Space Programme. The Indian Remote Sensing satellite system has one of the largest constellations of remote sensing satellites in operation in the world today. The first generation satellites IRS-1A and 1B were designed, developed and launched successfully during 1988 and 1991 with multispectral cameras LISS I and LISS II having spatial resolutions of 72.5 m and 36.25 m, respectively. It was launched on March 17, 1988 in sun-synchronous orbit, at a nominal altitude of 904 km. The orbital period was 103.2 minutes, with a repeat cycle of 22 days, crossing the equator at 10:26 AM. The IRS with high-resolution sensors and wide coverage capabilities provide with better resolution data and coverage to meet the growing applications needs (*https://calval.cr.usgs.gov/JACIE_files/.../Karnik_Deviprasad_JACIE2010FINAL.pdf*). **IRS-1B** provided better repetivity. Refer to Tables 3.5 and 3.9 for additional details.

Subsequently, the second generation remote sensing satellites **IRS-1C** and **-1D** with improved spatial resolutions have been developed and successfully launched in 1995 and 1997, respectively. The **PAN** and **WiFS** sensors on IRS-1C and -1D further strengthened the scope of remote sensing, with increased coverage and foray into application areas like resources survey and management, forest studies and disaster monitoring, environmental studies, cartographic and town planning. The satellites had three sensors, pan, LISS III and WiFS. IRS-1C/1D provided data at 5.8m resolution in panchromatic mode (0.5-0.75 μm), 6 bit data giving more information of the ground area covered (Annual Report, ISRO, 2018).

IRS-P6 payload was designed to provide continued remote sensing data for integrated land and water resources management. With the enhanced multi-spectral/spatial coverage and stereo imaging capabilities, further studies such as improved crop discrimination, crop yield estimation, forestry and disaster management can be carried out in advanced areas of applications. In order to have continuity, the LISS-III camera was included in the payload of IRS-P6, apart from the LISS-IV and AWiFS cameras.

Table 3.9: Some remote sensing satellites

Satellite	Launch date	Sensors	Spatial resolution (m)	Swath width (km)
Landsat-1	23. 07.1972	RBV MSS	80 80	185
Landsat-2	22.01.1975	RBV MSS	80 80	185
Landsat-3	05.03 1978	RBV MSS	40 80	185
Landsat-4	16.07.1982	MSS TM	80 30 and 120	185
Landsat-5	01.03.1984	MSS TM	80 30 and 120	185
Landsat-6	05.10.1993	ETM	could not achieve the orbit, and hence failed	
Landsat-7	15.04.1999	ETM+	30, 60 and 15	185
Landsat-8	11.02.2013	OLI TIRS	30 and 15 100	185
SPOT-1	21.02.1986	HRV PAN	20 10	60
SPOT- 2	22.01.1990	HRV PAN	20 10	60
SPOT-3	25.09.1993	HRV PAN	20 10	60
SPOT-4	24.03.1988	HR-VIR	20	60
SPOT-5	04.05.2002	HRG	10 and 5	60
SPOT-6	08 .09.2012	HRG	1.5	60
SPOT-7	30.06. 2014	HRG	8.0	60
IRS-1A	17.03.1988	LISS-I, LISS-II A/B	72.5 LISS-I 36.25 LISS-II	148 74 x 2 (148 km)
IRS-1B	29.08.1991	LISS-I and LISS-II A/B	72.5 LISS-I 36.25 LISS-II	148 74 x 2
IRS-P2	15.10.1994	LISS-II M	32 x 37	66 x 2 (131 km)
IRS-1C IRS-1D	28.12.1995 29.09.1997	LISS-III	23.5 and 70	142 and 148
		PAN	5.8	70
		WiFS	188	804
IRS-P3	21.03.1996	WiFS MOS-A MOS-B MOS-C	188 1500 520 550	804 195 200 192
IRS-P4 (Oceansat-1)	26.05.1999	OCM MSMR	360 x 236 105x68, 66x43, 40x26, 34x22 (km for frequency sequence)	1420 1360
IRS-P6 Resourcesat-1	17.10.2003	LISS-IV	5.8	70
		LISS-III	23.5	140
		AWiFS	70	740
IRS-P5 Cartosat-1	05.05.2005	PAN-F PAN-A	2.5 2.5	30 30
Cartosat-2	10.01.2007	PAN camera	< 1	9.6
Oceansat-2	23.09.2009	OCM SCAT ROSA	360 x 236 25 km x 25 km	1420 1400

Resourcesat-1 (IRS-P6), the tenth satellite in IRS series, was launched in October 2003. It was placed in 820 km high polar Sun Synchronous Orbit. The satellite is designed to provide both multi-spectral and panchromatic imagery of the Earth's surface. It has three sensors on-board: a Linear Imaging and Self Scanning sensor (LISS-III), an Advanced Wide Field Sensor **(AWiFS)** and a high resolution multi-spectral camera LISS-IV along with an On-Board Solid State Recorder (**OBSSR**). All the three cameras will be working on the 'pushbroom scanning' concept.

Resourcesat-3, a medium resolution, planned to be launched in September 2019, would ensure continuity of data services required for the operational programmes in the areas of land and water resources management. It will carry Advanced Linear Imaging Scanning Sensor-3 **(ALISS-3)** payload consisting of VNIR and SWIR bands. It would also carry Atmospheric Correction Sensor **(ACS)** for quantitative interpretation and geophysical parameter retrieval and to improve the data products. The ground sampling distances is expected to be 20m for VNIR and SWIR bands. Hyperspectral atmospheric correction bands will operate in VNIR bands and have ground sampling distances of 240m with a swath of 925 km at 795 km altitude orbit.

Oceansat-1 (IRS-P4) intended to study physical and biological aspects of oceanography, was launched in May 1999. It carries an Ocean Colour Monitor (OCM) and a Multi-frequency Scanning Microwave Radiometer **(MSMR)**. OCM operates in 402-422, 433-453, 480-500, 500-520, 545-565, 660-689, 745-785 and 845-885 nm bands with 360m spatial resolution and 1420km swath. **Oceansat-2** was launched on Sept. 23, 2009. It carries three payloads: Ocean Colour Monitor **(OCM)**, Ku-band Pencil Beam Scatterometer **(SCAT)**, and Radio Occultation Sounder for Atmosphere **(ROSA)**. **Oceansat-3** is a continuity mission of Oceansat-2 with enhanced imaging capability, planned to be launched in November 2018. It will carry Thermal IR sensor, 12 channels Ocean Color Monitor, Scatterometer and Passive Microwave Radiometer for simultaneous measurement of Ocean Color and SST, improvements in signal to noise ratio. IR Sensor and Ocean Color Monitor would be used in the analysis for operational Potential Fishing Zones. Satellite is mainly for Ocean biology and sea state applications (*http://www.eotec.com/images/IRS_Current_and_Future_Web.pdf*, Annual Report, ISRO, 2018).

Cartosat-1 is a state-of-the-art satellite which is mainly designed for 3D-mapping based on three or two cameras having different nadir angles in orbit direction for the generation of stereo models intended for cartographic applications. Cartosat-1 carries two state-of-the-art Panchromatic cameras that take B&W stereoscopic pictures of the Earth in the visible region. The swath covered by these high resolution PAN cameras is 30 km with a spatial resolution of 2.5 m. The cameras are mounted on the satellite in such a way that near simultaneous imaging of the same area from two different angles is possible. This facilitates the generation of accurate three-dimensional maps. The cameras are steerable across the direction of the satellite's movement to facilitate the imaging of an area more frequently. The unique high-resolution along-track stereo imaging capability, carried out for the first time anywhere in the world, enabled generation of the Digital Elevation

Models (DEM) and other value added products from Cartosat-1. The data provided enhanced inputs for large scale mapping applications and stimulate newer applications in the urban and rural development, land and water resources management, disaster assessment, relief planning and management, environment impact assessment and various other GIS based applications. The data was also used for updating topographic maps, besides generation of large-scale topographic maps.

Cartosat-2 is capable of providing scene-specific spot imagery, was launched in January 10, 2007. It carries a single panchromatic camera onboard capable of providing better than 1-meter spatial resolution imagery, with a swath of 9.6 km. The satellite has high agility with capability of steering along and across the track up to $\pm 45^0$ to facilitate imaging of any area more frequently. It has low revisit periods of 4 days and 1 day. **Cartosat– 2A** launched on 28 April 2008 can also provide scene specific spot imagery with Panchromatic Camera. The spatial resolution of this camera is better than 1m and swath of 9.6 km. Imageries from this satellite are used for cartographic applications like mapping, urban and rural infrastructure development and management in GIS. **Cartosat-2B** was launched on July 12, 2010, with a camera of spatial resolution of about one metre (0.8m).

Cartosat-3 is an advanced satellite to obtain panchromatic and multispectral imagery which is expected to be launched in 2018. The payload has the capability of imaging with 0.25m in Panchromatic and 1m in 4 bands of multispectral modes with a swath of 16km. Images would be useful for cadastre, infrastructure mapping and analysis, disaster monitoring and damage assessment.

National Remote Sensing Centre (NRSC), Hyderabad is the focal point for distribution of remote sensing satellite data products in India and its neighboring countries. NRSC has an earth station at Shadnagar, about 55Km from Hyderabad, to receive data from almost all contemporary remote sensing satellites. The National Data Centre (**NDC**) is a one-stop-shop for range of data products with a wide choice of resolutions, processing levels, product media, out scales, area coverage, revisit, season and spectral bands. Data products can be supplied on a wide variety of media and formats.

Some of the sensors onboard Landsats are explained below.

3.19.1 Linear Imaging Self Scanner

IRS-1A and 1B consist of Linear Imaging Self Scanning Sensor **(LISS)**-I and -2; each with a multispectral camera providing images in 4 bands (0.46 - 0.52 μm blue, 0.52 - 0.59 μm green, 0.62 - 0.68 μm red, and 0.77 - 0.86 μm NIR) at 7 bit radiometric resolution. The two LISS sensors aboard IRS-1A and 1B beamed down valuable data that aided in large scale mapping applications. Each LISS camera consists of the collecting optics, imaging detectors, inflight calibration system, the processing electronics, and data formatting electronics. LISS-I employs four 2048-element linear CCD detector arrays with spectral filters, and provides 76m resolution images with a swath of about 150 km. A LISS-I scene is 148 km x 174 km. The LISS-II features eight 2048-element linear CCD detector arrays with spectral filters. It provides images at 36.25m resolution. Four LISS-II scenes cover the area of one LISS-I scene.

LISS contains linear array of the sensor elements in this type of imaging/scanning system. For multispectral scanning, the along track scanner accommodates one line of detector array for each spectral band. However, IRS satellites use as many cameras as there are spectral bands; each with a characteristic filter and a linear array of CCD detectors. Under identical setup, it is found that along track scanner minimizes the detector size corresponding to a smaller IFOV producing higher spatial resolution and to narrow down the spectral bandwidth, thereby increasing the spectral resolution. However, if the user demands to observe a dynamic scene frequently, then there is a provision in IRS satellites to steer the cameras to look off-nadir at the required scene, some days before to some days after the normal nadir viewing date.

The IRS-LISS III was employed in IRS 1C and 1D. It provided 7 bits multispectral image with 23.5m ground resolution provides images in Green 0.52–0.59 μm, Red 0.62–0.68 μm, Near-Infrared 0.77– 0.86 μm, and Short-wave Infrared 1.55–1.7 μm band at 70.5 m resolution. WiFS sensor provided 7 bits data at 188 m resolution in two spectral band (0.62-0.68 μm and 0.77- 0.86 μm).

The LISS-IV data in IRS-P6 with 5.8 m resolution in multi-spectral mode, is helpful in improving the large scale mapping of natural resources and urban areas including infrastructure mapping such as road/rail network. This camera can be operated in two modes: Mono and Multi-spectral. In the multispectral mode, data is collected in three spectral bands viz, 0.52 to 0.59 μm (Green band 2) 0.62 to 0.68 μm (Red band 3), and 0.76 to 0.86 μm (NIR band 4). In the multispectral mode, LISS-IV sensor provides data corresponding to 23.5km swath. In Mono mode, the data corresponding to a swath of 70km, can be transmitted. Nominally, band-3 data will be transmitted in this mode. The LISS-IV camera has the additional feature of off-nadir viewing capability by tilting the camera by ± 26^0. This way, it can provide a revisit of 5 days for any given ground area.

3.19.2 Wide Field Sensor/Advanced Wide Field Sensor

Wide Field Sensor **(WiFS)** was employed by IRS 1C and 1D, with 188m resolution and providing images in 0.62-0.68 μm (red), 0.77-0.86 μm (near IR) and having a swath of 774km. Resourcesat employed Advanced Wide Field Sensor **(AWiFS)** with 56-70 m ground resolution, providing four images in 0.52-0.59μm (green), 0.62-0.68 μm (red), 0.77-0.86 μm (near IR), and 1.55-1.70 μm (mid-IR) having 370-470 km swath.

The availability of AWiFS data with improved spatial and spectral resolution helped in better classification accuracy of all agricultural related applications. It is a unique sensor with its high resolution and large swath enables monitoring large areas for flood inundation, vegetation stress etc. The AWiFS camera provides a combined swath of 737 Km. The AWiFS camera provides enhanced capabilities compared to the WiFS camera on-board IRS-1C/1D, in terms of spatial resolution (56m V/s 188m), radiometric resolution (10 bits V/s 7 bits) and spectral bands (4 V/s 2).

3.20 IKONOS

GeoEye Inc. (formerly Orbital Imaging Corporation or ORBIMAGE) operates with a growing constellation of high-resolution earth-imaging satellites (IKONOS, Orbview-2, Orbview-3, GeoEye-1, GeoEye-2) which are quickly becoming an important source of large scale mapping.

IKONOS is a commercial Earth observation satellite, launched in 24 September 1999, and derives its name from the Greek word eikôn for image. It is the first to collect publicly available high-resolution multispectral imagery with 3375 pixels and panchromatic (PAN) imagery with 13500 pixels, providing a swath width of 11.3 km. Spectral bands allow simultaneous acquisition of panchromatic and multispectral images: 1m (0.82m) Panchromatic 4m multispectral (Blue, Green, Red, and NIR 0.45–0.90 μm) and 1-m Pan sharpened. The revisit rate for IKONOS is 3-5 days off-nadir and 144 days for true-nadir, with a swath width of 11km × 11km (single scene). IKONOS orbits Earth every 98 minutes at an altitude of about 680 km, travelling in a sun-synchronous orbit.

IKONOS-2 developed by then Space Imaging, then GeoEye, now DigitalGlobe, was launched in September 1999 from Vandenberg Air Force Base (AFB), California. The satellite has a polar, circular, sun-synchronous orbit at an altitude of 681km. It provides multispectral data in B, G, R, and NIR bands with 4m resolution and a panchromatic band with 1m resolution. It has 2048 (11 bits) radiometric resolution. It covers 11km swath having up to 60^0 viewing angle.

3.21 QUICKBIRD

QuickBird-1, a very high resolution satellite, developed by then EarthWatch now DigitalGlobe was launched in November 2000, but was lost due to launch vehicle failure, **QuickBird 2,** owned and operated by DigitalGlobe, was launched from Vandenberg Air Force Base in California on 18 October 2001. It has resulted in the highest resolution commercial satellite until then. The satellite has 4 multispectral bands (B, G, R and NIR) with 2.4m resolution and a panchromatic band with 0.61m resolution with 2048 (11 bits) radiometric resolution. It was placed in Sun-synchronous polar orbit, at an altitude of 470 km, with 94 minutes of orbital period. The satellite has 1-5 days temporal resolution with up to 25^0 of viewing angle along-and cross-track covering 16.5km swath operating from 450km orbit

3.22 ORBVIEW

The **OrbView-2** was launched by GeoEye Inc. on August 1, 1997 from Vandenberg AFB, California. It was a low-resolution satellite (1km), capturing broad-area colour imagery of land and ocean surfaces for science research, agricultural and ocean monitoring. Launched in 2003 by GeoEye Inc, now DigitalGlobe, OrbView-3 acquired 1m panchromatic and 4m multispectral imagery (B, G, R, IR) in 8km-wide swath, having 2048 (11 bits) radiometric resolution. The satellite moves in 470km orbit with up to 45^0 of viewing angle. The satellite collected up to 210,000 km^2 of imagery each day, revisiting the entire Earth in less than 3 days.

3.23 GEOEYE

GeoEye-1 provides 253 million km^2 of satellite map images to Microsoft and Yahoo search engines with Google having exclusive online mapping access from the new **GeoEye-1** satellite. This satellite (also called **SeaStar**) collects real colour imagery of Earth's land and ocean surfaces on a daily basis. GeoEye-1 (formerly **OrbView 5**), developed by then GeoEye, now DigitalGlobe, was launched on September 6, 2008 from Vandenberg Airbase. The satellite provides 41cm resolution panchromatic and 1.65m resolution multispectral imagery in 4 bands (B, G, R and NIR) in 15.2km wide swath with 2048 (11 bits) radiometric resolution. The spacecraft was placed in a sun-synchronous orbit at an altitude of 684 km and inclination of 98° and can image up to 60° off-nadir viewing angle. GeoEye-1 offers 3m geolocation accuracy, which means that users can map natural and man-made features to within 3m of their actual location. This agile satellite can rotate or swivel forward, backward or side-to-side with robotic precision, and has a revisit capability of 1-3 days depending on latitude. The panchromatic and multispectral datasets can also be procured as combined (pan-sharpened) 0.41m resolution multispectral imagery. Images are very useful in studies related to telecommunications, infrastructure planning, mapping/surveying, civil engineering, mining & exploration, oil & gas, and DEM generation

3.24 WORLD VIEW

WorldView-1 was launched on September 18, 2007, and is owned and operated by DigitalGlobe. The high-capacity, panchromatic imaging system features 0.5m resolution imagery. WorldView-1 has an average revisit time of 1.7 days, and is capable of collecting in-track stereo. Operating at an altitude of 496km, WorldView-1 is capable of collecting up to 750,000 km^2 data per day. The satellite is also equipped with state-of-the-art geolocation accuracy capabilities and exhibits stunning agility with rapid targeting and efficient in-track stereo collection. It provides highly detailed imagery for precise map creation, and change detection studies in telecommunications, infrastructure planning, mapping/surveying, civil engineering, mining & exploration, oil & gas, and DEM generation. It also allows the creation of accurate maps in remote areas, maximising the utility of whatever resources are available.

WorldView-2 was successfully launched on October 8, 2009 from Vandenberg AFB, California, and was fully operational on January 6th 2010. It brings three numbers of DigitalGlobe's satellites providing sub-meter resolution, and is capable of collecting up to 975,000 km^2 of imagery per day. WorldView-2 was the first very high resolution satellite to offer 8-band multispectral imagery with sub-metre resolution, along with increased agility, accuracy and stereo capability. With the additional four spectral bands, WorldView-2 offers unique opportunities for remote sensing analysis of vegetation, coastal environments, agriculture, geology, environment, tourism and many others.

WorldView-3 was launched on August 13, 2014 from Vandenberg, AFB, California. It was placed in a Sun-synchronous orbit, at an altitude of 617 km, with orbital period of 97 minutes. It provides 31cm resolution in panchromatic, 1.24m resolution in multispectral, 3.7m resolution in SWIR (Short-Wave Infrared), and 30 m resolution in CAVIS (Clouds, Aerosols, Vapors, Ice, and Snow). **CAVIS** (Clouds, Aerosols, Vapors, Ice and Snow) will monitor the atmosphere and provide correction data to improve WorldView-3's imagery when it images Earth objects through haze, soot, dust or other obscurants. WorldView-3 has an average revisit time of <1 day and is capable of collecting up to 680,000 km^2 per day. It is very successful with its first super-spectral and high-resolution e.g., 31cm panchromatic resolution that collects five times more data than 70cm imagery, SWIR (Shortwave Infrared) bands that allow for accurate imaging through haze, fog, dust, smoke and other airborne particles; and eight multispectral bands. WorldView-3 offers unique opportunities for remote sensing analysis of vegetation, coastal environments, agriculture, geology, environment, tourism and many others.

WorldView-4 (formerly **GeoEye-2**) is DigitalGlobe's next very high resolution imaging satellite providing high resolution and color imagery to commercial, government and international customers. It was launched on November 11, 2016 in a Sun-synchronous orbit, at an altitude of 617 km, with 97 minutes orbital period. It crosses equator at 10:30 hours, having an effective revisit time capability of ≤ 3 days. The satellite provides 31cm resolution in panchromatic at nadir, 0.34 m at 20° off-nadir, 1m at 56° off-nadir, and 3.51m at 65° off-nadir, as well as 1.24m resolution in multispectral at nadir, 1.38m at 20° off-nadir, 4m, at 56° off-nadir, 14m at 65° off-nadir in 4 bands (B, G, R and NIR) in 13.1km wide swath with 2048 (11 bits) radiometric resolution.

Summary of some of the very high resolution satellites is given in Table 3.10.

3.25 HYPERSPECTRAL IMAGING SYSTEMS

Hyperspectral sensors (also known as Imaging Spectrometers) collects images of a scene in tens to hundreds of narrow spectral bands nearly simultaneously (Figure 3.36). They represent the next step in the spectral dimension of existing multispectral imaging radiometers currently represented by sensors, such as the Landsat TM which collects data in seven simultaneous bands. The hyperspectral sensors have two key component technologies (Chavez et al 1994). One is the spectral filtering technique by which the observed scene radiance is divided into narrow distinct bands. The other key is the detector array technology which allows multiple spatial and/or spectral samples through one- or two-dimensional arrays.

Table 3.10: Characteristics of high resolution satellites

Sensor	Resolution/Band*		Stero-capability	Swath (km)
	Panchromatic	Multispectral		
IKONOS	0.82 m 445-900 nm	4 m (Blue, green, red, NIR) bands	Yes	11.3
IKONOS-2	1.0 m 445-900 nm	4 m (Blue, green, red, NIR) bands	Yes	11
QuickBird	**Failed after launch**			
QuickBird-2	61cm 450-900 nm	2.4m (Blue, green, red, NIR) bands	Along track	16.5
OrbView-2	—	1 km, 8 bands	No	2800
OrbView-3	1 m 450-900 nm	4m (Blue, green, red, IR)	Yes	8
GeoEye-1	41 cm 450-800 nm	1.65 m Blue: 450-510 nm Green: 510-580 nm Red: 655-690 nm Near IR: 780-920 nm	Along track	15.2
WorldView-1	50 cm 400-900 nm	Not applicable	Along track	17.6
WorldView-2	50 cm 450-800 nm	2.0 m Coastal: 400-450 nm Blue: 450-510 nm Green: 510-580 nm Yellow: 585-625 nm Red: 630-690 nm Red Edge: 705-745 nm Near Infrared 1: 770-895 nm Near Infrared 2: 860-1040 nm	Along track	16.4
WorldView-3	31cm 450-800 nm	**Multispectral bands (1.24 m resolution)** Coastal: 400-450 nm Blue: 450-510 nm Green: 510-580 nm Yellow: 585-625 nm Red: 630-690 nm Red Edge: 705-745 nm Near Infrared 1: 770-895 nm Near Infrared 2: 860-1040 nm **SWIR bands (3.7 m resolution)** SWIR-1: 1195-1225 nm SWIR-2: 1550-1590 nm SWIR-3: 1640-1680 nm SWIR-4: 1710-1750 nm	Yes	13.1

		SWIR-5: 2145-2185 nm SWIR 6: 2185-2225 nm SWIR-7: 2235-2285 nm SWIR-8: 2295-2365 nm **CAVIS bands (30 m resolution)** Desert Clouds: 405-420 nm Aerosol-1: 459-509 nm Green: 525-585 nm Aerosol-2: 635-685 nm Water-1: 845-885 nm Water-2: 897-927 nm Water-3: 930-965 nm **NDVI-SWIR: 1220-1252 nm** Cirrus: 1365-1405 nm Snow: 1620-1680 nm Aerosol-3: 2105-2245 nm Aerosol-4: 2105-2245 nm		
WorldView-4 (formerly GeoEye-2)	31 cm 450-800 nm	1.24m Blue : 450 - 510 nm Green : 510 - 580 nm Red : 655 - 690 nm NIR : 780 - 920 nm	Yes	13.1

**Note: All data are 11 bit (2048 grey levels) radiometric resolution*

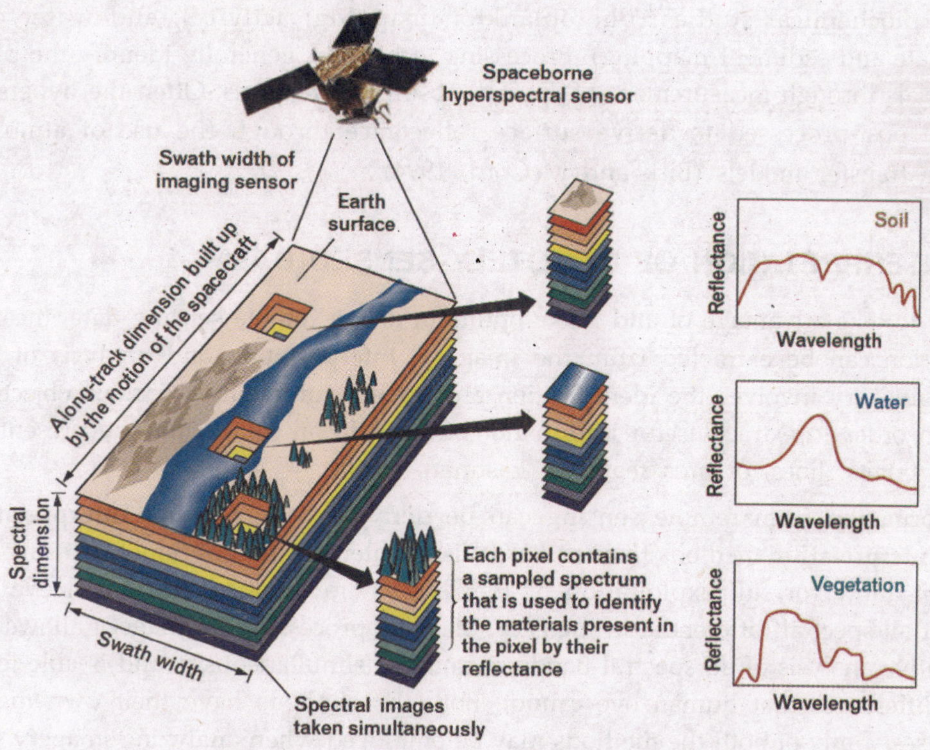

Figure 3.36: Hyperion imaging spectrometer

(*Source: http://www.markelowitz.com/Hyperspectral.html*)

NASA successfully launched the Hyperion imaging spectrometer (part of the EO-1 satellite) which produces 30m resolution images in 220 spectral bands (0.4-2.5 μm) with a 30m resolution. The data collected are often termed an **"image cube"** where the two spatial dimensions are joined by the third spectral dimension (Figure 3.36). The Hyperion instrument provides a new class of observation data for improved characterization of Earth surface. The instrument can image a 7.5 km by 100 km land area per image, and provides detailed spectral mapping with high radiometric accuracy to map complex land eco-systems (Birk and McCord, 1994).

Airborne Visible/Infrared Imaging Spectrometer **(AVIRIS)** is another example of NASA's hyperspectral airborne sensor. For example, AVIRIS collects data in 224 contiguous channels with wavelengths from 0.4-2.5 μm. One of the drawbacks with hyperspectral images is that it adds a level of complexity to reduce the redundancy from 200 narrow bands to work with. Hyperspectral images have many real world applications, and give higher level of spectral detail and better capability to *see the unseen*. For example, hyperspectral imagery has been used in mineral exploration.

Hyperspectral imaging is being used in vegetation studies (species identification, plant stress, productivity, leaf water content, and canopy chemistry), soil science (type mapping and erosion status), geology (mineral identification and mapping) and hydrology (snow grain size, liquid/solid water differentiation). Lake, river and ocean applications include biochemical studies (photoplankton mapping, activity), and water quality (particulate and sediment mapping). Processing techniques generally identify the presence of materials through measurement of spectral absorption features. Often the hyperspectral data are post-processed to derive surface reflectance through the use of atmospheric radiative transfer models (Birk and McCord, 1994).

3.26 INTERPRETATION OF REMOTELY SENSED DATA

In order to take advantage of and make optimum use of remote sensing data, meaningful information can be extracted from the imagery. Interpretation and analysis of remote sensing imagery involves the identification and/or measurement of various objects in an image in order to extract useful information. Objects in an image may be present in the form of points, lines, or area features (Eastman, 1999).

Information from remote sensing can be derived using **manual interpretation** or **digital interpretation** methods (Figure 3.37). Visual interpretation of remote sensing images does not allow for full exploitation of the data characteristics. A human eye cannot interpret all spectral differences in imagery. Machine processing of imagery allows for the quantitative analysis of all spectral bands in imagery simultaneously, and is able to detect subtle differences that human eye cannot. Both the methods have their own merits. In some cases, a mix of both the methods may be employed when analyzing imagery. In fact, the ultimate decision of the utility and relevance of the information derived at the end of the analysis is to be made by human-beings.

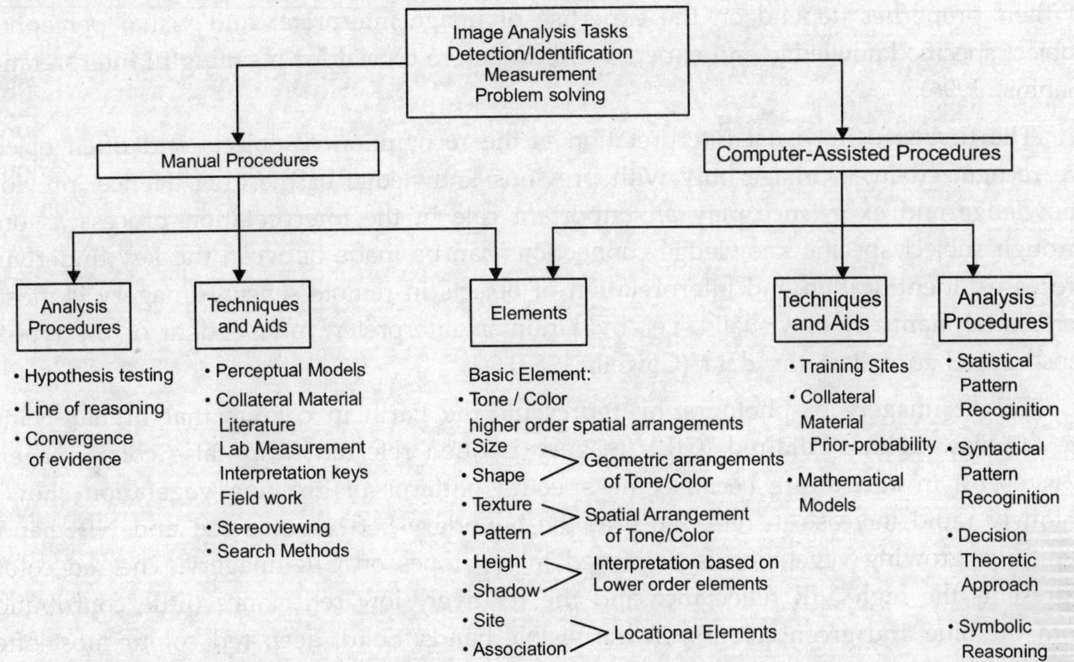

Figure 3.37. Interpretation methods and analysis procedure (*Source: Colwell, 1983*)

The interpreter must keep in mind that several features can change with time, and this can affect the appearance of the features recorded on the imagery. Some examples of dynamic situations are: (i) wetlands drying up, (ii) soil colour changing as it dries, (iii) crops growing and maturing, (iv) forest types, and (v) seasonal rivers. Additionally, the imagery is often collected under different atmospheric and sun angle conditions across a season, and will not show the same features exactly the way they were shown earlier. One way to verify it is to look at features that do not change in a short time, such as gravel roads or trees. If it is necessary, radiometric correction may be required to remove these apparent differences (Gibson, 2000).

Looking at familiar areas on the imagery is the best way of gaining experience in visual image interpretation. The interpreter can look at field changes i.e., temporal changes on the imagery within a season and across different years. Finally, image analysis is taken to the field in-hand for verification of accuracy of interpretation. Global positioning system (GPS) technology will be useful in field verification, particularly if a location grid is superimposed on the image.

3.27 VISUAL INTERPRETATION OF REMOTELY SENSED DATA

The visual interpretation of satellite images is a complex process. It includes recognition of objects and ascertaining their properties. The recognition of objects includes, such as roads, forest, agricultural fields, rivers, etc. The quality of recognition and determination of their properties depend on the expertise of image interpreter and visual perception. Subject specific knowledge and expertise are therefore crucial for meaningful interpretation (Sabins, 1996).

The first step in visual interpretation is the recognition of objects and often objects are recognized in an image only with previous knowledge of the area. Hence, previous knowledge and experience play an important role in the interpretation process as only through subject specific knowledge connections can be made between the key underlying processes. Identification and interpretation of objects in remote sensing imagery is mostly performed manually or visually, i.e., by a human interpreter, independent of the type of sensor used to collect the data (Cowell, 1983).

Colour imagery or photography represents the Earth in colours that human-beings are familiar. Colour Infra-red (CIR) imagery is often referred to as false color imagery. It is useful in agriculture because the spectral patterns of growing vegetation show a uniquely rapid increase in reflectance at the boundary between the red and NIR bands. Typically, growing vegetation is displayed in red tones on CIR imagery. The red colour represents the high NIR reflectance and the relatively low reflectance (little contribution from the blue and green colours) in the visible bands. Solid, deep red colour most often indicates healthy vegetation. The differences in the red tones within a field may be an indication of the variability in plant vigour, growth stage or plant population. Different crops will often appear in different shades of red colour depending on crop stage, vigour, wetness, weeds, etc. Since changes in reflectance of NIR region by plants is typically very sensitive, plant stress can often be detected.

Thermal imagery represents the apparent surface temperatures, which are in turn influenced by temperatures below the surface to a shallow depth. Moist soil will tend to be cooler than dry soil during the day. At night the opposite result occurs due to heat storage by the moist soil. Crop canopies are cool during the day because of evapotranspiration. Daytime rises in canopy temperature may indicate that some type of plant stress is happening, for example, moisture, disease, or insect problems. The spectral differences among different objects/surfaces are often subtle, whether at visible, NIR or thermal wavelengths, and will require field verification. Other times the spectral differences on the imagery will be clear, but there will be a need to visit the ground sites to determine what is represented by these differences. Once spectral pattern through ground observations are established, it is assumed that all similar signatures are probably the same within that image.

Visual interpretation is the best and convenient way to analyse the information from the imagery. This process utilizes the human brain and image characteristics to derive information through interpretation of remote sensing data. The strength of visual interpretation in remote sensing lies in efficiency of interpretation and extrapolation. The factors of visual interpretation are colour (or tone for black and white photos), texture, pattern, shape, size, shadow and location (Richards and Jia, 2013). Table 3.11 gives a summary of these interpretation elements. Tone is considered as the primary element, texture, size and shape are considered as the secondary elements, while pattern and shadow as tertiary and site and locations as lower order elements of interpretation (Figure 3.38).

Table 3.11: Quantitative and qualitative details of image interpretation elements

Element	Quantitative and Qualitative Details
Tone/ Color	**Grey tone**: light (bright), intermediate (gray), dark (black) **Color**: HIS = intensity, hue (color), saturation; RGB = red, green, blue
Texture	Characteristic placement of objects on the ground: systematic, random, linear, curvilinear, rectangular, circular, etc.
Pattern	Spatial arrangement of objects on the ground: systematic, random, linear, curvilinear, rectangular, circular, etc.
Shape	An object's geometric characteristics: linear, curvilinear, circular, elliptical, radial, square, rectangular, triangular, hexagonal, pentagonal, star, amorphous, etc.
Size	Length, width, perimeter, area (m^2) small, medium (intermediate), large
Shadow	Caused by solar illumination
Site/ Situation/ Association	**Site:** elevation, slope, aspect, exposure, adjacency to water, transportation, utilities **Situation**: objects are placed in a particular order or orientation relative to one another **Association**: related phenomena are usually present

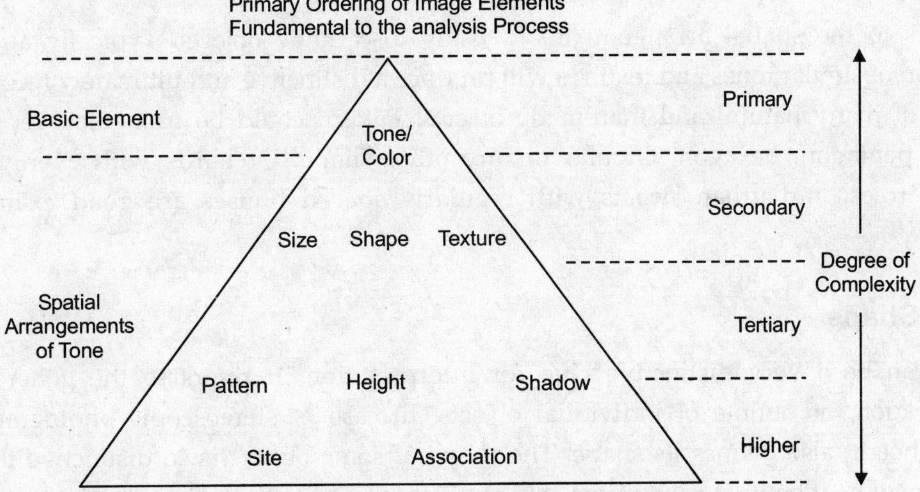

Figure 3.38: Image interpretation elements

(Source: https://www.e-education.psu.edu/geog160/node/1958)

3.26.1 Tone

It refers to the relative brightness or colour of objects on photographs/images. Generally, tone is the fundamental element for distinguishing between different objects or features. Variation in tone also allows the elements of shape, texture, and pattern of objects to be distinguished. Colour photography enables an interpreter to exploit differences in hue.

3.26.2 Texture

It is the arrangement and frequency of tonal variation in particular areas of an image. Texture is produced by an aggregation of unit features that may be too small to be discerned individually on the image, such as tree leaves. It is a product of their individual shape, size, pattern, shadow and tone. Texture is also one of the most important elements for distinguishing features from Radar images.

It determines the overall visual smoothness or coarseness of image features. As the scale of the image is reduced, the texture of any given object or area becomes progressively finer and ultimately disappears. An interpreter can often distinguish between features with similar reflectances based on their texture differences. An example would be the smooth texture of green grass as contrast with the rough texture of crowns of green trees on medium scale air-photos/images. Smooth textures would have very little tonal variation, e.g. fields, asphalt, or grasslands. Rough texture is found where the grey levels change abruptly in a small area, e.g. forest canopy. Sand has rough texture as compared to clay.

3.26.3 Pattern

It relates to the spatial arrangement of visibly discernible objects. Typically an orderly repetition of similar tones and textures will produce a distinctive and ultimately recognizable pattern of many natural and man-made objects. Pattern could be triangular, rectangular, square, pentagon, hexagon, circular or any other shape. Orchards with evenly spaced planted trees, and urban streets with regularly spaced houses are good examples of pattern.

3.26.4 Shape

Shape can be a very distinctive clue for interpretation. It refers to the general form, configuration, or outline of individual objects. In case of stereoscopic photographs, the object's height also defines its shape. The shape of some objects is so distinctive that their images may be identified solely from this criterion. Straight edge shapes typically represent urban or agricultural (field) targets, while natural features, such as forest boundary, lakes, are generally more irregular in shape. All shapes are not so distinct, but every shape has some significance to the interpreter.

3.26.5 Size

Size of objects in an image is a function of scale. It is important to assess the size of an object relative to other objects in a scene, as well as the absolute size. A quick approximation of target size can help in interpretation more quickly. For example, for zones of land use, large buildings such as factories or warehouses would suggest commercial property, whereas small buildings would indicate residential use. Relative sizes among objects on images of the same scale are also to be considered.

3.26.6 Shadow

Shadow is helpful in interpretation of images in two respects. Firstly, the shape or outline of a shadow gives an impression of the profile of objects which greatly aids in interpretation, and secondly the objects which cast shadow on the ground can be identified with respect to shape of the shadow. On the other hand, areas under shadow hinder the interpretation. For example, the shadows cast by various cultural features (bridges, silos, towers, etc.) can definitely aid in their identification on air-photos/images. In addition, the shadows resulting from even subtle variations in terrain elevations, especially in case of low sun angle photographs/images, can aid in assessing the natural topographic variations or geological landforms, particularly in Radar imagery.

3.26.7 Site/Association

It refers to topographic or geographic location, and is a particularly important clue in the identification of certain types of features. For example, certain tree species would be expected to occur on well-drained upland sites, whereas other tree species would be expected to occur on poorly drained lowland sites.

Association refers to the occurrence of certain features in relation to others. It takes into account the relationship between other recognizable objects or features in proximity to the object of interest. The features that one would expect to associate with other features may facilitate the identification. For example, the snow cover is related to higher elevation zones, commercial properties are associated with major transportation routes, and bridges are associated with rivers.

3.28 DIGITAL INTERPRETATION OF REMOTELY SENSED DATA

Like any raster image, remote sensing images consist of pixels. Raster images have a square grid like structure, where one square grid represents a pixel (i.e. the smallest element in a digital image). Each pixel is associated with a digital number in a particular wavelength of the electromagnetic spectrum. The pixel size defines its spatial resolution. Different satellites acquire data at different spatial resolutions in various wavelengths. Different types of features emit and reflect back different intensities of light, which is converted to digital numbers. Identification and separation of features with respect to their DNs in specific wavelength is called digital image processing (Jenson, 1986, Jain, 1989). A comparison between visual and digital methods of interpretation is given in Table 3.12.

Table 3.12: Visual interpretation versus digital image analysis

S.No.	Manual Interpretation	Digital Interpretation
1	Hard copy data are required.	Digital data are required
2	Requires simple and inexpensive equipment	Requires specialized, and often expensive equipment and software.
3	Limited to analyzing only a single channel of data or a single image at a time	Simultaneous interpretations of images with several wavelength.
4	It involves subjectivity. i.e., the results may vary with different interpreters.	It is an Objective process which is based on the utilisation of spectral signature of objects through a computer, so results are almost consistent.
5	Qualitative method	Quantitative method
6	Cost-effective for small areas and for one-time interpretation.	Cost-effective for large geographic areas, and for repetitive interpretations,
7	No algorithm is used	Possibility to explore alternatives with complex interpretation algorithms
8	Takes time	Speed may be an advantage
9	Output product is hard copy so not compatible with other data	Compatible with other digital data

The advantage of digital imagery is that it allows us to manipulate the digital pixel values in an image. The digital image processing is largely concerned with four basic operations: image pre-processing, image restoration, image enhancement, image transformation, and image classification (Eastman, 1999, Ricards and Jia, 2013).

3.29 IMAGE PRE-PROCESSING

The operation of image pre-processing involves the initial processing of raw image data to correct for geometric distortions, to calibrate the data radiometrically, and to eliminate the noise present in the data.

3.29.1 Geometric Correction

It is conversion of image to ground coordinates by removal of distortions caused by the sensor geometry. It enables mapping relative to data layers, mosaicking and scene comparison (e.g. change assessment). Raw remote sensing data contain distortions with no geographic coordinates, and therefore these are not as such useful for overlay with other map layers, or a comparison between image scenes. It has two steps-

3.29.1.1 Georeferencing

It is a process of locating an entity/object in real world coordinates, also called **geo-rectification** or **geo-registration**. It is required as the directions of satellite motion and on-board sensors while taking images is not exactly North-South or West-East respectively, so images are not perfect square but they have skewed shape. Georeferencing orients image to a known coordinate system, representing the Earth defined through projection systems so it can be viewed, compared, and analysed with other geographic data (Jenson, 1986, Richards and Jia, 2013). To georeference an image, the positions of known points, called **Ground Control Points (GCPs)**, are determined. The GCPs are normally selected as prominent objects whose geographical locations can be accurately determined either from the maps or GPS. At least four control points are required for georeferencing an image. Additional control points help increasing the accuracy. Once the image is georeferenced, each point on it has coordinates associated.

In brief, the process of georeferencing involves establishing the control points; inputs the known geographic coordinates of these control points, chooses the coordinate system and other projection parameters and then minimizes the root mean square (***rms***) error. The *rms* error is the difference between the actual coordinates of the control points and the coordinates predicted by the geographic model (polynomial) created using the control points. The accuracy of the georeferencing depends on the number, accuracy, and distribution of the control points and the choice of transformation model.

In image analysis, two or more images (at different scales) taken from various perspectives are merged into a common projection system. In this mathematical process, the geometry of an image is made planimetric. It involves the measurement of the image coordinates of selected GCPs on the reference map and the corresponding coordinates of the points on the other image (slave image) to correlate both with the real world. The coordinates of GCPs are measured on both the maps/images. The two sets of coordinates are used to solve a set of polynomial equations whose order would depend upon the amount of geometric distortion present in the raster image. Generally affine transformation is used for the purpose. As an example, Ist order transformation equations are given below:

$$X = ax + by + c \qquad ...(3.8)$$

$$Y = dx + ey + f \qquad ...(3.9)$$

Where X and Y are the coordinates from reference image/map, and, x and y are the coordinates from slave image. A minimum of three GCPs are required to solve these equations, though greater the GCPs more accurate would be the geo-referencing. In general, higher order of polynomial with more numbers of GCPs is preferred. Three GCPs would generate six equations. On solving the above equations, the values of the six (a, b, c, d, e and f) coefficients are determined. Any image coordinate can then be substituted in the equations to get the corresponding ground position on the used map coordinate system. The positions of the original grid cells will have to be interpolated in the mapping coordinate system.

The *rms* error is determined using the known coordinates of GCPs and computed coordinates of the same GCPs. This error should be within ± one pixel, to accept the results. If the value is higher, the GCPs selected which give higher *rms* error are to be modified/deleted/replaced. Again computation is [performed as above, till the threshold of ± one pixel *rms* error is achieved.

3.29.1.2 Resampling

After the coordinate transformation, the raster cells may have been oriented differently than the way they were originally in the raster coordinate system. The attribute value is to be interpolated for the cells oriented to the new coordinate system. This is called

resampling (Sabins, 1996, Richards and Jia, 2013). There are three common methods of resampling (Figure 3.39).

(a) Nearest Neighbour: In this method, the attribute value of the original cell nearest to a cell in the output raster layer is assigned to the corresponding cell.

(b) Bilinear Interpolation: It assigns the value to a cell in the output raster layer by taking weighted average of the surrounding four cells in the original grid nearest to it.

(c) Cubic Convolution: It assigns the value to a cell in the output raster layer by taking weighted average of the surrounding sixteen cells in the original grid nearest to it.

Among these three methods, the nearest neighbour is a preferred method as it doesn't change the values of the original grid cells assigned to the resampled grid cells but it produces a blocky image. The cubic convolution on the other side does change the values and more accurate but it generates a smoother image. The result of an image to map rectification is a geometrically correct grid of raster cells.

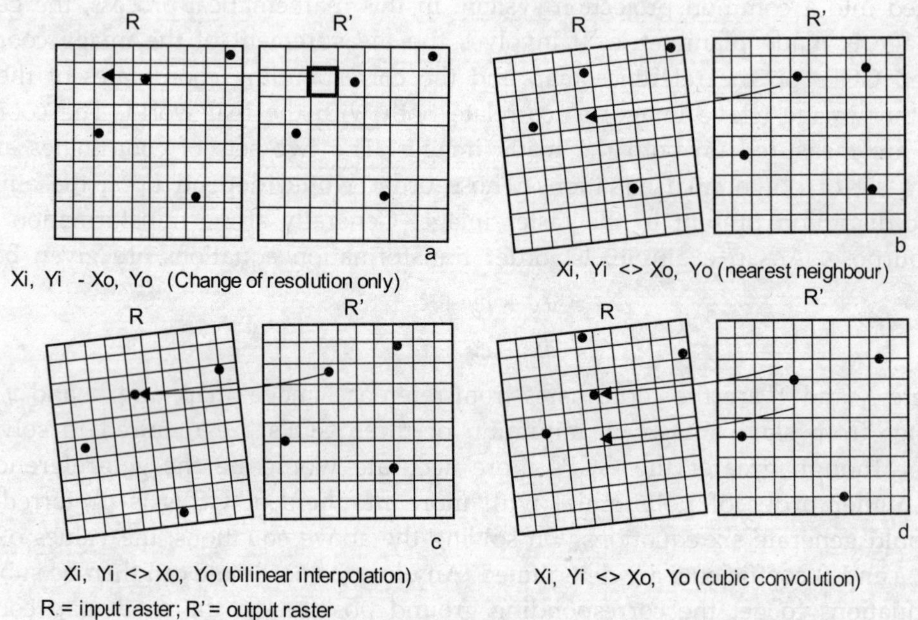

Figure 3.39. Resampling methods (*Source: Antrop and De Maeyer, 2005*)

3.29.2 Radiometric Correction

It involves removal of sensor or atmospheric 'noise', to more accurately represent the ground conditions. Radiometric correction is required to (i) improve variations within an image, (ii) correct for data loss, (iii) remove haze, (iv) create mosaicking, and (v) compare multi-bands and temporal images. Radiometric correction is done to modify DN values to account for noise, i.e. contributions to the DN that are a result of the intervening atmosphere and the sun-sensor geometry (Jain, 1989, Eastman, 1999).

(a) Atmospheric haze correction

Lower wavelengths are more subject to haze, which falsely increases the DN values. The simplest method for its correction is known as dark object subtraction method which assumes that in case of no haze, pixel will have zero DN value, e.g. deep water in near infrared will have complete absorption, and therefore those pixels will have zero DN values. For such image, lowest DN value is determined, and that is subtracted from all DN values in the image so that dark (water) pixel becomes zero.

(b) Cloud Removal

Clouds affect all visible and IR bands, hiding features twice: once with the cloud, another with its shadow. Clouds cannot be completely eliminated, although images can be corrected for cloud shadows by applying some advanced algorithms. If there are clouds in the image, it can be removed by creating a mosaic with another overlapping image.

(c) Reflectance to Radiance Conversion

DN reflectance values can be converted to absolute radiance values (*L*). This is useful when comparing the actual reflectance from different sensors e.g. TM and SPOT, or TM versus ETM (Landsat 5 versus 7), as below:

$$DN = a\,L + b \quad ...(3.10)$$

where a = gain and b = offset

The radiance value (*L*) can be calculated as:

$$L = [L_{max} - L_{min}]*(DN/255) + L_{min} \quad ...(3.11)$$

where L_{max} and L_{min} are known values from the sensor calibration (given in the Handbook of that satellite or supplied by the agency who designed the sensor).

3.30 IMAGE RESTORATION

The purpose of image restoration is to restore a degraded image to its original form. It is an objective process. For image restoration, a priori knowledge of the degradation is used, degradation is modelled, and the inverse process is applied (Jain, 1989, Castleman, 1996). Image degradation occurs in many forms, such as motion blur, noise, and camera shaken or not focussed. In motion blur, it is possible to come up with a good estimate of the actual blurring function and then "undo" the blur to restore the original image. To reduce the motion blur, one can also reduce the exposure time. If the image is corrupted by noise, it is compensated for the degradation.

There are many techniques to restore the degradation for the image; Mean/median filtering, Adaptive filtering, Homomorphic Filtering, Inverse and pseudo-inverse filtering, Wiener filtering, Blind deconvolution, Wavelet restoration etc (Jain, 1989). Inverse filtering is an easy and accurate way to restore an image provided no noise is present in the image. An inverse filter is a high pass filter, therefore it tends to amplify the noise. Wiener filter is more robust to noise, and preserves high-frequency details. Wiener filtering is the optimal trade-off between the inverse filtering and noise smoothing. It can be interpreted as an inverse filtering step followed by a noise attenuation step. Since the Wiener filtering contains the inverse filtering step, it amplifies the noise when the blurring filter is not invertible. To remove the amplified noise, wavelet thresholding is the best approach. In the blind deconvolution, images can be restored without having specific knowledge of degradation filter, or additive noise. All the homomorphic blind deconvolution techniques require iterations through either breaking up the degraded image or using multiple degraded images for estimation.

3.31 IMAGE ENHANCEMENT

The Image enhancement is predominantly concerned with the improvement of quality of images to optimise their appearance to the visual system. Although prior to distribution of data to the users, radiometric corrections for illumination, and atmospheric influences might have been applied, but the image may not still give the optimum contrast for visual interpretation. There is no generic algorithm available which could be universally applied for radiometric correction to produce the optimum brightness and contrast from a diverse range of objects (e.g. forest, deserts, snow, urban, water, etc.) present in the images. Enhancement of an image can be implemented by using different methods, and there is no general theory for determining the 'good' image enhancement, when it comes to human vision (Castleman, 1996). Thus, a custom adjustment of the range and distribution of brightness values is usually done individually for each image.

Enhancements are made to make visual interpretation and understanding of imagery easier. Enhancement is the modification of images to improve the interpretability through human vision. Visual inspection and analysis play a very strong role in all aspects of remote sensing. Image enhancement is the technique to improve the image quality so that the resultant image is better than the original image for a specific application. The main purpose of image enhancement is to bring out the details that are hidden in an image or to increase the contrast in a low contrast image. It does not add any additional information to the original image but it enhances the visual appearances of already captured features. Image enhancement can be done by improving the contrast and removing the noise or blurness from the image. It is necessary to understand the image characteristics through its histogram before doing the enhancement.

Various enhancement techniques manipulate the range of digital values in an image, graphically represented by its histogram.

3.31.1 Contrast Enhancement

Contrast is related to the color and brightness. The contrast is defined as the difference in color or intensity between two objects in an image. If the contrast is too low, it is impossible to distinguish between two objects and they are perceived as the same object. The contrast enhancement can be better understood by using the concept of an **image histogram**. Contrast enhancement involves changing the original values so that more available range is used, thereby increasing the contrast between objects and their backgrounds. Contrast enhancement is basically improving the interpretability for human viewers and providing 'better' input for automated image processing techniques (Richards and Jia, 2013).

There are many different techniques and methods of enhancing the contrast and details in an image. The contrast can be enhanced by either using linear or non-linear methods.

3.31.1.1 Linear contrast enhancement

The simplest type of enhancement is a **linear contrast stretch which** involves identifying the minimum and maximum brightness values in the image, and applying a linear transformation to stretch this range to occupy the full range (0-255). For example, the minimum value (occupied by actual data) in the histogram is 84 and the maximum value is 153. These 70 levels occupy less than one-third of the full 256 levels available. A linear stretch uniformly expands this small range to cover the full range of values from 0 to 255. This enhances the contrast in the image with light toned areas appearing lighter and dark areas appearing darker, making visual interpretation much easier. This graphic illustrates the increase in contrast in an image before (left) and after (right) a linear contrast stretch (Figure 3.40).

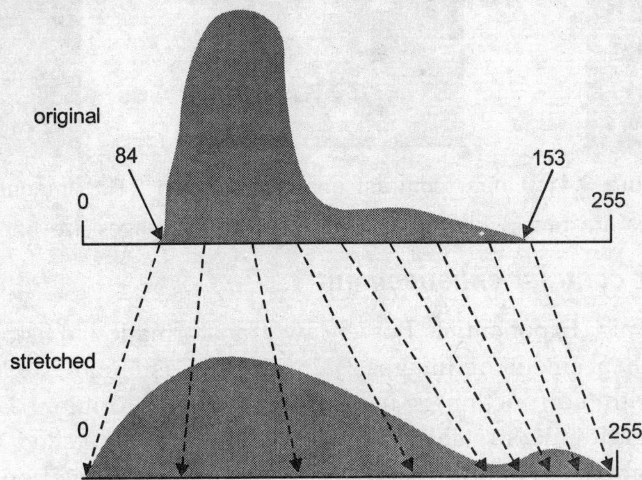

Figure 3.40: Histogram original (above) and after linear contrast enhancement (bottom)

(*Source: https://www.nrcan.gc.ca/earth-sciences/geomatics/satellite-imagery-air-photos/satellite-imagery-products/educational-resources/9389*)

Linear contrast enhancement, also known as contrast stretching, expands the original digital values of the remotely sensed data linearly into a new range. By expanding the original input values of the image, the total range of DN values can be utilized (Jenson, 1986, Jain, 1989). These types of enhancements are best applied to remotely sensed images with Gaussian type histograms, where all the brightness values fall within a narrow range of the histogram. There are three methods of linear contrast enhancement: (i) Minimum--Maximum Linear Contrast Stretch, (ii) Percentage Linear Contrast Stretch, and (iii) Piecewise Linear Contrast Stretch.

$$DN_{out} = ((DN_{in} - DN_{min})/(DN_{max} - DN_{min}))\text{*No. of grey levels} \quad ...(3.12)$$

Where, DN_{out} represents the output values in the image, while DN_{in} represents the DN value at that pixel location from input image. In this equation the "DN_{min}" and "DN_{max}" are the minimum and maximum DN value, respectively, in the input image. Here "No. of grey levels" shows the total number of intensity values that can be assigned to a pixel. For example, in 8 bit images, the maximum number of grey levels is 255. Figure 3.41 shows the results of linear contrast enhancement on Landsat ETM+ images.

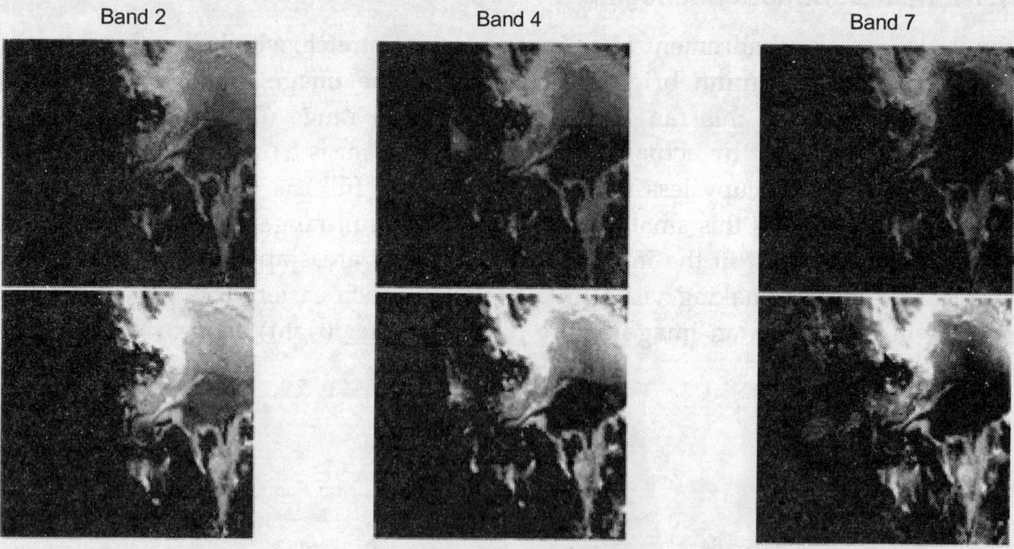

Figure 3.41: Linear contrast enhancement on ETM+ images.
(Top three images are raw, while bottom corresponding images are linearly enhanced)

3.31.1.2 Non-linear contrast enhancement

It includes Logarithmic, Exponential, Power-law transformation, Histogram Equalisation method etc., for enhancement of images (Jain, 1989, Castleman, 1996). In logarithmic stretching, the logarithmic function is used for scaling the original DN levels into the output range. In logarithmic stretching, smaller values are stretched to a wider range. This type of stretching is generally used to enhance the information contained in the darker pixels, during which process the information contained in the brighter pixels are compressed. Figure 3.42 shows the performance of logarithmic contrast enhancement applied to a retinal fundus image with their blood vessel segmentation outputs. General form of logarithmic stretching uses the following form.

$$DN_{out} = a \log_e (b^*DN_{in}) \quad ...(3.13)$$

where a and b are constants, and Dn_{in} is the input DN value from original image.

Application of exponential function stretches the image in an opposite way. It enhances the brighter pixels, while whilst decreasing the dynamic range in low value regions (dark). The equation used could be in the following form.

$$DN_{out} = a\, e^{\,b^*DNin} \quad ...(3.14)$$

where a and b are constants, Dn_{in} is the input DN value from original image.

Power-law transformations is an alternative to both the logarithmic and exponential transforms. It is the "raise to a power" in which each input pixel value is raised to a fixed power:

$$DN_{out} = a\,(DN_{in})^{\,b} \quad ...(3.15)$$

Where a and b are constants, if value of $b > 1$, it enhances the contrast of high-value portions of the image at the expense of low-value regions, whilst for $b < 1$, the effect is reverse. This gives the power-law transform properties similar to both the logarithmic ($\gamma < 1$) and exponential ($\gamma > 1$) transforms.

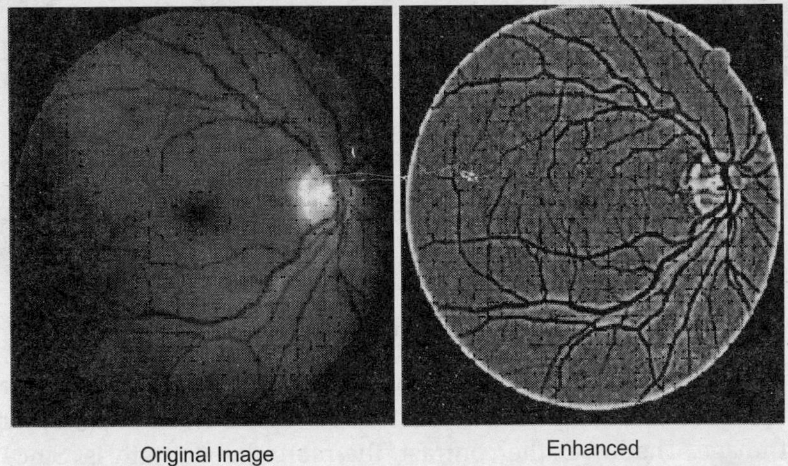

Figure 3.42: Logarithmic contrast enhancement applied to a retinal fundus image (*Source: https://www.codeproject.com/Articles/1203383/A-Fast-Simple-and-Powerful-Contrast-Enhancement-Al*)

3.31.1.3 Histogram equalization

Histogram equalization (**HE**) is the most popular non-linear algorithm for contrast enhancement due to its effectiveness and simplicity. A uniform distribution of the full input range of values across may not always be an ideal enhancement. In such cases, a **histogram-equalized approach** may give better results. Figure 3.43 shows the original image (left), and after histogram equalisation (right). This approach assigns more display values (range) to the frequently occurring portions of the histogram. In this way, the detail in these areas will be better enhanced relative to those areas of the original histogram where values occur less frequently. It accomplishes this by effectively spreading out the most frequent intensity values, i.e. stretching out the intensity range of the image. This method usually increases the global contrast of images when its usable data is represented by close contrast values. This allows for areas of lower local contrast to gain a higher contrast (Jain, 1989).

Histogram equalization transforms the gray levels of an image to a uniform histogram based on the probability of occurring gray levels in an input image. HE is one of the most useful forms of non-linear contrast enhancement. When a histogram of image is equalized, all pixel values of the image are redistributed such that there are approximately an equal number of pixels to each of the user-specified output gray-scale classes.

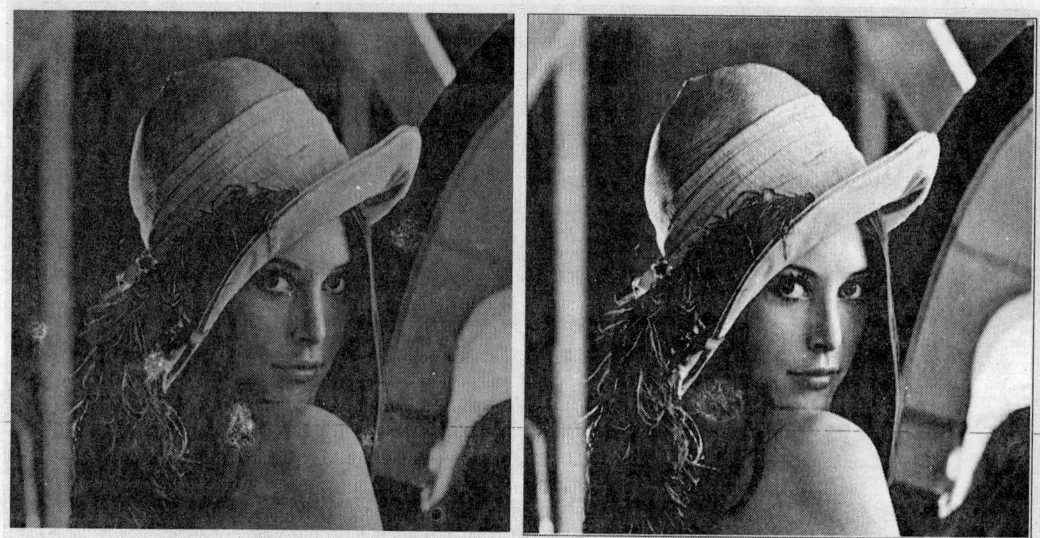

Figure 3.43: Original image (left), and after histogram equalisation (right) *(Source: Li, 2009)*

In general, by HE method it will flatten out the probability distribution of an image and increase its dynamical range. However, the strength of HE depends on the contrast of the original image. The lower the contrast, the more the strength is. Since its simplicity makes it easy to implement, it is usually applied in many areas, including texture synthesis, medical image processing and speech recognition. An advantage of this method is that it is a fairly straightforward technique and an invertible operator. So in theory, if the HE function is known then the original histogram can be recovered. A disadvantage of the method is that it is a general method. It will increase the contrast of background noise, while decreasing the usable signal (Richards and Jia, 2013).

3.32 IMAGE TRANSFORMATIONS

The image transformation refers to the derivation of new imagery as a result of some mathematical treatment of the raw image bands. It involves the transformation of images to get the additional synthetic images. Some examples of transformations are simple arithmetic operations, Vegetation Indices **(VI)**, Normalised Difference Vegetation Index **(NDVI)**, Principal Component Analysis **(PCA)** and Tasselled Cap Transformations **(TCT)** which could be used for creation of additional images, and alongwith the original raw images for the analysis and classification (Castleman, 1996, Gibson, 2000, Richards and Jia, 2013). With the availability of images from various sensors at different resolutions, it has become necessary to combine the images from two or more sensors to get the new image having optimum information content. This transformation, called image fusion, is also being used frequently in remote sensing data analysis.

3.32.1 Image Fusion

Data fusion approach combines the data from multiple sources to improve the interpretation performances and accuracy of the input images. It produces a high-quality visible representation of the images, and therefore it may be considered as image enhancement technique (Welch and Ehlers, 1987). Remote sensing data fusion is one of the most commonly used techniques, which aims to integrate the images acquired from sensors with different spatial and spectral resolutions to produce fused images that contain more detailed information than each of the input images. Fusion techniques are also used for a variety of applications; object detection, recognition, identification and classification, object tracking, change detection, computer vision, medical image analysis and defence security, etc.

Data fusion involves two major steps: (i) geometrical registration of two datasets, and (ii) mixture of spectral and spatial information contents to generate a new dataset that contains the enhanced information from both datasets. Registration between the two datasets is required to be done for extracting the information contents from both datasets, especially line features, such as roads and rivers. Radiometric and atmospheric calibrations are also needed to merge multi-sensor data (Lu and Weng, 2007).

Remote sensing based fusion techniques can be classified into three different levels; pixel/data level, feature level and the decision level (Pohl and Van Genderen. 1998). Pixel level fusion is the combination of raw data from multiple sources into single resolution data, which are expected to be more informative than either of the input data. Feature level fusion extracts various features, e.g. edges, corners, lines, texture parameters, etc., from different data sources and then combines them into one or more images that may be used instead of the original image that may be used for image segmentation or change detection. This is particularly important when the number of available spectral bands is large and it is impossible to analyse each band separately. Decision level fusion combines the results from multiple algorithms to yield a final fused decision. Methods of decision fusion include voting methods, statistical methods and fuzzy logic-based methods.

Pohl and Van Genderen (1988) provided a good review of literature on various methods of multi-sensor data fusion. Various methods, including colour related techniques (e.g. colour composite, intensity hue saturation or IHS, and luminance chrominance), statistical/numerical methods (e.g. arithmetic combination, principal component analysis, high pass filtering, regression variable substitution, canonical variable substitution, component substitution, and wavelets), were examined. IHS transformation was identified to be the most frequently used method for improving the visual display of multi-sensor data (Welch and Ehlers 1987), but the IHS approach can only employ three image bands, and the resultant image may not be suitable for further quantitative analysis such as classification. Principal component analysis is often used for data fusion because it can produce an output that can better preserve the spectral integrity of the input dataset.

The pixel level fusion methods are mainly applied to optical images, e.g., panchromatic (PAN) and multi-spectral images. High-level fusion includes feature level and decision level fusion of multi-source data, such as synthetic aperture radar (SAR), optical images, LiDAR, geographic information systems (GIS) data and ground data. Fusion of SAR and optical imagery has been applied to topography mapping, fused interferometric SAR and optical imagery to DEM extraction and fused optical and polarimetric SAR images for digital line graphics production. Fusion of LiDAR data and imagery has also been widely adopted for a variety of applications, ranging from DEM generation, 3D object extraction and modelling, and land cover mapping.

3.32.2 Vegetation Indices

Vegetation indices, for example, VI and NDVI images have been very frequently used world-wide for the study of forest cover, vegetation and crop classifications (Jenson, 1986, Gibson, 2000, Richards and Jia, 2013). Different bands of a multispectral image may be combined to highlight the vegetated areas. One such popular combination is the ratio of the near-infrared band to the red band, which is known as the Vegetation Index (VI)–

$$VI = NIR / Red \quad ...(3.16)$$

If both the Red and NIR bands (or the VIS and NIR) have similar reflectance, the value of Ratio is 1 or close to 1. Ratio values for bare soils generally are near 1; as the amount of green vegetation increases, the Ratio increases. The value of Ratio can increase far beyond 1 upto 30.

Most popular and commonly used vegetation index is Normalized Vegetation Difference Index **(NDVI)**. The NDVI is a measure of the vegetative cover on the land surface, but it also identifies water and soil. Vegetation differs from other land surface features because it tends to absorb strongly red wavelengths of sunlight and reflect in the near-infrared wavelengths. It is a measure of the difference in reflectance between these wavelength ranges. It is computed as-

$$NDVI = (NIR - Red) / (NIR + Red) \quad ...(3.17)$$

The NDVI values range between -1 and 1, with values 0.5 indicating dense vegetation and values < 0 indicates no vegetation. Since vegetation has high NIR reflectance but low red reflectance, vegetated areas will have higher values as compared to non-vegetated areas. Computation of NDVI values is shown in Figure 3.44. Stressed vegetation has low NDVI value (0.14) as compared to healthy vegetation (0.72), and this property helps in discrimination of different types of vegetation.

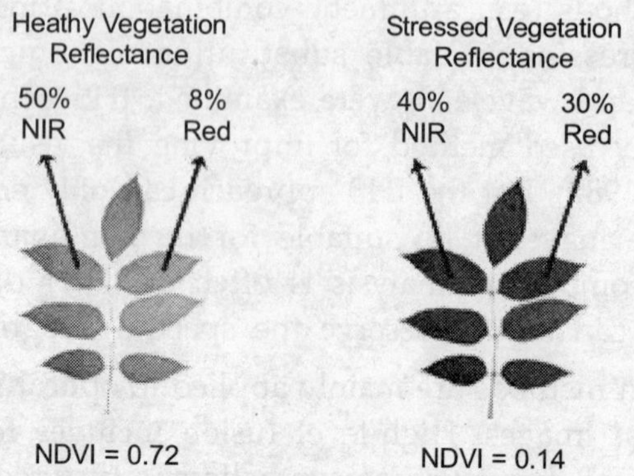

Figure 3.44: Computation of NDVI values (*Source: Perotti et.al. 2015*)

Many factors affect NDVI values, like plant photosynthetic activity, total plant cover, biomass, plant and soil moisture, and plant stress. Because of this, NDVI is correlated with many ecosystem attributes (e.g., net primary productivity, canopy cover, bare ground cover). Due to ratio of two bands, NDVI helps compensate for differences both in illumination within an image due to slope & aspect, and differences between images due to time of day or season when the images were acquired. Thus, NDVI makes it possible to compare images over time to study ecologically changes.

NDVI has an extremely wide range of applications. It is used to monitor vegetation condition, vegetation health, cover and phenology (life cycle stage) over large areas, and therefore can provide early warning on droughts and famines. Healthy vegetation (left) absorbs most of the visible light that hits it, and reflects a large portion of near-infrared light. Unhealthy or sparse vegetation (right) reflects more visible light and less near-infrared light.

3.31.3 Tasseled Cap Transformation

The tasseled cap transformation **(TCT)** was devised by R.J. Kauth and G.S. Thomas in 1976 based on a spectral analysis of the growth of wheat in fields. These researchers provided the rationale for Landsat MSS data from croplands as a function of the life cycle of the crop. In a real wheat field, there will be a distribution of the readings for bare soil along a ellipsoid as a result of variations in soil types and land angle relative to the sun angle. With growing wheat, there will be variation in the life cycle among the wheat plants. The transformation got it's name from the way that a graph looked (Figure 3.45) when the red band values of pixels were plotted against the near infra-red pixel values. The tasseled-cap transformation coefficients were defined against this graph to maximize the separation of the different growth stages of wheat. Thus the plot of the data for a wheat field resembles with a cap as shown in Figure 3.45, which is the basis of work of Kauth and Thomas.

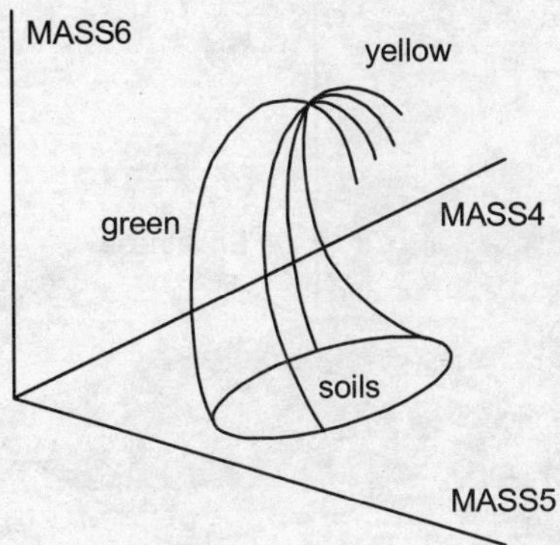

Figure 3.45: The graph between red and infrared bands to depict tasselled cap transformation (*Source: Kauth and Thomas, 1976*)

The tasseled-cap transformation is a conversion of the original bands of an image into a new set of bands that are useful for vegetation mapping. Originally constructed for understanding important phenomena of crop development in spectral space (Kauth and Thomas 1976), the transformation has potential applications in revealing key forest attributes including species, age and structure (e.g. Cohen et al. 1995). A tasseled-cap transform is performed by taking "linear combinations" of the original image bands - similar in concept to principal components analysis. It is the conversion of the DN values in various bands into composite values; i.e., the weighted sums (Chavez and Mackinnon, 1994). One component of their transformation is the weighted sum where the weights are statistically derived. Later analyses simplified the transformation to be the sum of the channel readings and called as "brightness." The second component is perpendicular to the first and its axis passes through the point of maturity of the plants, called as Greenness. The second tasseled-cap component "greenness" is typically used as an index of photosynthetically-active vegetation. The third component corresponds to an axis perpendicular to the first and second and passing through the point which represents "wetness" (e.g., soil or surface moisture) or "yellowness" (e.g., amount of dead/dried vegetation). These three components are shown in Figure 3.46. The fourth component represents the projection onto an axis perpendicular to other three, called as "non-such", and treated as random noise.

Brightness is defined in the direction of soil reflectance variation. It is obtained from a weighted sum of all bands. i.e., urbanized and bare soil areas. Greenness is defined in the direction of vegetation reflectance variation. It is obtained from the contrast of the visible bands (high absorption) with the infrared bands (high reflectance), i.e. the greater the biomass, the brighter the pixel value in the image (Cohen et al 1995). Wetness concerns the moisture status of the environment (soil & plant moisture). It is obtained from the contrast of the sum of visible and near-infrared with the sum of longer-infrared bands, i.e. water bodies are very bright. Greater the moisture content, brighter the response.

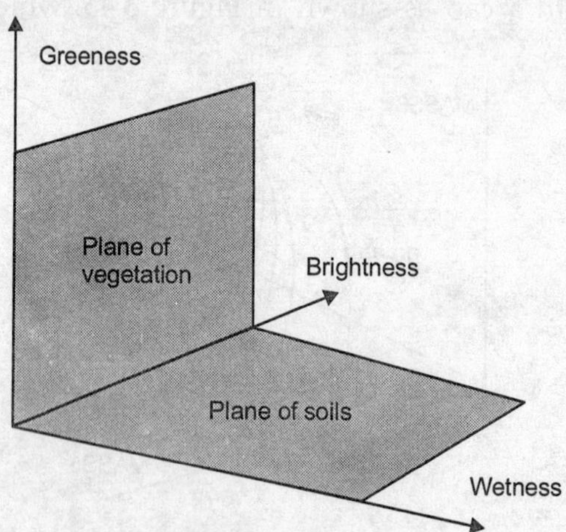

Figure 3.46: Representation of Greenness, Brightness and Wetness components on three axes.

Each tasseled-cap transformation is created by the summation of DN value of image band 1 times a constant plus DN value of image band 2 times a constant, and so on. The constants are like weights to create the tasseled-cap transformations which are derived statistically from images and empirical observations and are specific to each imaging sensor. The weights used by Kauth and Thomas for the tasseled cap transformation of Landsat MSS data are shown in Table 3.13.

A tasseled-cap transformation produces the same number of output components (Four) as input bands, but not all of the tasseled-cap components may be useful. The first tasseled cap contains the most information from the image and each subsequent component contains less of the original image information. Generally, the first three tasseled-cap components contain useful information and the fourth contains much of the image's "noise" and are not used.

Table 3.13: Coefficients for tasseled cap transformation of Landsat MSS and TM data

Weights for Landsat MSS Data						
Component	**Channel 1**	**Channel 2**	**Channel 3**	**Channel 4**	**Channel 5**	**Channel 7**
Brightness	0.433	0.632	0.586	0.264		
Greenness	-0.290	-0.562	0.600	0.491		
Yellowness	-0.829	0.522	-0.039	0.194		
"Non-such"	0.223	0.012	-0.543	0.810		
Weights for Landsat Thematic Mapper Data						
Brightness	0.3037	0.2793	0.4343	0.5585	0.5082	0.1863
Greenness	-0.2848	-0.2435	-0.5436	0.7243	0.0840	-0.1800
Wetness	0.1509	0.1793	0.3299	0.3406	-0.7112	-0.4572

Crist and Cicone (1984) adapted the tasseled cap transformation to the six channels of Landsat TM data. The weights are different and the third component was taken to represent soil wetness rather than yellowness as in Kauth and Thomas' original formulation. The weights found by Crist and Cicone for TM bands are given in Table 3.13.

3.32.4 Principal Component Analysis

The Principal Component Analysis **(PCA)** is a statistical technique used to reduce a set of correlated multivariate measurements to a smaller set where the features are uncorrelated to each other. The advent of multispectral and hyperspectral images in digital format has brought a new dimension in inventory, mapping and monitoring natural resources of the Earth. The techniques of PCA have been incorporated as a special transformation in digital image processing of satellite images where a number of correlated bands of the image data have been reduced to few uncorrelated bands. Two bands data from a sensor may be similar and convey essentially the same information. PCA therefore is a popular dimensionality reduction technique (i.e., compress the information contained in an original n-channel data set into fewer than n "new" channels or components) extensively used in studies, like change detection, image enhancement etc. (Jensen, 1986; Fung and LeDrew, 1987; Muchoney and Haack, 1994).

It is a linear transformation applied on highly correlated multidimensional (e.g. multispectral) data to reduce the dimensionality of the original bands and to maximize the amount of information from these original bands into the least number of principal components. Also, to save on data storage space and computing time, such bands could be combined into new, less correlated eigen images by PCA.

The power of PCA is that it creates a new dataset with only the essential information which is aggregated into groups called "**principal components**". Correlated original bands are transformed into uncorrelated principal components (in decreasing order) which contain the maximum original information (90%). Typically, the first few components contain most of the information in the data, so four bands of Landsat MSS data or six bands of the Thematic Mapper data may be reduced to just three principal components (called PC-1, PC-2, and PC-3). The components higher than three are usually treated as being noise without information. The first three principal components can also be used to create a false color composite (FCC) where the ground features are enhanced for visual interpretation. The FCC image may effectively be used as a base for ground truth collection in supervised classification of land use and land cover, or geologic interpretation etc. PCA has also been widely used in pattern recognition and remote sensing application, which mathematically establishes a new set of variables, describing the variance in the original data set. The principal component is also useful in providing maximum visual separability of image features. Therefore, principal component analysis can effectively be used in image classification to improve the accuracy of classification.

Principal component analysis is equivalent to transforming the data to a new coordinate system with a new set of orthogonal axes, like the tasseled cap transformation. Principal component analysis creates new variables as weighted sums of the different bands data. The weights used in principal component analysis are determined statistically and mathematically from the data. PCA translates the original axes to a new set of axes, with each axis orthogonal to the others Ist axis or PC is associated with the maximum amount of variance (the ellipsoid's major axis) 2nd axis (orthogonal to the 1st) contains the next highest amount of variation (Figure 3.47) and so on.

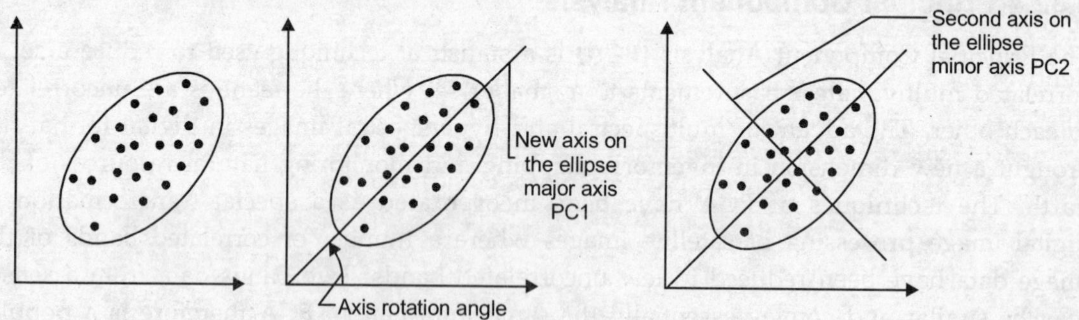

Figure 3.47: PC1 and PC2 components

The step by step procedure to compute the PC images is very well explained in *http://www.cs.otago.ac.nz/cosc453/student_tutorials/principal_components.pdf*. Matrix algebra used in PCA is computed from the covariance matrix. Eigenvector provides the direction of the new axes, and eigenvalues provide the length of the new axes. The basic steps of the transformation are: (i) organizing a dataset in a matrix, (ii) data centring (i.e. subtracting the dimensions means from themselves so each of the dimensions in the dataset has zero mean), (iii) calculate the covariance matrix (non-standardised PCA) or the correlation matrix (standardised PCA, also known as scaling), (iv) calculate either the eigenvectors and eigenvalues of the covariance (or the correlation) matrix, (v) sort variances in decreasing order (decreasing eigenvalues; this is default in eigenvalue analysis), and (vi) project original dataset signals (PC's or PC scores: eigenvector * input-data) to get PC images.

3.33 DIGITAL INTERPRETATION OF REMOTELY SENSED DATA

The image classification refers to computer-assisted interpretation of images. Image classification is a crucial and challenging task in various application domains, including biomedical imaging, video-surveillance, biometry, industrial visual inspection, robot navigation, and vehicle navigation. Digital image classification is a software based classification technique which involves automated information extraction based on identified spectral signature of cluster of pixels, and subsequently identifying the pixels with similar spectral signatures in the remote sensing image. It is the process of assigning a pixel (or groups of pixels) of an image to a land use or land cover class. Anderson et al (1976) have proposed the landuse and land cover classification scheme from remote sensing images. This scheme provides four levels of classification depending on the resolution and scale of remote sensing data, and is most widely used world-wide.

The objective of image classification is to categorise each pixel into at least one of the classes. There are statistical decision rules which are used to group the pixels in different feature classes (Castleman, 1996).

There are broadly two classification techniques; supervised and unsupervised classification. Both approaches of classification have their strengths and weaknesses associated with the classification process and results of the analysis. It is important to understand, however, that no particular classification method is inherently superior to any other (Jensen 2007). However, classifying a remotely sensed data into a thematic map is still a cumbersome job because of the landscape complexity, resolution of the image, and processing & classification approaches. Several steps are to be performed which include identification of suitable classification system, choosing appropriate training samples, processing of an image and extracting its features, applying a right classification method, post-classification and accuracy assessment.

3.33.1 Supervised Classification

Supervised classification has three distinct stages; namely training, allocation and testing. Training is the identification of a sample of pixels of known classes gathered from reference data, such as field visits, existing maps and aerial photographs. In supervised classification, an analyst uses previously acquired knowledge of an area, or a priori knowledge, to locate specific areas, or training sites, which represent homogeneous samples of known land use and/or land cover types. Based on statistics of these training sites, each pixel in an image is then assigned to a user-defined land use type (residential, industrial, agriculture, etc.) or land cover type (forest, grassland, paved surface, etc.) (Richards and Jia, 2013). The flow diagram in Figure 3.48 shows the procedure used (right diagram) in supervised classification.

In the second stage, the training pixels are used to derive various statistics for each class, and are correspondingly assigned signatures. In the third stage, the other pixels of the image are allocated to the same class with which they show greatest similarity based on the established signature files.

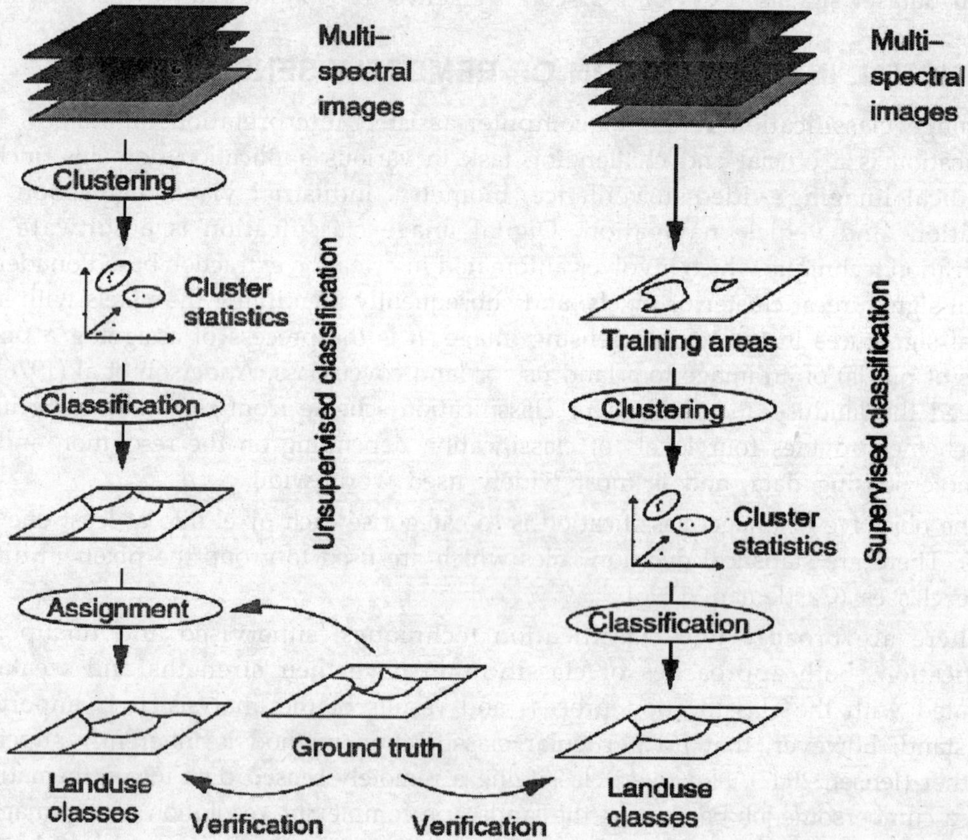

Figure 3.48: Steps used in supervised (right) and unsupervised (left) classification techniques

In a **supervised classification**, the analyst identifies homogeneous representative samples of different land use and land cover types (information classes) of interest in the imagery. The classification technique requires the training data set in order to teach the classifier to define the decision boundary. Information classes imply the actual land cover of the area under consideration which the analyst wants to classify, like vegetation cover, urban or water bodies (Figure 3.49). These samples are referred to as **training areas or samples which are** then used to extract statistical description of the reflectance of information for each class, which is known as **'Signature Analysis'**. There are two types of signatures; (i) **Parametric signature** - that is based on statistical parameters (e.g., mean) of the pixels that are in the training area (normal distribution assumption), and (ii) **Non-parametric signature -** that is not based on statistics, but on discrete objects (polygons or rectangles) in a feature space image.

Training process helps in assemblage of statistical parameters which describe the spectral response pattern for the information classes that are being considered for image classification. Thus, a sufficient number of homogeneous training sites for each class to represent the tonal variation present within each class in the image are required. The variation in spectral reflectances of a training set per class in multispectral bands is used to generate the statistics. It is important that the training sites be well distributed throughout the image, as far possible, as they become representative samples for the entire image, and also increase the chance to incorporate the site specific variations of that class in the training data.

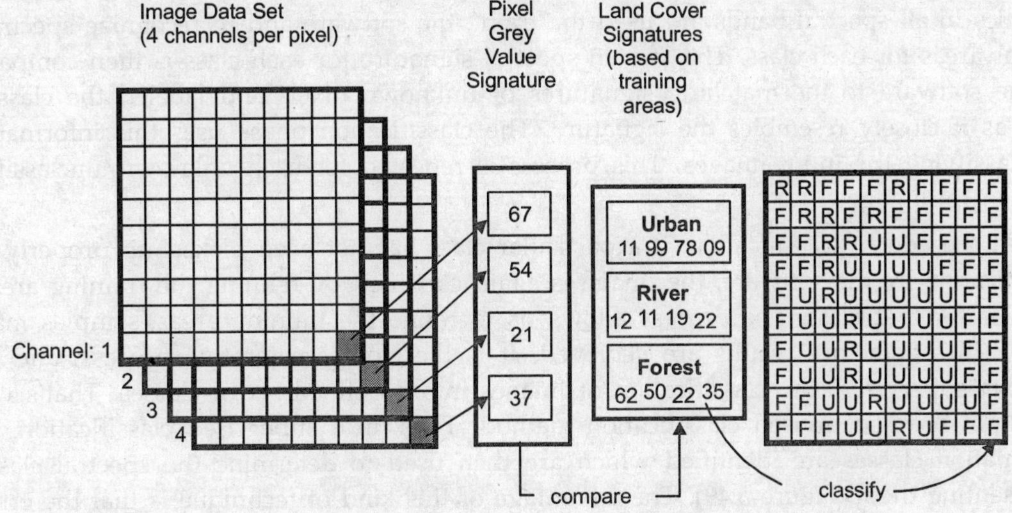

Figure 3.49: Steps in supervised classification

(*Source: http://www.sc.chula.ac.th/courseware/2309507/Lecture/remote18.htm*)

A histogram for each band of the training areas/samples can be drawn. The normal histogram with a single peak would indicate a single class but a bimodal response could point out to a sub-class present in the class. Thus, the classification accuracy may be improved if each of the class has one single peak in the histogram.

One of the important points in supervised classification is to avoid overlap in the training spectra for each class through the spectral plot. It is therefore easier to identify the combination of bands that might be best for discrimination through scatter plots for each class between any two spectral bands. The scatter plots provide with spectral separability. The training sample size varies from a minimum of 10*N* -100*N* per class, where *N* is the number of bands. Selection of sampling method is also very crucial for collection of training sample data and then using it for classification of entire image. Random sampling method, however, is the most popular approach, but other approaches of sampling have also been used (Section 3.34). Once the statistical characteristics are computed for each information class, the image is classified using any method, like Parallelepiped Classifier, Minimum distance classifier or Maximum likelihood classifier.

Training sites developed in one scene may or may not be replicable to entire study area due to variation in ground objects, ground conditions, illumination conditions, or atmospheric effects, which may change from one area to another. Similarly, training samples may not be usable directly across time due to lighting conditions, cloud cover response and due to growth period for various crops. Accuracy of supervised classification results depends entirely on the collection of a sufficient number of training sites, and purity of samples (Lillesand and Keifer, 1994).

The selection of accurate training areas is based on the analyst's familiarity and knowledge with the geographical area and actual surface cover types obtained through site surveys and present in the image. For each class, several training samples are identified from the images. For these areas/samples, the digital values (spectral signature) and their statistics in all spectral bands are used to "train" the software and to recognize spectrally similar areas for each class. The known spectral signature for each class is then compared by the software to the matching signatures of unknown pixels and labeled the class as soon as it closely resembles the signature. The classification phase uses this information for classifying the input images. This process is repeated for each unknown/unclassified pixel in the image.

At the end of classification, if a particular class has not been picked up properly for classification by the software, the image is again classified by refining the training areas/ samples for that class. The process allows us to refine the training areas/samples many times, till satisfactory results are achieved. It is therefore an iterative process, and the analyst "supervises" the classification of images into a defined set of classes. That's why it is known as supervised classification method. Thus, in a supervised classification, the information classes are identified which are then used to determine the spectral classes representing them (Figure 3.49). The advantage of this kind of technique is that the errors can be easily identified and solved. The only disadvantage is the large time required for training phase.

There are three main methods of supervised classification.

3.33.1.1 Parallelepiped

This classification method is used by determining the parallelepiped-shaped boxes for each pre-defined class. The parallelepiped bounday for each class is defined by the minimum and maximum of pixels in a particular class. The advantage of this method is that (i) it is easy to understand and implement, (ii) the speed of this classifier is high, and (iii) it is good for non-normal distributions. Though the above advantages are significant, it has a lot of disadvantages due to which practically it is not much used, e.g., (i) there can be significant gaps between the parallelepipeds, and the pixels within these regions will remain unclassified, (ii) does not incorporate variability, (iii) allows class overlap, and (iv) classes can include pixels spectrally distant from the signature mean.

3.33.1.2 Maximum likelihood

In this technique, the probability value of pixels is taken into consideration for classifying the pixels. The probability of each pixel belonging to a class is computed, and then compared. The pixel is assigned to the class where the probability value is highest. This method is highly efficient when it comes to classifying particularly the multi-spectral images. It is most accurate and considers the variability of signatures. Though this is an efficient technique, it requires larger computational time. It relies heavily on normal distributed signatures of the classes. In most cases, a maximum likelihood classifier is a better choice.

3.33.1.3 Minimum distance

In minimum distance classifier, the pixels are classified based on their distance from the mean spectra of the pre-defined classes. This type of classifier is mathematically simple, and therefore computationally less complex. It is fast and no pixels are left unclassified. It requires least time for computation among all the other supervised classification techniques. The disadvantage of this technique is that it takes into account only the mean value, and does not incorporate variability of signatures, so it is less efficient than the maximum likelihood technique.

3.33.2 Unsupervised Classification

This method is almost opposite to the supervised classification process. The unsupervised classification is very useful technique to classify the remotely sensed image where field data are not available, and the image is to be classified based on the spectral variations. Unsupervised classification techniques do not require training sample signatures, prior to analysis of scene. Image is analysed to identify the major land cover classes that already existed in the image. Statistical algorithms group similar pixels into various spectral classes which the software would analyse the scene, and later analyst will identify or combine into information classes (Jensen 2005). Spectral classes are grouped, solely based on DN values in the data, and then these DNs are matched by the analyst to information classes. **Clustering algorithms,** such as **K-means** and **ISODATA**, are used to determine the natural (statistical) groupings or structures in the data (Richards and Jia, 2013). Both the techniques are iterative. Thus, the algorithm classifies the pixel data based on similar properties of the data itself (Jenson, 2007). The basic assumption in unsupervised classification is that a particular land cover in a scene would form a single cluster. The flow diagram in Figure 3.48 shows the procedure used (left diagram) in unsupervised classification.

Unlike the supervised classification, only major land classes are separated as clusters, while for smaller classes it may be not be possible. The decision for the number of clusters may be based on histogram analysis of the reflectance values. Usually, the analyst specifies the number of groups or clusters (classes) to be looked in the scene. The analyst also specifies the parameters related to the separation distance among the clusters, number of iterations required, and the variation (like Standard Deviation) within each cluster, as input to software. Unsupervised learning explores the underlying structure of the data and automatically partitions them based on it. These are used for further classification. There are two clustering methods, namely Hierarchical clustering and Partitioning clustering. The former groups the data with a sequence of partitions, while the later one divides the data into pre-specified number of clusters. The most prominent number of peaks as seen in the histogram can also be considered as the number of clusters present in the scene. The iterative clustering process may result into some clusters that the analyst wants to subsequently combine, or clusters that should be broken down further, based on aerial photos and other ancillary data available for the site. Alternatively, the complete process can be re-started by changing the input parameters into the software, till satisfactory results are achieved. This technique is fast and automated. Thus, unsupervised classification is less dependent on human intervention, unlike supervised classification.

Image processing, neural network and other techniques are used to analyse the satellite imagery. The decision rule based on geometric shapes, sizes, and patterns present in the data is termed as **Spatial Pattern Recognition.** The pattern recognition of urban sprawl is identified after classification of the remote sensed images for the built-up area and is then further analysed. Table 3.14 lists the advantages and disadvantages of supervised and unsupervised classification techniques.

Table 3.14: Advantages and disadvantages of supervised and unsupervised techniques.

Techniques	Advantages	Disadvantages
Supervised	Generates informational classes representing features on the ground.	Information classes may not match spectral classes (e.g., a supervised classification of "crops" may mask the unique spectral properties of wheat and sugarcane that comprise the crops).
	Training areas are reusable (assuming they do not change; e.g. roads).	Homogeneity of information classes varies.
		Difficulty in selecting training sites.
		Training areas may not encompass unique spectral classes.
Unsupervised	No prior knowledge of the area is required.	Spectral classes do not represent features on the ground.
	Human error is minimized.	Does not consider spatial relationships in the data
	Unique spectral classes are produced.	Can be very time-consuming to interpret spectral classes.
	Relatively fast and easy to perform.	Spectral properties vary over time, across images.

Two popular methods of unsupervised classification techniques are briefly given below.

3.33.2.1 K-means

Image data clustering in remote sensing is usually based on the natural groupings in the image values of spectral reflectances. k-means is the most popular one due to its simplicity, efficiency, and empirical success in recognizing multivariate data. The objective of the k-means algorithm is to minimize within cluster variability. It assigns first an arbitrary initial cluster vector. The second step classifies each pixel to the closest cluster. In the third step the new cluster mean vectors are calculated based on all the pixels in one cluster. The second and third steps are repeated until either the distances the mean cluster vector that have changed from one iteration to another or the percentage of pixels that have changed between iterations, is small. The objective function (which is to be minimized) is the *sums of squares distances* (errors) between each pixel and its assigned cluster center. k-means is very sensitive to initial starting values. From a statistical viewpoint, the clusters obtained by k-mean can be interpreted as the Maximum Likelihood Estimates **(MLE)** for the cluster means if it is assumed that each cluster comes from a spherical Normal distribution with different means but identical variance (and zero covariance). k-means works best for images with clusters that are spherical and that have the same variance.

3.33.2.2 ISODATA

The Iterative Self-Organizing Data Analysis Technique **(ISODATA)** represents a comprehensive set of heuristic (rules of thumb) procedures that have been incorporated into an iterative classification algorithm. The ISODATA algorithm has some further refinement over the k-means clustering algorithm by splitting and merging of clusters (Jenson, 1996). Clusters are merged if either the number of members (pixel) in a cluster is less than a certain threshold or if the centers of two clusters are closer than a certain threshold. Clusters are split into two different clusters if the cluster standard deviation exceeds a predefined value and the number of members (pixels) is twice the threshold for the minimum number of members. ISODATA does not allocate its initial mean vectors based on the analysis of pixels in the first line of data the way the two-pass chain algorithm does. Rather, an initial arbitrary assignment of all clusters takes place along an n-dimensional vector that runs between very specific points in feature space. The region in feature space is defined using the mean and standard deviation of each band in the analysis. This method of automatically seeding the original vectors makes sure that the first few lines of data do not bias the creation of clusters. ISODATA is self-organizing because it requires relatively little human input. The ISODATA algorithm is similar to the k-means algorithm with the distinct difference that the ISODATA algorithm allows for different number of clusters while the k-means assumes that the number of clusters is known a priori.

3.33.3 Other Classification Techniques

There are many other classification methods, such as neural networks, fuzzy sets and expert systems are frequently used for digital image classification. These classification methods can be grouped as parametric and non-parametric or hard and soft classifiers or per pixel, sub pixel, per field. Per-pixel algorithms (Decision tree, Neural network, Support Vector Machine, sub-pixel algorithms (Fuzzy classifier, Fuzzy expert system), Contextual-based approaches **(ECHO)**, Knowledge-based algorithm **(Rule based)**, Object oriented classifiers **(E-cognition)** have been used for various applications and generation of specific thematic maps from remote sensing data (Lu and Weng, 2007, Richards and Jai, 2013, Prasad et al 2015, Thakur et al, 2017). Table 3.15 presents further summary of these classifiers used for image classification

The parametric and non-parametric image classification techniques are based on the supervised learning. The parametric classifiers use algebraic possibility for allocation to each class. Some of the parametric classifiers are Bayesian classifier and Decision tree. The parameters required, like mean and co-variance are taken from the training data, and used in these classifiers. The non-parametric classifiers, such as K-Nearest neighbor, Logical regression and Multilayer perceptron are used when no density function is available. It approximates the probability density function for further use. Advanced non-parametric classifiers, such as neural network, decision tree, and knowledge based classifiers, may be more suited to handle multi-source data, such as a combination of spectral signatures, texture and context information, and ancillary data, and therefore these techniques have gained increased attention in recent years (Kamavisdar, 2013). However, the selection of a suitable classifier may require consideration of many factors, such as classification accuracy, algorithm performance, and computational resources. Prasad et. al. (2015) presented a good summary of several of these classification approaches.

Table 3.15: Summary of some classifiers used for image classification
(Source: Lu and Weng, 2007)

Criteria	Categories	Example of classifiers
Whether training samples are used or not	Supervised classification approaches	Maximum likelihood, minimum distance, artificial neural network, decision tree classifier.
	Unsupervised classification approaches	ISODATA, K-means clustering algorithm.
Whether parameters such as mean vector and covariance matrix are used or not	Parametric classifiers	Maximum likelihood, linear discriminant analysis.
	Non-parametric classifiers	Artificial neural network, decision tree classifier, evidential reasoning, support vector machine, expert system.
Which kind of pixel information is used	Per-pixel classifiers	Most of the classifiers, such as maximum likelihood, minimum distance, artificial neural network, decision tree, and support vector machine.
	Sub-pixel classifiers	Fuzzy-set classifiers, sub-pixel classifier, spectral mixture analysis.
Which kind of pixel information is used	Object-oriented classifiers	eCognition.
	Per-field classifiers	GIS-based classification approaches.
Whether output is a definitive decision about land cover class or not	Hard classification	Most of the classifiers, such as maximum likelihood, minimum distance, artificial neural network, decision tree, and support vector machine.
	Soft (fuzzy) classification	Fuzzy-set classifiers, sub-pixel classifier, spectral mixture analysis.
Whether spatial information is used or not	Spectral classifiers	Maximum likelihood, minimum distance, artificial neural network.
	Contextual classifiers	Iterated conditional modes, point-to-point contextual correction, frequency-based contextual classifier.
	Spectral-contextual classifiers	ECHO, combination of parametric or non-parametric and contextual algorithms.

The hard classifiers e.g. ISODATA, Parallelepiped, Centroid (k means), Maximum likelihood develop classes by combining the spectra of all the pixels in a training set from a given feature. The classes contain the contribution of all the pixels in the training set. The hard classifiers assume that the pixels are pure and categorize them into one and only one class. In hard classifications, each pixel belongs to the class it most closely resembles. This makes the hard classifiers most inefficient in handling with the problem of mixed pixels. It treats the mixed pixels as noise, uncertainty or error. These classifiers work well in homogenous areas (e.g. croplands, water-bodies), and produces low classification accuracy in heterogeneous areas. The classification is dependent upon spatial scale and the variance of classes,

The soft classifiers work at the sub-pixel level but they cannot deal with pure pixels accurately. They treat them as mixed pixels, which produce large error. They group the mixed pixels into multiple classes, and handle this problem well. In soft classifications, each pixel can belong to more than one class and has membership grades for each class. Heterogeneous areas relative to spatial scale (e.g. residential areas, mixed forests) and gradients (e.g. clear to turbid water) are identified with greater accuracy. They determine membership grades for each class and display as brightness (classification certainty). These soft classifiers include; Linear mixture models, **FCM** (Fuzzy c-means) and **PCM** (Possibilistic c-means). The FCM has a probabilistic constraint and PCM is based on modified version of PCM. This classifier assigns the pixel fractions according to the area it represents inside a pixel, which makes it efficient in handling mixed pixels.

Per pixel classification is still most commonly used in practice. However, the accuracy may not meet the requirement of research because of the impact of the mixed pixel problem. Sub-pixel algorithms have the potential to deal with the mixed pixel problem, and may achieve higher accuracy for medium and coarser spatial resolution images. For fine spatial resolution data, although mixed pixels are reduced, the spectral variation within land classes may decrease the classification accuracy. Per-field classification approaches are most suitable for fine spatial resolution data (Thakur and Maheshwari, 2017).

Table 3.16 presents the advantages and disadvantages of some of the classifiers used in image classification.

3.33.3.1 Object oriented classifier

Object-oriented image classifier groups the pixels into representative shapes and sizes. This process is multi-resolution segmentation or segment mean shift. Multi-resolution segmentation produces homogenous image objects by grouping the pixels. Object-oriented classification based on image segmentation is often used for the analysis of high-spatial-resolution imagery. The object-oriented classification of a segmented image is substantially different from performing a per-pixel classification. The algorithm incorporates both spectral and spatial information in the image segmentation phase. The result is the creation of image objects defined as individual areas with shape and spectral homogeneity which may be recognized as segments or patches in the landscape. The analysis is not constrained to using just spectral information, but the mean spectral information along with various spatially distributed variables (e.g., elevation, slope, aspect, population density) associated with each object (polygon) in the dataset, may also be used. This introduces the greater flexibility and robustness for the use of this classifier. Once selected, the spectral and spatial attributes of homogeneous image objects are then analyzed using traditional classification algorithms (e.g., nearest-neighborhood, minimum distance, maximum likelihood) or knowledge-based and fuzzy logic classification approaches.

3.33.3.2 Artificial neural networks

Artificial neural networks **(ANN)** are non-parametric classifiers. The structure of the ANN is inspired from the human nervous system. ANN has a normal tendency for storing experiential knowledge, and consists of a sequence of layer; each layer consists of a set of neurons. All neurons of every layer are linked by weighted connections to all neurons on the preceding and succeeding layers. Each artificial neuron computes a weighted sum of its input signals and generates an output, based on certain activation functions, such as Piecewise linear, Sigmoid, Gaussian, etc. (Kamavisdar, 2013). ANN consists of one input layer, one output layer, and depending on the application, it may or may not have hidden layers. The number of nodes at the output layer is equal to the number of information classes, whereas the number of nodes at the input is equal to the dimensionality of each pixel. Feed-forward ANN with the back propagation learning algorithm is most commonly used method. In the learning phase, the network learns the connection weights iteratively from a set of training samples. The network gives an output, corresponding to each input, which is compared to the desired known output. The error between these two is used to modify the weights of the ANN. The training procedure ends when the error is below a pre-defined threshold. Thereafter, all the testing data are fed into the classifier to perform the classification.

3.33.3.3 Support vector machine

Support Vector Machine **(SVM)** is a non-parametric classifier. It is a binary classifier which separates the classes using a linear boundary. This classifier assumes that there is no prior information on how to classify the data. The SVM algorithm aims at finding a decision function, which minimizes the functional. The SVM permits the training, non-linear classifiers in high-dimensional spaces using a minute training set. This is enabled during the selection of a division of vectors (called the support vectors) which characterizes the right boundaries between the classes fit. The SVM optimizes the use of training data, which is the biggest advantage of this classifier over other classifiers, like Maximum likelihood classifier.

3.33.3.4 Decision tree

Decision tree, a non-parametric approach, is based on hierarchical rules. Decision tree calculates the class membership by repeatedly partitioning a dataset into uniform subsets Hierarchical classifier permits the acceptations and rejection of class labels at each intermediary stage. This method consists of three parts: partitioning the nodes, find the terminal nodes and allocation of class label to terminal nodes.

Table 3.16: Advantages and disadvantages of different classifiers

(Source: Kamavisdar, et al. 2013)

S.N.	Technique	Advantages	Disadvantages
1	Artificial neural network (ANN)	It is a non-parametric classifier.	It is semantically poor.
		It is an universal functional approximator with arbitrary accuracy	The training of ANN is time consuming.
		Capable to present functions, such as OR, AND, NOT	Encounters the problem of over-fitting.
		It is a data-driven self-adaptive technique	Difficult in choosing the type of network architecture.
		Efficiently handles noisy inputs	
		Computation rate is high	
2	Decision tree	Can handle non-parametric training data	The usage of hyperplane decision boundaries parallel to the feature axes may restrict their use in which classes are clearly distinguishable.
		Does not require an extensive design and training.	Becomes complex calculation when various values are undecided and/or when various outcomes are correlated.
		Provides hierarchical associations between input variables to forecast class membership and provides a set of rules that are easy to interpret	
		Simple and computationally efficient.	
3	Support vector machine (SVM)	It gains flexibility in the choice of the threshold.	Result transparency is low.
		Makes use of a non-linear transformation	Training is time-consuming.
		It provides a good generalization capability.	Structure of algorithm is difficult to understand
		The problem of over fitting is eliminated.	Determination of optimal parameters is not easy when there is non-linearly separable training data.
		Reduction in computational complexity.	
		Simple to manage decision rule complexity and error frequency.	
4	Fuzzy Measure	Efficiently handles uncertainty.	Without priori knowledge, output is not good
		Properties are described by identifying various stochastic relationships	Precise solution depends upon direction of decision.

3.33.3.5 Fuzzy classifier

In fuzzy classification, various stochastic associations are determined to describe characteristics of an image. Various types of stochastic are combined (set of properties) in which the members of this set of properties are fuzzy in nature (Kamavisdar, 2013). It provides the opportunity to describe different categories of stochastic characteristics in the similar form. Performance and accuracy depends upon the threshold selection and fuzzy integral.

3.34 ACCURACY ASSESSMENT

The increased usage of remote sensing data and techniques has made analysis faster and more powerful, but the increased complexity has also created increased possibilities for errors (Lillesand Kiefer, 1994). Thematic maps generated from remotely sensed image may contain errors because of (i) geometric error, (ii) atmospheric error, (iii) clusters incorrectly labeled after unsupervised classification, (iv) training sites incorrectly labeled before supervised classification, (v) un-distinguishable classes, and (vi) none of classification method is perfect.

Accuracy assessment of land-use or land-cover classifications obtained by remote sensing images is necessary to evaluate the quality of thematic maps. Validation or accuracy assessment is a critical step in the use and distribution of the results of analyses of remotely sensed data. A typical approach for validation and accuracy assessment is to use a statistically sound sampling design to select a sample of ground locations (number of pixels) in the study region. The land-use or land-cover classification assigned at these ground locations is actually compared with the true classification from image pixels to ascertain the accuracy. There are five important sampling techniques, often used for various purposes, as shown in Figure 3.50. These are used in the field for the data collection as well as determination of accuracy of image classification (Congalton, 1991).

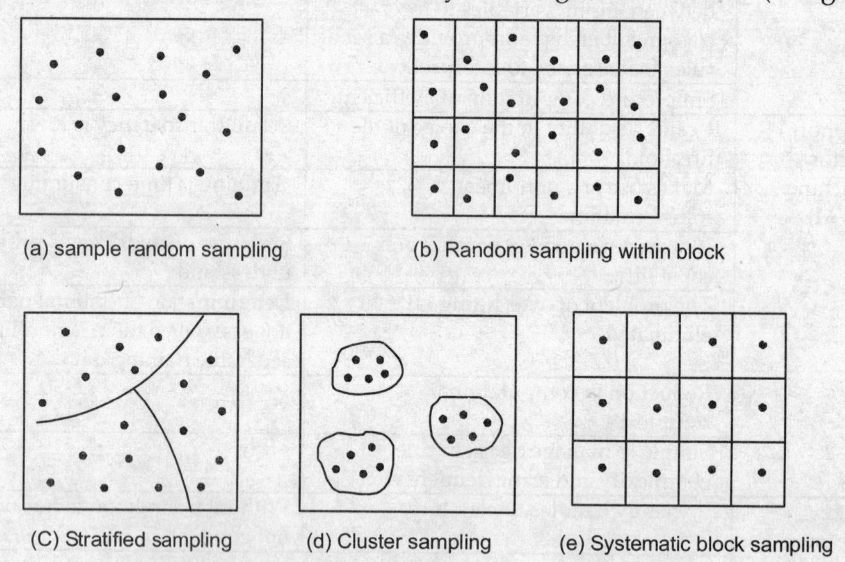

Figure 3.50: Five important sampling techniques

1. ***Simple random sampling***: observations are randomly placed, and no rules are used. It is done using a completely random process.
2. ***Random sampling with block***: a grid is laid out which provides even distribution of randomly placed observations.
3. ***Stratified random sampling***: a minimum number of observations are randomly placed in each class. Sampling points are generated proportionate to the distribution of classes in the image.

4. ***Cluster sampling***: randomly placed "centroids" used as a base of several nearby observations. The nearby observations can be randomly selected, systematically selected, etc.
5. ***Systematic block sampling***: observations are placed at equal intervals according to a planned strategy.

Image classification is considered to be incomplete without estimating the accuracy. It measures the agreement between a reference (assumed as 100% accurate) and a classified image of unknown accuracy. The accuracy assessment or error analysis permits the quantitative comparison to validate the classified map with the actual reference data/ image. The classification errors can occur due to a variety of reasons. Congalton (1991) suggests that the factors which are to be considered include error sources, sampling scheme, number of samples, and sample unit (ground data collection and sample size). Lunetta et al. (1991) list the errors associated with data acquisition, processing, analysis, conversion, and final product presentation (Figure 3.51). According to them, "in theory, the amount of error entering the system at each step can be estimated, but in practice, however, error is typically assessed only at the conclusion of data analysis, if it is to be assessed at all".

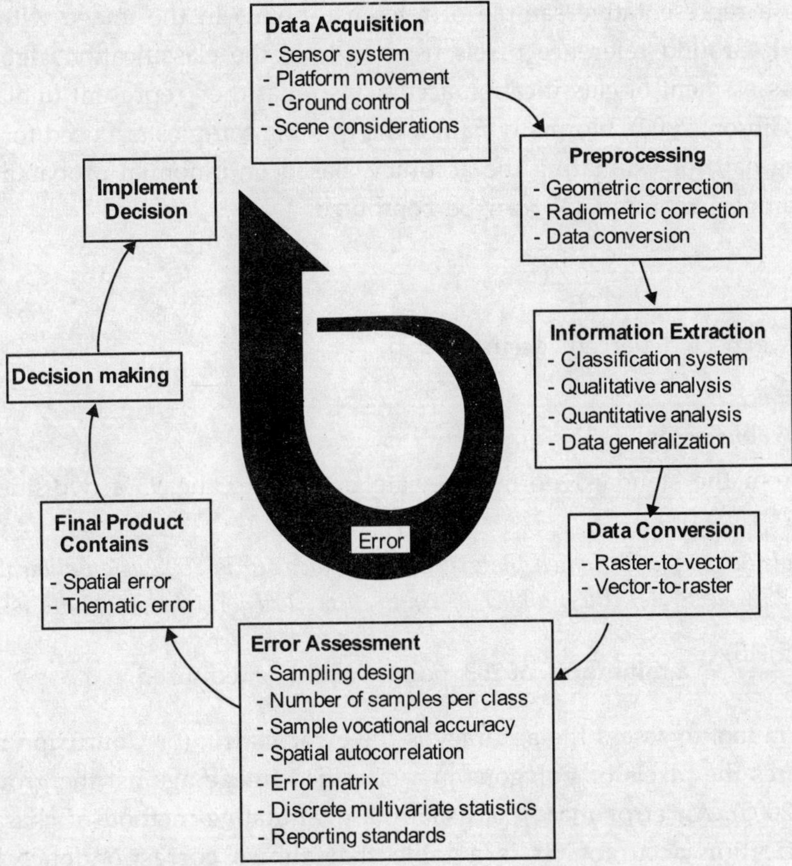

Figure 3.51: Sources of errors in remote sensing data *(Source: Lunetta et al., 1991)*

The accuracy of a classification can be defined as (i) Overall accuracy, (ii) Producer's accuracy, (iii) User's accuracy, and (iv) Kappa coefficient. The **overall accuracy** of the classification map is determined by dividing the total correct pixels (sum of the major diagonal) by the total number of pixels in the error matrix. The total number of correct pixels in a category is divided by the total number of pixels of that category as derived from the reference data (i.e., the column total). This statistics indicates the probability of a reference pixel being correctly classified, and is a measure of **omission error**. This statistics is the **producer's accuracy** because the producer (the analyst) of the classification is interested in how well a certain area can be classified. The **commission error** quantifies the **user's accuracy**. Thus, the errors in classification can further be obtained individually for each class. The **Kappa coefficient** reflects the difference between actual agreement and the agreement expected by chance. It is a measure of agreement or accuracy between the remote sensing–derived classification map and the reference data. The classification accuracy for each class indicates if there is any over-estimation or under-estimation in classification based on the input from reference data (Conglaton and Green, 1999).

It is not practically possible to test each and every pixel in the classification image, and therefore a representative sample of reference points in the image with known class values is used. Ground reference pixels used to train the classification algorithm are not used for the assessment of classification accuracy so that they represent unbiased reference information (Gibson, 2000). Normally half of the training samples are used for classification, and remaining half for estimating the accuracy. Based on binomial probability theory, the number of samples required (N) can be computed.

$$N = \frac{Z^2 pq}{E^2} \qquad \text{...(3.19)}$$

Where p- expected percent accuracy

$q = 100 - p$

E = allowable error

Z = 2 (from the standard normal deviate of 1.96 for the 95% two-sided confidence level).

For example, a sample for which the expected accuracy (p) is 85% at an allowable error (E) of 5% (i.e., it is 95% accurate), the number of points necessary for reliable results is:

$$N = \frac{2^2(85)(15)}{5^2} = \text{a minimum of 203 points would be reqiuired}$$

A common tool to assess the accuracy is the **error matrix** (or **Confusion matrix**). Error matrix compares the pixels or polygons in a classified image against the ground reference data (Jensen 2005). An error matrix is usually a quantitative method of characterising the image classification accuracy. It is a table that shows correspondence between the classification results with respect to a reference image. The error matrix is created with the help of reference data which includes thematic map, aerial photos, ground surveys, GPS surveys and a high resolution satellite data used for classification.

A typical confusion matrix is shown in Table 3.17. Columns of Table 3.17 are the ground truth classes, and rows of the table are the classes of classified image whose accuracy is to be assessed. Cells of the Table show number of pixels for all the possible correlations between the ground truth and the classified image.

Table 3.17: A typical confusion matrix

Classified Image	Number of Pixels in Reference Image (Ground truth)			Total
	Forest	Soil	Water	
Forest	37	3	7	Σ = 47
Soil	9	25	5	Σ = 39
Water	11	2	43	Σ = 56
Total	Σ = 57	Σ = 30	Σ = 55	N = 142

The diagonal elements of the matrix contains the number of correctly identified pixels. Classification of **overall accuracy** is obtained by dividing the sum of these diagonal pixels by the total number of pixels. It is computed as:

$\{(37 + 25 + 43) / 142\}\ 100 = 0.74$

The overall accuracy measures the accuracy of the entire image without reference to the individual categories. It is sensitive to differences in sample size, and biased towards classes with larger samples. Apart from the overall accuracy, the accuracy of individual class needs to be assessed. The non-diagonal cells in the matrix contain classification errors, i.e. the number of pixels in reference image and the classified image don't match. There could be two types of errors present: over-estimation (**commission errors**) and under-estimation (**omission errors**).

If the total number of correct pixels in a category is divided by the total number of pixels that were actually classified in that category, the result is a measure of **commission error**. This measure, called the **user's accuracy** or **reliability**, is the probability that a pixel classified on the map actually represents that category on the ground. For any class, error of commission occurs when a classification procedure assigns pixels to a certain class that don't belong to it in reality. Number of pixels incorrectly allocated to a class is found in column cells of the class above and below the main diagonal. The user's accuracy is the number of the correctly identified pixels of a class, divided by the total number of pixels in that class in the classified image. For class Forest, it is computed as:

$(37 / 47)\ 100 = 79\%$

The probability a reference pixel being properly classified, measures the **omission error** (reference pixels improperly classified are being omitted from the proper class). For any class, error of omission occurs when pixels that in fact belong to one class, are included into other classes. The omission error is an indicator of the **producer's accuracy.** For class Forest, it is computed as the number of the correctly identified pixels of a class, divided by the total number of pixels in that class in the referenced image:

(37 / 57) 100 = 65%

The overall accuracy of classification itself can be misleading, as it does not reveal whether the error was evenly distributed between classes or some classes were really bad and some were really good. Therefore, it is always better to compute the values of commission and omission errors. It is likely that the overall accuracy of an image classification might be quite high, whereas an individual class may have a considerable lower accuracy. If the accuracy of individual classes is most important to users, the classification results cannot be accepted as such, even if the overall accuracy is higher. Additionally, the producer's and user's accuracy cannot be separately used as an indicator of the classification accuracy, as these values do not provide complete details.

Another accuracy indicator is the **Kappa coefficient**. It reflects the difference between actual agreement and the agreement expected by chance. It is a measure of agreement or accuracy between the remote sensing–derived classification map and the reference data as indicated by a) the major diagonal, and b) the chance agreement, which is indicated by the row and column totals (referred to as **marginal**). Kappa of 0.85 means that there is 85% better agreement than by chance alone. Kappa coefficient is computed as–

$$\hat{K} = \frac{M \sum_{i=j=1}^{r} n_{ij} - \sum_{i=j=1}^{r} n_i n_j}{M^2 - \sum_{i=j=1}^{r} n_i n_j} \quad \text{...(3.20)}$$

Where:

r = number of rows in error matrix

n_{ij} = number of observations in row i, column j

n_i = total number of observations in row i

n_j = total number of observations in column j

M = total number of observations in matrix

So, Kappa coefficient is calculated as (from Table 3.17) -

$$= \frac{(142 \times 105) - [(47 \times 57) + (39 \times 30) + (56 \times 55)]}{142^2 - [(47 \times 57) + (39 \times 30) + (56 \times 55)]}$$

$$= \frac{14{,}910 - 6{,}829}{20{,}164 - 6{,}829} = \frac{8{,}081}{13{,}335}$$

$$= 0.606$$

Kappa coefficient is a measure of how the classification results compare well to the values assigned by chance. It varies between 0-1 (Congalton and Green, 1999). The value of 0 for coefficient indicates that there is a mismatch between the reference data and the classified image, and the classification is considered to be random. If the value is 1, the classified image and the reference data both have a true agreement with 100% accuracy. Thus, higher the value of Kappa coefficient, more accurate is the classification from remotely sensed image. Thus, if K> 0.80 it represents strong agreement and good accuracy. If it is between 0.40-0.80 (as in case of data given in Table 3.17), it is moderate accuracy, and K<0.40 is poor accuracy. The Kappa coefficient is not as sensitive to differences in sample sizes between classes, and is therefore considered a more reliable measure of accuracy.

3.35 APPLICATIONS OF REMOTE SENSING

Remote sensing has shown tremendous potential for applications in various fields, such as agriculture, forestry, cartography, hydrology & water resources, wetland mapping, geology, meteorology, land use mapping & modelling, urban & regional planning, environmental study, natural disaster assessment, archaeological applications and others. Because of its varied applications and ability to collect, interpret, and manipulate data over large areas, remote sensing has become a powerful tool for many applications. Remote sensing also plays a significant role in GIS, as thematic maps or digital elevation models (DEMs) generated from these images are used as the input. Some of the applications summarized here are only representative, and not exhaustive (Colwell, 1983, Fung and LeDrew, 1987, Jain, 1989, Gupta, 1991, Lillesand and Keifer, 1994, Castleman, 1996, Eastman, 1999, Gibson, 2000, Jenson, 2007, Richards and Jia, 2013).

3.35.1 Geology

Remote sensing data is helpful for updating the existing geological maps, rapid preparation of lineament and tectonic maps, identifying the sites for quarrying the minerals and locating fossil fuel deposits. Some of the remote sensing applications in geology include bedrock, lithological and structural mapping. Multispectral remote sensing data can provide information on lithology or rock composition based on their spectral reflectance pattern. Radar data provides an expression of surface topography and roughness, and thus is extremely useful, especially when integrated with another data source to provide detailed relief. Remote sensing based mapping and its integration in a GIS helps to map the mineral potential zones. With the help of spectral analysis, one can quickly identify and map mineral availability through special indicators. This will enable to narrow down the geo-physical, geo-chemical and test drilling activities to high potential zones (Gupta, 1991).

3.35.2 Hydrology and Water Resources

Remote sensing offers a synoptic view of the spatial distribution and dynamics of hydrological phenomena. Characterization of water bodies in terms of geological, geo-morphological, hydro- geological, soil and land use/land cover parameters enables conservation of land and water resources using remote sensing data. Remote sensing integrated with ground based information in GIS is useful for interpretation of land capability, irrigation suitability, water harvesting areas, monitoring the effects of soil & water conservation measures, estimation of runoff & sediment yields, and monitoring land use change, including land degradation. High spatial resolution satellite imagery can locate water shortages areas. This information is very useful to develop an action plan for providing drinking water to such areas.

In case of gauged reservoirs, remote sensing data can provide an assessment of sediment volume and reduction in the capacity of the reservoir. Remote sensing contributes to watershed delineation and management by providing accurate information on land use and land cover as well as elevation data. Remote sensing provides comprehensive, reliable and timely information on flood inundated and drainage congested areas, extent of damage to crops, river configuration, structures, silt deposits and vulnerable areas of bank erosion. Satellite data has been advantageously used to obtain such information on surface irrigation projects. The reflectance of water in satellite imagery increases with more suspended solids. Continual coverage and temporal images would be required to monitor the nutrient loadings.

3.35.3 Land use and Land Cover

Remote sensing data is extremely useful in obtaining up-to-date land use pattern of large areas, and monitor changes that occur over time. Land use and land cover mapping is one of the most important applications of remote sensing data. Land cover corresponds to the physical condition of the ground surface, for example, forest, grassland, concrete pavement etc., while land use reflects human activities, such as the use of the land, for example, industrial zones, residential zones, agricultural fields etc. Anderson et al (1976) proposed the land use and land cover classification upto four different levels from various remote sensing images. This scheme has been used world-wide.

The information on land use and land cover is required by regional planners and administrators to frame policy matters for development of the region. Urban planners have used land use change data to model an accurate measure of population growth. Land cover change detection is also necessary for the management and sustainable planning of natural resources. The change is usually detected by comparison between two multi-date images, or sometimes between an old map and an updated remote sensing image. Information on land cover change pattern is directly useful for determining and implementing the developmental policy, e.g. municipal authorities for tax assessment. Government also requires this information with the general protection of national resources, parks, wetland, wildlife sanctuaries etc.

3.35.4 Natural Hazards Study

Remote sensing can be used to study the damages caused by earthquakes, volcanoes, landslides, floods etc. Remote sensing along with other devices has also been used to predict the occurrence of some of the natural hazards. Geologists can identify the rock types, geomorphology, and changes from natural events, such as a flood or landslide. Landslides cause loss of life and damage to environment. The potential landslides are studied using stereo and optical images with slope. InSAR images can provide early warning signs for landslides. Assessment of affected area from earthquake is essential for planning rescue measures. Object-based image classification using change detection (pre- and post-earthquake) is a quick way to get the damage assessment.

3.35.5 Site Investigations and Regional Planning

Site investigations, in general, require topographical and geological information, which can easily be obtained through remote sensing data. Remote sensing is extensively used in site investigations for dams, bridges, roads, canals, pipelines, townships etc. High resolution images can be used to locate construction materials, like sand, gravel, boulders, quarry rock, sand–clay mixtures for the new projects, like dams, bridges, etc., across the rivers. By analyzing multi-date remotely sensed data of pre- and post-dam construction, the forest and other land at different water levels can be assessed. This would also help in preliminary investigation of locating suitable areas for human resettlement.

Geological information involves different soil and rock types and physical properties. In selecting suitable sites for bridges and dams, an important consideration is the stability of slopes; upstream and downstream of water crossing. Past data of river erosion and sedimentation would give clues needed for locating the sites where scour is likely to occur. High spatial resolution satellite data can be used for regional planning of large projects, like airports, harbors, industrial towns and recreational sites. The information on regional soils is also essential for general planning and site evaluation purposes.

3.35.6 Soil Mapping

The salinity, soil acidification and erosion are some of the basic problems in civil engineering projects. Remote sensing is ideal for mapping and prediction of salinity, and soil degradation. Soil layers that rise to the surface during erosion have different colors, tones and structures than non- eroded soils, thus easily identified on the images. Using multi-temporal images, the dynamic features e.g., the expansion of erosion, soil moisture, can be studied and mapped. Land degradation processes have been studied through the Universal Soil Loss Equation **(USLE)** erosion model. The necessary parameters for the model can be derived from satellite images. Microwave image have been successfully used for mapping and monitoring the soil moisture, which in turn is helpful in crop related and evapo-transpiration studies.

3.35.7 Transportation Network Mapping

Urban planners, emergency crews and navigation systems require up-to-date road networks. High resolution spatial data can be used for mapping of existing road and rail network, and planning the new ones. This also facilitates in locating the optimal routing for transport of construction materials. Object-based classification using multispectral images has automated the tedious process of generating road networks. In hilly areas, conventional survey for rail/road alignment is extremely time-consuming and tedious work which can be accomplished now with the help of high resolution satellite image.

3.35.8 Terrain Mapping and Analysis

Assessment of the terrain for specific developmental activities can be made through terrain evaluation. The terrain information can be acquired from remote sensing data by generating the Digital Terrain Model **(DTM)**. The DTM facilitates the investigation of alternative horizontal and vertical alignments of canals, roads, pipelines etc. For example, the construction of a dam requires the knowledge of terrain for proper planning, location, construction and maintenance of engineering facilities. High spatial resolution satellite data can be analyzed to delineate various landforms, mapping of soil classes, significant to engineering construction, delineation of landforms, soil relationships and grouping of landforms with various physiographic setting or terrain associations.

3.35.9 Urban Development

Systematic mapping and periodic monitoring of urban land use is necessary for proper planning and management. Master plan for development and management of urban settlements and other necessary facilities/amenities can be prepared efficiently using high resolution images. Sustainable development of urban agglomeration, optimal urban land use plans and resources development models need to be generated by integrating the information on natural resources mapped through satellite data.

3.35.10 3D City Models

These are digital models of urban areas that represent terrain surfaces, sites, buildings, vegetation, infrastructure and landscape elements of urban areas. Their components are described and represented by corresponding two-dimensional and three-dimensional spatial data and geo-referenced data. 3D city models support presentation, exploration, analysis, and management of tasks in a large number of different application domains. 3D GIS is the instant and effective solution for larger and remote locations where manual survey is not possible. Various urban/ rural planning departments require 3D GIS data, like, drainage, sewerage, water supply, road designing, etc. Many smart cities are being developed by generating and planning 3D models of the area.

Review Questions

1. Define remote sensing. What is its utility?
2. Enumerate the advantages and disadvantages of remote sensing.
3. Explain a typical remote sensing system.
4. Illustrate the electromagnetic spectrum (EMS), with an emphasis on optical visible spectral bands/
5. In remote sensing, what and why are the visible wavelength bands used so frequently?
6. State the characteristics of different frequencies in EMS.

7. Which part of the EMS is used in (i) optical and (ii) radar remote sensing? Discuss.
8. Discuss the interaction of electromagnetic radiation with the Earth's atmosphere.
9. Write a short note on black-body radiation.
10. Given the temperature of an object, write the equation or law which will be used to calculate the peak wavelength of radiation and total radiation emitance.
11. Define (i) Emissivity, (ii) Stefen Boltzmann law, and (iii) Wein's Displacement law.
12. The wavelength of an electro-magnetic wave is 100nm. What is the energy of that wave in Joules?
13. What is the wavelength of the signal from radio station located at 1.5 mHz (10^6 Hz) on the AM radio dial?
14. The light from a distant star displays an emission spectrum that peaks at a wavelength of 0.25 micrometers. What is its apparent surface temperature?
15. To study temperature of the soil, water, and rock on Earth's surface (average 300ºK), what wavelength (or spectral band) is best to use? Which satellites have the capability?
16. Explain four types of interactions between EMR and atmosphere.
17. What do you mean by atmospheric scattering? What are the main reasons for various colors of sky and clouds, explain.
18. Define Scattering. Explain the Mie Scattering?
19. What do you mean by atmospheric window? List the Atmospheric Window regions that are useful in remote sensing,
20. What is spectral signature of an object? How is this helpful?
21. Explain in detail the spectral reflectances of vegetation, water, soil and rock.
22. Explain the factors that influence the soil reflectance. Draw neatly the spectral signature curve for dry and moist soil.
23. Write a short note on spectral reflectance characteristics of rocks.
24. Discuss the use of a field spectro-radiometer.
25. Describe spectral properties of water bodies and how these can be used to differentiate between pure water and sediment-laden water.
26. Differentiate between Geostationary orbit and Polar sun synchronous orbit. Give examples.
27. Define the following terms with neat sketches; (i) Swath, (ii) Path-row number, (iii) Pixel, (iv) Digital Number and (v) Spectral band.
28. What do you mean by the histogram of an image? How does it help in image analysis?

29. What do you understand by the resolution of an image? What are the various elements of resolution?
30. Write short notes on (i) Spatial resolution, and (ii) Radiometric resolution.
31. Write short notes on (i) Spectral resolution, and (ii) Temporal resolution.
32. Define IFOV. What do you understand by 10 bit radiometric resolution image?
33. What are the different types of remote sensing data products?
34. What is difference among true color, false color, and pseudo colour images? What is the utility of FCC in recognizing terrain features?
35. Write a short note on multi-concept in remote sensing.
36. What are the different types of sensors based on energy source? How are active sensors different than the passive sensors?
37. Write the advantages of active sensors? Give examples of active sensors.
38. Draw a neat diagram for the classification of imaging sensor systems.
39. Define thermal infrared sensors. Discuss some important applications of thermal infrared sensors.
40. Write any four thermal sensors alongwith their salient features.
41. Discuss various microwave sensors.
42. What is RADAR? What are the advantages of microwave sensors over the optical sensors?
43. Enumerate various applications of microwave sensors.
44. Describe in detail about different types of satellite platforms based on resolutions.
45. Explain any three platforms used in remote sensing.
46. Describe in detail the characteristics of Landsats.
47. Write the details and applications of TM sensor.
48. Discuss the salient features of SPOT satellites.
49. Describe the characteristics of IRS satellites.
50. Discuss any two sensors providing stereo-pair images. What is the approach used to collect stereo-pairs?
51. Write a short note on the Indian remote sensing programme.
52. Describe high/very high resolution satellites/sensors. What are their main applications?
53. Discuss the characteristics of IKONOS image.
54. What is the major difference between visible, thermal infrared and microwave remote sensing?
55. Discuss the advantages of hyperspectral over multispectral remote sensing?
56. What are the two broad methods of interpretation of satellite images? Write their merits and demerits.

57. What is image interpretation? Write the objectives of image interpretation?
58. What is visual image interpretation? Discuss image interpretation elements quoting suitable examples.
59. Define a digital image. What is the objective of digital image processing?
60. Write a short note on pre-processing of remotely sensed data?
61. What is the geometric correction? Explain geo-referencing approach. What is the role of ground control points in geometric correction?
62. Discuss the re-sampling methods used in image processing.
63. Explain the procedure to apply radiometric correction to satellite images.
64. Differentiate between image restoration and image enhancement in remote sensing.
65. Discuss the broad two approaches used for image enhancement.
66. Explain the histogram equalisation technique. Why is this technique popular for enhancement of images?
67. Describe about image transformation. Why is it done?
68. Write a short note on data fusion in remote sensing.
69. Define (i) Ratio and (ii) NDVI. Why NDVI is most popular approach in image transformation?
70. What is Vegetation Index? Write its significance.
71. Discuss Tasselled Cap Transformations, along with their main utility.
72. Explain the utility of Principal Component Analysis. How do you generate principal component images?
73. Describe two broad digital image classification techniques used. List the advantages and disadvantages of each.
74. Explain the role of training samples in image analysis. How do you obtain these samples?
75. Discuss various supervised image classification techniques.
76. Discuss various unsupervised classification methods.
77. Describe the other modern techniques used in image classification. Write their advantages and disadvantages.
78. Describe ANN method of image classification.
79. Discuss various methods of accuracy assessment of a classified image.
80. Explain the following terms (i) Error of omission, (ii) Error of commission, (iii) User's accuracy, (iv) Producer's accuracy, and (v) Kappa coefficient.
81. Discuss the application of remote sensing in hydrology and water resources.
82. Describe application of remote sensing images for mapping urban land use.
83. Describe the use of remote sensing images in urban and utility planning.
84. Write in brief various applications of remote sensing data.

85. The figure below shows the Landsat-4 mapping geometry. The Landsat tracks the Earth surface from north to south, as shown. Scan width, swath width, spatial resolution, the altitude of the satellite are all shown in the figure. Compute the following :
   (a) What is the scanning configuration of the system?
   (b) What is the type of orbit of the satellite?
   (c) How many pixels each scan line has?
   (d) If the satellite moves at a speed of about 7 km/second, how many scans will be in each second, and how much the scan frequency (Hz) will be?

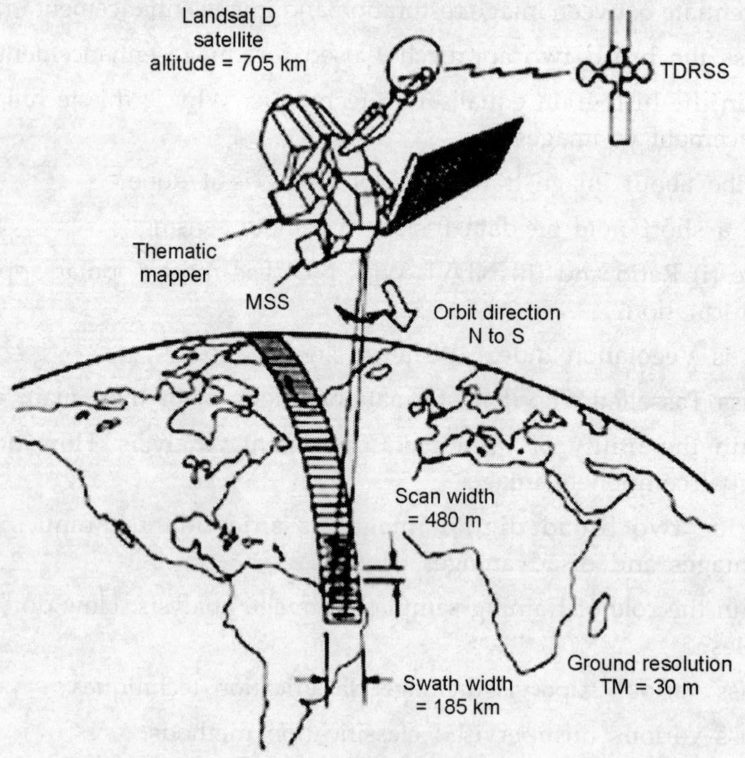

Figure Landsat-D mapping geometry

References

1. Albertz, J., (2007), Einführung in die Fernerkundung Grundlagen der Interpretation von Luftund Satellitenbildern. 3, aktual. und erw. Aufl. utg. Darmstadt: Wiss. Buchges. X, 254 S. S
2. Anderson, J. R., Hardy, E.E., Roach, J.T., and Witmer, R.E., (1976), A Land Use And Land Cover Classification System for Use With Remote Sensor Data, Geological Survey Professional Paper 964, U.S. Geological Survey Circular 671, United States Government Printing Office, Washington.

3. Antrop, M., and De Maeyer, Ph. (2005) *Theoretische basisconcepten van GIS*. Gent: Academia Press.
4. Annual Report (2017-2018) ISRO, Bangalore, Department of Space, Govt. of India.
5. Birk, R.J. and T.B. McCord, (1994), Airborne Hyperspectral Sensor Systems," IEEE AES Systems Magazine, October 1994, pp. 26-33.
6. Calla, O.P., (2010), Applications of Microwaves in Remote Sensing IP Multimedia Communications, In Special Issue of IJCA -www.ijcaonline.org.
7. Castleman, K. R. (1996) *Digital Image Processing*, Prentice-Hall, London
8. Chavez, P.S., and Mackinnon, D.J. (1994) Automatic Detection of Vegetation Changes in the South-western U.S. using Remotely Sensed Images. Photogrammetric Engineering Remote Sensing, 60 (5), pp.571-583.
9. Chavez, Jr., P.S., Marino, C.M. and Schowengerdt, R.A., (1994) (Eds) *Recent Advances in Remote Sensing and Hyperspectral Remote Sensing*, SPIE Vol. 2318.
10. Cohen, W.B., Spies, T.A. and Fiorella, M. (1995) Estimating the Age and Structure of Forests in a Multi-ownership Landscape of Western Oregon, U.S.A., Int. J. Remote Sensing, 1995, Vol. 16, No.4, 721-746.
11. Colwell, R. N. (1983), *Manual of Remote Sensing*, Published by American Society of Photogrammetry, USA.
12. Congalton, R. (1991), A Review of Assessing the Accuracy of Classifications of Remotely Sensed Data, Remote Sensing of Environment, 37: 35, 46.
13. Congalton, R. G. and Green, K.. (1999), *Assessing the Accuracy of Remotely Sensed Data: Principles and Practices*, Lewis Publishers, Boca Raton.
14. Crist, Eric P. and Cicone, Richard C., (1984) A Physically-Based Transformation of Thematic Mapper Data-The TM Tasseled Cap, IEEE Transactions on Geoscience and Remote Sensing, Volume: GE-22, Issue: 3, May 1984.
15. Eastman, J R. (1999), IDRISI 32- Guide to GIS and Image Processing, Vol. 1 & II, Worcester, MA, Clark University, USA.
16. Fung, T. and LeDrew, E. (1987), Application of Principal Components Analysis to Change Detection, ISPRS Journal of Photogrammetry and Remote Sensing, Vol. 53, No. 12, 1987, pp. 1649-1658.
17. Gibson P.J. (2000), *Introductory Remote Sensing - Principles and Concepts*, Routledge, London.
18. Gillespie, A., Rokugawa, S., Matsunaga, T., Steven Cothern, J., Hook, S., and Anne Kalhe, A. (1998), A Temperature and Emissivity Separation Algorithm for Advanced Spaceborne Thermal Emisssiona and Reflection Radiometer (ASTER) Images, IEEE Trans. Geoscience and Remote Sensing, Vol 36, pp 1113-1126.
19. Green, R.O., (1995) (Ed), Summaries of the Fifth Annual JPL Airborne Earth Science Workshop, Vol. 1. AVIRIS Workshop, NASA JPL, January, 1995.
20. Gupta, R.P. (1991), Remote Sensing Geology, Springer Verlag, Berlin.

21. Holland, D., Guilford, R. and Murray, K. (Eds), 2003. *Topographic Mapping from High Resolution Space Sensors*, OEEPE Official Publication No. 44.
22. Hunt, G. R, Sailsbury, J, W. and Lenhoff, C.J., (1971) Visible and near-infrared spectra of minerals and rocks: III. Oxides and hydroxides. *Modem Geology*, (2), 195–205.
23. Imhoff, M.L., (1995) A Theoretical Analysis of the Effect of Forest Structure on Synthetic Aperture Radar Backscatter and the Remote Sensing of Biomass, IEEE Transactions on Geoscience and Remote Sensing, Vol 33, pp 341–352
24. Jain, A.K. (1989) *Fundamentals of Digital Image Processing*, Prentice-Hall, London.
25. Jensen, J. R. (1986), *Introductory Digital Image Processing. A Remote Sensing Perspective*, Englewood Cliffs: Prentice-Hall, London.
26. Jensen, J. R. (2007) *Remote Sensing of the Environment: An Earth Resource Perspective*. 2nd Edition, Pearson Prentice Hall, Upper Saddle River.
27. Kahle, B. (1998) A temperature and emissivity separation algorithm for Advanced Spaceborne Thermal Emission and Reflection Radiometer (ASTER) images. IEEE Transactions on Geosciences and Remote Sensing, 1998. 36(4): p. 1113-1126. 2.
28. Kamavisdar, Pooja, Saluja, Sonam and Agrawal, Sonu (2013) A Survey on Image Classification Approaches and Techniques, International Journal of Advanced Research in Computer and Communication Engineering, Vol. 2, Issue 1, January 2013
29. Kasischke, Eric S., Melack, John M. and Dobson, Craig M., (1997) The Use of Imaging Radars for Ecological Applications—A review, Remote Sensing of Environment, Vol 59, Issue 2, February 1997, Pages 141-156
30. Kauth, R. J. and Thomas, G.S., (1976), The Tasseled Cap-A Graphic Description of the Spectral-Temporal Development of Agricultural Crops as Seen by LANDSAT, Proceedings of the Symposium on Machine Processing of Remotely Sensed Data, Purdue University of West Lafayette, Indiana.
31. Li, Gang 2009, Image Local Contrast Enhancement Based on Grey Relational Analysis, International Symposium on Computer Network and Multimedia Technology, pp1-4.
32. Lillesand, T.M. and Kiefer, R.W., (1994), *Remote Sensing and Image Interpretation*, 3rd Ed. John Wiley & Sons, New York.
33. Lillesand, T. M., Kiefer, R.W. and Chipman, J. W., (2004), *Remote Sensing and Image Interpretation*, Fifth Edition, Wiley, Chichester. pp 35-38
34. Lunetta, R., Congalton, R., Fenstermaker, L., Jensen, J., McGwire, K. and Tinney, L. (1991) Remote Sensing and Geographic Information System Data Integration: Error Sources and Research Issues. Photogrammetric Engineering and Remote Sensing, 57(6):677{687.
35. Lu. D. and Weng, Q. (2007) A Survey of Image Classification Methods and Techniques for Improving Classification Performance, International Journal of Remote Sensing Volume 28, 2007 - Issue 5.

36. Manjul, S. S., (2002) Design and Development of Ratio Radiometer for Snow and Glacial Studies, Proc. ISSN 1682-1777, SPRS TC-VII and ISRS Symposium, Hyderabad from December 3–6, 2002, pp. 34–39.

37. Manjul S. S. and Kulkarni A.V. (2004) Design and development of Near Infrared Ground Truth Radiometer (NIGTR) for Spectral Signature Studies in Spectral Bands of MODIS and AWiFS Spaceborne Sensors. Proceedings on International Symposium on Snow and Monitoring and Avalanches (ISSMA-2004), Snow and Avalanche Studies Establishment (SASE), DRDO, Manali, India, pp. 467–474

38. Morisette, J.T, Privette, J. L, Justice, C. O [2002], A framework for the validation of MODIS Land products. Remote Sensing of Environment, 83 (2-Jan), 77-96.

39. Muchoney, D.M. and Haack, B.N. (1994) Change Detection for Monitoring Forest Defoliation. Photogrammetric Engineering and Remote Sensing, 60, 1243-1251.

40. Perotti L., Lasagna M., Clemente P., Dino G.A., De Luca D.A. (2015) Remote Sensing and Hydrogeological Methodologies for Irrigation Canal Water Losses Detection: The *Naviglio di Bra* Test Site (NW-Italy). In: Lollino G., Arattano M., Rinaldi M., Giustolisi O., Marechal J.C., Grant G. (Eds) Engineering Geology for Society and Territory - Volume 3. Springer, Cham.

41. Pohl, C. and Van Genderen, J.L. (1998) Multisensor Image Fusion in Remote Sensing: Concepts, Methods and Applications. International Journal of Remote Sensing, 19, 823-854. https://doi.org/10.1080/014311698215748.

42. Poon, J. and Fraser, C.S., (2006) High-Resolution Satellite Imagery in Remote Regions, a Case Study in Bhutan. Australian Remote Sensing and Photgrammetry Conference, ARSPC-2006, Canberra, 20-24 Nov, 5pages

43. Prasad, S.V.S. Satya Savithri, T. and Murali Krishna, I.V. (2015), Techniques in Image Classification; A Survey, Global Journal of Researches in Engineering: Electrical and Electronics Engineering, Volume 15, Issue 6, Version 1.0.

44. Richards, J.A. (1990) Radar Backscatter Modelling of Forests: a Review of Current Trends. International Journal of Remote Sensing, 11, pp. 1299-1312.

45. Richards, J. A. and Jia, X., (2013), *Remote Sensing Digital Image Analysis*, Springer-Verlag, Berlin.

46. Rowan, L.C., Mars, J.C. and Simpson, C.J. (2005), Lithologic mapping of the Mordor, NT, Australia ultramafic complex by using the Advanced Spaceborne Thermal Emission and Reflection Radiometer (ASTER), Remote Sensing of Environment,99, 105–126

47. Sabins, F.F. (1996) *Remote Sensing Principles and Interpretation.* 3rd Edition, W.H. Freeman and Company, New York.

48. Schmugge, T., Hook, S.J. and Coll, C., (1998) Recovering Surface Temperature and Emissivity from Thermal Infrared Multispectral Data. Remote Sensing of Environment, 65, pp. 121-131.

49. Special Issue on Airborne Imaging Spectrometry, Remote Sensing of the Environment, Vol. 44, May/June 1993.

50. Thakur, Nupur and Maheshwari, Deepa (2017) A Review of Image Classification Techniques, International Research Journal of Engineering and Technology (IRJET) e-ISSN: 2395-0056 Volume: 04 Issue: 11 | Nov -2017
51. Tolhurst, Jeff, (2016), Drones in GIS, Columbia College GIS Program, Sonora, CA
52. Vane, G., *Imaging Spectrometry of the Terrestrial Environment*," edited by, SPIE Vol. 1937, April 1993.
53. Welch, R. and Ehlers, M. 1987. Merging Multi resolution SPOT HRV and Landsat TM data.. Photogrammetric Engineering and Remote Sensing, 53: 301–303.
54. Wulder, M.A., White, J.C., Goward, S.N., Masek, J.G., Irons, J.R., (2008) Landsat continuity: issues and opportunities for land cover monitoring. Remote Sensing of Environment, 112: 955–969
55. Zhang, L. and Gruen, A., 2006. Multi-Image Matching for DSM Generation from IKONOS Imagery. ISPRS Journal of Photogrammetry and Remote Sensing, Vol. 60, pp. 195-211.

Web Resources:

http://what-when-how.com/remote-sensing-from-air-and-space/atmospheric-absorption-scattering-and-turbulence-visible-imagery-remote-sensing/

http://www.nrcan.gc.ca/node/9295

http://labs.cas.usf.edu/geodesy/sar.html

http://www.markelowitz.com/Hyperspectral.html

https://www.e-education.psu.edu/geog160/node/1958

https://crisp.nus.edu.sg/~research/tutorial/spot.htm

Source: http://web.sonoma.edu/users/f/freidel/techniques/exer/rem_sens/remsen_e.html)

http://hyperphysics.phy-astr.gsu.edu/hbasees/quantum/radfrac.html

http://www.harrisgeospatial.com/Support/SelfHelpTools/HelpArticles/HelpArticles-Detail/TabId/2718/ArtMID/10220/ArticleID/17333/Atmospheric-Windows-and-Optical-Sensors.aspx

https://www.nrcan.gc.ca/earth-sciences/geomatics/satellite-imagery-air-photos/satellite-imagery-products/educational-resources/9389

http://www.sc.chula.ac.th/courseware/2309507/Lecture/remote18.htm

https://www.researchgate.net/publication/290899564_Satellite_Hyperspectral_Earth_Observation_Missions_-_A_Review [accessed Feb 03 2018].

https://www.geoimage.com.au/satellite/geoeye-1

https://www.geoimage.com.au/satellites/very-high-resolution-satellites

https://www.itc.nl/Pub/sensordb/AllSensors.aspx

http://instruct.uwo.ca/earth-sci/300b-001/remote.htm

https://crisp.nus.edu.sg/~research/tutorial/opt_int.htm

https://www.spectravista.com/ger1500/

http://gisknowledge.net/topic/remote_sensing_and_dia/tutorial_true_ colour_composite.htm

http://www.euroargo-edu.org/argoeu_4.php.

http://forsys.sefs.uw.edu/fusion.html

https://www.satimagingcorp.com/services/resources/

eoedu.belspo.be/en/satellites/spot. htm).

https://landsat.usgs.gov/

http://digipiczone.com/editing-techniques-for-contrast-enhancement

https://www.codeproject.com/Articles/1203383/A-Fast-Simple-and-Powerful-Contrast-Enhancement-
http://www.eotec.com/images/IRS_-_Current_and_Future_-_Web.pdf

https://calval.cr.usgs.gov/JACIE_files/.../Karnik_Deviprasad_JACIE2010FINAL .pdf

Chapter 4

GLOBAL POSITIONING SYSTEMS

4.1 INTRODUCTION

Navigation systems have been in use since pre-historic times. Human-beings have always been concerned about where they are, where they are going, and how they are going to get there, and back again to their destination, using an appropriate route. Earlier civilizations developed unique ways for their navigation systems to do their daily works, like travelling, jobs, boating, hunting etc (Smith, 1997). They used directions, objects, etc., to fix their routes, and subsequently they noted down on stones, paper, cloth or leaves that can be retained for longer duration. Various methods have been used in the past from simply leaving markers, stone structures, along a coastline or river to charting the stars. In later years, compass and sextants were developed for navigation purposes. As technology developed, the need for a more accurate system with wider coverage that can help in faster navigation also increased (Agrawal, 2004).

The Global Positioning System (GPS) was designed to show the exact position of objects on the Earth anytime, anywhere, and in any weather condition. It is the most advanced and popular system of navigation. This system was launched into space in 1978 with the first GPS satellite (Herring, 1996). In the early 20th century, ground-based radio-navigation systems were developed.

Today, the technology has benefitted various applications like, Highways, Remote sensing, GIS, Railroads, Mining/Geology, Surveying and mapping, Agricultural, Environmental management, Geodesy, Resources, Power, Telecommunications, Health, Law enforcement, Emergency, Crustal movement, Disaster response, Weather, Aviation, Maritime, Precise timing, Automobile, Tracking objects, Sports, Construction, Recreation, etc. Now a days, GPS are used extensively mainly by navy, airforce, army, coast guard, rescue & relief personals, civilian carriers, surveyors, commercial transport, hikers, and trekkers (El-Rabbany, 2006). World-wide, there are a large number users of GPS enabled gadgets, like mobile phones, wrist watches etc., for a variety of utility (Xu, 2010).

4.2 HISTORY OF GPS

The first man-made **SPUTNIK** satellite was launched into the space on 4th October 1957 at an altitude of 985 Km above the Earth's surface, with the revolution period of 98 minutes. It carried a unique navigation system i.e., **Doppler's shift**. Dr. Ivan Getting, president of the Aerospace Corporation, in October, 1958 designed a three-dimensional, position-finding system based on time difference of arrival of radio signals which was the revolutionary in the field of space sciences and history of mankind (Hoffmann et al 1994). As early as 1962, he saw the need for a new satellite-based navigation system, and envisioned a more accurate positioning system that would be available in three dimensions, 24 hours a day, seven days a week (Smith, 1997). The history of satellite navigation is shown in Figure 4.1.

Frank McClure of the Applied Physics Laboratory made a suggestion in 1958 that it is possible to turn the problem upside down, and using a known satellite position, a navigator could determine his/her location anywhere in the world after receiving and processing the satellite signal for 15 minutes. This idea gave birth to Navy Navigational Satellite System or **TRANSIT** in 1958 (Kaplan, 1996). TRANSIT was an US based military satellite at an altitude of 1100 Km, with the revolution period of 108 minutes. It used observed measurements in Doppler shift to calculate distance and position to satellites, and remained operational till the end of year 1996 (Sickle, 2001).

GPS, a satellite based navigation system, was developed first by the Department of Defence, USA, which is a part of Global Navigation Satellite System (**GNSS**). In 1973, the US decided to establish, develop, test, acquire, and deploy a first space borne GPS, resulting in the Navigation Satellite Timing and Ranging (**NAVSTAR)** GPS. Initial satellites were launched between 1974 and 1977 for use in precision weapon delivery. GPS was designed as an all-weather, space based navigation system to satisfy the requirements for the Defence. It accurately provided the position (longitudes, latitudes, and altitudes), velocity, and time at a common reference system, anywhere in the world for 24 hours. At least four satellites are used to estimate four quantities, longitudes, latitudes, altitudes, and GPS time for each point to be surveyed. At initial stages of GPS, 10 development satellites were launched between 1978 and 1985. The initial constellation of 24 satellites was deployed within 1989 to 1994. The complete system was fully operational in 1995. Later, in May 2000, the military accuracy was made available to all users (El-Rabbany, 2006).

USA is the world leader of developing and launching GPS satellites, with worldwide coverage. Other nations have also developed their own navigation systems, for example USSR has developed their navigation system, called Global Navigation Satellite System (**GLONASS**) while European Union developed a system known as **GALELIO** navigation satellites. Figure 4.1 gives a summary view of the history of U.S. satellite-based navigation, particularly GPS. Details of the Russian GLONASS and the European GALILEO systems are not included as they arrived later, and generally mimicked the GPS development albeit with their own, locally developed detailed designs.

GPS technology was introduced to the Indian market in Mid 90's and since then there have been advances in technology that are leading the evolution of GPS and its tracking capabilities. Indian system, known as the Indian Regional Navigation Satellite System (**IRNSS**), is using its seven satellites. It will beam accurate navigation signals over India and up to 1,500 km from its borders. India's own GPS "Navigation with Indian Constellation" (**NavIC**) whose Hindi meaning is 'sailor' or 'navigator', is the operational name of IRNSS. It is currently in its nascent stage and Indian GPS is most likely to be available in the market for public use early next year. It is designed to provide accurate position information to users within the country, and is supposed to be more accurate than the US GPS system.

China is creating the **BeiDou** Navigation Satellite System; regional service has already been launched and it intends to achieve global coverage by around 2020.

Today GPS is considered as a global leader in navigational systems all over the world. The use of the system's additional bandwidth was opened for civilian use. This move, combined with recent advances in personal technologies was the catalyst for an explosive surge in GPS market opportunities and intelligent applications (El-Rabbany, 2006).

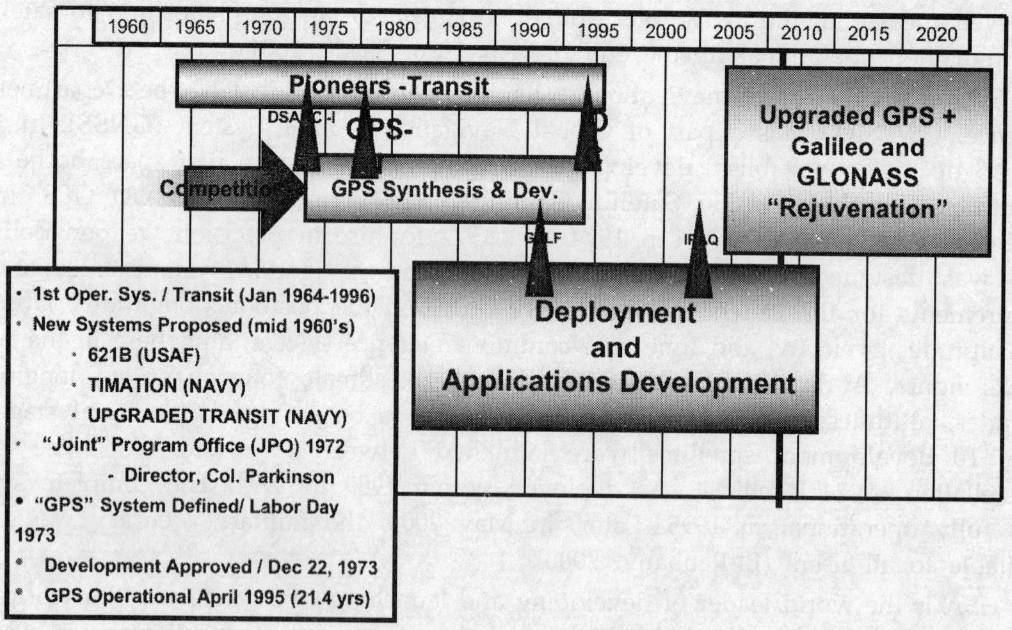

Figure 4.1: The history of satellite navigation *(Source: Parkinson et al, 2010)*

4.3 ADVANTAGES AND DISADVANTAGES OF GPS

The GPS was initially invented for defense and military purposes, but looking at its enormous advantages to provide 3-dimensional coordinates and time data, it is being used today world-wide for varied applications. Like any other technology, GPS technology also has some advantages and some disadvantages, as briefly given below.

4.3.1 Advantages

1. GPS provides real word geographical coordinates (Latitude, Longitude and Elevation with respect to WGS-84 datum) of any point on the Earth surface at any time and at any place.
2. In addition to three dimensional coordinates, it provides accurate time from atomic clock onboard GPS satellites.
3. GPS works day and night (24 x 7) under all weather conditions.
4. Signals received by the device from the GPS satellites are free of cost.
5. The data (output) is in the digital form which can be directly stored in the GPS device and further used directly in GIS.
6. GPS can also be used to prepare the spatial maps of the area surveyed.
7. Due to its low cost, it is easy to integrate into other technologies, like cell phone. Many smartphones feature a GPS based navigation system which greatly helps the users in navigation.
8. GPS can be used to track the things, irrespective of it being static or dynamic mode.
9. GPS devices can find a desired location for specific landmarks, such as the restaurants and hospital, police stations, within a specific radius of your current location.

4.3.2 Disadvantages

1. GPS devices rely on the power from batteries working for 8-12 hours in the field. So extra pair of charged batteries is required for taking continuous measurements.
2. GPS can provide mm accuracy, but are expensive. Low accuracy GPS have lesser features.
3. The accuracy of the coordinates is an issue. It requires clear visibility to the GPS satellites in the sky. The ionosphere and the troposphere cause slow down of the signal propagation speed and error in the coordinates.
4. Accuracy of observation depends on signals received from sufficient number of satellites as well as their distribution in the sky.
5. GPS signal also gets affected due to multipath from high rise buildings, towers and tress, the electromagnetic interference (electric wires, geomagnetic storms) etc., and cause errors in the measurements.
6. The GPS signals are unable to pass through solid structures so it can not work indoors, underground, under water, under forest, or under a bridge.

4.4 COORDINATE SYSTEMS

Data in a GPS is represented in a simplified view of the real world. Physical entities or phenomena on the Earth are approximated by data in a GIS. These data include information on the spatial location and extent of the physical entities, and also information on their non-spatial properties (attribute data). In geographical data, each physical entity or phenomena is associated with a location defined in a given space. Coordinates are used to define the spatial location and extent of geographic objects. A coordinate most often consists of a pair of numbers that specify the location in relation to an origin. The coordinate systems are usually based upon standardized map projections. Typically, there are two distinct types of data used to define geographical objects. First, coordinates or geometric data define the location and shape of the objects (Seebar, 2003). Second, attribute data, such as a name, color, pH, or soil moisture value, are collected and referenced to each object.

The geographical data, collected through GPS or any other method, are therefore often represented as an (x, y, z) triplet, where x refers to the x-coordinate and y to the y-coordinate in a (x, y) Cartesian coordinate system (Figure 4.2a), and z is its attribute data (e.g., elevation, landuse, soil type, rainfall, geology, snow depth). Since at a single location, there may be many attribute data present (e.g., snow depth may be related to elevation and temperature, a property called association), the data can be generalized to $(x, y, z_1, z_2, ... z_n)$ where n is the number of attributes at that location. Attribute data and their relative positions collected through GPS provide the advantage of using these for geographical analysis in a geographic information system (GIS) and solve complex problems (Smith, 1997).

Coordinate data may also be specified in a spherical coordinate system using angular measurements on a spherical Earth. The most common spherical system uses two angles of rotation to specify locations on an Earth surface (Figure 4.2b). These angles of rotation occur around a polar axis to define a **longitude** (λ) and with reference to an equatorial plane to define **latitude** (φ). Latitudes increase from zero at the equator to 90° at the poles. Northern latitude is written as N55°, and similarly southern latitudes are preceded by S. The longitudes increase east and west of an origin, and longitude values are preceded by an E and W, respectively, e.g., W45°. Latitude defines a position for any point on the Earth surface in terms of "**Northing**" (y) and Longitude in terms of "**Easting**" (x) relative to origin (0, 0). Spherical coordinates are recorded in a degrees-minutes-seconds, e.g. N55°10′05", signifying 55 degrees, 10 minutes, and 05 seconds of latitude. Minutes and seconds range from zero to sixty.

A geographic coordinate system is based on a three-dimensional ellipsoidal or spherical surface, and locations in GPS are defined using angular measurements, usually degrees of longitude and latitude. Horizontal coordinate systems are either geographic or projected. A projected coordinate system is based on a geographic coordinate system and a map projection. The vertical coordinate system provides a reference for z-coordinates, which are measurements of the height or depth of features with respect to a datum, such as world geodetic system- 1984 (**WGS-84)** datum (Seeber, 2003).

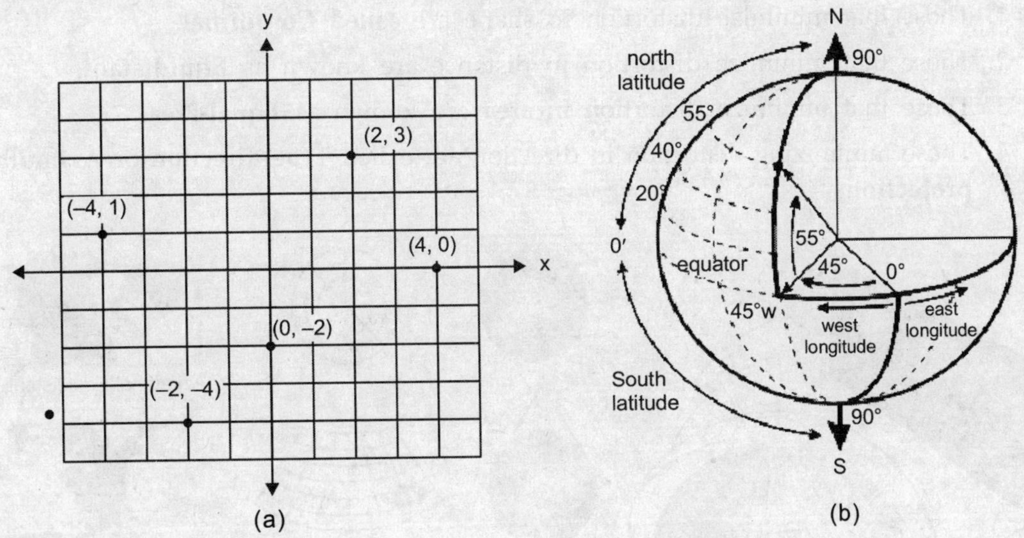

Figure 4.2: Coordinate system (a) rectangular, and (b) polar system (*Source: Smith, 1997*)

4.5 MAP PROJECTION

A global or spherical coordinate system, such as latitude-longitude, is often referred to as geographic coordinate systems. If two datasets are not referenced to the same geographic coordinate system, there is a need to perform a geographic (datum) transformation. This is a well-defined mathematical method to convert coordinates between two geographic coordinate systems. There are several pre-defined geographic transformations in GPS as well as GIS software. It is important to correctly use a geographic transformation, particularly in a large area; else analysis may give wrong location by up to a few hundred meters (Agrawal, 2004).

Projection is a fundamental component of map making. It is a mathematical means of transferring information from the Earth's three-dimensional curved surface to a two-dimensional medium (paper or computer screen), as shown in Figure 4.3a. It is done through a systematic mathematical transformation of the Earth's graticule of lines of longitude and latitude onto a plane. Projected coordinate systems are referred to as map projections. Different projections are used for different types of maps because of their appropriateness for certain uses. One map projection might be used for large-scale data in a limited area, while another is used for a small-scale map of the world.

A projected coordinate system, such as **Azimuthal Equidistant, Lambart Conical, Miller Cylindrical, Universal Transverse Mercator (UTM), Albers Equal Area,** or **Robinson**, provides various mechanisms to project maps of the Earth's spherical surface onto a two-dimensional cartesian coordinate plane (Smith, 1997). The Earth's spherical (or rather ellipsoid/spheroid) surface needs to be depicted as a flat surface for maps. The Indian grid uses the Lambert Conformal Conic Projection system (also known as Conic Orthomorphic Projection) with 2 standard parallels.

Figure 4.3b shows some of these projections. There are different classes of projections that minimize the distortion.

1. Those that minimize distortion in shape are called **Conformal**.
2. Those that minimize distortion in distance are known as **Equidistant**.
3. Those that minimize distortion in area are known as **Equal-area**.
4. Those minimizing distortion in direction are called **True-direction** or **Azimuthal projections**.

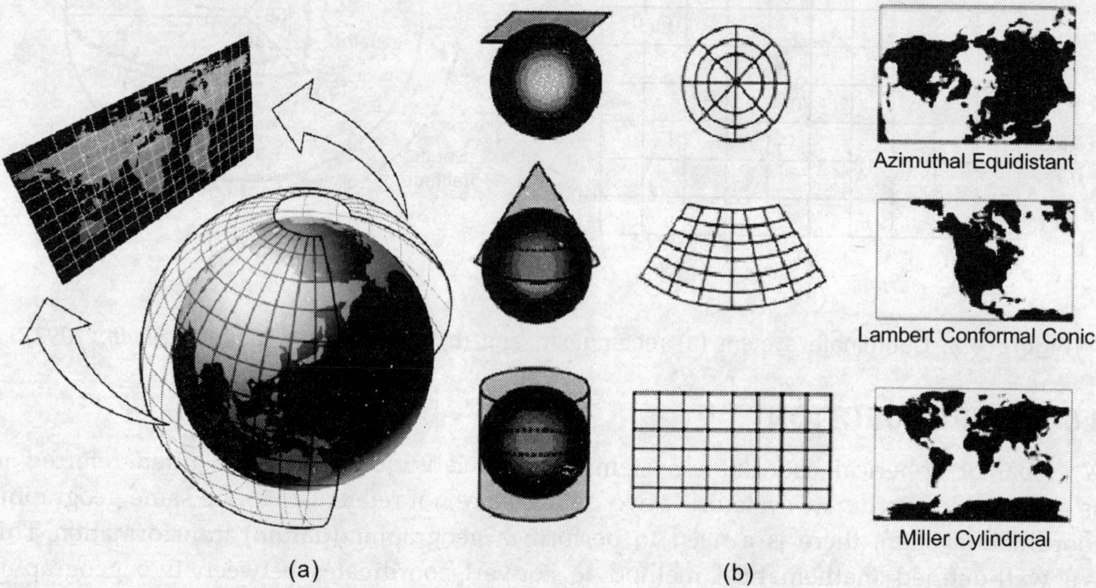

Figure 4.3: (a) Transferring Earth's three-dimensional curved surface to a two-dimensional flat surface (b) Some project coordinate system onto a two-dimensional cartesian coordinate plane (*Source: Seeber, 2003*).

4.5.1 Choosing a Map Projection

The selection of a map projection for a particular area can be made on the basis of (i) ***shape*** of the area, (ii) ***location*** (and orientation) of the area, and (iii) ***purpose*** of the map. For data collection and mapping & analysis work, it is to be ensured that the right type of projection is used. A preferred map projection is that where scale distortions remain minimum and map properties match to the purpose of the mapping (Seeber, 2003).

Generally, normal cylindrical projections are used to map the world. Conical projections are often used to map the different continents, while the polar azimuthal projections may be used to map the polar areas. Transverse and oblique aspects of many projections can be used for most parts of the world, though they are usually more difficult to construct. The general ***shape*** of the mapping area should match with the distorted pattern of a specific projection. If an area is approximately circular, an azimuthal projection will minimize the distortion, whereas, the cylindrical projection is best for a rectangular area and a conic projection for a triangular area. The choice of the aspect of a map projection depends largely on the ***location*** (and orientation) of the geographic area to be mapped. The most appropriate type of distortion property for a map depends largely on the ***purpose*** for which it will be used (Smith, 1997).

Angles and local shapes (e.g., in aeronautical charts, sea, air or meteorological charts, topographic maps) are correctly represented with a ***conformal map projections***, but for larger regions, they show considerable area distortions. Map projections with an ***equal-area distortion property*** represent areas correctly, so maps which are to be used for measuring areas (e.g. thematic and distribution maps) often make use of this projection system. The ***equidistant map projection*** is achievable only from one or two points to any other point on the map or in certain directions. Maps (e.g. air-route, radio or seismic maps) which require correct distances measured from the centre of the map to any point often make use of this projection (Well, 1989). In general, the ***ideal map projection*** for any country would either be an azimuthal, cylindrical, or conic projection, depending on the shape of the area, and purpose of maps (Seeber, 2003). For topographic and small-scale maps, ***Transverse mercator*** and the ***Lambert conical projections*** are used.

4.6 DATUMS

Datums are sets of parameters and ground control points defining local coordinate systems. Because the Earth is not a perfect sphere, but is somewhat "egg-shaped," **spheroids** and **ellipsoids** are used to model the 3-dimensional shape of the Earth (Smith, 1997). A datum is created to account for these local variations in establishing a coordinate system.

In engineering and mapping work, a datum is a reference point, or surface with respect to which coordinates are measured. The ***geoid*** is defined as the surface of the Earth's gravity field, which is approximately the same as *mean sea level*. It is perpendicular to the direction of gravity pull. Since the mass of the Earth is not uniform at all points, and the direction of gravity changes, the shape of the geoid is irregular. A ***geodetic datum*** is a coordinate system and a set of reference points, used to locate places on the Earth. The local datum, known as mean sea level, can vary from one country to another. Different datums use different mathematical relationships for considering the precise shape and size of the Earth (reference ellipsoid). Because the Earth is an imperfect ellipsoid, localised datums can give a more accurate representation of the area.

In Figure 4.4, the Earth is shown as the irregular surface (thick blue line). A generalized Earth-centered coordinate system, called World Geodetic System (**WGS-84**, in red colour) provides a good overall mean solution for all places on the Earth. However, WGS-84 cannot account for local variations; therefore local datums have been developed world-wide. For example, mean seal level datum of India (green line) which more closely fits the earth's surface at that location of the country. Local datum fits best only for that country, so it will result in serious errors in measurement if used in another part of the Earth (Seeber, 2003).

At global level, however the use of WGS-84 datum, as shown in Figure 4, is becoming increasingly adopted. The constants and model parameters which describe the Earth's size, shape, gravity and geomagnetic fields is the basis of WGS 1984 (Xu, 2010). NAVSTAR GPS also uses this reference system as it follows the criteria outlined in the International Earth Rotation Service **(IERS)**. The geometric centre of the WGS-84 ellipsoid coincides with the origin of the WGS-84 coordinate system, and Z axis serves the rotational axis of this ellipsoid of revolution. Reference ellipsoid of WGS 84 generates its own geodetic coordinates.

GPS receivers provide WGS-84 coordinates to GPS users if no changes to the reference frame are selected or made. At the beginning of each calendar year, the software that generates GPS broadcast orbits are updated with an epoch at the half-year mark to account for plate tectonic motion. This method results in a yearly step-wise adjustment of WGS-84 coordinates delivered through GPS broadcast orbits (Smith, 1997).

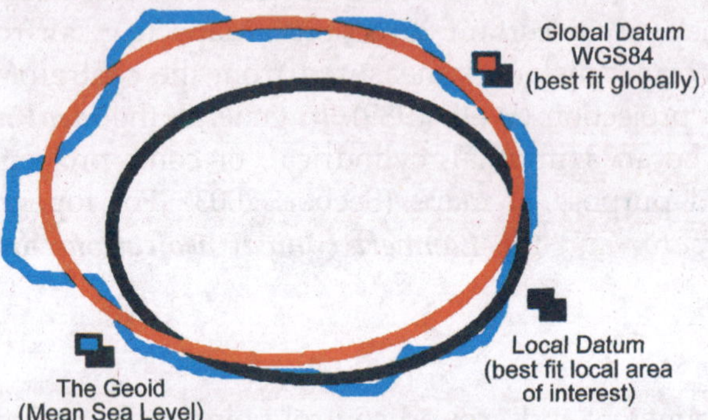

Figure 4.4: The shape of the Earth and WGS 84 datum (*Source: Smith, 1997*)

The Indian Geodetic Datum uses the Everest Spheroid as reference surface to define the shape of the Earth. It was originally defined in 1830 by Colonel George Everest (Surveyor General of India from 1830 to 1843) based on Great Trigonometrical Survey initiated in 1802. This was subsequently updated in 1888 and then in 1956. Kalyanpur (Madhya Pradesh, 77.65489°E 24.11981°N) in Central India was chosen as initial point of origin. India and adjacent countries cover a very large area, and therefore to minimise errors in scale, and to improve correctness of shape, this area is divided into a total of nine zones, as below and shown in Figure 4.5. Each of the zones has its own unique set of parameters.

Figure 4.5: Approximate layout of zones in Indian grid.

1. Zone 0 - India and Pakistan North of 35°35′N.
2. Zone IA - India and Pakistan 28°N-35°35′N.
3. Zone IB - Unknown parts of China (Tibet).
4. Zone IIA - India 21°N-28°N & West of 82°E and Pakistan South of 28°N.
5. Zone IIB - Complete Bangladesh, India North of 21°N & East of 82°E and Myanmar (Burma) North of 21°N.
6. Zone IIIA - India 15°N-21°N.
7. Zone IIIB - Myanmar (Burma) 15°N-21°N.
8. Zone IVA - India South of 15°N.
9. Zone IVB - Myanmar (Burma) South of 15°N.

For Indian grid, 'Indian (India and Nepal)', Datum may be used with following parameters:

(a) Everest 1956 Ellipsoid
  (i) Semi-Major axis/Equatorial Radius - 6,377,301.243m.
  (ii) Inverse flattening (1/f) - 300.8017.
  (iii) Semi-Minor axis/Polar Radius - 6,356,100.228m (calculated from 1/f).

(b) Datum Transformation Parameters to WGS 1984
  (i) Delta X - 295m.
  (ii) Delta Y - 736m.
  (iii) Delta Z - 257m.

4.7 VARIOUS SEGMENTS OF GPS

There are mainly three segments of GPS; **space segment, control segment**, and **user segment** (Jeffery, 2015). These are shown in Figure 4.6, and briefly explained below.

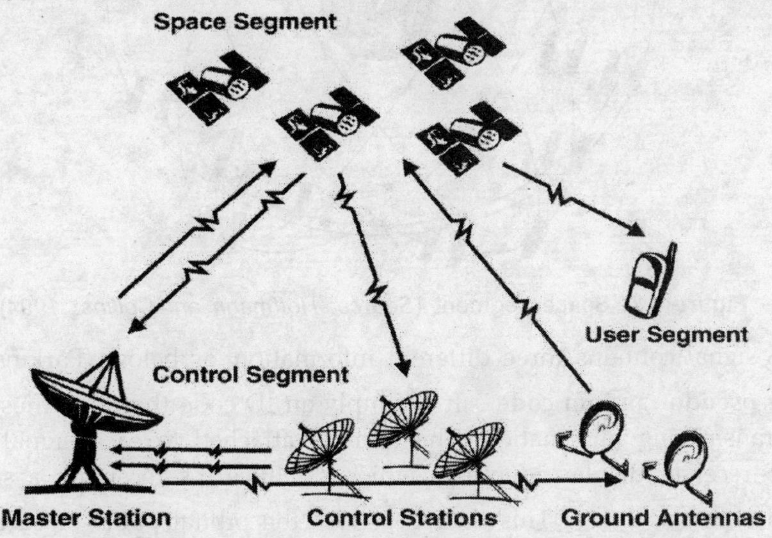

Figure 4.6: Various segments of a GPS (*Source: Herring, 1996*)

4.7.1 Space Segment

The space segment includes constellation of NAVSTAR Earth orbiting satellites with a design life of for about 7.5 years. Primarily, a GPS requires 24 satellites for full global coverage. Four satellites are launched in 6 orbital planes which are inclined at 55^0 with respect to equator, and orbits separated by 60^0. They revolve around the Earth at the altitude of about 12000 miles (~20,000 km) above Earth's surface. Orbital period of each satellite is approximately 11hr 55minutes (Sickle, 2001). This arrangement provides visibility between five and eight satellites at any given time from any point on the Earth (Figure 4.7).

Each satellite consists of four precise atomic clocks; only one of which is used at a time. It has a micro-processor on board for limited data processing. Each satellite carries three nickel-cadmium batteries, two solar panels, battery charger, S band antenna-satellite control, and 12 element L band antenna-user control. These satellites are equipped with thrusters which can be used to maintain or modify their orbits. The GPS satellites use a ranging system (trilateration). At a given time, several satellites send their signals to a GPS receiver. Each transmission of signal is time-tagged, and contains the satellite's position (Parkinson, and Spilker, 1996, Xu, 2010). The time-of-arrival of signal at GPS receiver is compared with the time-of-transmission. The time is multiplied by the speed of light to obtain the corresponding distance between that satellite and GPS receiver. The location of the user is determined by the intersection of several of these ranges.

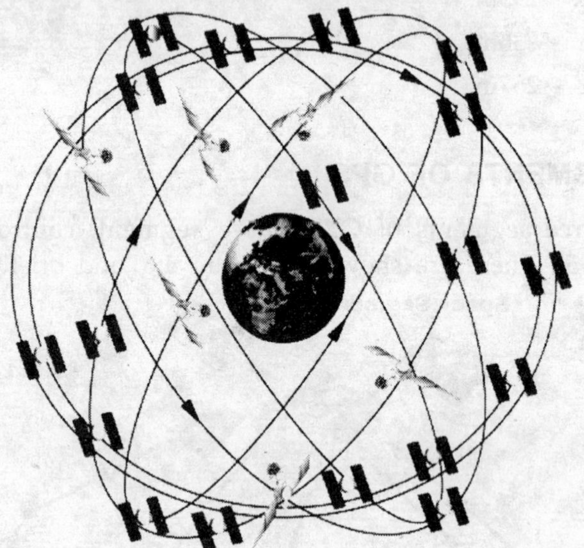

Figure 4.7: Space segment (*Source: Hoffmann anf Collins, 1994*)

The GPS signal contains three different information, as below (Parkinson et al 2010):

1. **The pseudo random code** – It is simply an ID code that identifies which satellite is transmitting information. The number attached to each signal bar visible on GPS receiver display identifies which satellites it's receiving a signal from.
2. **The almanac data** – This data describes the orbital paths of each satellite. GPS receiver uses this data to determine which satellites it should track. With almanac

data, the receiver can concentrate on those satellites it can see and neglect those that would be over the horizon and out of view.

3. **The ephemeris data** – It provides information to the GPS receiver where each satellite should be at any time throughout the day. Each satellite will broadcast its own ephemeris data showing the orbital information. Ephemeris data consists of very precise orbital and clock correction information necessary for precise positioning, but it keeps on changing after short time.

4.7.2 Control Segment

The control segment is administered by the Department of Defence **(DoD)**, US government who is responsible for construction, launching, maintenance and monitoring the performance & health of all GPS satellites. Primarily, one master control station is established in USA, and several ground monitoring stations and 4 antenna stations for whole GPS throughout the world (NAVSTAR, 2003). Various stations in control segment are represented in Figure 4.8.

The DoD monitors these stations and tracks all GPS signals for controlling the satellites and predicting their orbits. The **master control station** is responsible for collecting and tracking the data from the monitoring stations, and computes satellite orbits & clock parameters. Other monitoring stations are responsible for measuring the pseudo range data. This orbital tracking network is used by master control station to calculate satellite ephemeris and clock correction coefficients, and to forward them to ground antenna. The antenna transmits the data to each satellite at least once a day. The satellites then send subsets of the orbital ephemeris to GPS receivers over radio signals. Along with the other information, meteorological data are also collected by the monitoring stations, thus allowing for an accurate evaluation of the tropospheric delays of GPS signals (NIMA, 1997). The satellite tracking data from these monitoring stations are transmitted to the master control station for processing.

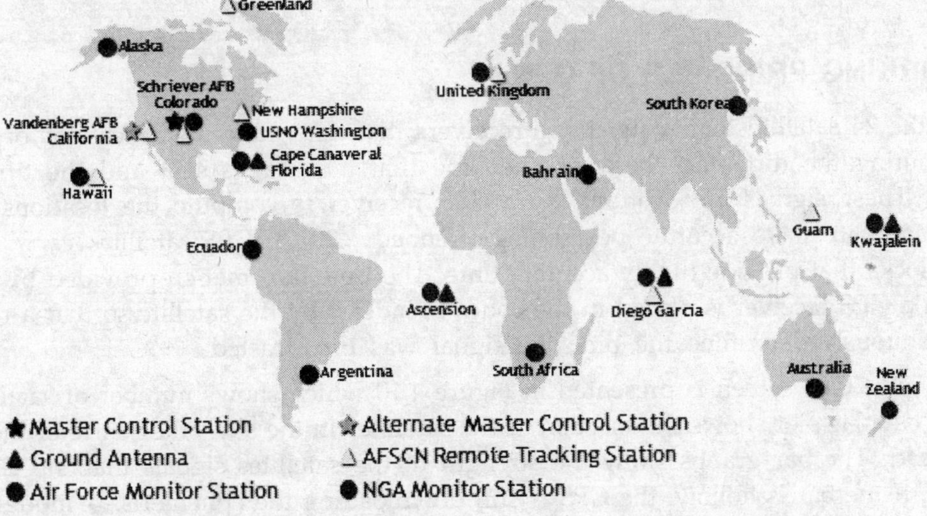

Figure 4.8: Control segment (*Source: Jacobson, 2007*)

4.7.3 User Segment

It consists of GPS receivers that receive signals from the GPS satellites (Figure 4.9). The typical receiver is composed of an antenna and a pre-amplifier, radio signal microprocessor, control and display device, data recording unit, and power supply. GPS receivers convert satellite signals into position, velocity, and time estimates. A minimum of four satellites are required to compute four dimensions i.e., x, y, z (position) and time. The GPS receivers come in different sizes and shapes. A receiver is often described by its number of channels, signifying how many satellites it can monitor simultaneously. Originally, GPS receiver was designed to work in four or five channels, but it has typically increased over the years after 2007; and presently, the receivers can operate between 12 and 20 channels (Key, 2004).

GPS receiver collects two types of data from satellites to get an exact location i.e., almanac and ephemeris which is continuously transmitted by GPS satellites, and receiver collects & stores the data (Kennedy, 2010). The almanac gives the exact status of satellites and its approximate orbital information which are used to estimate visibility of satellites. Ephemeris data gives the accurate information about the orbit of the satellite which can be used to calculate the location of satellite with one meter or two. It is updated every two hours and usually valid for 4 hours.

In this segment, the observations are taken by the user both for civilian and military uses (Boa and Yen, 2004). Navigation in three dimensions is the primary function of GPS. Navigation receivers are made for aircraft, ships, ground vehicles, and for hand carrying by individuals. Geodetic receivers are used for positioning, time dissemination, measuring atmospheric parameters, surveying, geodetic control, and plate tectonic studies. Precise positioning is possible using GPS receivers at reference locations providing corrections and relative positioning data for remote receivers (Hoffmann and Collins, 1994). While all three segments operate at one time, but the typical user is normally unaware about the control segment, and only concerns with the receiver in hand and the satellites actually visible at that location during use.

4.8 WORKING PRINCIPLE OF GPS

Each of the 24 satellites emits signals to receivers that determine their locations or ranges by computing the difference between the time that a signal is sent and the time it is received. These signals are captured by a GPS receiver to compute the locations of the satellites and to make accurate positioning (Kennedy, 2010). GPS satellites carry precise atomic clocks that provide highly accurate time. The time information provided by atomic clocks in a GPS receiver is placed in the codes broadcast by the satellite so that a receiver can continuously determine the time the signal was broadcasted.

A typical GPS screen is presented in Figure 4.10 which shows number of satellites in use. The circular plot shows the location of the satellites in the sky - the centre of the circle is overhead. The bar graphs show the strength of the satellites signals that the GPS has acquired. If the bar is hollow, the GPS is still downloading the ephemeris. A modern GPS receiver will typically track all of the available satellites simultaneously, but only a selection of them will be used to calculate the position (Jefffery, 2015).

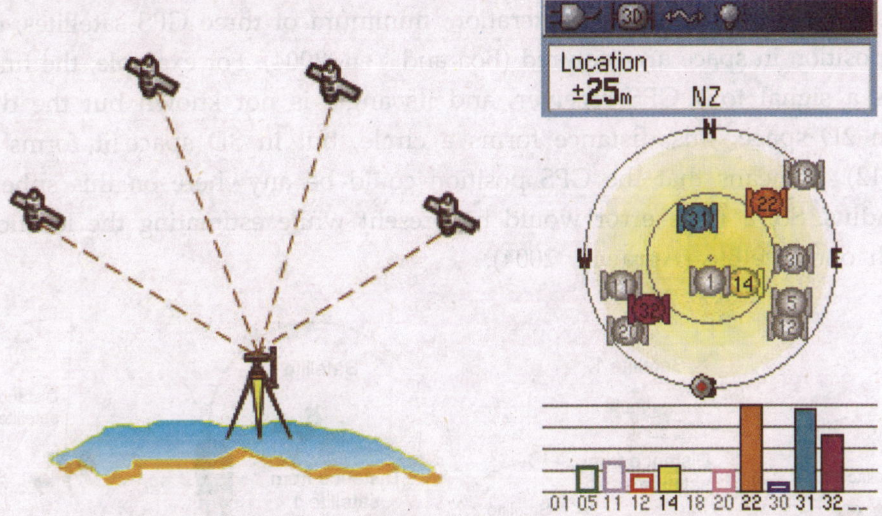

Figure 4.9: Users segment (*Source: Kaplan and Christopher, 1996*)

Figure 4.10: Typical features on display of a GPS

When signals are received from a satellite, the receiver monitors the navigation message from the satellite which contains the current GPS time, a set of numbers called the ephemeris. These data describes the satellite's orbit in space, and the exact location of the satellite where the satellite is in that orbit at a particular time. The result is a set of x, y and z coordinates with respect to a coordinate system referred to as WGS-84 where the satellite was when the signal was transmitted (Kulshreshta, 1997).

With information about the ranges from at least four satellites and the location of these satellites when the signal was sent, the GPS receiver computes its own three-dimensional position. Since, the satellites broadcast radio signals (EM radiation), simple distance calculation can be made by the simple mathematical relationship: $d = v * t$, where v = speed of light 3.0×10^{8} m/s, t = known time difference between send and receive signals, as shown in Figure 4.11.

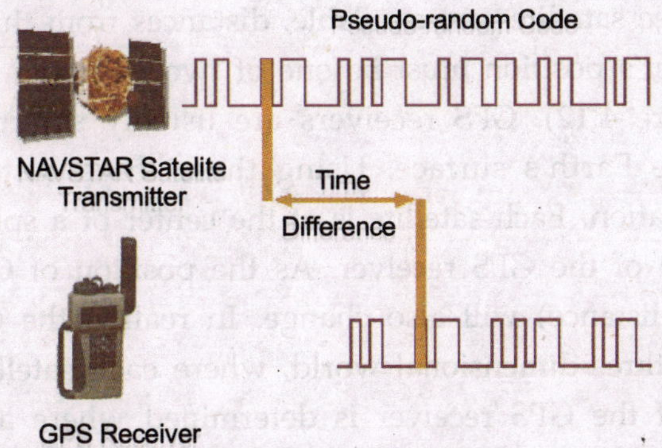

Figure 4.11: Computation of distance (*Source: Hurn, 1989*)

4.8.1 Trilateration

GPS receivers use a technique called **trilateration** which involves computing distance with the help of known distances. In trilateration, minimum of three GPS satellites; each with a known position in space are required (Boa and Yen, 2004). For example, the first satellite broadcasts a signal to a GPS receiver, and its angle is not known but the distance is known. In 2D space, this distance forms a circle, but in 3D space it forms a sphere (Figure 4.12). It means that the GPS position could be anywhere on this sphere at this specific radius. So, a large error would be present while estimating the location on the Earth with one satellite (Agrawal, 2004).

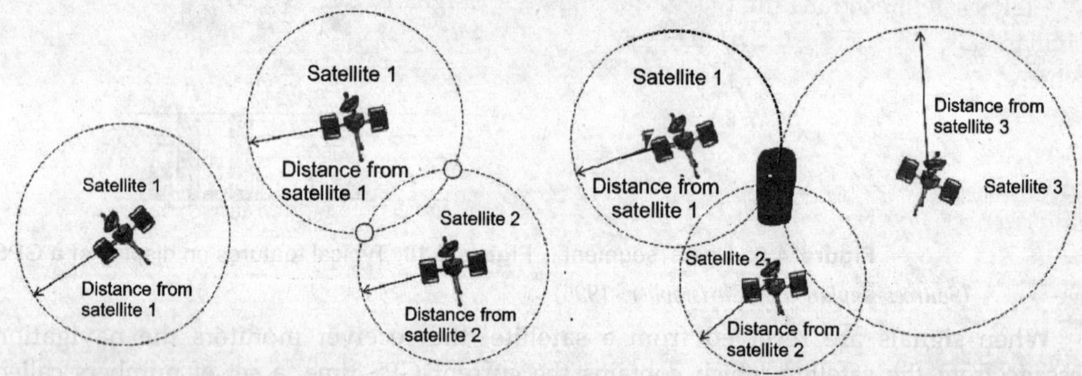

Figure 4.12: Determination of location from 1 Satellite, 2 Satellites, and 3 Satellites using trilateration method (*Source: Hinch, 2010*)

When signals from two satellites are available, a receiver can find its position somewhere along a circle formed by the intersection of the two spherical ranges (Figure 4.12). This means that the GPS position could be anywhere on that circle. But this time, there are two known distances from two satellites. With two signals, the precise position could be any of the two points where these two spheres intersect (Leick, 1995). The receivers normally select the point out of two, which is closer to the Earth. Even this process incurs error in measurement of location.

If signals from three satellites are available, distances from three satellites are known. In this case, the receiver's position must be one of two points at the intersection of three spherical ranges (Figure 4.12). GPS receivers are usually smart enough to choose the location nearest to the Earth's surface. Using these three distances, trilateration can determine a precise location. Each satellite is at the center of a sphere and where they all intersect is the position of the GPS receiver. As the position of GPS receiver moves, the radius of each circle (distance) will also change. In reality, the GPS satellites broadcast signals as a sphere in three-dimensional world, where each satellite is at the center of a sphere. The position of the GPS receiver is determined where all spheres intersect (El-Rabbany, 2006).

At a minimum, three satellites are required for a two-dimensional (horizontal) fix. Four ranges are however needed for a three-dimensional fix (horizontal and elevation).

4.9 GPS SATELLITE SIGNALS

The signal that is sent out from GPS satellites is a random sequence; each part of which is different from every other, called **pseudo-random code**. This random sequence is repeated continuously. All GPS receivers know this sequence and repeat it internally. Therefore, satellites and the receivers must be in synchronisation. The receiver picks up the satellite's transmission and compares the incoming signal to its own internal signal. By comparing the lag in these signals, the travel time is computed (Misra, 2016).

GPS satellites transmit two radio signals; designated as L1 and L2 (Figure 4.13). A civilian GPS uses the L1 signal frequency (1575.42 MHz) in the UHF band. The L1 code, which is available for civilians, is the Course/Acquisition-code **(C/A- code)**, which has a wavelength of approximately 300 meters (NAVSTAR, 1996). The C/A-code is modulated only upon L1, and its non-availability in L2 allowed the government to control the level of accuracy available to civilian users. The L1 frequency carries the navigation message and the standard positioning code signals (**SPS**). Civil users worldwide use the SPS without restrictions. Most receivers are capable of receiving and using the SPS signals. The SPS accuracy is intentionally degraded by the DOD by the use of Selective Availability (**SA**). SPS provides 100 m horizontal, 156 m vertical, and 340 nanoseconds time accuracy (Wells, 1989, Xu, 2010). The signals travelling from satellite to receivers will pass through clouds, dust, gas, particles etc., but will not travel through solid objects, such as buildings and mountains.

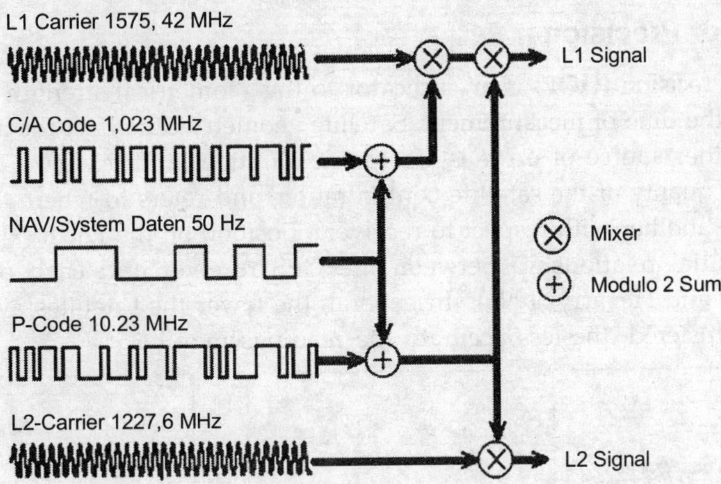

Figure 4.13: Carriers of GPS signals (*Source: Leick, 1995*)

Dual frequency receivers get signals in L1 and L2 carrier wave at frequency 1227.60 MHz (wavelength 24.45 cm). These dual frequencies receivers are chosen to eliminate the ionospheric dispersion which is one of the major sources of systematic range error. The pseudo-ranges, which are derived from signal travel time to the receiver, use two pseudorandom noise (**PRN**) codes. These codes are modulated onto the carrier frequencies

(Sickle, 2001). The carrier frequency with PRN codes is modulated for the real time positioning through GPS signals. The travel time of a PRN signal code can give pseudo-ranges. The Precision-code (**P-Code**) modulates both the L1 and L2 carrier phases found in military receivers. It is only used by receivers which are designed for precision positioning code signals (**PPS**) (Boa and Yen, 2004).

P-code, with a wavelength of approximately 30 meters, is encrypted into the **Y-Code** in the Anti-Spoofing (**AS**) mode of operation. The encrypted Y-Code requires a classified AS module for each receiver channel. The P (Y)-Code is the basis for the Precise Positioning System (PPS). Authorized users with cryptographic equipment & keys, and specially equipped receivers use the PPS. PPS provides 22 m horizontal, 27.7 m vertical, and 200 nano-second time accuracy (Kulshrestha, 1997, Key 2004).

As the satellite system was fully operational in 1992, access to the P-code was denied to the public by US Government NAVSTAR, 2003). In order to maintain control over the navigation system, the US military wanted to have most accurate GPS measurements with them only. Therefore, by altering the satellites clocks slightly according to a specific code, civilians used to get some errors in measurements as a result of time error. These signals allow non-military GPS users to obtain measurements that were accurate to approximately 100 meters (Boa and Yen, 2004).

Later, methods have been developed, where civilians have accurately calculated the receiver's position by comparing the GPS-measured position of a known location with its actual coordinates. The corrections were broadcasted to the GPS receiver, and thus it was possible for civilians to determine the positions with an accuracy of millimetres (Kulshreshtha, 1997).

4.9.1 Dilution of Precision

The Dilution of Precision **(DOP)** is an indicator to the geometrical strength of the satellites being tracked at the time of measurement. Satellite geometry can affect the accuracy of GPS positioning. Another source of error is Geometric Dilution of Precision (**GDOP**) which is a measure of the quality of the satellite configuration, and refers to where the satellites are in relation to one another with respect to receiver's position on the Earth (Figure 4.14). This indicates the spatial relationship between the GPS receiver and each of the potential satellites (Kaplan and Hegarry, 1996). In general, the fewer the satellites available and the closer they are clustered, the less accurate the readings may be.

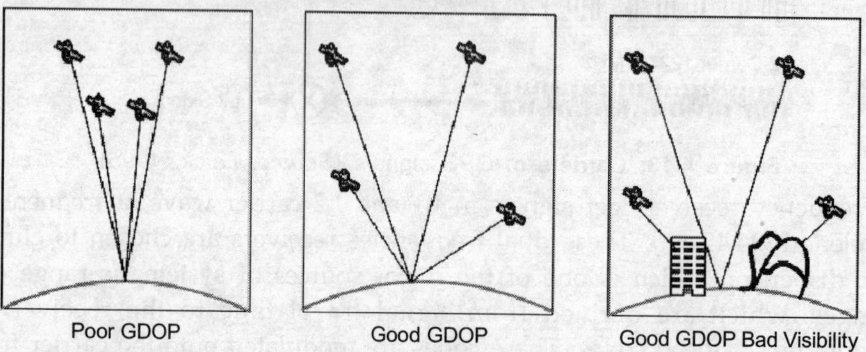

Figure 4.14: Geometric dilution of precision (*Source: Sickle, 2001*)

The GDOP has two components; one related to the receiver's position (**PDOP**) and one related to the time determination (**TDOP**). While PDOP is related to the satellite geometry (Figure 4.15), its value between 2 and 4 is excellent, between 4 to 6 is good, between 6 to 8 is fair, between 8 to 10 is poor, and 10 to 12 is marginal, and values above 12 is not recommended to use. PDOP mask or filter can be used in receiver as a tolerance setting for acceptability of signal quality. Overall estimate of accuracy = PDOP * GDOP (Herring, 1996).

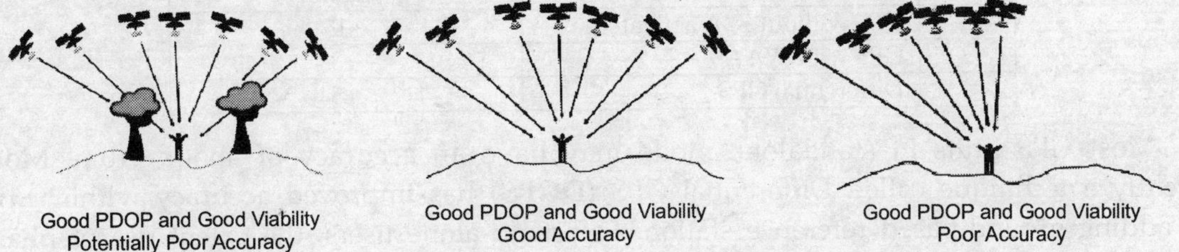

Figure 4.15: Position dilution of precision (*Source: NAVSTAR, 2003*)

4.9.2 Accuracy

GPS is an utterly pervasive and wonderful technology. GPS accuracy is sufficiently accurate for most applications. There are different levels of accuracy that can be achieved using appropriate equipment and techniques (Figure 4.16). There are two main factors that determine the accuracy of a GPS position: (i) Error on range measurement (Noise + Systematic), and (ii) Geometry of the satellites (Boa and Yen, 2004). The first factor has many components that are controlled by the receiver and the local environment of the system. The second factor is not under the control of the user, except by using a receiver with more channels. The position error may be computed as (Position Error = DOP x Range Error), where DOP is the Dilution of Precision (NAVSTAR, 2003)

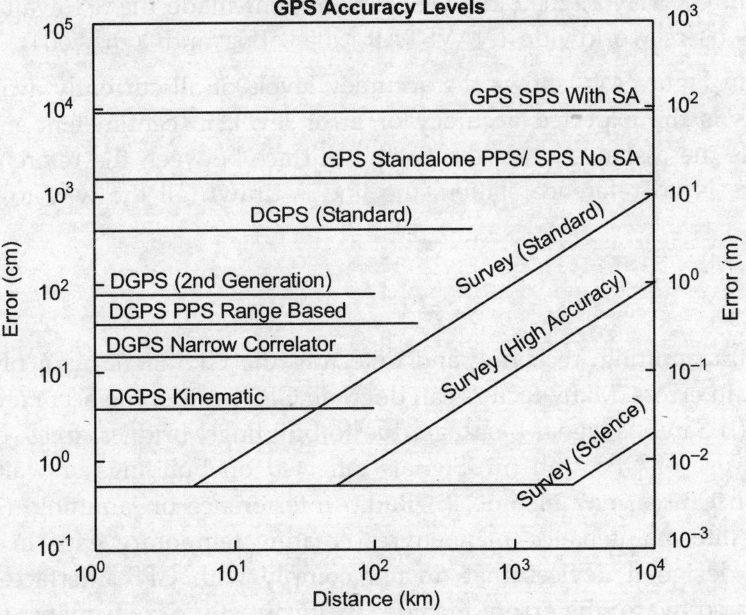

Figure 4.16: Various accuracy levels (*Source: Clynch, 2001*)

The accuracy expected to be obtained using a GPS receiver will vary according to the overall system used (Figure 4.16). While accuracy level actually achieved will depend upon many factors, typical estimations of the level of GPS accuracy is presented in Table 4.1.

Table 4.1: GPS system with expected accuracy

S.No.	GPS system	Expected accuracy (m)
1	GPS with S/A activated	±100
2	GPS without S/A activated	±15
3	GPS with WAAS	±3
4	Differential GPS	±5

Most GPS units in standalone mode may have an accuracy of about ±10m. More recently a technique called Differential GPS (**DGPS**) has improved accuracy within ±1m by adding ground-based reference station. For stand-alone users, the extent use of phase is a major factor in achieving the accuracy. The noise on the phase is typically 1 mm to provide the range 10 cm to 1 m (Jeffery, 2015). Therefore, the use of phase data in a way can improve the accuracy. The multipath also drastically reduces the phase measurement. In point positioning mode, accuracy within meter with 1 epoch solution and 24 hours of observation may be possible (depends on SA). In differential mode accuracy in cm (in P Code) and 1-5 m (in CA Code) may be obtained, while accuracy of 5 mm ± 1 ppm may be obtained in differential phase mode (Hurn, 1993, Xu, 2010).

Special techniques (called **Kinematic**) make use of the phase to achieve higher accuracies. However, they normally are to be used to range 25 to 50 km of baslines. GPS position errors are always about twice as bad in height as along either horizontal axis. Horizontal errors for PPS and SPS modes in the 3-5 m range are common. During 1990, the intentional degradation of accuracy was in place (called Selective Availability) and SPS accuracy was 100 m horizontal. On May 1, 2000, the U.S. government made the SA available to all civil and commercial users worldwide (NAVSTAR, 2003, Boa and Yen, 2004).

The graph in Figure 4.16 shows the accuracy levels of all currently available systems. The vertical axis is the expected accuracy or error level, in centimeters and meters. The horizontal axis is the distance along the Earth's surface between the reference station and the user. If there is no reference station, the line is drawn all the way to 10,000 km, all over the Earth.

4.9.3 Errors

The process of transmitting, receiving and detecting the GPS signal is a physical process which may contain errors. Many factors can degrade GPS positioning accuracy, but common causes include: (i) Satellite signal blockage due to buildings, bridges, trees, etc., (ii) Indoor or underground use of GPS, and (iii) Signals reflected off buildings or walls (**multipath**). Far less common causes may include: (i) Radio interference or jamming, (ii) Major solar storms, (iii) Satellite maintenance/manoeuvres creating temporary gaps in coverage, and (iv) Improperly designed devices that do not comply with GPS interface specifications. Due to mapping software, the errors include: (i) Incorrectly drawn maps, (ii) Mislabelled businesses and other points of interest, and (iii) Missing roads, buildings, communities, etc (Parkinson and Spilker 1996). The other reasons of the errors (Figure 4.17) could be (Sickle, 2001, Boa and Yen, 2004) -

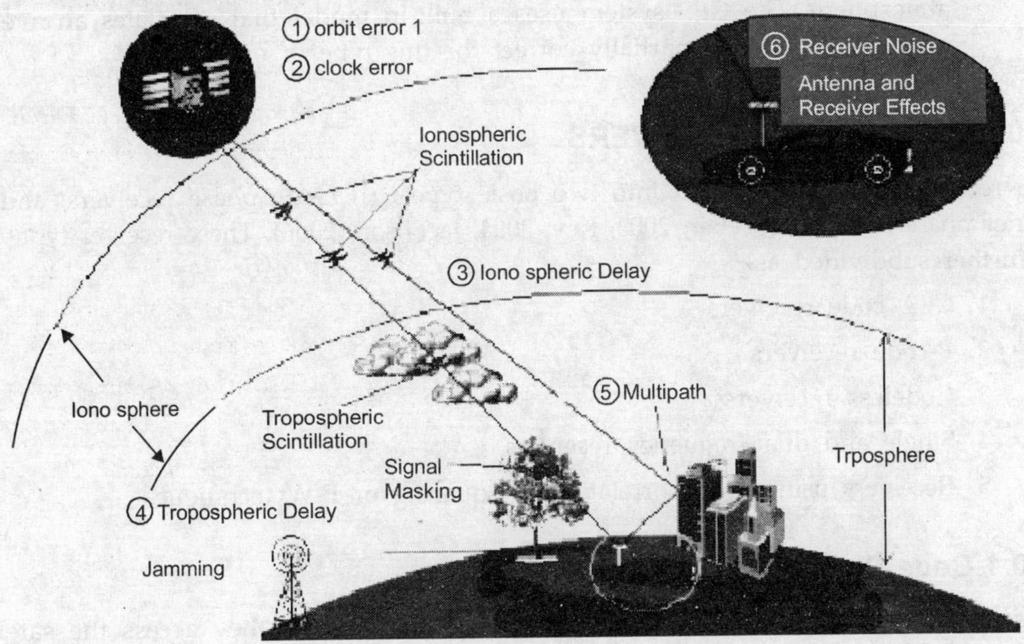

Figure 4.17: Various sources of errors in signals (*Source: Andrejs, 2010*)

1. *Signal multipath-* This occurs when the GPS signal is reflected off the objects falling in the path of satellite signals, such as tall buildings or dense forest or large mountain, before it reaches the receiver. This increases the travel time of the signal, thereby causing errors.
2. *Receiver clock errors-* A receiver's built-in clock is never as accurate as the atomic clocks onboard satellites, therefore, the data may have very slight timing errors.
3. *Orbital errors-* These are also known as ephemeris errors, these are inaccuracies in the reported locations of the satellites.
4. *Number of satellites visible-* The more the number of satellites visible to a GPS receiver, higher the accuracy of observations.
5. *Interferences-* Magnetic terrain, magnetic ores, electronic interferences, electric poles, etc., can cause position errors.
6. *Under cover-* Typical GPS units do not work indoors, underwater or underground.
7. *Satellite geometry-* This refers to the relative position of the satellites at any given time, which may not be desirable positions, and may give errors in observations. In an ideal satellite geometry, these are located at wide angles relative to each other.
8. *Intentional degradation of the satellite signal-* Selective Availability **(SA)** was an intentional degradation of the signal once imposed by the US DoD. The SA was intended to prevent military adversaries from using the highly accurate GPS

signals. The government turned off SA in May 2000, which significantly improved the accuracy of civilian GPS receivers.

9. *Ionosphere and troposphere delays-* The satellite signal slows as it passes through the atmosphere. The GPS system uses a built-in model that calculates an average amount of delay to partially correct for this type of error.

4.10 TYPES OF GPS RECEIVERS

GPS receivers can be classified into two basic types: (i) Code phase receivers, and (ii) Carrier phase receivers (Seeber, 2003, Key, 2004, Jacobson, 2006). These receiver types can be further subdivided as-

1. C/A code receivers
2. P-code receivers
3. Codeless receivers
4. Single and dual-frequency receivers
5. Receivers using cross-correlation or squaring or P-W techniques

4.10.1 Code Phase Receivers

These receivers are also called code correlating receivers as they access the satellite navigational P- or C/A-code signal for their operation. They have a unique capability to begin calculations without having an approximate location and time. Code phase receivers provide real-time navigation using almanac data from satellite message for operation and signal processing. These receivers have anywhere-fix capability as they can synchronize themselves with GPS time at a point with unknown coordinates (Boa and Yen, 2004). For this purpose, they need to lock the signals of four satellites to commence the survey with a quicker start-up time.

In code based receivers, phase position of the received code sequence is compared with the phase of an identical code replica, generated by the receiver (using the same algorithm as used for the code from the satellites) via a correlation technique. Hence, the observable is also called the code phase (Seeber, 2003). These receivers can be used for the rapid calculation of baselines when high accuracy is not required, for instance in exploration or offshore work. The two code sequences are shifted stepwise in phase until a maximum correlation is obtained. These have a complete code dependent correlation channel which produces: code phase, carrier phase, change of carrier phase (Doppler frequency), and satellite message.

4.10.2 Carrier Phase Receivers

These receivers utilize the actual GPS signals to calculate a position. Two common types of such receivers (Single frequency and Dual frequency) are explained below (Kaplan and Hegarry, 1996, Boa and Yen, 2004), and a comparison is given in Table 4.2.

Table 4.2 A comparison of single and double frequency receivers

S.No.	Single Frequency	Double frequency
1	Access to L1 only	Access to L1 and L2
2	Mostly civilian users	Mostly military users
3	Much cheaper	Very expensive
4	Modulated with C/A and P codes	Not possible for civilian users if Y code is present.
5	Affected by ionospheric delay	Almost independent of ionospheric delay
6	Used for short base lines	Used for both long and short base lines
7	Most receivers are coded	Most receivers with dual frequency are codeless

(a) **Single frequency** – These receivers track L1 frequency signal only, and are cheaper than dual frequency receivers (Figure 4.18a). They can be effectively used in relative positioning mode for accurate baselines of less than 50 km or where ionosphere effects can normally be ignored.

(b) **Dual frequency** – Theses receivers track both L1 and L2 frequency signals, and are expensive than single frequency receivers. They can effectively be used to measure longer baselines of more than 50 km where ionosphere effects have a larger impact, as ionosphere effects are eliminated by combining L1 and L2 observations.

4.10.3 Geodetic Receivers

These receiver are essentially used for geodetic/surveying applications with the carrier phase data available (Kulshrestha, 1997, Boa and Yen, 2004, Jacobson, 2006). These receivers are available in both the frequencies; L1 and L2 (Figure 4.18b). They have access to P code, at least for larger distances, and in geographical region with strong ionospheric disturbances (low and high latitudes). A modern geodetic receiver is able to measure accurately and reliably anywhere under any condition. It can be used for applications related to geodetic, geodynamic, detailed GIS and topographic engineering survey, etc (Jeffery, 2015).

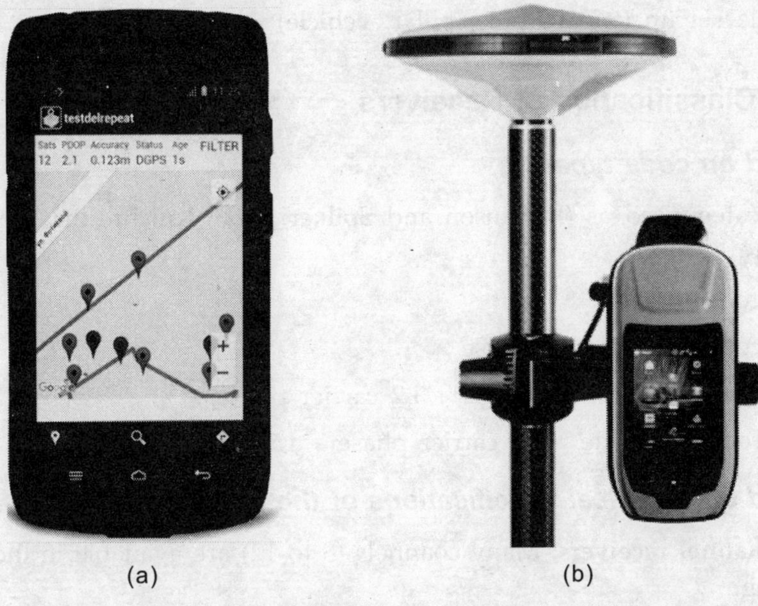

(a) (b)

Figure 4.18: (a) Navigational receiver (b) Geodetic receiver

Following factors are to be kept in mind while selecting the receivers (Wells, 1989, Seeber, 2003, Xu, 2010):

1. Capability of tracking all signals from each visible satellite at any time (as GPS+GLONASS system needs 20 dual frequency channels)
2. Have low phase and code noise
3. Contain high data rate (> 10Hz) for kinematic applications with high memory capacity
4. Low power consumption, low weight and small size
5. Full operational capability under AS
6. Capability to track weak signals (under foliage, and difficult environmental conditions)
7. Able to do multipath mitigation, interference suppression, stable antenna phase centre
8. Have DGPS and RTK capability
9. 1 pps timing output
10. Ability to accept external frequencies
11. Fast data transfer to computer
12. Few or no cable connection
13. Availability of radio modem
14. Can operate over difficult meteorological conditions
15. Ease of interfacing with other GPS systems.
16. Flexible set up (tripod, pole, pillar, vehicle)

4.10.4 Other Classification of Receivers

4.10.4.1 Based on code types

These may be categorised as (Parkinson and Spilker, 1996, Kulshrestha, 1997, Key, 2004, Jacobson, 2006)-

(i) C/A code

(ii) C/A code + L1 carrier phase

(iii) C/A code + L1 carrier phase + L2 carrier phase

(iv) C/A code + P code + L1 carrier phase + L2 carrier phase

4.10.4.2 Based on technical specifications of the channels

(i) Multi-channel receivers: Many channels (8 to 12) are available in the receivers for satellite tracking.

(ii) Sequential receivers: Such receivers can lock one satellite at a time. The operation is repeated for four satellites before giving navigational solution. It takes more time to get position fix.

(iii) Multiplexing receivers: It is a single channel receiver in which the hardware channel is time shared. The receiver switches rapidly between satellites being tracked and collect data to maintain two to eight signal processing algorithms in the software.

(iv) All in view receivers: It can view all satellites in view so as to choose four satellites out of them having the best geometry. These receivers have more complex and expensive hardware

(v) Integrated GPS receivers: It can work with both NAVSTAR and GLONASS signals.

4.11 GPS SURVEYING TECHNIQUES

The GPS technology has two major advantages over conventional survey i.e., weather does not disrupt the observations, and an intervisibility between stations is not so important. In addition, if two or more receivers are used in surveying work, the data are stored in a file in a common format. The file format is known as the receiver independent exchange format, or **(RINEX)**. It was developed by the Astronomical Institute in 1989, and is very useful, because the files that are downloaded from different receivers can be brought together in a single format and used. The GPS survey technique used in a given work depends on the (i) Accuracy requirements, (ii) Time to complete the work, (iii) Local terrain conditions, and (iv) Available equipment (Sickle, 2001). There are various methods available for some specific tasks (Jeffery, 2015), which may be kept in mind while collecting the data from GPS. Popular method employed in the field are summarised below.

4.11.1 Static Surveying

Static GPS surveying was the first method of GPS surveying used in the field, and it continues to be the primary technique for GPS/GNSS control even today. Relative static positioning requires several stationary receivers simultaneously collecting data from four or more satellites during observation session from 30 minutes to 2 hours, under an unobstructed sky. A typical application of this method would be the determination of baselines to accuracies ranging from 1 ppm to 0.1 ppm over tens of kilometres (Sickle, 2015). The line between any two receivers is called a baseline. The data are collected for a longer duration of time to achieve higher accuracy of the baseline.

This method is used in surveying works that require reasonable high accuracy, e.g., control surveys from local to state-wide extent, and will probably continue to be the preferred method in that category. In this method, receiver at each point collects data continuously for a planned length of time. Figure 4.19 shows the field set up of static method. The duration of data collection will depend on (i) Required precision, (ii) Number of visible satellites, (iii) Satellite geometry (DOP), (iv) Single frequency or Dual frequency receivers, and (v) Distance between receivers (Rahman and Fazal, 2017).

In static method, the reference receiver is placed at a known point. A second receiver (called the "rover") at the other end of the baseline is placed. Table 4.3 presents the guidelines that would help while selecting the Reference Receiver and Rover Receiver during GPS survey. Data are recorded for longer duration, depending on how long the line is, how many satellites are in sight, and their relative geometry. The observations are taken twice to avoid any mistakes. The rover is moved to the next baseline, and the process is repeated. For greater speed and multiple baselines, rovers can be increased to measure each baseline. When the baseline between a known point and a new point is measured, the new point can be used as a known point for other baselines, and this process continues further. To strengthen the network of baselines, control points should be situated at commanding locations. The number and location of control points will depend on the size and shape of network. To achieve higher accuracy, the post processing software should not take time more than the duration of data collection (Xu, 2010)

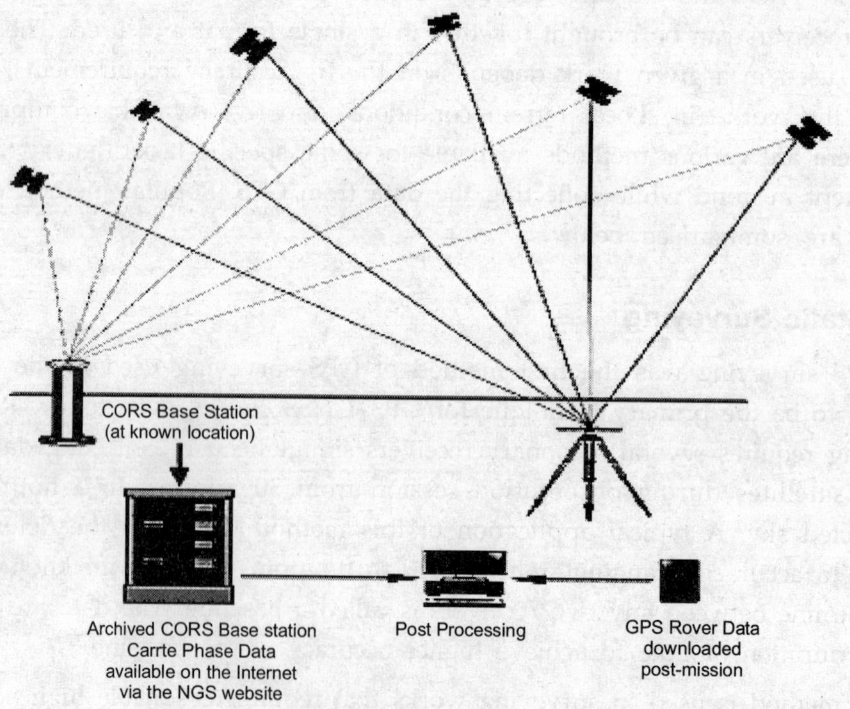

Figure 4.19: Static Method *(Source: Sickle, 2015)*

Table 4.3: Guidelines for selecting the reference receiver and rover receiver during GPS survey.

S.No.	Reference Receiver	Roving Receiver
1	No obstructions above 15° cut-off angle.	15° cut-off angle.
2	No reflecting surfaces nearby (multipath).	Obstructions should not block signals.
3	Safe location, as equipment may be left unattended.	No reflecting surfaces nearby (multipath).
4	No transmitters in vicinity.	No transmitters in vicinity.
5	Reliable power supply to GPS.	Fully-charged battery.
6	Ample memory capacity.	Sufficient memory capacity.
7	Correct selection of configuration parameters (e.g. recording rate).	Correct selection of configuration parameters (e.g. data-recording rate).
8	Antenna height and offset to be checked.	Antenna height and offset to be checked
9	Not necessarily to have a known point.	Observe in good weather
10	It is better to establish temporary reference stations at good sites rather than at unsuitable known points.	The GDOP should be ≤ 8.
11	For precise GPS surveying, WGS 84 coordinates for one point have to be known to about 10 m accuracy.	Use Stop and Go Indicator as a guide.

4.11.2 Rapid Static Surveying

The rapid static method is still an attractive method of surveying with GPS. This method is developed for duel frequency phase measurements or pseudo range measurements GPS receivers. It is east, quick and efficient. Short-time measurements are taken in this method. The rapid-static technique is well suited, for short range applications, such as control densification and engineering surveys or surveying many points (Parkinson and Spilker, 1996, Xu, 2010). Several points with known coordinates are to be established in order to start the work and to calculate the transformations. The basis of this technique is the ability of the software to resolve the ambiguities using a very short observation period. Unlike kinematic and stop-and-go techniques, there is no need to maintain lock on satellites when moving from one point to another.

Rapid static observations are taken when there are four or more satellites with GDOP < 8. The required observation time is mainly a function of the baseline length, number of satellites and ionospheric disturbance. Ionospheric disturbance varies with time, day/night, month, year, position on Earth's surface. As ionospheric disturbance is much lower at night, and therefore night observation time for rapid static can often be halved, or the baseline range doubled. Thus at night, it might be advantageous to measure baselines from 20 to 30 km. Observations with a minimum of 5 satellites above 15° and a good GDOP (< 8) should preferable be used (Kennedy, 2010). Table 4.4 provides an approximate guide to baseline lengths and observation times for mid latitudes under the ionospheric activity when using a dual frequency sensor.

Table 4.4: Summary of number of satellites, baseline lengths and observation times for static and rapid static methods

Obs. Method	No. of Satellites GDOP ≤ 8	Baseline Length (Km)	Approximate time observation	
			By day	By night
Static				
	4 or more	15 to 30	1 to 2 hours	1 hour
	4 or more	Over 30	2 to 3 hours	2 hours
Rapid Static				
	4 or more	Up to 5	5 to 10 mins	5 mins
	4 or more	5 to 10	10 to 20 mins	5 to 10 mins
	5 or more	10 to 15	Over 20 mins	5 to 20 mins

4.11.3 Kinematic Surveying

Kinematic surveying uses differential carrier phase tracking with two receivers to record observations simultaneously. In this method, relative positioning is used as one receiver is stationary and another one is in motion. It is used in most surveying applications where reference receiver remains stationary and placed at the known point, while other rover receiver will visit the unknown points for a very short time. The recording interval for Static observations could be 10 sec, for Rapid Static observations 5-10 sec, and for kinematic observations 0.2 sec or more (Agrawal, 2004).

Kinematic GPS surveying is generally suitable for any type of surveying or mapping where there are no high rise buildings, overhanging trees, dense forest, over-passes or such structures in rover's route. Kinematic GPS can use multiple bases and/or multiple rovers in the same survey, if necessary. Possible errors in kinematic surveying could be (Herring, 1996) (i) antenna height may change between points, especially if a prism pole with a sliding mechanism is used, and (ii) not properly plumbing the antenna over the point at time of measurement.

The development of **OTF-AR** (On-The-Fly–Ambiguity Resolution) algorithm is a dramatic step forward because static ambiguity reinitialization is no longer necessary for any positioning technique. The ambiguity will be resolved while the antenna is moving to the next stationary survey point. New ambiguities can be resolved On-The-Fly as the antenna moves with uninterrupted tracking. The kinematic GPS survey is undergoing rapid improvement, and OTF-AR is making it ideal for road centre line surveys, topographic surveys, hydrographic surveys, airborne applications and many more (Xu, 2010).

4.11.4 Stop and go Kinematic Surveying

This is the kinematic technique because the user's receiver continues to track satellites while it is in motion. The base receiver remains stationary and placed at the known point while other rover receiver will visit the unknown points for a very short time (less than two minutes). It is known as stop-and-go technique because only the coordinates of the receiver are used when it is stationary ('stop' part) but the receiver continues to function while it is moving (`go' part) from one stationary station up to the next station (Boa and Yen, 2004). The software sorts out the recorded data for different points and differentiates the kinematic or go data (not of interest) from the static or `stop' (data of interest) (http://www.gisresources.com/gps-surveying-techniques_2/).

The initial ambiguity must be resolved by the software before the Stop-and-Go survey commences. Once the ambiguities are resolved, the user's receiver is moved from point to point, collecting data just for a minute or so. It is vital that the antenna continues to track the satellites. In this way, the resolved ambiguities are valid for all future phase observations. One negative characteristic of this technique is the requirement that signal lock must be maintained as the satellites by the user receiver as it moves from point to point. This may require special antenna mounts on vehicles if the survey is carried out over a large area (Kennedy, 2010).

Stop-and-Go kinematic method is suitable for details surveys as topographic mapping or boundary survey work when many points close together have to be surveyed, and the terrain poses no problems in terms of signal disruption. It is possible to combine both continuous and 'stop & go' techniques in same survey but it gives low accuracy than the static surveying method, however it is better than the most other surveys. Speed is the main advantage of the kinematic survey (Agrawal, 2004, Misra, 2016). The technique can also be implemented in real time if a communication link is provided to transmit the data from the reference receiver to roving receiver.

This method also has certain limitations (Boa and Yen, 2004)–

(a) An initialization process to determine the integer biases of at least 4 satellites is needed at the beginning, which can be determined by (i) Using a known baseline less than 20 km in length and having an accuracy of less than 5 cm, and (ii) Perform a static mode survey first for one of the base lines.

(b) The lock on the same four or more satellites must be maintained during the entire survey. If for any reason a cycle slip occurs, the rover must return to any previous point which had been determined without cycle slip.

4.11.5 Real Time Kinematic Surveying

Real-Time Kinematic **(RTK)** is an attractive technique for many survey applications as it provides positioning in real-time. There is no post processing of the carrier phase data required. RTK method provides positional accuracy nearly as good as static positioning method using carrier phase, but it is faster (Wells, 1989, Sickle, 2001). It involves the use of at least one reference receiver, and at least one rover receiver, as well as the data link (Figure 4.20). RTK is based on transmitting reference station carrier phase data to the user's receivers. All the receivers involved observe the same satellites (five satellites minimum) simultaneously. Once set up, the reference receiver will continuously transmit its carrier phase measurements to the roving receiver.

The rover receiver gets signals from the reference receiver, but because it also has its own GPS antenna, it receives satellite signals directly instead of through the reference receiver. The rover then processes both signals to resolve the ambiguity. Start by setting up the reference receiver is et up on the known point. When the rover starts tracking both the satellites and the signals from reference receiver, the rover will initialize, resolve ambiguities, and be ready to record both points and coordinates. Baseline measurements are accurate between 1 cm and 3 cm. The contact with the reference receiver should not be lost, which causes the rover to lose the ambiguity calculations and thus affects the accuracy. The antennas on both the transmitting and receiving radios should not be blocked by tall buildings, and that the cable to the antenna should not be so long that the signals are degraded.

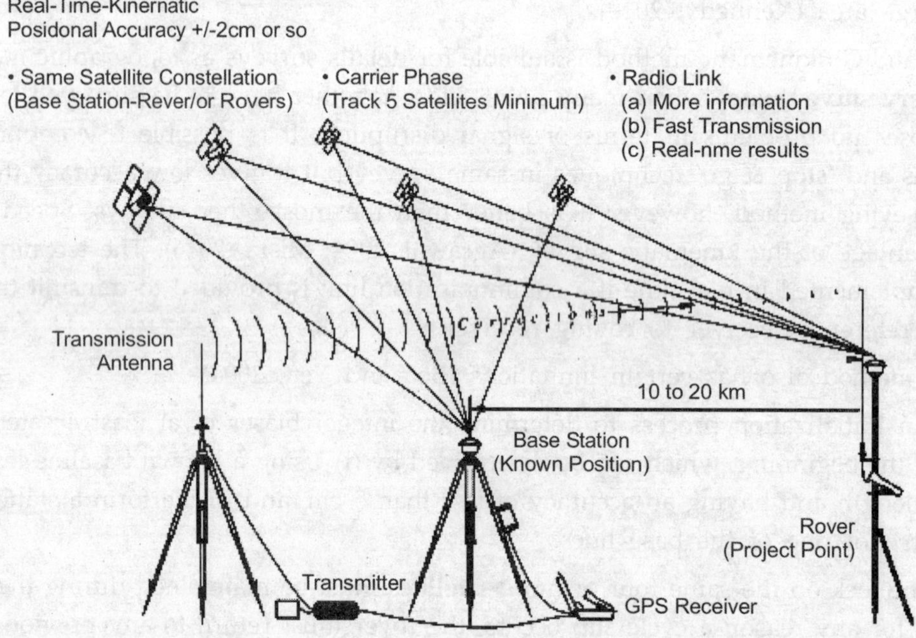

Figure 4.20: Real-time kinematic surveys (*Source: Sickle, 2015*)

It mainly refers to a stop-and-go method where coordinate points are available in real time. A radio communication link is maintained between the base receiver and the rover, and the pseudo range is supplied by base receiver through carrier phase measurements to the rover which in turn computes its position and displays the coordinates. The rover keeps updating coordinates of the locations while moving as long as lock on satellites is maintained. The baselines are typically at 10 to 20 km, which is considerably shorter than DGPS's effective range (Xu, 2010). The RTK method is most suitable for stakeout surveys. On The Fly **(OTF)** mode, there is no need to maintain the lock on satellites while the rover is in motion (Rahman and Fazal, 2017).

Table 4.5 presents the advantages and disadvantages of various GPS survey methods.

Table 4.5: Advantages and disadvantages of various GPS survey methods

(Source: http://www.gisresources.com/gps-surveying-techniques_2/)

	Conventional static GPS		Rapid-static, Stop and go, Kinematic GPS	
S. No.	**Advantages**	**Disadvantages**	**Advantages**	**Disadvantages**
1	Highest accuracy	Long observations session	Higher accuracy than pseudo range solution	Special Hardware & Software
2	Robust technique	Inappropriate for engineering and cadastral application	Appropriate for many survey applications	Susceptible to atmospheric and multi path biases
3	Ambiguity Resolution not critical		High productivity	Higher capital costs
4	Minor effect on multipath		Similar procedures to modern terrestrial surveying	Ambiguity fixed or continuous lock required
5	Undemanding on Hardware/ software			

4.11.6 Differential GPS Surveying

The differential GPS **(DGPS)** technique improves the accuracy and integrity of standard GPS, as it works by placing a GPS receiver at a known location, called a reference station (Boa and Yen, 2004). This might be a benchmark whose exact location is already known, and which is to be used as a starting point for a survey (Figure 4.21). Thus, the difference between the GPS derived position and the true position is determined. The station actually calculates the difference between the measured and actual ranges for each of the satellites visible from that station (Kennedy, 2010, Hurn, 1993). This calculated difference is called the "differential correction" for that satellite. Most of the wide variety of DGPS services was not originally designed to augment surveying and mapping applications of GPS; they were established to aid GPS navigation.

The DGPS technique is based on pseudo ranges, and code phase. Although the accuracy of code phase applications improved a lot with the elimination of Selective Availability (SA) in May 2000, yet reduction of the effect of correlated ephemeris and atmospheric errors by differential corrections still requires achieving the consistent accuracy better than the 2 to 5 m range. DGPS based on C/A code SPS signals can however offer meter or even sub-meter accuracy. Pseudo-range formulations can be developed from either the C/A-code or the more precise P-code. These formulations with the C/A-code can provide a precision of around 3 m can be achieved with a range measurement. Point positioning accuracy for a differential pseudo-range formulated solution is generally found to be in the range of 0.5-10 m (Hurn, 1993).

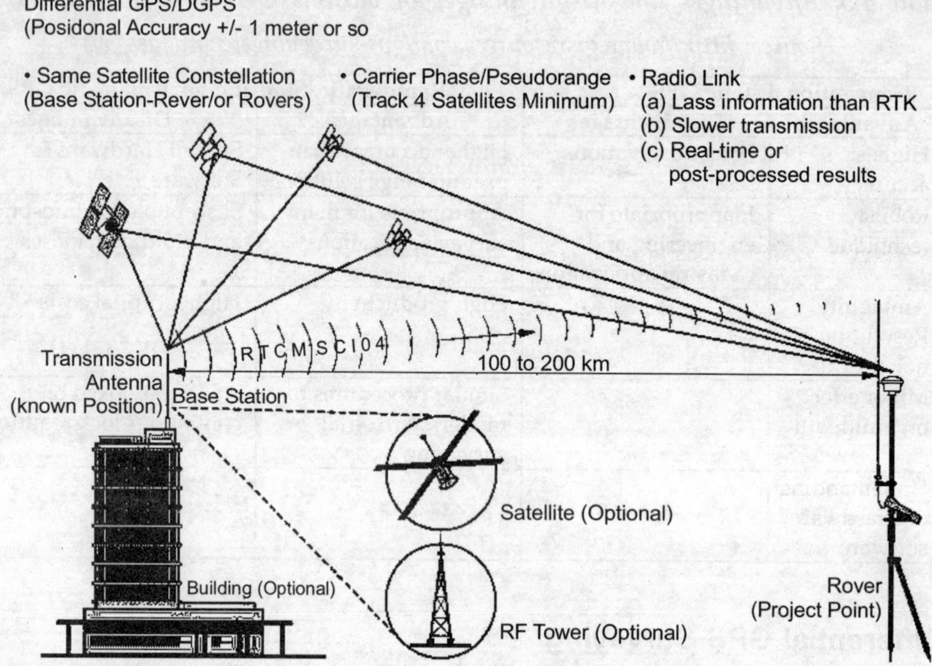

Figure 4.21: The DGPS survey *(Source: Sickle, 2015)*

Differential corrections may be used in real-time or later, with post-processing techniques. Usually, pseudo-range corrections are broadcast from the base to the rover or rovers for each visible satellite. Using the computed satellite position and its own known location, it computes the mathematical, or model, range to the satellite. Rovers can receive the correction signal and calculate coordinates. The real-time signal comes to the receiver over a data link. Some systems require two-way, some one-way, communication with the base stations. Radio systems, Internet, radio signal, or cell phone, geostationary satellites, low-earth-orbiting satellites and cellular phones are some of the options available for two-way data communication (Kennedy, 2010).

4.12 APPLICATIONS OF GPS

The technology of GPS was initially developed for military applications, but during 1980, the US Government decided to make it available for the civilian use as well. With the surge in popularity of GPS receivers over the past several years, the civilian community has its own large and diverse user segment. GPS today has become an efficient tool in the field of science, commerce, surveillance and tracking. Data collection from several hundred locations can be done in quickly with the GPS, and the resulting data can be processed to have an accuracy of less than 1 meter (Jacobson, 2007, Jeffery, 2015).

GPS receivers have been used in numerous applications (El-Rabbany, 2006); most relate either to the ability of the receiver to determine the position or time to great precision. However, the ability to determine position is the most widely used application of the GPS system. The use of GPS systems has revolutionized the practice of surveying.

Instruments and computer software to process the GPS results have been developed specifically for various surveying applications. Surveyors use GPS to save time over standard survey methods. They use GPS receivers to survey locations that are located at a distance and a direct line of sight had to be established by connecting points over obstructions, like a mountain or forest or lake. By conventional method, this work was often be very time consuming and even dangerous in hazardous terrain.

Many utility companies use GPS who survey the locations of their poles, pipe line etc. Highway departments survey existing roads and plan new routes with the GPS. At the high-precision end, the scientists measure the movements of tectonic plates, or establishing major political boundaries. Receivers are used that are able to measure the locations with a repeatability of only a few millimeters over baselines that extend several hundred kilometers. When an earthquake occurs, observations can determine which parts of the area actually moved, and in which directions and how far.

GPS is available as an in-car navigation aid, and is used by hikers and hunters. Automobile vehicle, such as a car, truck, ship or aircraft can have a receiver that constantly keeps track of position. Some automobile companies connect receivers into radio systems that use satellite communications to allow one master control center to track all vehicles in the fleet anywhere available. GPS tracking systems are used to route and monitor delivery vans and emergency vehicles. Many emergency vehicles have also been fitted with receivers so that the vehicle closest to an emergency could be located quickly (Kennedy, 2010).

GPS is used by ships at sea and aircraft flying in bad weather to keep track of position and speed, regardless of visibility or time of day. GPS is used for enroute navigation and for airport or harbor approaches. Some aircrafts have been equipped with two or more GPS antenna, with the signals from all antennas sent to one receiver to compute the attitude of the aircraft also. The aircraft also has an inertial navigation system (INS - a navigation system to sense changes in a vehicle's attitude and velocity) which along with GPS can greatly improve overall navigation.

Military GPS has been integrated into fighters, bombers, tankers, helicopters, ships, submarines, tanks, jeeps, and soldiers' equipment. In addition to basic navigation activities, military applications of GPS include target designation, close air support, "smart" weapons, and rendezvous (Kennedy, 2010).

In precision agriculture farming, GPS is used to accurately guide farm machinery engaged in ploughing, planting, fertilizing, and harvesting. Most smart phones feature GPS map for navigation applications. Some civilian as well as military applications are listed below (El-Rabbany, 2006, Jacobson, 2007):

4.12.1 Civilian Applications

1. *Navigation* – Used by navigators for locating path, orientation purposes.
2. *Geotagging* – Map overlays can be created by applying location coordinates to images and other documents.

3. *Surveying* – Surveyors verify the length of roads and boundaries of the property.
4. *Map-making* – Used by civilians and military cartographers for map making.
5. *Tectonics* – Detect the precise motion of land in earthquakes.
6. *Geofencing* – Vehicle, person or pet can be detected by using GPS tracking system.

4.12.2 Military Applications

1. *Navigation* – Soldiers can find location of objects in the dark and unknown regions with the help of GPS.
2. *Search and rescue* – Knowing the position, rescue work can be undertaken easily.
3. *Reconnaissance* – Movement of troupes can be handled.
4. *Target tracking* – Military weapon systems use GPS to track ground and air targets.
5. *Missile and projectile guidance* – can be used to target military weapons, such as cruise missiles, precision – guided munitions.

4.13 FUTURE USES OF GPS TECHNOLOGY

GPS enhances and improve aviation, search and rescue, surveying and mapping, trucking and shipping, fishing, tracking, space exploration, offshore drilling, and many more scientific uses. GPS has been used in planes, cars, trains, boats, watches and cell phones, as well as for improving productivity and efficiency in many areas (Kennedy, 2010). GPS also furthers scientific aims, such as weather forecasting, earthquake prediction, and environmental protection. Furthermore, the precise GPS time signal, derived from atomic clocks, is embedded in critical economic activities, such as synchronising communication networks, managing power grids, and authenticating electronic transactions.

As of February 2017, there are 31 operational GPS satellites in the orbit; nineteen of these satellites broadcast L2C and the other twelve broadcast L5 signals. Each of the GPS surveying technique has its own strengths and weaknesses. Often a combination of conventional static and GPS technique makes an ideal solution to a surveying problem. One of the challenges for GPS surveyors is to select the best combination of techniques for the terrain, distance and logistic constraints. The OTF-AR (on-the-fly–Ambiguity Resolution) algorithm is very useful for any positioning technique. GPS researchers are developing algorithms that are able to reliably resolve the ambiguities with a single epoch of data (Xu, 2010).

The L2C-band in the future will be the next major band for general use. Operating on new satellites, which will replace dated GPS satellites, the L2C band will provide an improved and greater precision. Also, backward compatibility with current devices will not be an issue; as it will work on current receivers while increasing transmission power and compatibility with GNSS signals. High-precision location systems may also pave the way for the spread of driver-less cars. The GPS is expected to undergo a major upgrade in coming years. It currently uses the L-band wavelength, which is not as accurate as S, C, and X signals. The only reason GPS system operators use the L--band signals is their ability to penetrate clouds, fog, and adverse weather obstructions (Sickle, 2015).

GPS system is available in smart phones, and can access maps within seconds. GIS and GPS along with nano-technology are two of the fastest growing technology fields which create the opportunity in future for developing micro-GPS units. While GIS is a powerful technology for government and military uses, the general public would like to derive the benefits to utilize the convenience of nano-GPS technology. These nano-GPS units will open up the possibility for people to be able to track not only their own items, but other peoples' items, or other people. Nano-GPS could also be used to assist in a large range of crimes, stalking, burglary or murder.

The new GPS signals are designed to enable interoperability between international satellite navigation systems, such as Galileo and GLONASS. The main focus of the new GPS program is to add new signals to the satellite constellation. The United States and Europe originally developed L1C as a common civil signal for GPS and Galileo. Japan's Quasi-Zenith Satellite System **(QZSS)** and China's BeiDou system are also adopting L1C-like signals (Jeffery, 2015). To enable worldwide usage of satellite positioning (GNSS), GPS receivers can receive signals in future from USA's NAVSTAR, Russia's (GLONASS), India's Regional Navigational Satellite System (IRNSS), Japan's Quasi-Zenith Satellite System (QZSS), China's BeiDou and Europe's Galileo satellite systems

A new generation of GPS satellites is currently in production. GPS III is the newest block of GPS satellites which is expected to begin launching in 2017, and all 24 satellites to be made available in the late 2020s. These will have 4 civil signals: L1 C/A, L1C, L2C, and L5. First set of satellites will broadcast common L1C signal. GPS III will have 4 military signals: L1/L2 P(Y), L1/L2M with 3 improved Rubidium atomic clocks. The new constellation of satellites will enhance signal reliability and accuracy and have a 15-year design lifespan (https://www.rewiresecurity.co.uk/blog/future-of-gps-and-global-positioning-locating (Future of GPS Tracking).

As of today, GNSS receivers have been used in drones, Internet of things (IOT) products, sensors, intelligent transport systems and GPS tracking systems, and half of all current GPS receivers in use can receive signals from two or more GNSS systems. Seven billion GPS receivers are being used in all sorts of vehicles and devices in 2017, and it is supposed to reach ten billion by 2023 (https://castnav.com/future-gps- location-technology/ (Future of GPS and Location Technology)

GPS is an outdoor technology, as its signals are lost under forest cover, in underground buildings, and even in high-rise buildings. Radio frequency identification (**RFID**) is rapidly becoming an important form of positioning technology, which can be used, for example, to track the movement of goods from manufacturer through retailer to consumer, to track pets and animals, and to manage building materials on construction sites. The positioning technologies (GPS and RFID) are already widely used and suggest that there is a need to anticipate a world in which it will be possible to know *where everything is, at all times.*

There are already substantial domains over which this kind of knowledge is at least partially available. For example, it is now already known where every mobile phone is, provided it is turned on and within the range, and with the most advanced phones location based on GPS is known to better than 10 m. RFID may yet prove to be the best technology for indoor tracking, though many other possible solutions are being developed (Goodchild, 2009).

The technology has been moving at a rapid pace in the 21st century, and GPS is no exception. After the deployment of new satellites, the accuracy, uptime and accessibility of GPS will improve all around the world. With the development of new software, the new generation of GPS vehicle trackers in the 2020s will have an increased accuracy, up to centimetres close to an asset. The future of GPS tracking is going to be more accurate and effective for personal tracking, as well as business use.

Review Questions

1. What is GPS? What does it give?
2. Write the historical developments of GPS.
3. List the advantage and disadvantages of GPS.
4. Define, (i) Latitude, (ii) Longitude, and (iii) Meridian, and (iv) Mean sea level.
5. Explain the coordinate systems used in geodesy.
6. Discuss different types of map projections? Which are the commonly used map projection ?
7. Define (i) Geoid and (ii) Spheriod, and (iii) Datum. Explain the utility of datum.
8. Explain various segments of a GPS. Also discuss their roles and functions.
9. Discuss the task of control segment.
10. Discuss the space segment in NAVASTAR GPS system.
11. Explain various components of a GPS receiver.
12. Discuss the principles of trilateration used in GPS.
13. Explain the GPS satellite signals in details.
14. Explain PDOP and GDOP in GPS data collection. What is the utility of these in GPS observations?
15. What is ambiguity? Explain the selective availability?
16. Describe the accuracy achieved from different GPS receivers.
17. Discuss various sources of errors in GPS observations.
18. Briefly explain about different classification of GPS receivers.
19. Discuss code phase receivers. How is code phase receiver different from carriers phase?
20. Explain carrier phase receivers. Write the application of code phase and carrier phase receivers.

21. Describe geodetic receivers.
22. What are the different survey techniques employed in GPS survey? Discuss all methods in brief.
23. Explain the static method of GPS survey. Write its applications.
24. Describe real-time kinematic method of GPS survey. Write its applications.
25. Discuss the advantages and disadvantages of various GPS survey methods.
26. What is differential GPS? What are the main advantages of DGPS?
27. Describe various applications of GPS technology.
28. Explain the future uses of GIS

References

1. Agrawal, N. K., (2004), *Essentials of GPS* , Spatial Networks: Hyderabad.
2. Andrejs (2010) Easy Way Boost GPS Signal, GPS Navigation System, (https://gpsnavigationsite.com/easy-way-boost-gps-signal/amp/)
3. Boa, James and Tsui, Yen (2004) *Fundamentals of Global Positioning System Receivers: A Software Approach*, John Wiley & Sons.
4. Clynch, James R. (2001) Lecture notes on GPS Accuracy Levels, Naval Postgraduate School, Department of Oceanography, CA, USA, February 2001.
5. Defense Mapping Agency Technical Manual (1996) - Datums, Ellipsoids, Grids and Grid Reference Systems, DMA TM 8358.1, Defense Mapping Agency, Fairfax, Virginia, USA.
6. Dhunta, P. S., (2001), *Principles of GPS* , Deep: New Delhi.
7. El-Rabbany, Ahmed (2006) *Introduction to GPS: The Global Positioning System*, 2nd Edition, Artch House, Boston.
8. Goodchild, Michael F (2009) Geographic information systems and science: today and tomorrow, Annals of GIS, 15:1, 3-9, DOI: 10.1080/19475680903250715.
9. GPS for Land Surveyors From: Federal Geographic Data Committee FGDC-STD-007.2-1998 Draft Geospatial Positioning Accuracy Standards Part 2: Standard for Geodetic Networks
10. GPS Joint Program Office. (1997). *ICD-GPS-200: GPS Interface Control Document*. ARINC Research. Available on line from United States Coast Guard Navigation Center.
11. Herring, Thomas A. (1996), *The Global Positioning System*. Scientific American, February 1996: p. 44-50.
12. Hinch, S.W. (2010). *Outdoor Navigation with GPS. Birmingham, Alabama:* Wilderness Press Keen Communications.
13. Hoffmann-Wellenhof, Lichtenegger, B.H. and Collins, J. (1994). *GPS: Theory and Practice*. 3rd Ed. New York: Springer-Verlag.

14. Hurn, Jeff (1989) GPS: A Guide to the Next Utility, Trimble Navigation Ltd, Sunnyvale.
15. Hurn Jeff (1993) Differential GPS explained, Trimble Navigation Ltd., Sunnyvale.
16. Institute of Navigation, (1993), *Global Positioning System monographs*. Washington, DC: The Institute of Navigation.
17. Jacobson, Len (2007) *GNSS Markets and Applications*, Artech House Publishers
18. Jeffery, Charles (2015) *An Introduction to GNSS: GPS, GLONASS, Galileo and other Global Navigation Satellite Systems*, NovAtel.
19. Kaplan, Elliott D. and Hegarty, Chirstopher (1996). *Understanding GPS: Principles and Applications*. Boston: Artech House Publishers.
20. Kennedy, Michael (2010) *Global Positioning System and ArcGIS*, CRC Press, Taylor and Francis.
21. Key, H., (2004), Product Survey on Geodetic GPS receivers, GIM International, April 2004, pp. 46 - 51.
22. Kulshrestha, A, (1997), GPS Receivers for Civil and Military Applications - Requirements for Type Certification, National Conference on Global Positioning System, 21-23 Feb, 1997, IIT Kanpur, India.
23. Leick, Alfred. (1995). *GPS Satellite Surveying*. 2nd. Ed. New York: John Wiley & Sons.
24. Misra, Pratap (2016), *GPS for Everyone: You are Here*, Ganga-Jamuna Press.
25. National Imagery and Mapping Agency (NIMA) (1997). Department of Defense World Geodetic System 1984: Its Definition and Relationship with Local Geodetic Systems. NIMA TR8350.2 Third Edition. 4 July (1997). Bethesda, MD: National Imagery and Mapping Agency. Available on line from National Imagery and Mapping Agency.
26. NAVSTAR (1996) GPS User Equipment Introduction, Available on line from United States Coast Guard Navigation Center.
27. NAVSTAR (2003) Global Positioning System Surveying, US Army Corps of Engineers, Engineering Manual, EM-1110-1-1003, 1 July 2003.
28. Parkinson, Bradford W. and Powers, Stephen T. with Gaylord Green, Hugo Fruehauf, Brock Strom, Steve Gilbert, Walt Melton, Bill Huston, Ed Martin, James Spilker, Fran Natali, Joe Strada, Burt Glazer, Dick Schwartz, Tom Stansell, and others (2010), Part 1: The Origins of GPS, and the Pioneers Who Launched the System, GPS World, May 2010.
29. Parkinson, Bradford W. and Spilker. James J. (1996). *Global Positioning System: Theory and Practice. Volumes I and II.* Washington, DC: American Institute of Aeronautics and Astronautics, Inc.
30. Rahman, Atiqur and Fazal, Sahab (2017) *Global Positioning System: Concept, Technique and Application*, New Age International Publishers.

31. Seeber, G, (2003), *Satellite Geodesy* , 2nd edition, de Gruyter: Berlin.
32. Sickle, J. V, (2001), *GPS for Land Surveyors*, Taylor and Francis.
33. Sickle, J. V, (2015), *GPS for Land Surveyors*, CRC Press, Taylor and Francis.
34. Smith, James R (1997) *Introduction to Geodesy*, The History & Concepts of Modern Geodesy, Wiley Interscience.
35. Wells, David, (1989). *Guide to GPS positioning*. Fredericton, NB, Canada: Canadian GPS Associates.
36. Xu, Guochang (2010), *GPS: Theory, Algorithms and Applications*, Springer.

Web Resources

https://www.e-education.psu.edu/geog862/node/1674

http://www.gisresources.com/gps-surveying-techniques_2/

https://www.rewiresecurity.co.uk/blog/future-of-gps-and-global-positioning-locating (Future of GPS Tracking)

https://castnav.com/future-gps-location-technology/ (Future of GPS and Location Techno

Chapter 5

GEOGRAPHIC INFORMATION SYSTEMS

5.1 INTRODUCTION

Spatial information is always related to geographic space, i.e., large-scale space. Geographic space that represents the surrounding geographic world is the space of topography, land use/land cover, climate, geology, water, forest, cadastral, and other features. Geographic Information Systems (GIS) - a geospatial technology - can be used to create spatial databases, analyze spatial patterns, and produce maps that communicate more effectively (Star and Estes, 1990). Location has always been important to humans. Stone-age hunters anticipated the location of their quarry, early explorers lived by their knowledge of location, and current societies work based on their understanding of who belongs where. Location in the form of maps and spatial information has served discovery and planning for years in the past.

The spatial data generally is in the form of maps, such as topography, geology, soil types, forest and vegetation, land use, water resource availability etc., stored as layers in a digital form. Integrating a database of multiple information layers can produce new thematic maps. Thus, GIS can be used to create maps, integrate information, visualise scenarios, solve complicated problems and develop effective solutions. These capabilities distinguish GIS from other information systems and make them valuable to a wide range of modelling applications, such as assessing trends and patterns of the events, predicting outcomes, and planning strategies (Bolstad, 2002).

With the advent of computers, GIS applications drew attention in various fields to get to where they are today. In the 1980s, most GIS applications ran on workstation computers tied to mainframe computers but today personal computers are fast, capable of storing and processing large datasets, and can process multiple tasks simultaneously (Moyer, 1989). Creating good maps and analyzing spatial data may be a time-consuming process and challenging practice, but powerful mapping tools of GIS has enabled users to make maps and to perform analyses easily (Burrough, 1986). Today GIS technology is used to manipulate objects in geographic space and to acquire knowledge from spatial information.

GIS technology integrates common database operations, such as query and statistical analysis with the unique geovisualization and geographic analysis benefits offered by maps (Doellner, 2005). It can be used for updating maps much easier than updating maps manually. GIS system can be used to produce three-dimensional images or view of the terrain. It has the potential to help decision makers and planners by further developing it as an Expert System or Decision Support system (DSS) to provide best solution to make decisions and solve problems (Davis, 2001, Eldrandaly, 2007).

There are lot of applications where GIS can be used. Being a useful tool for multi-disciplinary applications, many professionals can involve themselves into it. For example, an urban planner can understand the growth of the city and quantify the future growth. A forest manager can measure the forest cover and assess its health, and also plan to combat with forest fire. Water resources scientist can carry out the water quality analysis, watershed analysis, hydrologic modelling and flood management studies. A Civil Engineer would be interested to align a new road, or railway line or finding a suitable site for dam construction or development of a smart city. GIS can also be used effectively for asset management, crop studies, archaeology, criminology, sales marketing, logistics, health, resource studies and environmental impact management etc. (Leipnik et al 1993, Gruen et al 2004, Campbell and Shin, 2011, Poux and Suemnichet, 2012, Aher et al 2016, Adrees et al 2016, Iftikhar, 2016, Hersh, 2017, Tripathi and Banker, 2017).

5.2 DEVELOPMENTS IN GIS

Dr. John Snow's Cholera map is a great example of manual GIS. In 1840s, a cholera outbreak killed several hundred residents in London's Soho area. Dr. Snow, a physician, located the address of each fatality on a hand-drawn base map and soon a cluster of cases was visible (Figure 5.1). Then on the base map, over the streets and fatalities, he drew the locations of water wells. Familiar with the idea of distance decay, he knew that people would go to the nearest well because water was free and heavy to carry. Dr. Snow could see that the fatalities clustered largely among those who lived near the Broad Street water well. He and his students took the handle off the water pump, and new cholera cases dropped down rapidly. By disabling the pump, Dr. Snow demonstrated the spatial relationship between cholera fatalities and the Broad Street water well, and, more importantly, he established the relationship between cholera and drinking water.

In the 1950s, maps were very simple. They had their uses in vehicle routing, new development planning and locating places of interest. But none of this was done on computers.

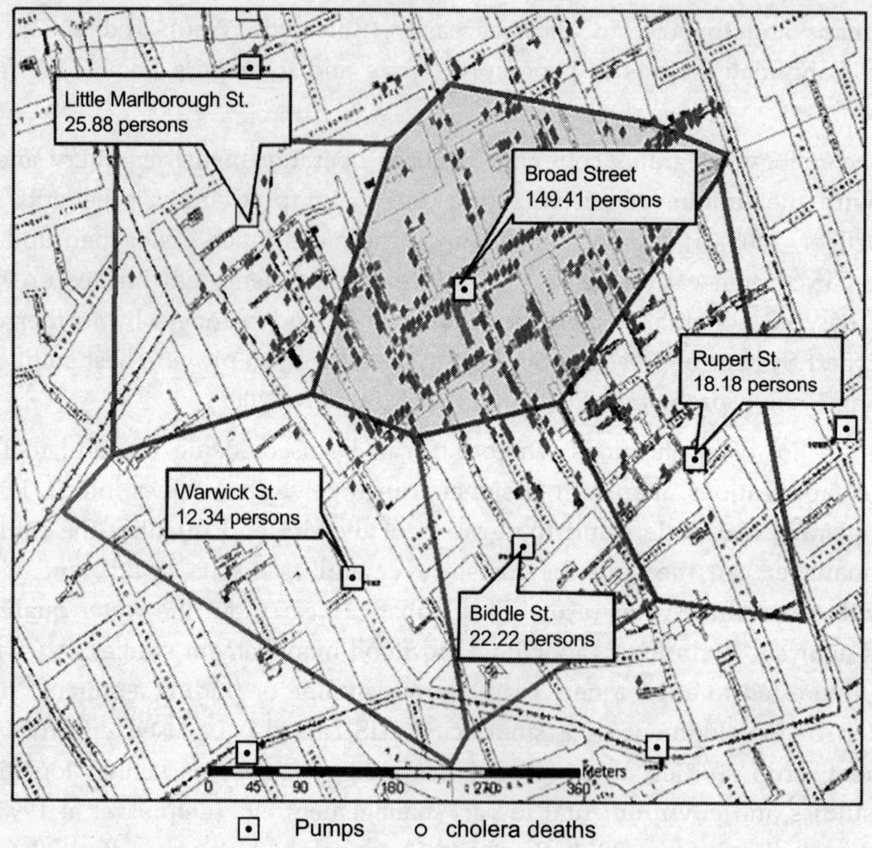

Cholera Mortality per 1,00 persons for central pump catchments.

Figure 5.1: Dr. John Snow's cholera map of London's Soho-1954. *(Source: Star and Estes, 2010)*

In 1960s, Dr. Roger Tomlinson, called the father of GIS, created and developed Canadian Geographic Information System to store, analyze and manipulate data that was collected for the Canada Land Inventory. Because of the vast amount of territory Canada occupies, the idea for Canada Land Inventory was developed in 1964. This software had the capability to overlay, measurement and digitizing (converting scan hardcopy map to digital data).

Figure 5.2 shows that the changes in GIS technology over decades. The main reason for its growing uses is continuously expanding capabilities of GIS as a "technical tool" for integrating vast amount of spatial data, including remote sensing images for GPS navigation, creating interactive maps, 3D mapping, asset management, queries, etc.

In 1970s, the GIS community emphasized the use of data structures, display capabilities and a few basic operations. In early 1970's, computer mapping started as an automated map drafting. The points, lines and areas defining the geographic features on a map were represented as an organized set of x, y coordinates. These data were used to redraw the maps into variety of colors, scales, and projections as compared to original maps. An added advantage with computer mapping was the ability to change a portion of a map and quickly redraft the entire area, as well as update the resource maps (Burrough, 1996).

The 1980s saw a steady growth in GIS, and the community expanded to a few thousand researchers which included more traditional programmers on the systems and systems managers, data providers and GIS specialists. In 1980s, most efforts focused on vector processing of spatial objects (point, line and polygon features). Early development of GIS used two data structures for encoding maps; the vector data model that represents map features (as discrete spatial objects), and the raster data model that stores map features over an imaginary grid, and processes the information for each cell in the grid (continuous map surface). Increasing demands for mapped data focused attention on data availability, accuracy and standards. Hardware continued to improve with time, for example, the manual digitizing tablets were replaced by automated scanners for GIS work. National and international organizations began addressing the necessary standards for digital maps to ensure compatibility among various systems (Campbell and Shin, 2011).

During 1980's, the change in data format was attempted. Spatial database management systems **(SDBMS)** were developed that linked computer mapping capabilities with the traditional database management capabilities. In these systems, a user was able to instantly retrieve the location as well as information about that location with the help of unique identification number assigned to a feature. Efforts were also made on developing cartographic modeling for map analysis, such as intersection, overlay, buffer and geo-query (Bolstad, 2002).

In 1990s, professional programmers restructured, extended and enhanced the old unstructured programs into comprehensive GIS systems with graphical interface. The GIS developers used the toolkits to develop customized solutions for individual industries and organizations (Berry and Marble, 1998). As GIS continued its evolution, the emphasis turned from descriptive query to prescriptive analysis of maps. If early GIS users had to repeatedly overlay several maps, or if repeated distance or area calculations were needed, the GIS systems were now programmed with a mathematical solution to save time by automating the tedious and repetitive operations.

In 1990s, attention was paid to map analysis, as digital representation provided a wealth of quantitative (as well as qualitative) processing possible through spatial statistics and spatial analysis. The spatial statistics described the spatial variation in the data, rather than assuming a uniform response every where, using both the location and the measurements at sample locations to generate a spatial map. Spatial analysis applications, on the other hand, involve context-based processing. Spatial mathematics evolved similar to traditional algebra in which basic operations (e.g., add, subtract, multiply, divide, exponential, root, log, cosine, differentiate) are logically sequenced to form equations. Advanced GIS operations, such as minimum area, effective distance, optimal path routing, etc., were developed in modern GIS software. These along with new tools and modeling approach extended the capabilities of decision-making models into effective decision support systems (Bernhardsen, 1992). On the application side, Global Positioning System (GPS) was fully integrated with GIS with varying backgrounds and application interests (Carter, 1992).

Figure 5.2 indicates that there are large numbers of GIS experts, and also more users of technology. It was obvious as all computer-based disciplines brought Internet connections in 2000s. The dominant focus was to have access to spatial information from webmaster to the end users. The GIS systems gave way to web services and tailored application solutions. There was growing number of websites with extensive sets of map layers that enabled users to mix and match their own needs. Data exchange and interoperability standards extended this flexibility to multiple nodes on the web, with some data from one source and analytic tools from another source. Coupled with the current multimedia and 3D geovisualization, such as Google Earth, a whole new form of mapping started in GIS (Doellner, 2005). Another characteristic of the new processing environment was the full integration of the GPS and remote sensing imagery with other web-based maps, bringing geographic positioning to the palm computers or smart phones. Ancillary systems, such as robotics to new automated procedures for data collection and on-the-fly gave birth to many new applications (Carter, 1992; Bolstad, 2002).

The 2010s witnessed a whole new community on the right (GIS specialist, General users and Public users) emphasizing applications involving millions, and on the left (General programmers, GIS developers and System managers) emphasizing systems involving thousands (Figure 5.2). This dualistic community is expected to change the evolutionary character of the GIS community into a radically different revolutionary group. This decade will likely to see billions of general and public users with the knowledge of science and technology supporting GIS (Campbell and Michael, 2011). GIS technology has reached to masses today through a simple set of highly useful apps on smart phones that can provide location of desired facilities or guide users while driving.

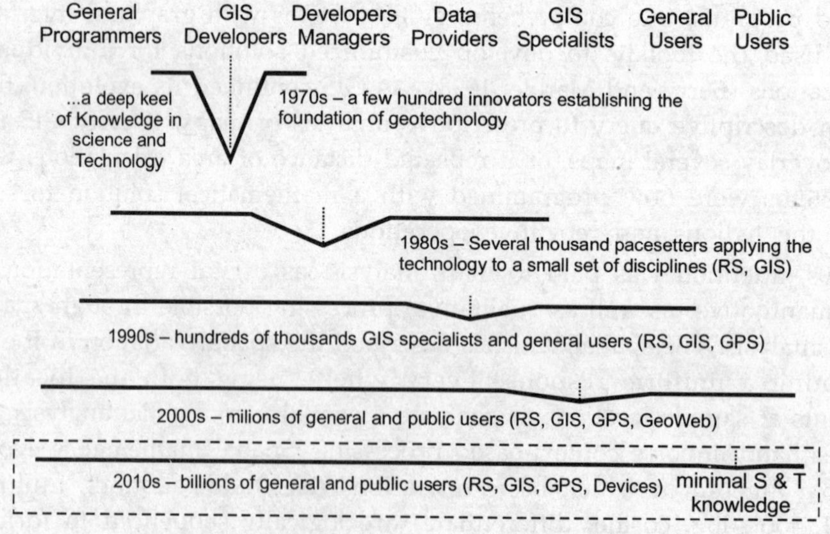

Figure 5.2: Growth of GIS (*Source: Berry, 2013a*)

Today, it is possible to drape spatial information on a 3D view of the terrain. Virtual reality transforms the information from spatial 2D maps to rendered 3D objects of trees, roads and buildings for near photographic realism (Eldrandaly, 2007). Embedded hyperlinks provide access to actual photos, video, audio, text and data associated with map locations.

Immersive imaging enables the users to interactively pan and zoom the display in all directions (Davis, 2001). 4D GIS (*X, Y, Z* and time) is the next major frontier (Berry, 2013b). Time is handled as a series of stored map layers that can be animated to view changes on the landscape. On the basis of past trend, predictive modeling can provide solutions to proposed management actions in the future (Eldrandaly, 2007). Tomorrow's data structures will accommodate time as a stored dimension and completely change the conventional mapping paradigm.

5.3 DEFINITIONS OF A GIS

Over past 20 to 30 years, many authors (Parker 1988; Moyer, 1989, Star and Estes, 1990; Burrough and McDonnell, 1998, Davis, 2001; Bolstad 2002, and Longley et al. 2005) have defined GIS; and most of their definitions are more or less similar. These definitions generally refer to a system of computer hardware, software and people that support the capture, management, analysis and visualisation of spatial data.

Star and Estes (1990) defined GIS as *"an information system that is designed to work with data referenced by spatial or geographic coordinates. In other words, a GIS is both a database system with specific capabilities for spatially–referenced data, as well as a set of operations for working with the data"*.

Burrough and McDonnell (1998) defined GIS as *"a powerful set of tools for storing and retrieving at will, transforming and displaying spatial data from the real world for a particular set of purposes"*.

Davis (2001) defined GIS as *"a computer–based technology and methodology for collecting, managing, analyzing, modeling, and presenting geographic data for a wide range of applications."*

Longley et al. (2005) defined GIS as *"a special class of information systems that keep track not only of events, activities, and things, but also of where these events, activities, and things happen or exist"*.

A GIS therefore can be defined as an information system which is capable of integrating, storing, editing, analysing, sharing and displaying spatially referenced data of the Earth (Jones, 1997). GIS can be used to visualize, query, analyze, and interpret data to understand relationships, patterns, and trends. By relating seemingly unrelated data, GIS can help to better understand the spatial patterns and relationships. GIS application tools allow end users to perform spatial query, analysis, edit spatial data and create maps (Lo and Yeung, 2002). In a simple way, GIS consists of images that are geo-referenced to the Earth or have x,y coordinates and their attribute values that are stored in the table. GIS can use any information that includes location. These locations can be expressed in many different ways, such as latitude and longitude, address, or ZIP code (Moyer, 1989).

5.4 TERMINOLOGY USED IN GIS

Some technical terms frequently used in GIS work are explained below (Parker, 1988, Moyer, 1989, Marble and Peuquet, 1983, Maguire et al 1991, Lo and Yeung, 2002 Star and Estes, 2010) -

Arc: Arcs are lines or polygon boundaries, represented as a series of vertices or coordinate points.

Attribute data: Tabular or textual data or non-spatial data describing the geographic characteristics of features is called attribute data. An attribute table stores this data about the geographic data in columns and rows – similar to a spreadsheet.

Boolean algebra: These are conditions used to select features with a set of algebraic conditions which include AND, OR or NOT. Venn diagrams are often used to represent Boolean operations.

Buffer: The buffer tool is a proximity function that creates a polygon at a specified distance surrounding a selected feature, i.e., point, line or polygon feature.

Cartography: Cartography is the science of representing real-world features on maps as spatial information in two or three dimensions.

Control point: Control points are known XY location having a high degree of accuracy. They are used for georeferencing of hard copy maps and satellite images to a standard map projection before using in GIS.

Database management system (DBMS): A DBMS is a collection of tools that permits an interface between users and their database for the entry, storage, input, output and organization of data.

Field: A field (or item) is the characteristic used to describe each feature in a geographic data set usually viewed as columns in an attribute table.

Geographic object (Spatial feature): A feature is a cartographic point, line or polygon object with a spatial location in the real-world that can be used in a GIS.

Interpolation: It is the computation of values at unsampled locations based on known values at sampled locations, for example, rainfall, elevations, temperature, soil moisture values.

Network: A network in a GIS is a connected set of line features (arcs) used to represent the real-world networks, such as roads, rivers, pipe lines, etc.

Node: A node is an important point at the intersection of two line features.

Query: A query is a request or search of spatial or tabular data based on user-define criteria.

Raster: A cellular data structure composed of rows and columns for storing images. Each unit in the grid is assigned a value associating it with the corresponding attribute data.

Record: A record in an attribute table is the row that specifies an entity. It represents a spatial feature in the dataset in a one-to-one relationship.

Registration: Registration is the assignment of coordinates from one coordinate system (of a map) to another coordinate system (of another map) so that both the maps have similar coordinate system.

Spatial analysis: It is the process of examining the locations, attributes, and relationships of features in spatial data through overlay and other analytical techniques in order to address a question or gain useful knowledge. Spatial analysis extracts or creates new information from the spatial data.

Spatial data: It is geographically referenced data that describe both the location (geometry) and the characteristics of spatial features.

Spatial relationship: A spatial relationship that links GIS features with a table by unique identifiers, which are stored in a relational database management system.

Thematic layer: A thematic layer represents a distinct entity in a spatial data layer, for example, rivers, roads, forest, urban, elevation etc.

Topology: Topology is a set rules that dictates the spatial properties of point, line and area features such as connectivity, adjacency and contiguity.

Vector: Vector data comprised of x-y coordinate representations of locations on the earth that take the form of single points, strings of points (lines or arcs) or closed lines (polygons) known as features. Each feature has an associated attribute code for identification.

5.5 ADVANTAGES AND DISADVANTAGES OF A GIS

Today, GIS is used as a multi-disciplinary tool. It has found its applications in large domains, such as natural resources, industry, administration, education, hospitals, schools, etc. it has the capability to integrate large amount of spatial and non-spatial data to derive the useful results. Some of the advantages and disadvantages of using GIS are given below.

5.5.1 Advantages:

1. GIS offers quick collection and analysis of data to provide solutions for the problems.
2. It integrates large amount of spatial and non-spatial data, which is very useful for making querries and generating new thematic maps.
3. It helps in answering questions as well as solve complex problems through looking at the data in a way which is easily and quickly shared.
4. It can be used for better management of natural resources.
5. GIS can be used for better and improved decision making with the help of layered information
6. It can save costs due to faster analysis.
7. GIS can make better predictions and analysis.
8. Study can be performed in 3D environment, and fly through model can be developed to understand the characteristics of terrain.
9. It helps in visualisation of terrain.
10. Since the data are digital, the same layers can be used for other applications.
11. Digital data in a GIS is easily updated. Change of scale of output is possible.

12. GIS allows viewing, questioning, understanding, visualizing and interpreting the data into number of ways. The results can be represented pictorially or graphically or in tabular form, depending upon the input data.

5.5.2 Disadvantages:

1. Initial cost of establishment of GIS lab is high.
2. Expertise is required to carry out modelling and analysis work, particularly when integrating large amount of data.
3. It requires huge data input to derive the results.
4. There is a loss of information and shape of the objects while working at various resolutions in Raster format.
5. There is a loss of information while converting raster maps into vector maps.

5.6 COMPONENTS OF A GIS

A GIS is much more than the software package as it involves the geographical data the computer hardware, the computer peripherals, the trained operator and the experts who will derive the output information from GIS. There are five important components of a GIS, as shown in Figure 5.3 (Marble and Peuquet, 1983, Moyer, 1989, Star and Estes, 1990).

1. Hardware
2. Software
3. Data
4. Methods
5. People

The hardware consists of equipment needed to run a GIS including a computer system with enough power to run the software, enough memory to store large amount of data, and input and output devices, such as scanners, digitizers, media disks, and printers (Carver, 1998).

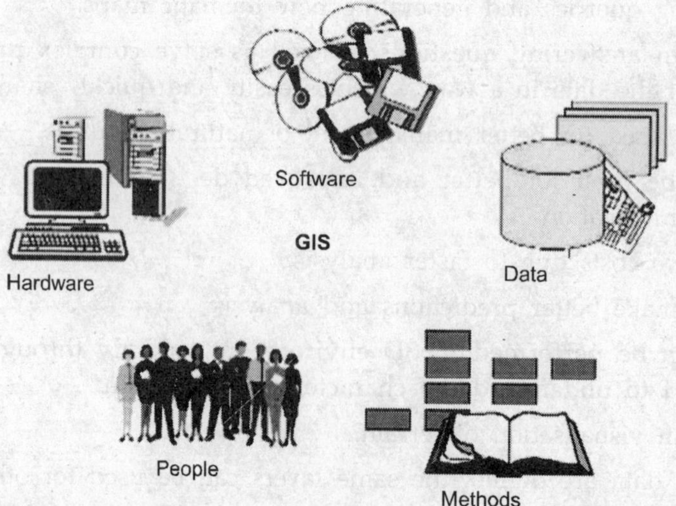

Figure 5.3: Major components of a GIS (*Source: Longley et al, 2005*)

There are many GIS software packages available today. Whereas, most of the packages (e.g. **ArcGIS, QGIS, GRASS GIS, ILWIS, GeoMedia, Mapinfo, IDRISI, SuperGIS, SAGA GIS to JUMP GIS**) are capable of data input, storage, management, transformation, analysis, and output, but the appearance, methods, resources, and ease of use of various packages may be different (Davis, 2001). Available GIS software are now capable of allowing both spatial and non-spatial data to be stored in a single database, known as the object-relational model. The modern packages usually come with a set of tools that can be customized to the users' needs (Lo and Yeung, 2002). Longley et al. (2005) classified the main GIS software packages into four main types as follows (Eldrandaly, 20017):

(a) Desktop GIS software: Desktop GIS software originated to be used in personal computers with Microsoft Windows as operating system, and are considered the mainstream workhorses of GIS today. They provide tools for a wide variety of users. The desktop GIS software include a range of options from simple viewers (such as ESRI ArcReader, Intergraph GeoMedia Viewer and MapInfo ProViewer) to desktop mapping and GIS software systems (such as Autodesk Map 3D, ESRI ArcView, Intergraph GeoMedia, and MapInfo Professional), and at the high-end, full-featured professional editor/analysis systems (such as ESRI ArcGIS ArcInfo, Intergraph GeoMedia Professional, and GE Smallworld GIS).

(b) Server GIS: Server GIS runs on a computer server that can handle concurrent processing requests from a range of networked clients. In addition to display and query applications, the software offer mapping, routing, data publishing, and suitability mapping. Third generation server GIS offer complete GIS functionality in a multi-user environment. Examples of server GIS include AutoDesk MapGuide, ESRI ArcGIS Server, GE Spatial Application Server, Intergraph GeoMedia Webmap, and MapInfo MapXtreme.

(c) Developer GIS: Developer GIS are toolkits of GIS functions (components) that a programmer can use to build a specific-purpose GIS application. They are of great interest to developers because such components can be used to create highly customized and optimized applications that can be either stand alone or embedded with other software systems. Examples of component GIS products include Blue Marble Geographics GeoObjects, ESRI ArcGIS Engine, and MapInfo MapX. Most of the developer GIS products from mainstream vendors are built on top of Microsoft's COM and .Net technology standards, but there are several cross platform choices (e.g., **ESRI ArcGIS Engine**) and several Java-based toolkits (e.g., **ObjectFX Spatial FX**).

(d) Hand-held GIS: Hand-held GIS are light weight systems designed for mobile and field uses. Hand-held GIS software are available on high-end 'smart phones' which can deal with comparatively large amount of data for sophisticated applications. These systems usually operate in a mixed connected/disconnected environment, and can make active use of data and software applications held on the server and accessed over a wireless telephone network. Examples of hand-held GIS include Autodesk OmSite, ESRI ArcPad, and Intergraph Intelliwhere.

Collecting the geographic data and creating a database is perhaps the most time-consuming and costly aspect of using a GIS. Before acquiring geographic data, it is crucial to check the quality of data. As the database is normally generated using various data (such as, Topographic maps, Aerial photographs, Remote sensing images, GPS data, Laser scanner data, etc.) which are normally available at different scales and collected by various modes of acqtuisition, there may be chances to have erroneous results when these are integrated in GIS due to varying errors present in these data sources, unless these errors are eliminated before their uses in GIS.

Methods include the procedure the data will be input into GIS system, stored, retrieved, managed, transformed, and analyzed to finally derive the output. In methods, steps are used to perform overlay analysis, spatial analysis, and modelling to derive the desired results and output. The transformation processes include, such as changing the coordinate system, setting a projection, correcting any digitized errors in the data set, and converting data from vector to raster or raster to vector (Carver, 1998). For successful GIS operation, a well-designed plan and business operation rules are important.

The people are one of the important components who actually work with GIS, such as GIS managers, database administrators, application specialists, systems analysts, and programmers. Other people performing professional services and making decisions on GIS work may include facility managers, resource managers, planners, scientists, engineers, industry personnel, etc. People use all above components to run a GIS system. Today's computers are fast and user friendly which make it easy to perform geographic queries, analysis and displaying maps.

5.7 BASIC TASKS OF A GIS

GIS has four basic tasks (Aronoff, 1989):

1. **Create** geographic data
2. **Manage** it
3. **Analyze** it, and
4. **Display** it on a map.

Geographical data are distinguished from non-spatial data in that every value in spatial data is associated with a location. Geographic data or information, such as city, reservoir, national park, etc., that identifies the geographic location of features and boundaries on Earth, is called spatial data. Spatial data is usually mapped and can be stored as coordinates and topology. Attribute data are used to record the non-spatial characteristics of a feature. Attributes or variables may be envisioned as a list of characteristics that help describe and define the features to represent in a GIS. Color, depth, height, weight, age, vegetation type are some examples of variables that may be used as attributes (Bernhardsen, 1992). These are normally presented in tables with attributes arranged in rows and columns. Each row corresponds to an individual spatial object, and each column corresponds to an attribute. Tables are organized and managed using a specialized computer program, called a database management system (DBMS) (Bailey and Gatrell 1995).

In most GIS software, data are organized in themes as data layers, often referred to as thematic layers. Each layer organizes the spatial and attribute data for a given set of cartographic objects in the region of interest. Figure 5.4 presents an example of several thematic layers derived from a piece of real world. This approach allows data to be input as separate themes and overlaid based on analysis requirements. This can be conceptualized as vertical layering the characteristics of the Earth's surface.

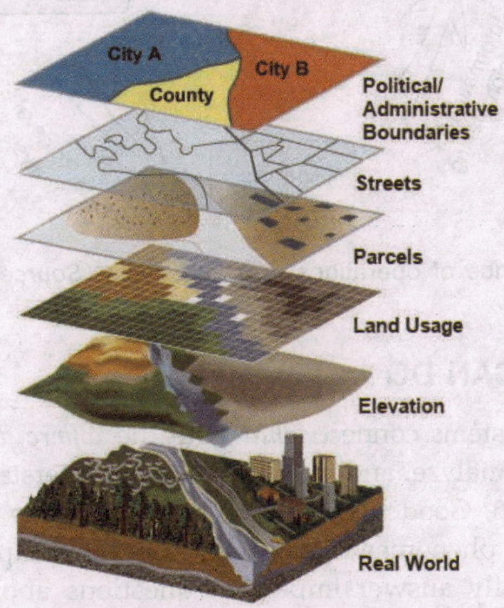

Figure 5.4: Abstracting real world into GIS layers (*Source: Hersh, 2017*)

It's easy to visualize and understand the locations (latitudes and longitudes coordinates) of geographic information (such as land use, elevation, etc.) from a map than a spreadsheet. Everyone knows that maps are easier to understand. It had been estimated that 80% of the informational needs of local government policy makers are related to geographic location (Berry and Marble, 1998). By making the link between the map and the attributes, GIS becomes a powerful tool for addressing and analyzing geographic data for desired applications.

A GIS is often used in a sequence of processes or operations that is referred to as the GIS cycle (Figure 5.5). This cycle starts with the real world (see top) and then moves through input of data after data collection from real world, retrieval and analysis, data analysis, output, decision-making on the output and action taken on information and applied back to real world. Thus, GIS has great utility as a decision-making and management tool.

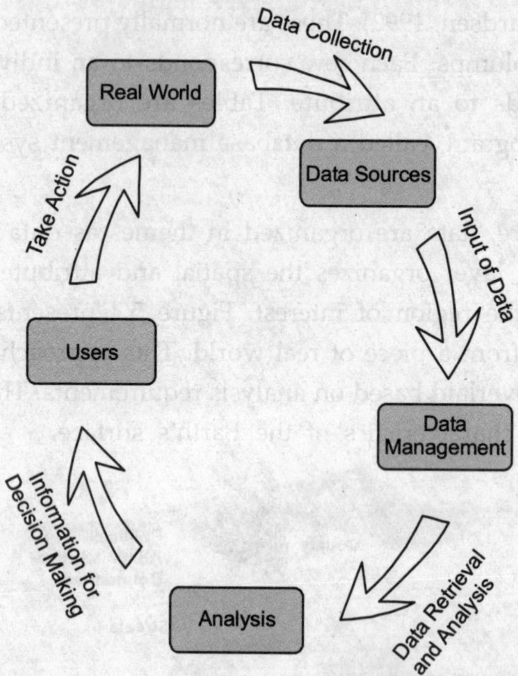

Figure 5.5: Sequence of operations in a GIS cycle (*Source: Burrough, 1986*)

5.8 ANSWERS A GIS CAN DO

Geographic Information Systems connect ***what*** with the ***where***, and discovers ***how***. A GIS lets us visualize, question, analyze, and interpret data to understand relationships, patterns, and trends (Burrough, 1986, Goodchild, 1990). These questions examine the relationships among various geographic phenomena using GIS tools, and explore & help answer these questions. A GIS can easily answer important questions about location, patterns and trends. For example:

1. **What is at?** This is basic question on GIS; what at a particular location is situated. For example, what is at the last north end of Akbar Road?
2. **Where are land features found?** It includes points, lines, and polygons. If you need to find the closest Restaurant or Hospital, GIS can display the path. The question can be a more challenging that explores the locations meeting a specific condition. For example, a city might identify all of the land parcels that are larger than 2 acres, vacant without vegetation, zoned as commercial land, and within ½ km of highway.
3. **What geographical patterns exist?** This question describes and compares spatial patterns at different locations, and can establish the relationship between two or more datasets that occupy the same location. For instance, there might be a direct relationship between a region's varying elevation and the amount of rainfall that falls on it.

4. **What changes have occurred over a given period of time?** GIS is able to present the change scenario due to variation in climate using time-series data. For example, it can predict the changes in the size of Nainital lake over past 40 years.
5. **What-if scenario?** It can predict the impact of a new facility over the existing scenario. For example, it can produce the scenario of environmental and safety implications affecting nearby homes, if a transmission line is laid out.

5.9 REPRESENTATION OF GEOGRAPHICAL DATA

Data in a GIS is represented in a simplified view of the real world, and is often represented as an (x, y, z) triplet. These data include information on the spatial location and extent of the physical entities, and information on their non-spatial properties (attribute data). The geographical data therefore, is represented in cartesian coordinate system or spherical coordinate system (latitude-longitude) where z is its attribute data (may be many e.g., elevation, landuse, soil type, rainfall, geology, snow depth), so the data can be generalized as $(x, y, z_1, z_2,...z_n)$ where n is the number of attributes at that location (Campbell and Shin, 2011). The digital data are converted to a common datum and projection system, as already explained in Chapter on GPS, before its analysis in GIS. Attribute data and their relative positions provide the advantage of using GIS for complex geographical analysis.

The digital datasets that are currently not in a GIS format are often converted to create GIS layers. The conversion process varies based on the format of the dataset and the import/export capabilities of both the host software and the GIS program, to be easily analysed by GIS. Other than GIS software, there are additional software (like AutoCAD, MicroStation, Corel Draw) that display, create, and edit vector spatial data (Parker, 1988, Star and Estes, 1990). For example, before capturing and importing CAD and drawing data, they need to be saved in DXF format before many GIS programs can read them.

Shape of a feature is important which is to be represented on a map in GIS. Single or multiple paired coordinates (x, y) associated with real world coordinate systems locate individual features in space and define their unique shape in the form of points, lines and polygons (Lo and Yeung, 2002), as shown in Figure 5.6.

5.9.1 Points

Points are zero dimensional features (with only one x, y coordinate set) whose location is depicted by a small dot. Ideally, there is no feature on the Earth with zero dimension but many features are represented as point features depending on the scale of map or purpose of study. Examples include electric poles, individual trees, wells, houses, schools, etc.

5.9.2 Lines

Line features are formed from a sequence of at least two paired coordinates. The first pair starts the line and the last ends it. A line feature is one-dimensional feature and its paired coordinates are used to compute the length of line. Additional paired coordinates can form vertices between the starting and ending points that will give the shape to the line. Examples include utility lines, canals, railroads, rivers, etc.

5.9.3 Polygons

Polygon features have closed boundaries which are formed by a sequence of lines. In a closed polygon, starting point is also its ending point. The sequence of coordinates forming the polygon provides with both perimeter and area. Examples include lakes, ponds, forest cover, agriculture land, countries, states, districts and census districts.

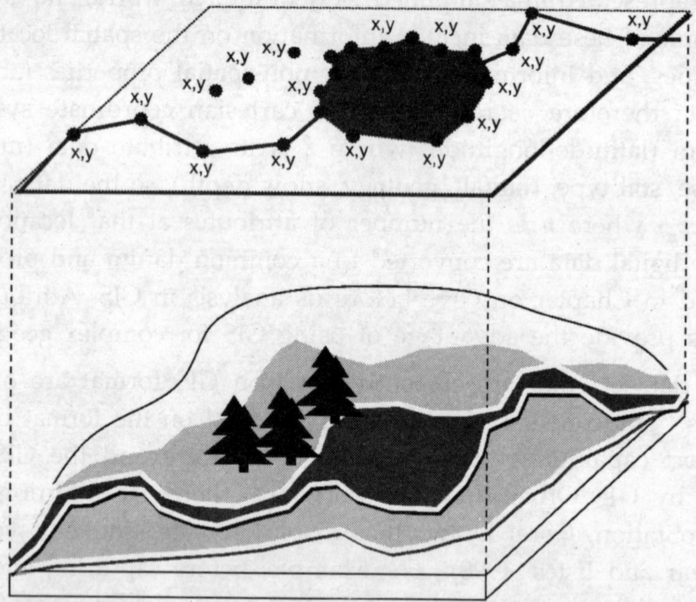

Figure 5.6: Point (trees), line (river), and polygon (water pond) features along with their coordinates (*Source: http://grindgis.com/what-is-gis/what-is-gis-definition*)

5.10 CONVERTING THE GEOSPATIAL DATA

Hard-copy maps (topographical maps, thematic maps) and aerial photographs/images are a major source of spatial data for GIS. Different processes, including digitizing, and scanning, can be used to convert these into digital format before input into GIS (Longley et. al., 2005). However, in many cases there will be a need to capture both the spatial locations of the features and its associated attributes in the field, depending on the GIS application. Data input is usually the major bottleneck in the development of a GIS database in developing countries like India, as converting hard-copy data from maps, images, and printed reports is tedious and time consuming task.

5.10.1 Scanning

It is the most popular way to convert hard-copy maps and images into digital layers. Scanners may be B&W or colour that capture the intensity of gray shade or colour of the objects on the original document, and convert these to pixel values arranged in rows and columns. The scanned image is a raster file, arranged as an array of pixels in columns and rows, depending on the resolution of the scanner device used in the process (Maguire et al 1991). Figure 5.7 shows the flatbed scanner and wide-format, sheet-fed scanner used in GIS work.

For many GIS applications, resolution and bit depth of the scanners may be important. Scanners support resolutions from 72 to 1200 dpi (dots per inch), but most scanning for GIS applications is done at resolutions between 200 and 600 dpi. Higher resolutions create higher quality images, but they also create substantially larger file sizes. Bit depth is the number of bits used to represent each pixel on a raster image. The greater the scanner's bit depth, the more colors and shades of gray a digital image can represent with larger sizes (Marble and Peuquet 1983). For example, a 24-bit color scanner can represent 2 to the 24th power or 16.7 million colors.

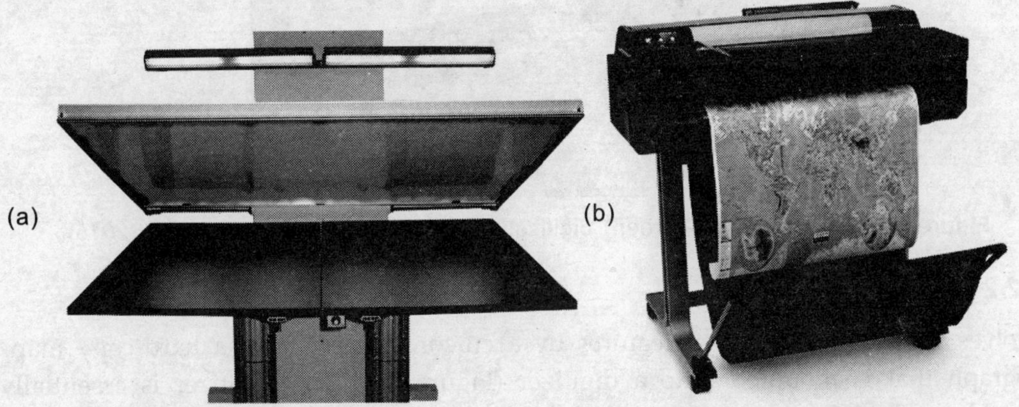

Figure 5.7: (a) Flat bed scanner, and (b) Wide-format, sheet-fed scanner

5.10.2 Digitisation

It is the transformation of information from analog format, such as a paper map, to digital format, so that it can be stored and displayed with a computer. Manual digitising involves an operator using a digitising table (or tablet) (known as heads-down digitising), or with the operator using a computer screen (heads-up digitising) (DeMers, 2000, Longley et al 2005). Digitisation process may introduce other type of errors which could be undershoots, overshoots, triangles, and sliver polygons. Editing of digitised features is done to remove such errors, and enter missing data to form the topology.

5.10.2.1 On-screen digitization

On-screen digitising is an interactive process in which a map is created using previously digitised or scanned information. Scanned (Raster) image is geo-referenced before its digitization (Davis, 2001). It is displayed on the computer screen as a background image in GIS, and the desired features are digitized (vectorised) with the help of a mouse

(Figure 5.8). This process, called "heads-up" digitization (or on-screen digitization), is similar to manual digitizing but without having a physical digitizing board. On a display screen, mouse is moved over the features and clicked; thus the positions of point, line, and polygon features are digitized and stored into new or existing layers. In heads up digitization, background images can be zoomed to clearly see the features of interest, enhancing the accuracy of identification and location of features, which is not possible in manual digitization using a tablet. Due to the increased popularity of heads-up digitizing as it is more convenient, manual digitizing is less frequently used.

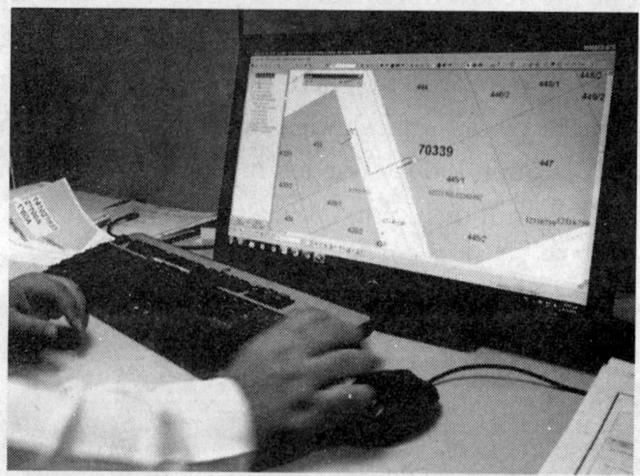

Figure 5.8: Heads up (on-screen) digitization process (*Source: Arc News, 2015*)

5.10.2.2 Manual digitization

It involves tracing the extent of features by a cursor directly from a hard-copy map or photograph that is mounted onto a digitizer (Figure 5.9). The digitizer is essentially a large table or board with an imbedded fine copper wire meshed electronic grid that senses the position of a pointer, called a puck or a cursor. Manual digitizing involves three steps; mounting the map on the digitizer, establishing control points, and digitizing map features (Jones, 1997). In the first step, map is mounted on the digitizer with its surface flattened and without any wrinkles by fixing with tape at its four corners. If working for several days with the same map, humidity might create wrinkles in paper maps, and therefore it has to be stretched out and re-mounted carefully to minimise the digitisation errors. It is tedious, time consuming and more laborious approach than the on-screen digitizing approach.

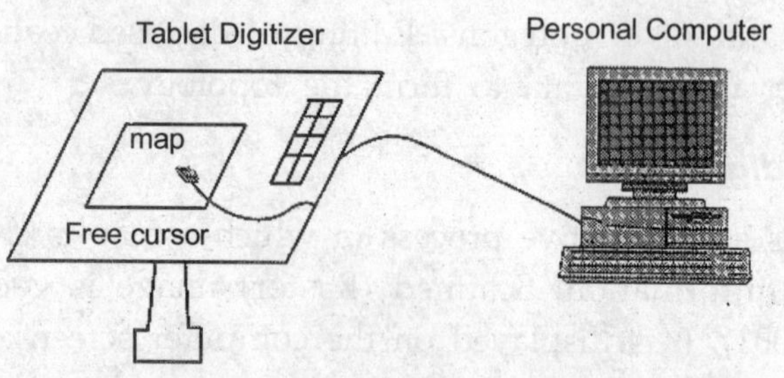

Figure 5.9: Digitizing tablet

5.11 DATA MODELS

There are two fundamental data models in GIS: raster and vector (Figure 5.10). Each model has its advantages and disadvantages (Goodchild, 1990, DeMers, 2000), and one data model may prove best for a certain types of application better than the other.

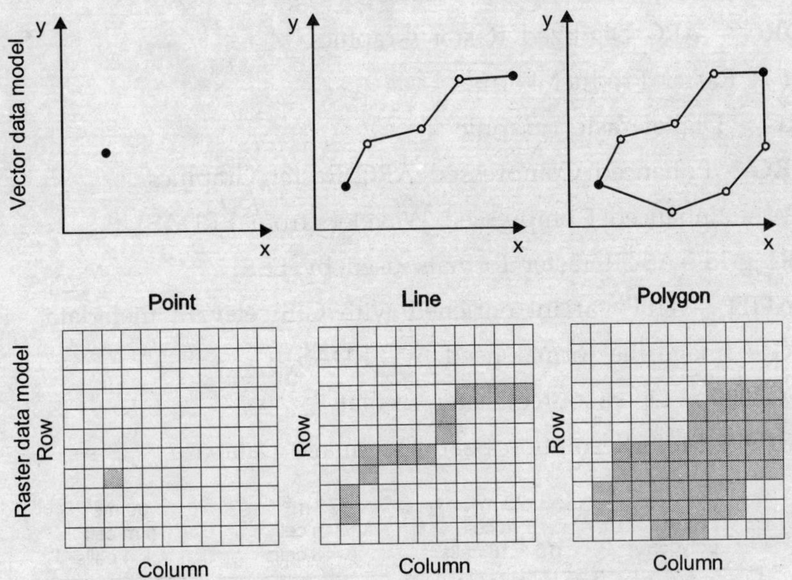

Figure 5.10: Raster and vector representation of features

5.11.1 Raster Data

The raster data model has a matrix of rows and columns with associated (field) values, and represents features of the Earth's surface through grid cells or pixels so that the geographic position of any feature or pixel can be determined. Pixels are the building blocks of any raster data model, which represent the value of that cell. They are usually square of consistent size within each layer. In raster model, larger the grid size, lower is the storage space and more is the distortion in the shape of features (Davis, 2001, Campbell and Michael, 2011), as shown in Figure 5.11.

The grid size in GIS analysis should be selected in such a way that it is much larger than the minimum mapping unit **(MMU)** at working scale. The minimum mapping unit is determined by the simple thumb rule relationship: MMU = 0.25mm x scale. Here, 0.25mm distance is taken using the concept that cartographically within 1mm distance five dots can be distinctly drawn, and the separation between each dot is 0.25mm. The MMU defines that any object or feature smaller than this unit cannot be shown on thematic map, while the grid cell size defines a unit of a piece of land which is considered to be homogeneous/ uniform for spatial analysis.

In addition to geographic position, a specific attribute value, representing that feature is [illegible] with the pixel. The second raster layer of the same area will provide a second attribute of that feature. A third layer will give a third attribute of that feature, and so on. Feature represented by a point fills one cell while lines and polygons are represented as a string or contiguous group of cells. Raster layers requires larger storage space; as every pixel gets a value, and cells with no features (empty cell) also get a "0" value. Conceptually, the raster model is simple and easy to use.

There are various raster formats available, as given below:

- **ADRG** – ARC Digitized Raster Graphics
- **RPF** – Raster Product Format
- **DRG** – Digital raster graphic
- **ECRG** – Enhanced Compressed ARC Raster Graphics
- **ECW** – Enhanced Compressed Wavelet (from ERDAS)
- **ESRI grid** –ASCII raster formats used by ESRI
- **GeoTIFF** – TIFF variant enriched with GIS relevant metadata
- **IMG** – Image file format used by ERDAS
- **JPEG2000** – Open-source raster format
- **MrSID** – Multi-Resolution Seamless Image Database

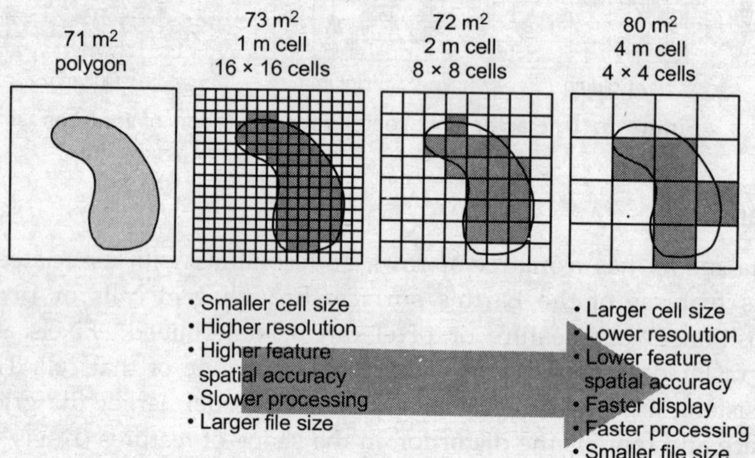

Figure 5.11: Effect of grid cell size on shape of the feature (*Source: ESRI, 2015*)

5.11.2 Vector Data

The vector data model uses discrete point and line segments to represent the locations of the Earth's features. Vector features are located with x, y coordinates, and therefore points are easy to store as they have one coordinate pair, called node. A node is a location in space that defines the shape of point, line, and polygon features. Lines have at least two nodes at their end points, and polygons have a minimum of three nodes to form an area. Lines and polygons usually have many more nodes that would define the line or the polygon (Aronoff, 1989, Star and Estes, 1990).

Vector objects usually require much less storage space than the raster layers. The vector data model can handle many attributes for each feature type as opposed to raster systems that record one attribute per layer. The link between the spatial and attribute data files is made with a unique identifier. Each feature on the map and its corresponding attributes has a unique identifier that links the map feature to its database attributes.

There are various vector formats available, as given below:

- **AutoCAD DXF** – AutoCAD DXF format by Autodesk
- **Cartesian coordinate system (XYZ)** – simple point cloud data
- **DLG** – Digital Line Graph (USGS format)
- **GML** – Geography Markup Language – Open GIS format used for exchanging GIS data
- **GeoJSON** – a lightweight format based on JSON, used by many open source GIS packages
- **GeoMedia** – Intergraph's Microsoft Access based format for spatial vector storage
- **ISFC** – Intergraph's MicroStation based CAD solution
- **KML** – Keyhole Markup Language a XML based
- **MapInfo TAB format** – MapInfo's vector data format
- **NTF** – National Transfer Format
- **Spatialite** – a spatial extension to SQLite,
- **Shapefile** – Most popular vector data developed by ESRI
- **Simple Features** – Specification for vector data
- **SOSI** – a spatial data format used for all public exchange of spatial data in Norway
- **Spatial Data File** – Autodesk's high-performance geodatabase format
- **TIGER** – Topologically Integrated Geographic Encoding and Referencing
- **VPF** – Vector Product Format

5.11.3 Raster Versus Vector

It is difficult to say that which model (Raster or Vector) is better for all applications as there are advantages and disadvantages to both data models. While raster data analysis is faster, the vector output is more accurate (Heywood et al 1998, Bolstad, 2002, Lo and Yeung, 2002). Table 5.1 presents some of the advantages and disadvantages of both the data models.

Table 5.1: Advantages and disadvantages of vector and raster data models

Data model	Advantages	Disadvantages
Raster	Simple data structure, Easy to understand	The features may not depict their true shapes as these are represented cell by cell. The accuracy of these shapes will depend upon the cell size.
	Data are arranged into columns and rows.	Cell size determines the resolution at which the data is represented. Smaller the cell size better the representation of information and more is the storage space.
	Computation of area of any polygon is easy and faster, as it is number of cell multiplied by the cell area.	Requires more storage space than vector data.
	Compatible with remote sensing or scanned images	Accuracy of locating a feature within the cell may be a problem, for example, locating electric poles in a raster map with 50m grid cell.
	Analysis process is faster, like overlay and buffering.	Projection transformations are time consuming
	Spatial analysis is easier. Surface analysis and neighborhood functions are only feasible in raster systems	Network linkages are difficult to establish
	Simulation and modelling is easy because each layer has the same size and shape of the cell.	
	Earth surface can be better represented in third dimension through (DEM).	
Vector	Data is represented in its original shape without any generalization.	Overlay analysis based on criteria is difficult and complicated
	Require less space to store vector layers.	Spatial analysis is cumbersome.
	Editing of vector data is faster and convenient.	It is slow to process complex datasets.
	Spatial accuracy is higher.	Simulation is difficult because each unit has a different topological form
	The vector systems depict how the features are related to one another using the topology.	Since the computation is more complex, Innovation on new analysis function is less.
	Network analysis is much faster.	
	Projection transformations are easier	

5.12 TOPOLOGY AND ITS COMPONENTS

Everything is related to everything else, but near things are more related than the distant things. A topology is a mathematical procedure that describes how features are spatially related and ensures data quality of the spatial relationships. These relationships may be in the form of simple distance calculations from one feature to another, and also include the more complicated relations of adjacency and connectivity (Marble and Peuquet, 1983, Star and Estes, 1990). This type of topology looks at the spatial relationships of existing features. Topological relationships include following three basic elements (Figure 5.12).

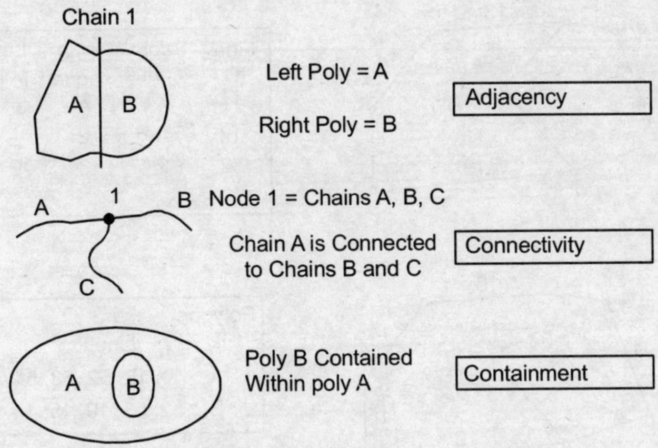

Figure 5.12: Topological spatial relationships

(a) Connectivity: It provides information about linkages among spatial objects. It is also called Arc-Node topology. Points along an arc that define its shape are called vertices. End points of the arc are called nodes, and arcs join only at the nodes. For example, spatial relationship exists between the locations of streets, sidewalks and streetlights.

(b) Contiguity/Adjacency: It provides information about neighbouring spatial object. Every arc has a defined direction. A GIS database maintains the list of polygons on the left and right side of each arc. The software then uses this information to determine which features are next to one another. Adjacency focuses on a single type of feature and establishes the topological relationship to describe how surrounding features are related to that feature.

(c) Containment: It provides information about inclusion of one spatial object within another spatial object. It is also called Polygon-Arc topology. Polygons are represented as a series of (x, y) coordinates that connect together to define an area. Various arcs define boundaries and closed areas are maintained.

One of the most important concepts associated with GIS is topology which is used for spatial analysis of features. Topology expresses explicitly the spatial (mathematical) relationships between connecting or adjacent vector features (points, lines and polygons) in a GIS (Burrough and McDonnell, 1998, DeMers, 2000). Figure 5.13 shows the topology of three basic types of features which can be used to establish the relationship through attribute tables of these features.

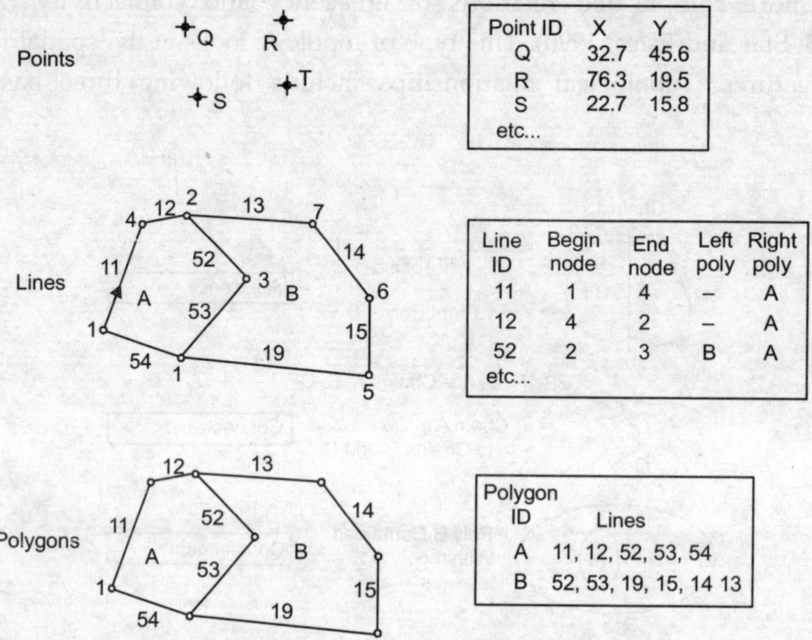

Figure 5.13: Topology of three basic types of features (*Source: Bolstad, 2010*)

In GIS map, two lines meeting perfectly at a point have an explicit relationship; left side and right side. Topologic data structure ensures that information is not unnecessarily repeated (Lo and Yeung, 2002). For example, if there is a common line between two adjacent polygons, the database would store the coordinates of common line only once in order to represent boundaries of two polygons (as opposed to two lines, one for each polygon). The database thus indicates that the line is the "left side" of one polygon and the "right side" of the adjacent polygon. For example, Figure 5.14 shows three

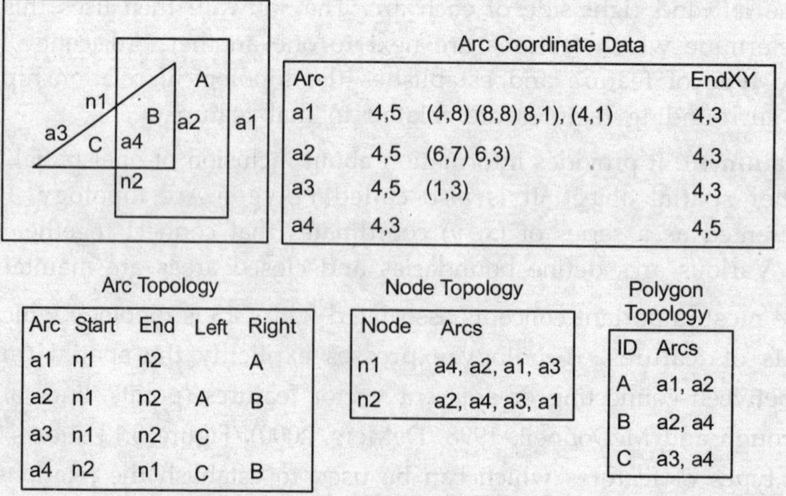

Figure 5.14: Arc-node topology of polygon features

polygons, *A*, *B* and *C*, with their arcs lengths *a1*, *a2* and *a3*, respectively. Line *n1n2* with arc length *a4* is common to two polygons *B* and *C*. Here *n1* and *n2* denote the node points or break points. Arc coordinate table shows the coordinates representing the *a1*, *a2*, *a3* and *a4* arcs, whereas arc topology, node topology and polygon topology are shown separately.

Figure 5.15 depicts some other topological relationships which can be established using three basic types of features in combination, such as point-point, point-line, point polygon, line-line, line-area and area-area. This figure is self-explanatory.

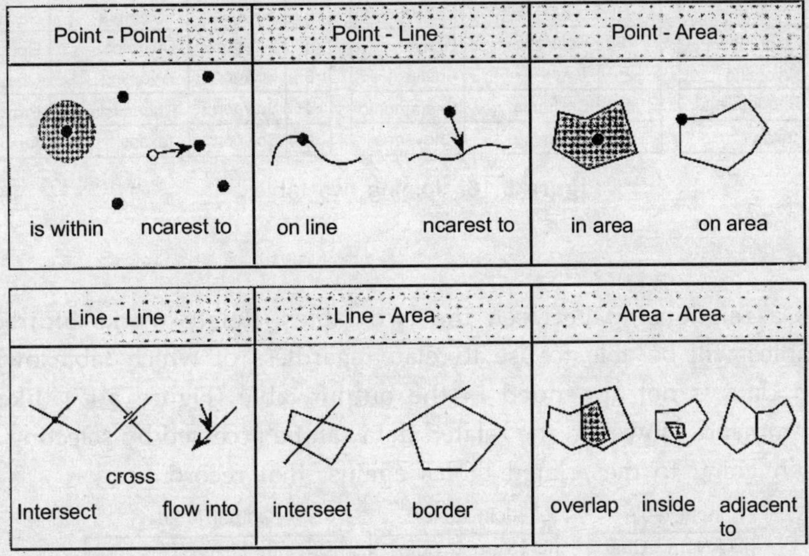

Figure 5.15: Topological relationships from three basic features (*Source: Islam, 2008*)

5.13 GEODATABASE

The term **'Geodatabase'** is defined as a collection of geographic datasets of various types that are held in a common file system folder, such as MS Access database, Oracle, SQL server, DB2 etc (Campbell and Shin, 2011, Berry, 2013a). The geodatabase is built on extended relational database. It supports various elements of GIS, such as attribute data, CAD data, geographic features, aerial and satellite images, GPS data and LiDAR survey measurements. These types of data can be represented as data objects viz. annotation, dimension, feature class, geometric network, raster dataset, tables, topology, relationship class etc. (Eldrandaly, 2007).

Most databases instead of keeping their data together in a single table, organize the data into multiple tables; each focusing on a specific theme. A user can link these tables through a common field, and can produce another table by linking the records in one table with the records in the other table. The associations can be made by using Join and Relate commands (Star and Estes, 2010), as presented below.

5.13.1 Join

Joining appends the fields of one table to fields of another through an attribute/field common to both the tables. Figure 5.16 shows the results after joining database of two table using *State Name* as the common key.

States Shapefile

FID	Shape	Satte_Name
1	Polygon	Califomia
2	Polygon	Colorado
3	Polygon	Wyoming
4	Polygon	Rhode Island
5	Polygon	Texas

Capitals Data Table

FID	Satte_Name	Capital
1	Rhode Island	Providence
2	Colorado	Denver
3	Texas	Austin
4	Califomia	Sacramento
5	Wyoming	Cheyenne

Result of Table join
Notice the name of the data table precedes the name of the field after the join

FID	Shape	Satte_Name	Capitals_Capital
1	Solygon	California	Sacramento
2	Solygon	Colorado	Denever
3	Solygon	Wyoming	Cheyenne
4	Solygon	Rhode Island	Providence
5	Solygon	Texas	Austin

Figure 5.16: Joining two tables.

5.13.2 Relate

Relate defines a relationship between the two tables. Relate works bidirectional that means both tables will be able to use to relate regardless of which table owns to relate. The associated data is not appended in the output table (Figure 5.17), like it is done through Join command. However, the related data can be accessed by selecting a particular record and then going to the related tables against that record.

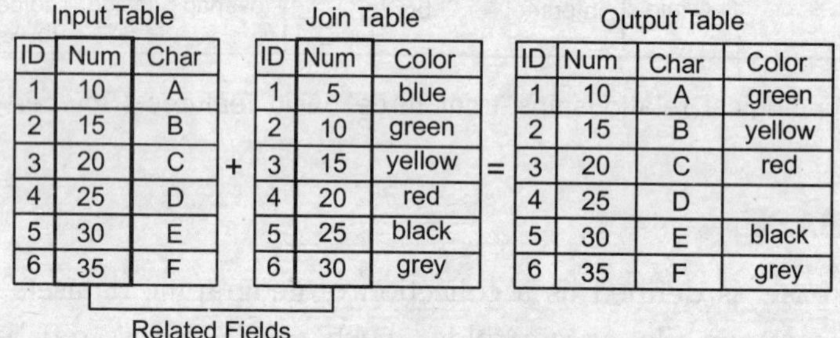

Input Table

ID	Num	Char
1	10	A
2	15	B
3	20	C
4	25	D
5	30	E
6	35	F

\+ Join Table

ID	Num	Color
1	5	blue
2	10	green
3	15	yellow
4	20	red
5	25	black
6	30	grey

= Output Table

ID	Num	Char	Color
1	10	A	green
2	15	B	yellow
3	20	C	red
4	25	D	
5	30	E	black
6	35	F	grey

Related Fields

Figure 5.17: Relating two tables

5.13.3 Relational Database

Relational database stores the data in multiple files, and makes it easier to extract information from these files at any given time through the use of a common field (Figure 5.18). It consists is a series of standard database tables, column types, indexes, and other database objects, and this grouping is called a "Relational Database Management System **(RDBMS)**" (Jones, 1997). The tables in these databases are often linked with inter-tabular relationships, hence the name "relational" database. A relational database aims to achieve normalization of data which helps to reduce the redundancy and anomalies. Outside of a GIS, database tables are created and manipulated in relational databases, such as **dBASE, rBase, ACCESS, Oracle, SQLServer, INFORMIX,** etc. (Longley et al 2005).

A flat file structure is used with a relational database model where data are stored in different tables. The columns of a table are named by attributes, and row in the table is called a tuple which represents the basic data (Heywood et al 1998). It is not necessary that two rows of the same table may have identical values in all columns. There are two crucial data viz. primary key and foreign key in the tables. A primary key is an attribute whose value is unique across all tuples (rows) in a relation (table). The primary key of one table appearing as an attribute of another table is known as a foreign key in that table.

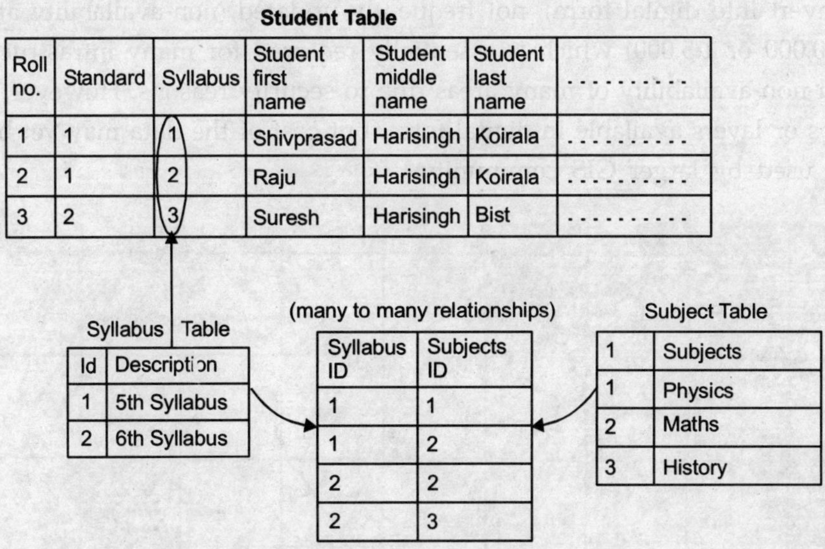

Figure 5.18: A relational database

The analysts need not to be aware of any data structure or data pointer, and can easily add, update, delete or create records using simple logic (Goodchild, 1990). A few search commands in a relational database require more time to process as compared to other database models.

5.14 SOURCES OF GIS DATA

5.14.1 Topographic Maps

Topographic maps are the best source to provide basic ground information quickly at a reasonable low cost. In India, topographic maps are produced by the Survey of India (SOI), Dehradun at three different scales; 1:250,000, 1:50,000 and 1:25,000. Figure 5.19 shows a sample of topographic map and various features on it at 1:50,000 scale. These maps are true representation of the objects on the Earth surface with Latitudes and Longitudes as well as contours (elevations) marked on it (Figure 5.20) which could be used to get three dimensional coordinates of ground objects. One can see the Latitude (N 20^0 45' 00") and Longitude (E 84^0 00' 00") values at the right hand corner of map as well as brown lines which depict elevation contours (e.g. 120, 140 m). Green colour indicates the forest cover while agricultural land is shown by yellow colour. These maps are popular in India as they are used to compute the coordinates of control points for geo-referencing of other data in a geodatabase, and also to create a Digital Elevation Model (DEM) from the digitized elevation contours of the area (Gruen et al, 2004).

In India, the disadvantages of using these maps are that they are in hard copy format (need to convert into digital form), not frequently updated, non-availability at large scale (such as 1:10,000 or 1:5,000) which is essentially required for many infrastructure related projects, and non-availability of many areas due to security reasons. However, SOI is now making maps or layers available in digital form, but cost of the data may yet be a limiting factor to be used by larger GIS community.

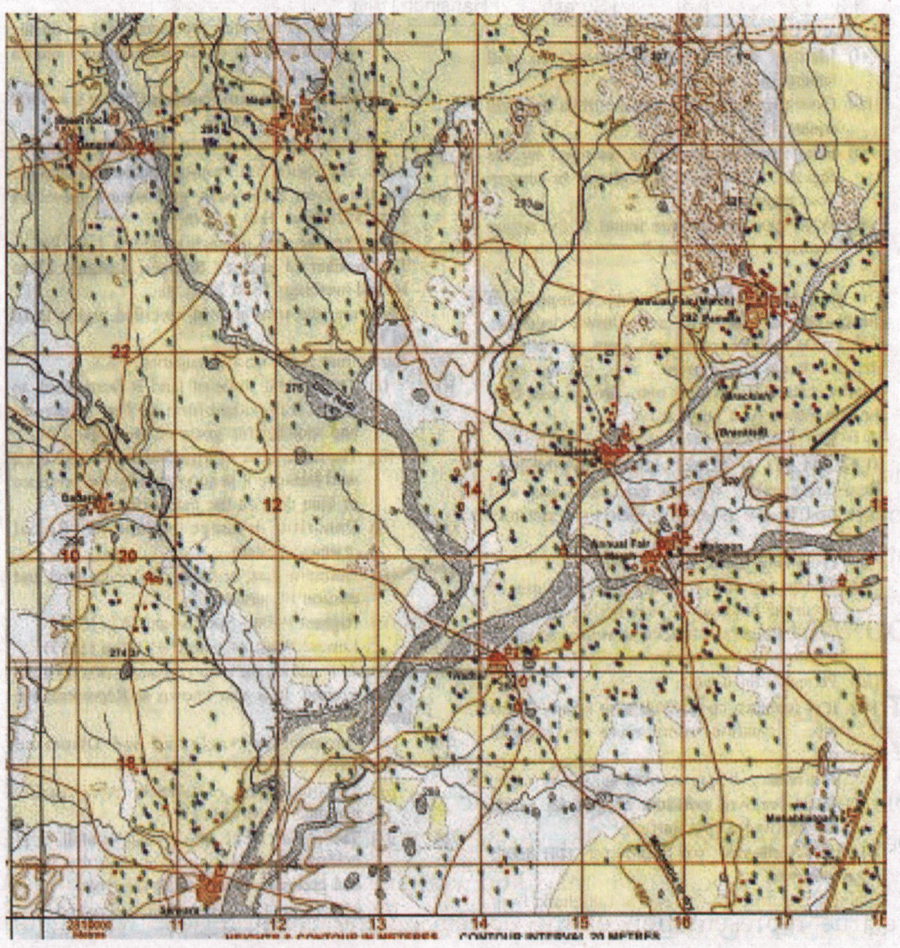

Figure 5.19: A sample of topographic map at 1:50,000 scale

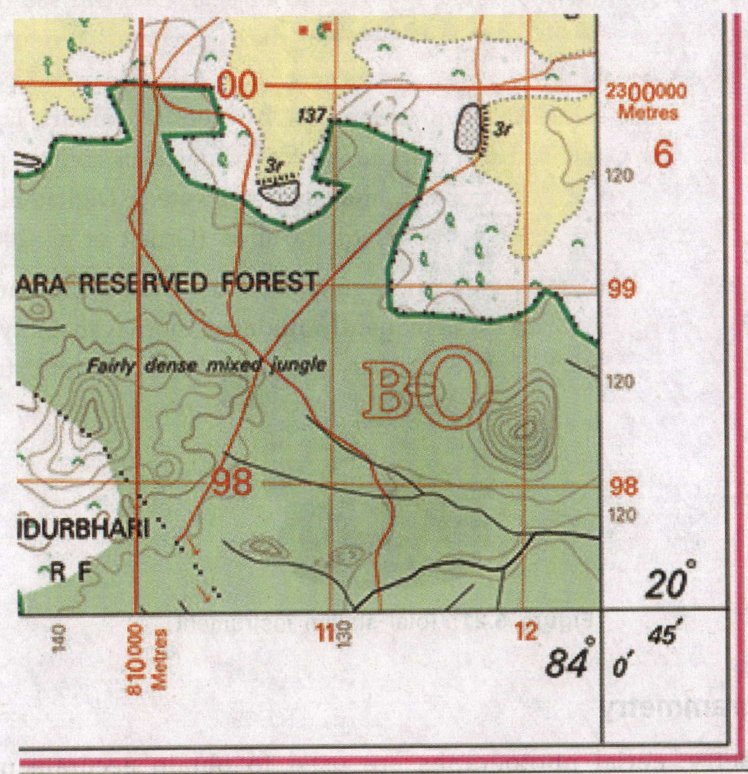

Figure 5.20: Latitude, longitude and contours values on a topographic map

5.14.2 Thematic Maps

Many government organisations produce their own thematic maps, such as soil, forests, water, road, rails, urban, etc. Survey of India **(SOI)** Dehradun and National Atlas Thematic Mapping Organisation **(NATMO)** Kolkata are also responsible to generate large number of thematic maps for entire India at different scales. These maps provide a good source of information in GIS based analysis.

5.14.3 Automated Surveying

It uses instruments, like laser levels, electronic distance measurement **(EDM)** systems, and total stations to capture spatial data, electronically. The most sophisticated of these instruments is the total station (Figure 5.21) that combines angle-measuring capabilities with the distances, and ultimately computes three dimensional coordinates of ground objects (*x*, *y* and *z*, where *z* denotes the elevation of the object). The data from these instruments can be directly uploaded into many vector-based GIS systems, and requires pre-processing before these can be used to make a spatial map.

Figure 5.21: Total station instrument

5.14.4 Photogrammetry

In photogrammetry, aerial photographs are used to obtain accurate measurement. Photogrammetric techniques determine ground distances and directions, heights of features, and terrain elevations, and three dimensional coordinates of ground objects that can be used into the GIS. Stereo photogrammetric techniques are applied to get the reliable three dimensional coordinates of ground objects. These techniques are very popular to create a DEM of area which can be straightaway used in GIS, being in raster format, along with other datasets (Maguire et al 1991).

A DEM is the digital representation of the land surface elevations with respect to any reference datum (Figure 5.22). As a regular arrangement of cells, DEM on its simplest form is the digital representation of topography. The quality of a DEM depends on its horizontal and vertical accuracy. The size of the grid cell is a critical parameter which determines the accuracy of interpolated elevation values (Poli et al 2004). DEM provides several useful inputs, such as elevations, ground slope, aspect, flow direction, catchment area etc to a large number of applications. DEMs are widely used in hydrologic and geologic analyses, hazard monitoring, natural resources exploration, agricultural management, groundwater modelling, estimation of the volume of proposed reservoirs, determining probability of landslide, flood prone area mapping, terrain visualisation, virtual sites etc (Lo and Yeung, 2002).

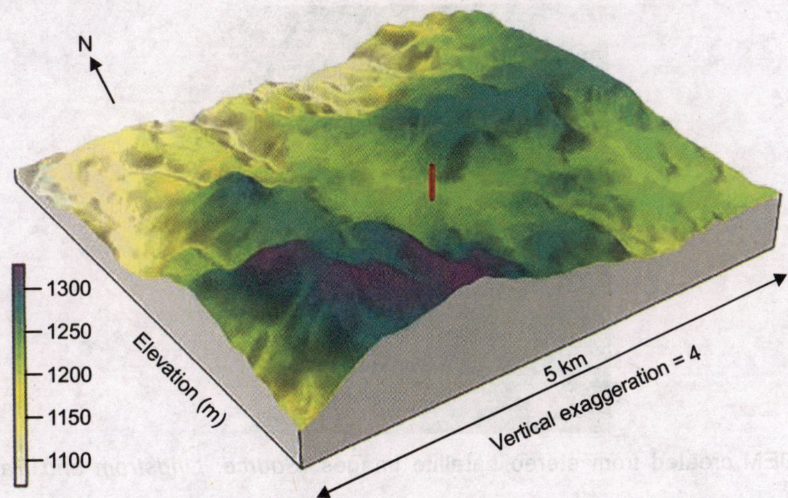

Figure 5.22: DEM of the area showing elevation values in feet

5.14.5 Remote Sensing

Satellite images (Hard copy or Digital) are an important source of data in a GIS. Digital image processing of remotely sensed images is done through specialised software packages, like ERDAS Imagine, ILWIS, etc. After processing images, the thematic layers can be generated and directly used in GIS being in raster format. Most popular thematic layer which is generally used in a large number of applications in GIS by the analysis of satellite images is the landuse and landcover maps (Carter, 1992, Berry, 2013a). The hard copy images can be digitized to create thematic layers in vector format, and used in GIS based analysis.

In addition to thematic layers, another important source of input to GIS from satellite images is DEM (Figure 5.23). For DEM data to be used in GIS, the Shuttle Radar Topography Mission **(SRTM)** is a good source of DEM data for almost entire world. The SRTM digital elevation data, produced by NASA originally, is a major breakthrough in digital mapping of the world. It provides a major advancement in the accessibility of high quality elevation data for large portions of globe. Satellite interferometry with synthetic aperture radar, such as SRTM uses two radar images from antennas at the same time to create DEM (Toutin et al., 2002). This data is currently distributed free of charge by the USGS.

According to previous studies on the evaluation of DEM generated by ASTER, a vertical accuracy of approximately ±15m can be achieved (Cuartero et. al., 2004). Poli and Dolci (2004) used ASTER images for the generation of DEM, the points are automatically extracted in the images at sub-pixel accuracy. DEM from various stereo satellite sensors, including WorldView-4 and WorldView-3 at 30cm resolution have been generated to support project planners. Among the high resolution satellite images that have been successfully used for DEM generation and objects extraction, Cartosat, OrbView-3 and IKONOS stereo images (Fraser et al., 2002; Toutin et al., 2002, Yanalak, et.al., 2012) and SPOT-5 stereo images (Gruen et al., 2004) have been successfully used.

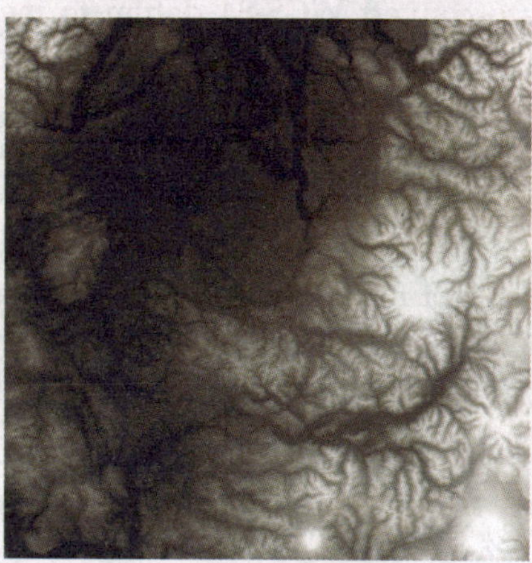

Figure 5.23: DEM created from stereo satellite images (*Source: Lindstrom and Pascucci, 2001*)

A Google Earth image of Mount St. Helens is shown in upper-left portion of Figure 5.24. A three-dimensional rendering of geography of the area is shown with peaks and valley. A DEM showing the topographic undulations is created to establish its relative height above mean sea level.

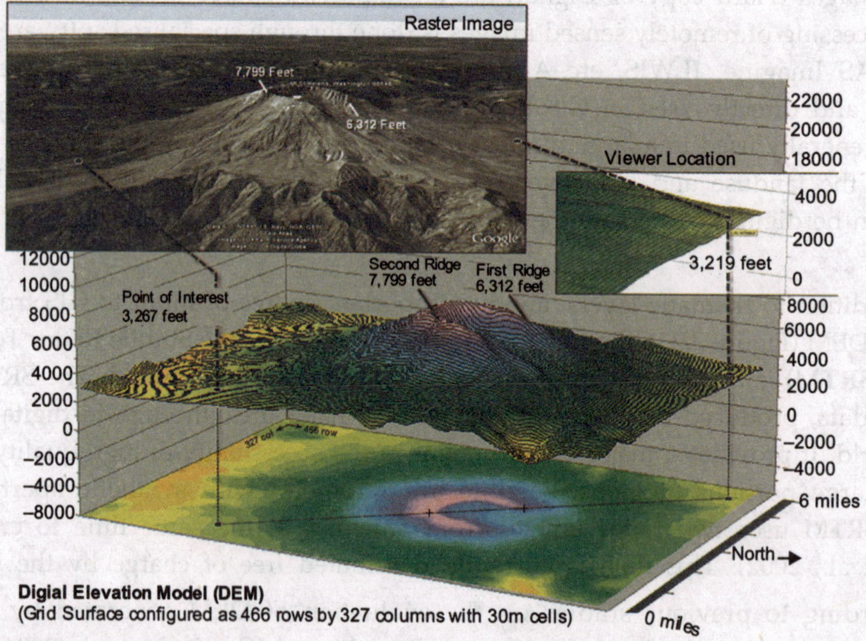

Figure 5.24: The DEM of Mt St. Helen's by storing elevation values in a matrix of 30 meter grid cells of 466 rows by 327 columns (152, 382 values) (*Source: Berry, 2013b*).

5.14.6 Global Positioning System

GPS, a radio-based navigation system, computes accurate locations (Latitude, longitude and elevation) of objects on the Earth's surface. It is to be noted that the elevation of object is obtained with respect to **WGS-84** datum, and not the mean sea level. Many GPS or GIS software are capable to convert WGS-84 datum to mean sea level of the country. With hand-held GPS receivers, the locations of objects can be determined within a reasonably accuracy. Using two GPS receivers simultaneously (called Differential GPS or DGPS) or using a Wide Area Augmentation System **(WAAS)**-enabled GPS receiver, which use satellites and ground stations that provide GPS signal corrections, users can get sub-meter accuracy in locations.

GPS is a major data input tool for GIS work (Venkatraman and Anitha, 2017). Many GPS units have "feature lists" that streamline the data entry process. Feature lists are databases that are defined to locate each feature type, along with their associated attributes. Both the feature locations and their associated attributes can be downloaded into GIS.

5.14.7 Light detection and ranging

Laser based technology uses laser light pulses to measure the distance to a surface. Light detection and ranging **(LiDAR)** sensors operate on the same principle as that of laser equipment. It is similar to other types of radar, but uses light instead of radio waves. Pulses are sent from a laser onboard an aircraft and the scattered pulses are recorded. The time lapse for the returning pulses is used to determine two-way distance to the object. LiDAR uses a sharp beam with high energy, and hence high resolution data can be achieved (Berry, 2013a).

Ground-based or airborne LiDAR systems provide very dense data (cloud) points with their three dimensional coordinates of the objects having high accuracy. The cloud data result in thematic layers depicting the ground features better than the traditional remote sensing and radar methods. LiDAR based systems are gaining popularity to provide input to GIS, as data collection is much faster and accurate as well as all their weather operation capability. The disadvantage is that the technology is expensive for a country like India, and the collected data volume is huge even for a small area. Therefore, it requires high speed computer to do lot of editing before processing the data to transform into thematic layers (Berry, 2013b). These systems have lot of potential to provide data for proper planning the urban area or transforming the cities into smart cities.

Both vector and raster data models use LiDAR data. Many GIS programs have functions to convert points data (x, y and z) into vector layers, which may also be converted into raster layers (Yanalak et al, 2012). In vector systems, LiDAR points frequently generate topographic layers, called Triangular Irregular Networks **(TIN)**, which can be used to represent terrain in vector-based systems. DEM can also be generated quickly from these data for a large area.

5.14.8 Unmanned Aerial Vehicle/Drone

An unmanned aerial vehicle **(UAV)**/Drone represents a new type of remote sensing platform that is easy to use and does not carry a human operator. It uses aerodynamic forces to provide vehicle lift, which can fly autonomously or be piloted remotely. It provides users with many new options regarding where, when, and how geospatial imagery and data are collected (Figure 5.25). System includes: Aircraft, Sensor (NIR/SWIR, MIR, TIR,

Multispectral/hyperspectral, LiDAR etc), Camera, GPS, Radio Controlled device, and Wifi. Vector and raster layers from UAV/Drone after processing can be used in GIS (Berry, 2013b).

With the advancement, Drone technology and autonomous flights are expected to have a dramatic increase in the use for GIS mapping applications. At present the limitations could be (i) regulations surrounding their usage, which vary from country to country (ii) maximum speed of 30mph (iii) low flying height (150m vertical flight), (iv) limited time of flight for data collection (~15 to 20 minutes flight time per battery), and (v) non-working in rains, wind, snowfall, fog, etc. Nonetheless, the UAV/Drone based technology is revolutionizing both spatial data collection and geographic analysis at a large scale. This paradigm shift brings new perspectives on GIS to a wide range of applications as below:

1. Surveying
2. Remote sensing
3. Precision agriculture
4. Terrain mapping/modeling
5. 2D and 3D image analysis
6. 3D topographic image analysis
7. Ortho-mosaicking
8. Weather monitoring
9. Oil and Gas exploration
10. Mining
11. Transmission line monitoring
12. Disaster response and relief, and many more

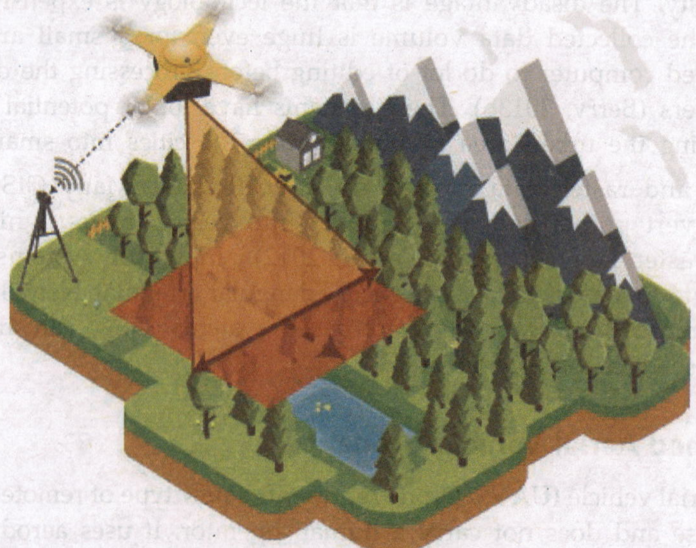

Figure 5.25: Data collection using Drone/UAV
(*Source: http://www.yellowscan.fr/event/yellowscan-surveyor-demo*)

5.15 INTERPOLATION OF DATA

Interpolation is the method of predicting the value of attributes at unknown sites from the measurements made at known point locations within the area (Sibson, 1981). The rationale behind interpolation is that the values at unknown points are more likely to be similar to the values present in the vicinity in space. Interpolation finds its applications in many areas, such as interpolation of rainfall or soil moisture or elevations with few available values (Star and Estes, 2010). The difference (absolute or squared difference) between the measured and predicted values at data points is an indicator of the quality of the interpolation.

There are two methods of interpolation; (i) Global method, and (ii) Local method. Global methods predict values at unknown locations using the values of entire dataset, while, local methods predict using the value of known points within a neighbourhood (such as 3 x 3 cell size, buffer zone etc). Global methods usually create smooth surfaces, which are sensitive to outliers (values that are significantly different as compared to the other values). Local methods yield less smooth surfaces and are not sensitive to outliers as the value has been interpolated using neighbourhood operation (Sibson, 1981, Burrough and McDonnell, 1998).

Interpolation predicts values for cells in a raster from a limited number of sample data points. There are several interpolation techniques available in GIS software (Campbell and Shin, 2011), as explained below.

5.15.1 Inverse Distance Weighted

The inverse distance weighted **(IDW)** method estimates cell values by averaging the values of sample data points in the neighborhood of each processing cell. The nearer a point is to the center of the cell being estimated, the more influence, or weight, it has in the averaging process.

5.15.2 Kriging

Kriging is an advanced geo-statistical procedure that generates an estimated surface from a scattered set of points with z-values. More so than other interpolation methods, a thorough investigation of the spatial behavior of the phenomenon represented by the z-values should be done before the best estimation method is selected for generating the output surface.

5.15.3 Natural Neighbour

Natural neighbor interpolation finds the closest subset of input samples to a query point and applies weights to them based on proportionate areas to interpolate a value (Sibson, 1981).

5.15.4 Spline

The spline method estimates values using a mathematical function that minimizes the overall surface curvature, resulting in a smooth surface that passes exactly through the input points.

5.15.5 Trend

Trend is a global polynomial interpolation that fits a smooth surface defined by a mathematical function (a polynomial) to the input sample points. The trend surface changes gradually and captures coarse-scale patterns in the data.

5.16 VARIOUS OPERATIONS IN GIS

GIS applications are tools that allow users to create interactive queries (user-created searches), analyse spatial information, edit data in maps, and present the results of all these operations. Spatial analysis is core to the GIS and an important outcome. Through spatial analysis, a range of questions can be answered which may help in decision making. The range of methods deployed for spatial analysis varies with respect to the type of data model used. GIS can also be used in statistical analysis by applying geo-statistics over geographic data. GIS can relate unrelated information by using location as the key index variable (Davis, 2001).

GIS software does simple querying operations with the spatial data, like feature selection, and perform spatial querying, like buffering and overlay operations (Goodchild, 1990). In the spatial operations, a logical operation is applied to the spatial data in order to display only those features which satisfy the logical condition. GIS can manipulate the data in single layer, like merging, dissolving and append operation but the full potential of GIS lies in the ability to integrate data from the variety of spatial layers (DeMers, 2000). It starts from combining two vector layers or takes one raster layer and place the other vector layer on it to place the one vector layer on another and compare features from both layers. Spatial analysis functions can also be classified in regards to the data type involved in the spatial analysis (point, line, network, polygons/areas, surface), the data structure (vector and raster), or the conceptual model of space (discrete entity vs. continuous field (Burrough et al. 1998). Albrecht (1996) provides a detailed classification of spatial analysis functions available in GIS software (Figure 5.26).

Another unique characteristic of the GIS is spatial modelling. In the spatial modelling, manipulation of geographic information in multiple steps is done which may represent stages in some complex analysis. Spatial models are classified as data models, static modelling and dynamic modelling. Also, they are classified based on their purpose, based on their methodology and based on logic (Heywood et al, 1998). Spatial models used spatial data, and makes use of combined functional capabilities, such as analytical tools for computation and programming languages. The aim of spatial modelling is to derive a meaningful representation of events, occurrences or processes by making use of the power of spatial analysis.

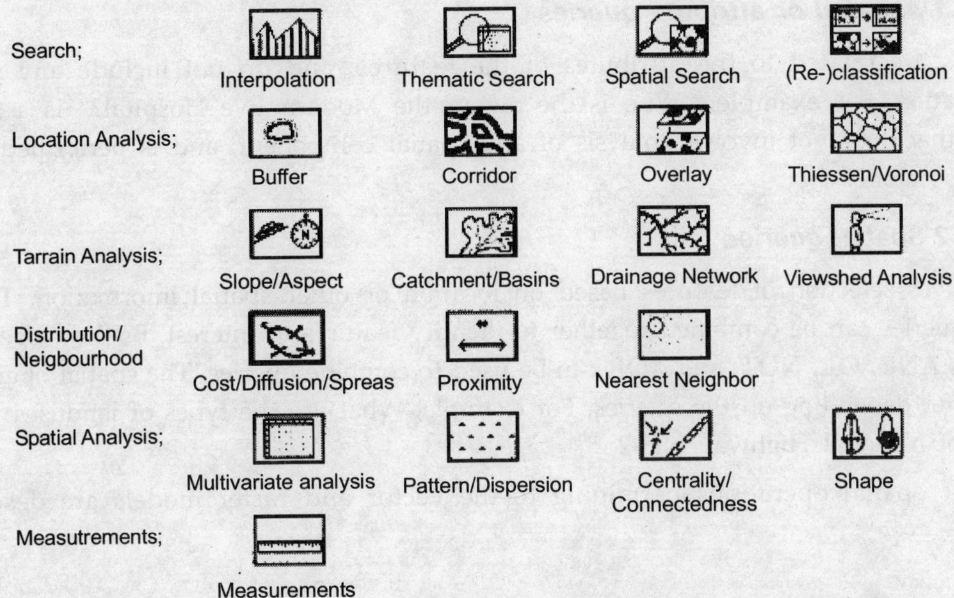

Figure 5.26: Classification of spatial analysis functions (*Source: Albrecht, 1996*)

In GIS, various analyses can be done, like surface analysis, network analysis, spatial interpolation, grid (raster) analysis and analytic modelling. In the network analysis, nearest route can be determined. In grid analysis, it calculates output grid values based on the values from multiple grids at the same location. Local statistics can be done on two or more grid themes, like majority, maximum, mean, median, minimum, sum etc. By spatial interpolation, spatial values of unknown points can be determined. Terrain analysis includes computation of slope, aspect, hill shade, contour and curvature etc. Proximity analysis is a useful in various processes, like site selection which can be critical for business administration (Longley et al, 2005).

5.16.1 Measurement

Measurement of length, perimeter and area of the features is a common requirement in spatial analysis. Perimeter is calculated by counting the number of cells in each side that is making the boundary of the feature and then multiplying the count by resolution (cell size) of the raster grid. All the sides of the feature are then added. In vector data model, distance between two points is measured using the Euclidean distance method. Perimeter is calculated by adding the measurements of straight lines forming the feature. To calculate the area, the feature is sub-divided into geometric shapes and then the areas of the geometric shapes are totalled.

5.16.2 Query

Query is a logical question which is performed on the database to retrieve specific data. Queries are useful for deriving the desired results. There are two types of queries that can be performed in GIS (Lo and Yeung, 2002).

5.16.2.1 Aspatial or attribute queries

Queries are related to the attributes of the features, and do not include any spatial information. For example, "Who is the owner the Modern Eye Hospital?" is a simple query that does not involve analysis of any spatial component, and is performed using database alone.

5.16.2.2 Spatial queries

It involves selection of features based on location or other spatial information. Two or more queries can be combined together to identify features of interest. Boolean operators, such as **AND, OR, NOT,** and **XOR** can be used to combine queries. The spatial operations can differ depending on the queries. For example, What are the types of landuses within 500m of National Highway NH-2 ?

The spatial operations pertaining to the vector and raster models are described below.

5.16.3 Raster Operations in GIS

Both operators and functions evaluate the expression only for input cells that are spatially coincident with the output cell. Mathematical operators apply a mathematical operation to the values in two or more input raster layers. Figure 5.27 shows how local, focal, zonal and global operations can be applied on raster layers.

5.16.3.1 Arithmetic operators

A range of arithmetic operations, such as addition, subtraction, multiplication, and division can be applied to two or more raster layers (Moyer, 1989). If the data in grids is in the form of integer then after any mathematical operation, the data in the output grid would also be integer.

5.16.3.2 Local operations

Local functions process a grid on a cell-by-cell basis. The output value of each cell depends on the values of corresponding cells in the raster input layers for analysis.

5.16.3.3 Neighbourhood analysis

The value of a cell in the output raster depends upon the value of the corresponding cells and their neighbouring cells in the input raster (Sibson, 1981). The neighbourhood for a cell is generally taken as a matrix (window) or a region in which the cell itself occupies the centre, and is surrounded by the others cells. Neighbourhood analysis is used to compute the average value of the cells over the defined window, and is placed as the value of the computed central cell. It can also be used to compute the mean, median value of all the cells over the window.

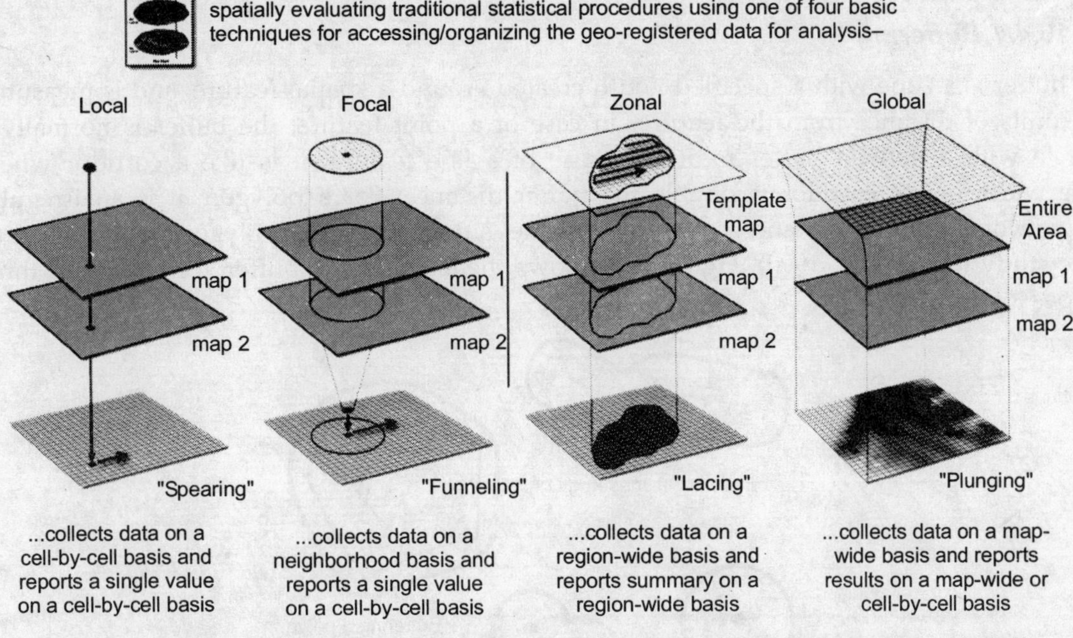

Figure 5.27: Local, focal, zonal and global operations in a GIS (*Source: Barry, 2013b*)

5.16.3.4 Boolean operators

Boolean operators use Boolean logic (**True** or **False**) on input raster, cell-by-cell basis (Shahabi et al, 2014). Output values of **True** are written as 1 and **False** as 0.

- **AND** (&): Finds where values are true (non-zero) in the cells of both input raster.
- **OR** (|): Finds where non-zero values are present in the cells of one or both input raster.
- **XOR** (!): Finds where non-zero values are present in the cells of one input raster or another input raster, but not both.
- **NOT** (^): Finds where non-zero values are not present in the cells of a single input raster.

5.16.3.5 Relational operators

Relational operators evaluate specific relational conditions (Maguire et al, 1991). If a condition is **True**, the output is assigned 1; if a condition is **False**, the output is assigned 0.

- = (Equal to)
- > (Greater than)
- < (Less than)
- ≥ (Greater than or equal to)
- ≤ (Less than or equal to)
- ≠ (Not equal to)

5.16.4 Vector Operations in GIS

5.16.4.1 Buffering

A buffer is a zone with a specified width created around a spatial feature, and is measured in units of distance from the feature. In case of a point feature, the buffer is normally a circle with a defined buffer radius. In case of a line feature, it is like a corridor where the width of the corridor is double the buffer distance. For a polygon, it is an irregular region of the buffer distance, inside or outside, surrounding the polygon, as per need of the study (Goodchild, 1990). Figure 5.28 shows the examples of buffer zones around three types of features.

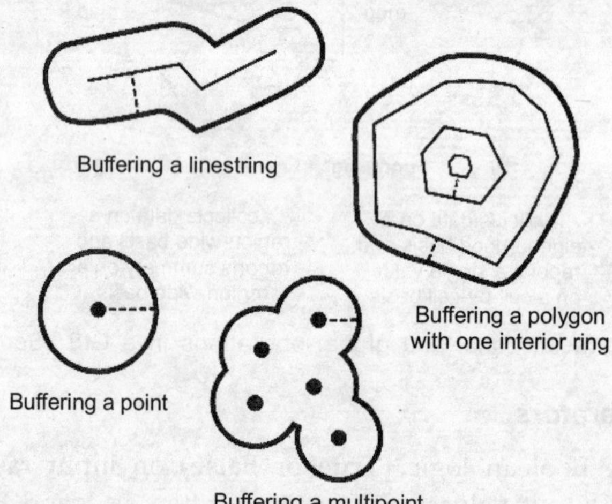

Figure 5.28: Buffer zones around three types of features.

Buffering is used for neighbourhood or proximity analysis which aims to evaluate the characteristics of the buffered area surrounding the spatial feature. Common examples of point, line and polygon features include (i) the identification of hospitals within a certain distance of a house, area served by a Bus Station, (ii) the number of commercial complexes present around 500m of a road, and (iii) hotels around 1000m of buffer zone of a lake.

5.16.4.2 Dissolve

It merges the adjacent features having same attribute value, and thus reduces the number of records from the attribute table. Dissolve is shown in Figure 5.29.

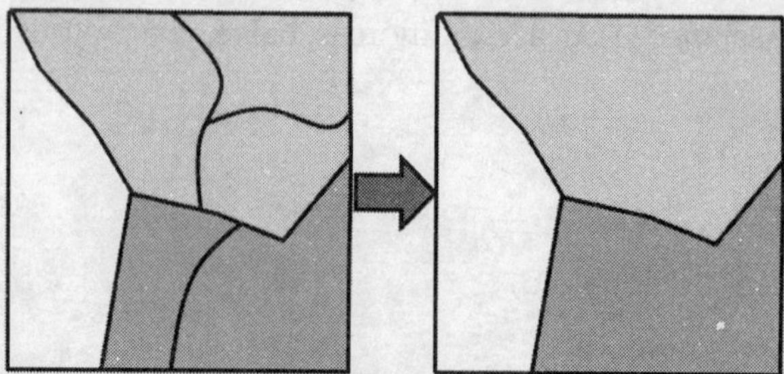

Figure 5.29: Output from dissolve function *(Source: Campbell and Shin 2011)*

5.16.4.3 Union

Union creates a new theme by overlaying two polygon themes. It is same as 'or' Boolean operator. The output theme contains the combined polygons and attributes of both themes. Only polygon themes can be combined using union (Figure 5.30a).

5.16.4.4 Intersect

Intersect creates a new theme by overlaying a point, line or polygon theme with an intersecting polygon theme. It is same as 'and' Boolean operator. The output theme contains only the feature inside the intersecting polygons (Figure 5.30b).

5.16.4.5 Identity

It creates a new theme by overlaying a point, line, or polygon theme with an intersecting polygon theme. The output theme contains all the original point, line, or polygons as well as the attributes transferred by the intersecting polygon theme (Figure 5.30d).

5.16.4.6 Clip

Clip is used to subset a point, line or a polygon theme using another polygon theme as the boundary of the area of interest (Figure 5.30e).

5.16.4.7 Erase

Erase removes polygons in a theme from the area covered by polygons of another theme. The output feature class only contains those features of the input polygon theme that falls outside the polygons of the second theme (Figure 5.30f).

5.16.4.8 Split

It causes the input features to form subset of multiple output feature classes. The split field's unique values form the names of the output feature classes (Figure 5.30g).

5.17 FREE (OPEN) GIS RESOURCES

5.17.1 GIS Data

The Internet is a great place to start looking for data. The users can find existing GIS datasets on internet that may serve the purpose and meet specifications and requirements, as it saves significant time and money. A large number of base map data (countries, states, district, forest, lakes, major roads, rails, tourist places, rivers, township etc.) as well as spreadsheets already exist on the Internet. Large quantity of raw data (such as satellite images, maps, digital files etc) may be free download for use in GIS work. While using these data, there is a word of caution that its reliability and authenticity must be ascertained (including its metadata, if possible) before use, else the accuracy of the derived results cannot be determined.

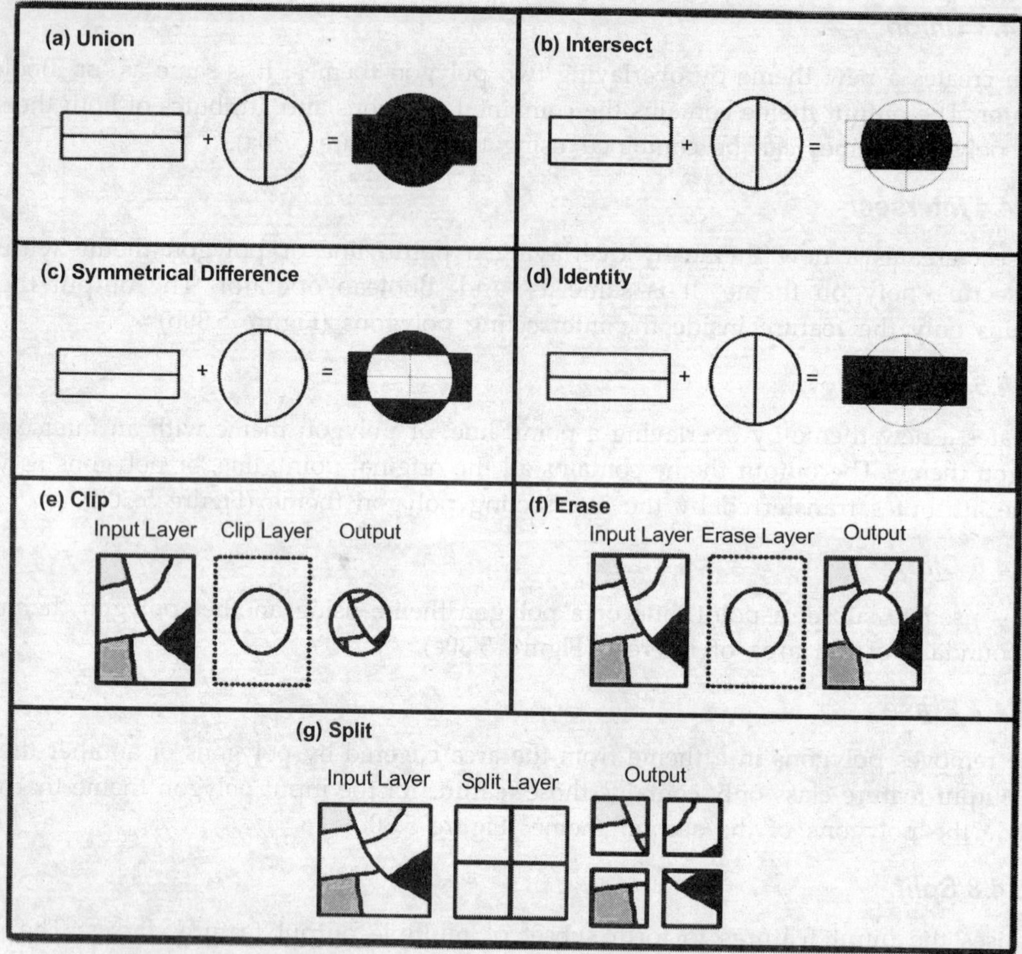

Figure 5.30: Various operations on vector layers *(Source: Campbell and Shin 2011)*

For GIS work, many government agencies (like IMD, GWB, CWC, NATMO, Google, Earth, BHUVAN, etc), and commercial organizations (like Google Earth) may also be a better source of data/information provider. Landsat data may be freely downloaded with USGS website. Figure 5.31 shows the screenshot of main page of BHUVAN site of Department of Space, Government of India where large amount of free satellite images and other thematic data are available. To its credit, Bhuvan is unique and most importantly, regularly updated and upgraded and perhaps the best geoportal for Indian data. It also boasts of a rich ensemble of value-added products and analysis models (Datta, 2016). But, Bhuvan has its limitations. The fact that it caters to 1 meter data makes it good only for thematic visualization, not for engineering grade work. Further, Bhuvan can provide limited solutions as it is devoid of elevation data and ground-verified attributes which SoI alone can provide (Datta, 2016). Many government organisations provide various maps, tabular and graphical data, and private agencies modify "public" data to create a "value-added" product that can be purchased for GIS work.

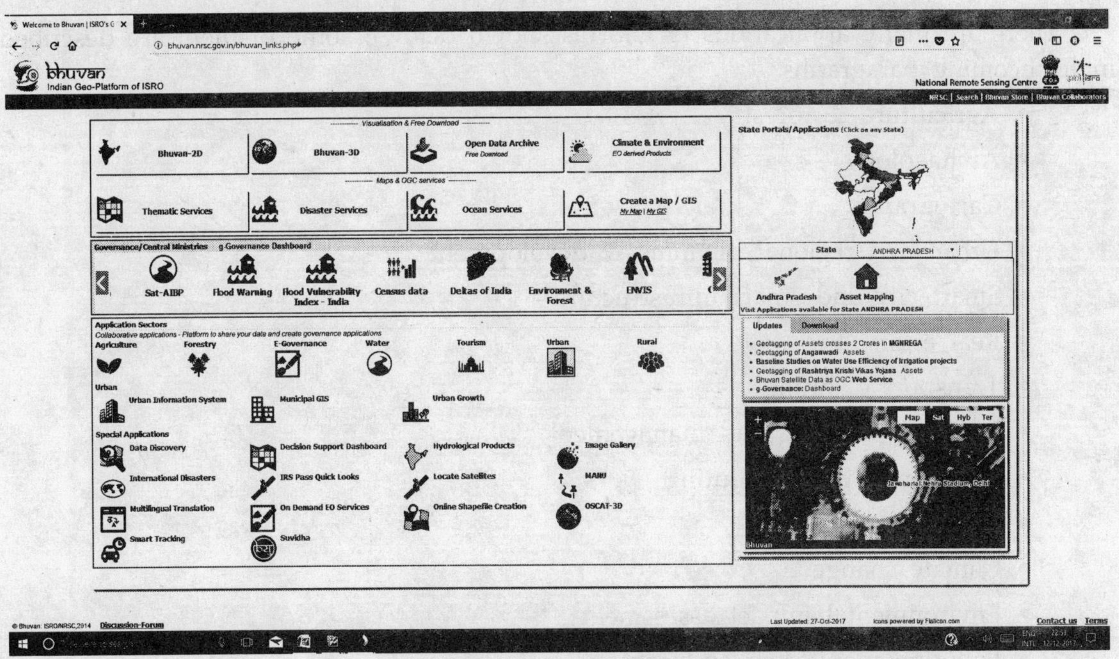

Figure 5.31: A glimpse of BHUVAN mainpage (*Source: http://bhuvan.nrsc.gov.in/bhuvan_links.php*)

5.17.2 Software

There are many image processing and GIS software available as Open Resources to analyse the data. Some of the software include; Geographic Resources Analysis Support System **(GRASS)**, Geoda, GeoServer, GDAL, OGR, gvSIG, Integrated Land and Water Information Management **(ILWIS)**, MapWindow GIS, OpenJump GIS, Quantum GIS **(QGIS)** System for Automated Geo-scientific Analyse **(SAGA)** GIS, PostgreSQL + PostGIS: TerraLib, uDig, Whitebox **GAT** (Geospatial Analysis Toolbox). These software are used for geospatial data analysis and management as well as visualization of output graphics/ maps.

5.18 APPLICATIONS OF GIS

GIS is used to analyse, study, search and select databases for a specific purpose and application. Spatial information is the base for natural resource management planning and monitoring using temporal distribution of the resource. Geospatial tools are much more reliable, precise and efficient in resource assessment, change detection, suitability analysis, scenario study impact assessment etc. GI|S can combine layers of data to find the best alternatives for routes and optimum sites for development projects, saving invaluable time for the government or organisations. GIS makes map data interactive and, thus, more useful. It can easily identify land owners affected by the development project so that they may be assessed for land compensation. GIS is also diverging into location-based services **(LBS)**. LBS allows GPS enabled mobile devices to display the locations on GIS maps in relation to fixed assets (nearest restaurant, bus station, police station), or mobile assets (friends, children, taxi, trucks). It helps the businesses to learn the locations about their customers as well as help for better decision making and improved communication.

There are many applications of GIS (as shown below); some of them are described in forthcoming paragraphs.

- Agriculture & forestry
- Archaeology
- Cartography
- Urban and regional planning & development
- Smart city and smart infrastructure
- Real estate
- Transport planning
- Logistics planning and management
- Emergency vehicle routing
- Telecommunication
- Climate change
- Environmental impact assessment
- Pollution monitoring and control
- Public health
- Landfill site selection for solid waste disposal
- Resource management
- Water resource planning and management
- Watershed analysis
- Groundwater potential zones
- Glaciology
- Wetlands management
- Petroleum (exploration mapping)
- Geology (mineral/rocks identification & mapping)
- Soil conservation
- Natural disasters and hazard mapping (*Landslide, Earthquakes, Floods, Hurricane)*
- Population census analysis
- Crime mapping
- Military - logistics and battle plans

5.18.1 Civil Engineering Projects

Flexible GIS models that manipulate, compile and process the spatial data have provided a powerful tool in civil engineering applications (Priya et al 2009). Advancement and availability of GIS technology plays a vital role and serves as a complete platform in every phase of infrastructure project life cycle, including planning and design, data collection and management, spatial analysis, construction, and operations management and maintenance (ESRI, 2008).

In planning, GIS helps professionals to combat complex scenarios relating to the selection of site, environmental impact, economic analysis, study of eco-system, managing risks regarding the use of natural resources, sustainability issues, managing traffic congestion, routing of roads and pipelines, what-if -scenarios, visualization of concept options, and benefit/cost alternatives analysis etc. GIS is equipped with almost all those tools and functions that enable users to have quick access to the required data. Some of the analyses in civil engineering projects that can be performed by GIS are: site suitability, terrain, visibility, hydrology analysis, volume calculations, soil load analysis, traffic capacity, environmental impact, slope stability, materials consumption, runoff, erosion control, and air emissions (Venkataraman and Anitha, 2017). Analysis of the environment within a GIS allows users to view patterns, trends, and relationships that were not clearly evident without the visualization of data (ESRI, 2008). GIS software greatly enhances the optimum use of land, the functional efficiency of a proposed design, its marketability, and the overall cost-effectiveness of a project.

GIS allows creation of new infrastructure data for civil works, including grading, contouring, specifications, cross sections, design calculations, mass haul plans, environmental mitigation plans, and equipment staging. The GIS helps the professionals to understand the site conditions that affect the schedule baseline and cost baseline. To keep the construction within budget and schedule, GIS guides as to how to utilize the resources on site efficiently (ESRI, 2008). Operations are controlled by modeling of site data and compared by the baselines prepared in planning phase. Modeling of site may be in the form of raster images or CAD drawings. These can help us to keep track of timely operations of activities. GIS can help to make a record of work that has been completed and can give users visualization in the form of thematic maps which will guide users about rate of operations, completed operations and pending operations.

5.18.2 Site Selection

In past, many studies has been carried out for the selection of suitable sites by using GIS for example, landfill (Shahabi et al., 2014), hospital (Soltani and Marandi, 2011), geothermal (Poux and Suemnicht, 2012) and others. Site selection is also critical for planning a real estate project. It is a core component of the pre-planning phase, after which the project life cycle will commence.

A GIS can be used effectively to combine hydrological, geological and socio-economic parameters objectively and analyze these systematically for identifying suitable area for water reservoir (Ali Ahmad et al 2015) and a dam. GIS can find the best location for a dam, away from natural hazards, like earthquake and volcanic eruption. The GIS is used to study geologic features, analyze soils and strata, assess seismic information, and create three dimensional displays of geographic features. This information in GIS can also be used to analyze rock information characteristics and identifying the best dam site (Iftikhar, 2016).

Site selection for bridges includes the stability of slope leading down to and up from the water crossing, historical data on erosion & sedimentation, the amount of river channel contraction, degree of curvature of river bend, nature of bed and bank materials including the flood flow and the flow depth. Based on the prescribed criteria to integrate the information, GIS will provide the suitable site for bridge on a river.

5.18.3 Urban Planning

GIS technology provides planners, surveyors, and engineers with the tools they need to design and map their neighborhoods and cities for decision-making process (ESRI, 2008). It is used to analyze the urban growth and its direction of expansion, and to find suitable sites for future urban development (Dekolo and Oduwaye, 2005). GIS is also used for different types of utility mapping, like pipeline, electricity, telecom and cooking gas to have proper inventory systems, track maintenance, monitor regulatory compliance, model the distribution analysis, transformer analysis and load analysis. GIS can be used by facility managers for space management, visualization and planning, emergency and disaster planning and response. GIS technology is faster, better and more efficient in pipeline route planning and selection. Accurate pipeline route selection brings about risk and cost reduction as well as better decision making process. GIS least cost path analysis have been effectively used to determine suitable oil and gas pipeline routes *(Source: http://grindgis.com/blog/gis-applications-uses.*

5.18.4 Terrain Mapping and Analysis

Terrain slope and characteristics are important for planning any developmental activities on the land surface (Lindstrom and Pascucci, 2001). DEM along with satellite images and other relevant data are thus important for proper analysis of the terrain (Campbell and Shin, 2011). For example, the slope of the river and adjoining land is important to protect the land from floods. Remote sensing based inventory of construction material, such as boulders, quarry rock, sand–clay mixtures etc., would help to locate suitable sites of construction materials for building up of water resources engineering projects, like dams, bridges, etc., across the rivers.

5.18.5 Water Resources

Various parameters of the watershed, i.e. stream network (drainage), soil, geology, topography, physiography, land use, vegetation/forest cover and snow cover can be integrated together in GIS for better watershed planning. This is essential for the conservation and management of water and land resources of watersheds for optimum productivity. Water resources planning and management and hydrologic modeling have been successfully carried by using GIS models (Leipnik et al 1993; Aher et al 2014). By analyzing multi-date remote sensing data in GIS, it would be possible to monitor the impact of dam construction. It requires information on land use / land cover, soil and geological mapping, terrain evaluation, etc. Remote sensing data in GIS can provide an assessment of sediment volume and reduction in the capacity of sediment volume and reduction in the capacity of the reservoir.

5.18.6 Solid Waste Management

Municipal solid waste management is among the most significant threat to the global health. For proper management of soild waste, appropriate site selection may be done on technical, economical and socio-environmental issues and meet multiple criteria by using the capabilities of GIS. Multi-criteria decision analysis in GIS provides necessary conditions for site selection evaluation problem, and therefore helps creating a decision supporting system (DSS) which can assist decision makers in site selection as an effective tool (Aziz and Khodakarami, 2013). With the help of GIS, users can identify the places suitable for waste treatment plant. GIS based process is cost effective to identify suitable dumping sites for further investigations.

5.18.7 Natural Resources Management

The most common role of GIS technology in land use and land cover applications is to determine the changes in land use/land cover types, and finding the change pattern with time, and possible causes, like natural, seasonal, or man-made (e.g. deforestation). With the help of GIS technology, agricultural, water, soil and forest resources can be well monitored, maintained and managed. Water is one of the most essential constituents of the environment, and GIS is used to analyze geographic distribution of water resources. Forest condition can easily be monitored in GIS environment. Vegetation cover is interrelated with water, i.e. forest cover reduces the storm water runoff.

Environmental impact assessment (EIA) is an important policy initiative to conserve natural resources and environment. Many human activities produce potential adverse environmental effects which include the construction and operation of highways, rail, roads, pipelines, airports, radio-active waste disposal and more. The EIA can be carried out efficiently by the help of GIS, by integrating various GIS layers, and assessment of natural features can be made (Ainhoa, 2012).

5.18.8 Traffic and Transportation Engineering

GIS can be used in managing transportation and logistical problems. A new railway or a road can be planned by using engineering, environmental and topographical data into GIS platform. GIS provides a valuable tool in the process of planning and design of highways. GIS can also help in monitoring rail systems and road conditions. GIS can be used as a key tool to minimize accident hazard on roads, by optimising the existing road network and also improving the road safety measures. By identifying the accident locations, remedial measures can be planned. GIS can effectively be used for the management of traffic problems. By creating an extensive database of traffic information, such as speed data, road geometry, traffic flow and other spatial data and processing this information in GIS will help in traffic management (Adrees, 2016). Web-based navigation maps encourage safe navigation on land and waterway by providing accurate topographic and hydrographic data.

5.18.9 Disaster Management and Mitigation

GIS can help with risk management and analysis by displaying which areas are likely to be prone to natural or man-made disasters. When such disasters are identified, preventive measures can be developed (Tripathi and Bankar, 2017). GIS has made it possible to efficiently collect, manipulate and integrate a variety of spatial data such as geological, structural, surface cover and slope characteristics of an area, which can be used for hazard zonation. These layers can be integrated using GIS and weighted analysis used to find landslide prone area. GIS can also help in risk assessment and can reduce the losses of life and property. GIS helps to provide information for disaster relief funds, and can be utilized by insurance agencies to assist in assessing monetary value of property loss.

The seismo tectonics of a region can be displayed in a GIS to mark all active faults and select earthquakes within a certain distance from these faults, and calculate the density of seismic events (Source: http://grindgis.com/blog/gis-applications-uses). GIS based maps of flooding risk areas are much needed to evaluate the flood potential level in area and to estimate the damage. The GIS based platforms enable users to find out the damage and rapid response against volcanic activities may helps to reduce the loss to human life and environment.

5.19 FUTURE USES OF GIS TECHNOLOGY

GIS development has been more evolutionary than revolutionary. It responds to contemporary needs as well as technical breakthroughs. With the advent of high speed computers, most of the spatial and non-spatial data and procedures for their analysis have been automated. As a result, the focus of GIS has expanded from descriptive inventories to entirely new applications, involving prescriptive analysis (Godchild 2009). Therefore, the map analysis has become more quantitative. This new processing capabilities provides an opportunity in GIS based research to address complex spatial issues. Comprehensive spatial databases are being developed, and applications of GIS are accelerating around the globe (Rhind, 20017). GIS provides is a convenient way to expand our abilities to do better research in much less time and to bring interdisciplinary approaches to scientific studies by allowing efficient ways to integrate multiple data sets.

As shown in Figure 5.32, the evolution of GIS is more cyclical than linear. In the 1970s the research and early applications centered on *Computer Mapping* that yielded to *Spatial Data Management* (data structure/management focus) in the next decade, linking digital maps to attribute databases for geo-query. The 1990s centered on *GIS Modeling* (analysis focus) that laid the foundation of new ways of addressing spatial patterns and relations, as well as new applications. Today, GIS is centered on *Multimedia Mapping* (mapping focus). Advances in virtual reality and 3D geovisualization represent incremental progress in visualizing maps that use computer hardware/software (Doellner 2005; Godchild, 2009). The truly geospatial innovation awaits the next re-focusing on data/structure and analysis.

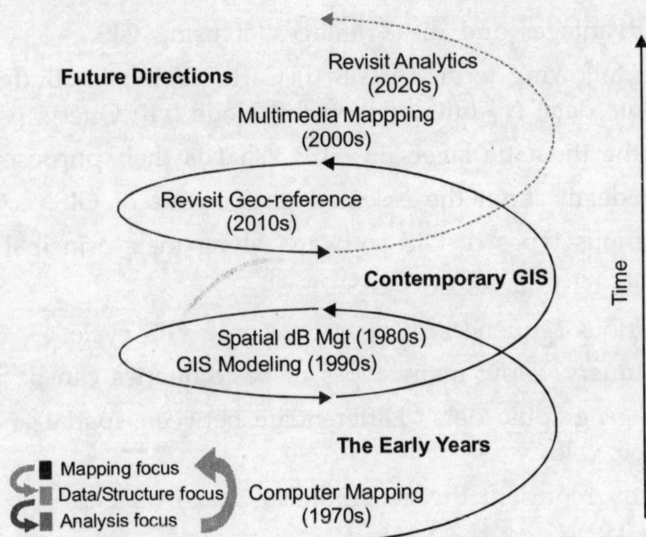

Figure 5.32: Future directions and uses of GIS technology (*Source: Berry, 2007b*)

The bulk of the current state of geospatial analysis relies on "*static coincidence modeling*" using a stack of geo-registered map layers. But the frontier of GIS research is shifting focus to "*dynamic flow modeling*" that tracks movement over space and time in three-dimensional geographic space. Advanced map analysis applications may represent natural extensions of geospatial conceptualization and analysis, built upon an entirely new set of analytic tools, geo-referencing framework and a more realistic paradigm of geographic space.

GIS technology has greatly changed our perspective of reading a map. The role of mapping has changed from an input provider to decision-making. The digital nature of modern maps has completely changed than what it used to be. There is a need to formulate innovative applications that would meet the complexity and accelerating needs of 21st century. Much attention is required to go into training and development of geospatial applications as has been given to hardware, software and database development. Much more attention needs to be focused beyond mapping to that of spatial reasoning. The biggest challenge is educating future GIS professionals and users to understand these requirements. Map analysis capabilities will serve as the catalyst to fully address cognitive aspects of geographic space as well as characterizing discrete physical features. The future also will build on the cognitive basis as well as the databases of GIS technology.

In future, there is a need to have people oriented GIS which have high technology impact but simple to use for the end-users. The modern GIS should be interactive, real-time system with capabilities of using artificial intelligence, fuzzy logic, and expert systems (knowledge-based systems).

Review Questions

1. Write three frequently used definitions of GIS.
2. Write a short note on historical developments of GIS.

3. List the advantages and disadvantages of using GIS.
4. Define the following terms in GIS (i) Cartography, (ii) Buffer, (iii) Spatial data, (iv) Attribute data, (v) Interpolation (vi) Node (vii) Query, (viii) Spatial analysis.
5. What are the thematic layers in GIS? What is their purpose?
6. Explain in detail about the essential components of GIS.
7. Discuss various types of GIS software, along their principal uses.
8. Explain four basic tasks of a GIS.
9. Discuss various sequences of operations in a GIS cycle.
10. What is a query? How many types of basic queries can be made with a GIS?
11. What is a geographic data? Differentiate between spatial and non-spatial data. Specify their roles.
12. How do you represent the geographical data in a GIS?
13. Explain point, line and polygon features in GIS with examples.
14. Explain digitization process and write its advantages.
15. What is the role of a scanner in GIS? Describe different types of scanners used in GIS work.
16. Explain in detail about two data models used in GIS.
17. What is vector data representation? Explain it with suitable examples.
18. Write the advantages of vector and raster data in GIS.
19. What is the role of grid or cell structure in data representation? How a minimum mapping unit is different from the size of a raster cell?
20. What is topology? Discuss its importance in GIS
21. Write three basic elements of topological consistency.
22. Describe the Arc-Node Data structure with a neat sketch.
23. What is a geodatabase? Explain its utility.
24. Discuss the Relational Data Base Management System?
25. Discuss the different data sources in GIS?
26. Explain in detail the data utilized from Total Station, LiDAR, and UAV in GIS work.
27. Differentiate between DEM and DTM.
28. Explain different sources of DEM creation in GIS. Explain their applications.
29. Discuss various data interpolation techniques used in GIS.
30. What are various vector operations in GIS? Explain with examples.
31. What are various raster operations in GIS? Explain with examples.
32. Discuss overlay operation in GIS?
33. Explain with suitable examples how buffering is carried out for three basic types of features.

34. Write about the uses of logical operators in spatial analysis.
35. Discuss the characteristics of BHUVAN Indian site.
36. List the major application areas of GIS.
37. Write various civil engineering applications of GIS.
38. Discuss the application of GIS in site selection and highway alignment studies.
39. How is GIS used in urban planning and terrain analysis.
40. What are the applications of GIS for water resources?
41. How is GIS helpful in disaster management?
42. Write a short note on future uses of GIS.

References

1. Abler, R. F. (1987) The National Science Foundation Centre for Geographic Information and Analysis. Intl. Journal of Geographical Information Systems, 1, 303, 26.
2. Adrees, Mohamed S., Abdalla, Amar Ibrahim, and Karrar, Abdelrahman (2016) A Proposed Framework for Using GIS to Enhance Traffic Safety in Sudan: A Case Study, American Journal of Traffic and Transportation Engineering, Volume 1, Issue 1, May 2016, Pages: 1-6
3. Aher, P.D., Adinarayana, J, Gorantiwar, S.D. and Sawant, S. A. (2014) Information System for Integrated Watershed Management using Remote Sensing and GIS, In Remote Sensing Applications in Environmental Research, P. K. Srivastava et al. (Eds.), Society of Earth Scientists Series, Springer International Publishing Switzerland.
4. Ainhoa González Del Campo, (2012) GIS in Environmental Assessment: A Review of Current Issues and Future Needs, J. Env. Assmt. Pol. Mgmt., 14, 1250007 (2012)
5. Ali Ahmad, Bakhtyar, Shahabi, Himan and Ahmad, Baharin Bin. (2015), Application of GIS Based Multi-criteria Analysis in Site Selection of Water Reservoirs (Case Study: Batu Pahat, Malaysia). Research Journal of Applied Sciences, Engineering and Technology, 9, 995-1005.
6. Arc News (2015), ESRI, California, USA.
7. Aronoff, S., (1989), *Geographic Information System: a management perspective*. Ottawa: WDL Publications.
8. Aziz, R. S. and Khodakarami, L. (2013), Application of GIS Models in Site Selection of Waste Disposal in an Urban Area, First International Symposium on Urban Development, WIT Press.
9. Bailey, T.C., (1994), A Review of Statistical Spatial Analysis in Geographical Information Systems, *Spatial Analysis and GIS*, Fotheringham, S. and Rogerson, P. (Eds) Taylor and Francis, London, 13-44.

10. Bailey, T.C. and Gatrell, A.C., (1995), *Interactive Spatial Data Analysis*, Harlow-New York: Longman.
11. Batty, M., Bracken, I., Guy, C. and Spooner, R. (1985), Teaching Spatial Modelling using Interacting
12. Computers and Interactive Computer Graphics, Journal of Geography in Higher Education, 9 (1), 25-36
13. Bernhardsen, T. (1999), *Geographic Information Systems: an introduction*, Wiley, New York.
14. Berry, B.J.L. and Marble, D.F., (1998), *Spatial Analysis: A Reader in Statistical Geography*. Englewood Cliffs, New Jersey: Prentice Hall.
15. Berry, Joseph K. (2013a), *Beyond Mapping III*, Compilation of Beyond Mapping columns appearing in GeoWorld magazine 1996 to 2013, BASIS **Press.**
16. Berry, Joseph K. (2013b), *Beyond Mapping IV*, Compilation of Beyond Mapping columns appearing in GeoWorld magazine 1996 to 2013, BASIS **Press.**
17. Bracken, Ian, Higgs, Garry, Martin, David and Webster, Chris (1989), *A Classification of Geographical Information Systems Literature and Applications*, CATMOGS (Concepts and Techniques in Modern Geography) edited by Quantitative Methods Study Group of the Institute of British Geographers. University of Wales College of Cardiff.
18. Bolstad, Paul V. (2002), *GIS Fundamentals*, Eider Press.
19. Burrough P A (1986), *Principles of Geographical Information Systems for Land Resources Assessment*, Clarendon Press, Oxford, 194 pp.
20. Burrough, P., and McDonnell, R., (1998), *Principles of Geographical Information Systems*, Oxford University Press, New York.
21. Campbell, Jonathan and Shin, Michael, (2011), *Essentials of Geographic Information Systems*, Flatword Unlimited.
22. Carter, James R., (1992), Perspectives on Sharing Data in Geographic Information Systems, Photogrammetric Engineering and Remote Sensing, Vol. 58, No. 11, pp. 1557-1560.
23. Cuartero, A., Felicisimo, A.M. and Ariza, F.J., (2004), Accuracy of DEM Generation from TERRA-ASTER Stereo Data, International Archives of Photogrammetry and Remote Sensing, 35 (B2), pp. 559–563.
24. Davis, B.E. (2001) *Geographic Information Systems: a visual approach*, Onword Press, Canada.
25. Dekolo, Samuel and Oduwaye, Leke. (2005), GIS in Urban and Regional Planning. Conference: Conference: Nigerian Institute of Town Planners CPD Workshop, January, Lagos, DOI:10.13140/2.1.1613.2482.
26. DeMers, M.N. (2000), *Fundamentals of Geographic Information Systems*, (2nd Ed), Wiley & Sons.

27. Doellner, J. (2005), *Geo-visualization and real-time computer graphics*. In J. Dykes, A.M. MacEachren and M. J. Kraak, eds. Exploring geovisualization. Amsterdam: Elsevier. Chapter 16, pp. 325_344.

28. Eldrandaly, Khalid. (2007), *Expert Systems, GIS, and Spatial Decision Making: Current Practices and New Trends*. Chapter 8 in Expert Systems Research Trends, A.R. Tyler (Ed), Nova Science Publishers, Inc., USA.

29. ESRI (2015), *Arc Map*, Version 10.3, ESRI, California, USA.

30. ESRI (2008), *Application of GIS in Civil Engineering*, ESRI, California, USA.

31. Fraser, C., Baltsavias, E.P., and Gruen, A., (2002), Processing of IKONOS Imagery for Sub-metre 3D Positioning and Building Extraction, Photogrammetric Engineering and Remote Sensing, 56(3), pp. 177-194.

32. Goodchild, M.F., (1990), Spatial Analysis Using GIS, Fourth International Symposium on Spatial Data Handling, Zurich: University of Zurich.

33. Goodchild, Michael F. (2009), Geographic information systems and science: today and tomorrow, Annals of GIS, 15:1, 3-9, DOI: 10.1080/19475680903250715.

34. Gruen, A., Remondino, F., and Zhang, L., (2004), 3D Modeling and Visualization of Large Cultural Heritage Sites at Very High Resolution: the Bamiyan valley and its standing Buddhas. The International Archives of the Photogrammetry, Remote Sensing and Spatial Information Sciences, Vol. 35, Part B5.

35. Hersh, Cora A. (2017) Using Geographic Information Systems to Improve Exposure Assessment in Epidemiological Studies of Cancer, News and Events, Division of Cancer Epidemiology and Genetics (DCEG), National Cancer Institute, Bethesda, Maryland 20892.

36. Heywood, I., Cornelius, S. and Carver, S. (1998), *An Introduction to Geographical Information Systems,* Longman.

37. Iftikhar, S, (2016), Site Suitability Analysis for Small Multipurpose Dams using Geospatial Technologies, Journal of Remote Sensing & GIS, 5 (162).

38. Islam, Akm, Saiful (2008), Lecture Notes on Data Model and Structure, "WFM 6202: Remote Sensing and GIS in Water Management", Institute of Wtaer and Flood management, Bangladesh University of Engineering and Technology, Nov.

39. Jones, C. (1997), *Geographic Information Systems and Computer Cartography*, Longman Publishers, Singapore.

40. Leipnik, Mark R., Kemp, Karen and Loaiciga, Hugo. A. (1993), Implementation of GIS for Water Resources Planning and Management, Journal of Water Resources Planning and Management-ASCE, 119. 10.

41. Lindstrom, Peter and Pascucci, Valerio (2001), Visualisation of Large Terrains Made Easy, IEEE Visualization '01 Conference Proceedings, October 2001.

42. Lo C.P. and Yeung A.K.W., (2002), *Concept and Techniques of Geographic Information System*, Prentice-Hall of India, New Delhi.

43. Longley, P., Goodchild, M., Maguire, D., and Rhind, D., (2005), *Geographic Information Systems and Science*, Wiley, New York.

44. Maguire D J, Goodchild M F, and Rhind D. W. (1991), (Eds.) *Geographical Information Systems: principles and applications*, Longman, London, pp. 403-12, Vol 1.

45. Marble, D. F. and Peuquet, D. J. (1983), *Geographic Information Systems and Remote Sensing*, In R. N. Colwell (Ed.) Manual of Remote Sensing, Vol. 1, Falls Church, VA., ASPRS.

46. Moyer, D. David, (1989), Geographic Information Systems: Definitions, Concepts, and Applications,

47. Symposium on the Potential for Geographic Information Systems in Agricultural Economics, Louisiana State University, Baton Rogue, July, 13 pp.

48. Parker, H. Dennison, (1988), The Unique Qualities of a Geographic Information System: A Commentary, Journal of Photogrammetric Engineering and Remote Sensing, Volume 54, No. 11, November, pp. 1547-49.

49. Poli, D., Remondino, F., and Dolci, C. (2004), Use of Satellite Imagery for DEM Extraction, Landscape Modeling and GIS Applications, Institute of Geodesy and Photogrammetry, ETH Zurich, 8093 Zurich, Switzerland.

50 Poux, Bastien and Suemnicht, Gene (2012), Use of GIS Geoprocessing to Select the Most Favorable Sites for Geothermal Exploration in Oregon, GRC Transactions, Vol. 36, 2012.

51. Priya, Satya, Sharma, Puneet and Mehta, Premal (2009), GIS Software for Civil Engineering Verticals: An Overview, Geospatial World, September Issue. 1, 2009.

52. Rhind, David (2017) A GIS Research Agenda, International Journal of Geographical Information Systems, 2:1, 23-28.

53. Shahabi, H., Keihanfard, S., Ahmad, B.B., Javad M., and Amiri, T. (2014), Evaluating Boolean, AHP and WLC Methods for the Selection of Waste Landfill Sites using GIS and Satellite Images, Environmental Earth Sciences, Vol. (71)(9) pp 4221-4233

54. Sibson, R. (1981), A Brief Description of Natural Neighbour Interpolation. In: V Barnett, (Ed), Interpreting Multivariate Data, Wiley, New York, USA, pp 21-36.

55. Soltani, Ali and Marandi, Ebrahim Zargari, (2010), Hospital Site Selection using Two-Stage Fuzzy Multi-criteria Decision Making Process, Journal of Urban and Environmental Engineering, Vol.5, No.1, p.32-43.

56. Star, J., and Estes, J., (1990), *Geographic Information Systems: An Introduction*, Englewood Cliffs, NJ: Prentice Hall.

57. Toutin, Th. and C Heng, Ph. C., (2002), Comparison of Automated Digital Elevation Model Extraction Results using Along-track ASTER and Across-track SPOT Stereo Images, Optical Engineering, 41, pp. 2102–2106.

58. Tripathi, Jai Prakash and Bankar, Anand D. (2017), Disaster Management and It's Planning. IOSR Journal of Business and Management, 19, pp44-52.

59. Venkatraman, S, and Anitha K. (2017), Applications of GIS and GPS in Civil Engineering, International Journal of Pure and Applied Mathematics, Volume 116, No. 14, 1-7.

60. Yanalak, Mustafa, Nebiye Musaoglu, Cengizhan Ipbuker, Elif Sertel and Sinasi Kaya (2012), DEM Accuracy of High Resolution Satellite Images, International Conference on Computational Science and its Applications, pp 471-480.

Web Resources

http://grindgis.com/what-is-gis/what-is-gis-definition

http://www.yellowscan.fr/event/yellowscan-surveyor-demo

http://envi-logic.com/en/What-is-geographic-information-system-(GIS).html

http://giscommons.org/output/

http://gisgeography.com/what-gis-geographic-information-systems/

http://www.geo.umass.edu/courses/geo494a/Chapter2_GIS_Fundamentals.pdf

http://www.innovativegis.com/basis/MapAnalysis/Default.htm

PRINCIPLES AND THEORY OF GEOINFORMATICS

P.K. GARG

FEEDBACK FORM

1. Which topics from your examination point of view are inadequately or not covered in this book?

2. Is there any misprints/ mistakes/ factual inaccuracy in this book? If so, please specify.

3. What is your assessment of this book as regards the presentation of the subject-matter, expression, precision and price in relation to the other recommended books available on this subject?

4. Which competing books you regard as better than this? Please mention their author and publishers.

5. Any further suggestions/comments you would like to make for the improvement of the book?

PS: If needed, please attach a separate sheet.

Name :

College :

Address :

Email :

Mobile :

Please mail the feedback form at:

KHANNA BOOK PUBLISHING CO. (P) LTD.

4C/4344, Ansari Road, Daryaganj, New Delhi-110002

You can also email this feedback form at contact@khannabooks.com or Whatsapp at +91 – 99109 09320

BEST FEEDBACK WILL BE REWARDED SUITABLY

5.15 Interpolation of Data 249

5.15.1 Inverse distance weighted 249

5.15.2 Kriging 249

5.15.3 Natural neighbour 249

5.15.4 Spline 250

5.15.5 Trend 250

5.16 Various Operations in GIS 250

5.16.1 Measurement 251

5.16.2 Query 251

5.16.3 Raster operations in GIS 252

5.16.4 Vector operations in GIS 254

5.17 Free (Open) Source GIS Software 255

5.17.1 GIS data 255

5.17.2 Software 254

5.18 Applications of GIS 257

5.18.1 Civil engineering projects 258

5.18.2 Site selection 259

5.18.3 Urban planning 260

5.18.4 Terrain mapping and analysis 260

5.18.5 Water resources 260

5.18.6 Solid waste management 261

5.18.7 Natural resources management 261

5.18.8 Traffic and transportation engineering 261

5.18.9 Disaster management and mitigation 262

5.19 Future Uses of GIS Technology 262

Review Questions 263

References 265